The Architecture of Art Museums

As a building type, art museums are unparalleled for the opportunities they provide for architectural investigation and experimentation. They are frequently key components of urban revitalization and often push the limits of building technology. Art museums are places of pleasure, education, and contemplation. They are remarkable by their prominence and sheer quantity, and their lessons are useful for all architects and for all building types.

This book provides explicit and comprehensive coverage of the most important museums built in the first ten years of the twenty-first century in the United States and Europe. By dissecting and analyzing each case, Ronnie Self allows the reader to get under the skin of each design and fully understand the process behind these remarkable buildings. Richly designed with full technical illustrations and sections, the book includes the work of Tadao Ando, Zaha Hadid, Peter Cook & Colin Fournier, Renzo Piano, Yoshio Taniguchi, Herzog & de Meuron, Jean Nouvel, SANAA, Daniel Libeskind, Diller Scofidio + Renfro, Steven Holl, Coop Himmelb(l)au, Bernard Tschumi, Sauerbruch Hutton, and Shigeru Ban & Jean de Gastines.

Together these diverse projects provide a catalogue of design solutions for the contemporary museum and a snapshot of current architectural thought and culture. One of few books on this subject written by an architect, Self's analysis thoroughly and critically appraises each project from multiple aspects and crucially takes the reader from concept to building. This is an essential book for any professional engaged in designing a museum.

Ronnie Self is Associate Professor of Architecture at the Gerald D. Hines College of Architecture at the University of Houston, USA. He received a Bachelor of Architecture from the University of Texas at Austin and advanced degrees in Theories of Architecture from the École d'Architecture Paris-Villemin and Philosophy of Art from the Université de Paris I, Panthéon-Sorbonne. He is a registered architect practicing in Houston and previously worked in the Paris office of Renzo Piano Building Workshop for 12 years where, among other projects, he was the Architect in Charge of the Atelier Brancusi for the Centre Georges Pompidou. He writes regularly on recently completed projects throughout the United States for American and French magazines.

The Architecture of Art Museums

A DECADE OF DESIGN: 2000–2010

Ronnie Self

Routledge
Taylor & Francis Group
LONDON AND NEW YORK

First edition published 2014
by Routledge

2 Park Square, Milton Park, Abingdon, Oxon OX14 4RN

Simultaneously published in the USA and Canada
by Routledge
711 Third Avenue, New York, NY 10017

Routledge is an imprint of the Taylor & Francis Group, an informa business

British Library Cataloguing in Publication Data
A catalogue record for this book is available from the British Library

Library of Congress Cataloging in Publication Data
Self, Ronnie.
The architecture of art museums : a design and planning guide / Ronnie Self.
pages cm
Includes bibliographical references and index.
1. Art museum architecture--Themes, motives. I. Title.
NA6695.S45 2014
727'.709051--dc23
2013031876

ISBN: 978-0-415-50651-9 (hbk)
ISBN: 978-0-415-50652-6 (pbk)
ISBN: 978-1-315-81714-9 (ebk)

Typeset in ITC Officina Sans Std 9/12.5 pt
by Fakenham Prepress Solutions, Fakenham, Norfolk NR21 8NN
Printed in Great Britain by Bell & Bain Ltd, Glasgow

MIX
Paper from responsible sources
FSC® C007785

Contents

Introduction

The *Architecture of Art Museums* evolved out of articles I wrote over a period of nearly ten years between 2000 and 2010 for the French architectural magazine Archicréé. As a correspondent, the projects reviewed were essentially assignments – important buildings in the United States that the editor-in-chief and I felt would be of interest mainly to a European audience. Though various types of buildings were reviewed during the period, the majority were art museums designed by European, Japanese, as well as American architects. They were the most notable buildings – and museums – in the United States in the first decade of the twenty-first century. All of the projects were visited personally, generally at the time of the inauguration. At the opening events there were often presentations made by the architects as well as the museums, and there were opportunities for discussion and questions. Beyond the galleries and other public spaces I also visited behind the scenes areas such as art storage, conservation, administrative offices, loading docks, mechanical rooms, etc. Information was also acquired through conversations with associate architects, engineers, and other consultants. I also looked into each architect's thoughts on museums and architecture in general especially through their own writings and published interviews. In that way this book is a synthesis of what has been said about museums by these "museum architects" and a snapshot of current ideas on architecture.

When I first began to write for Archicréé I asked the editor, Joelle Letessier, for tips on how to approach a critique. Her advice was to look at the building and write like an architect. Writing like an architect should mesh the theoretical with the technical and address the many unrelated influences that go into making any project. The success of a space for art is determined at many levels from the conceptual to the experiential to the detail. My personal interest in the building type was influenced by the several museum projects I was in charge of or involved in as a collaborator in the Paris office of Renzo Piano Building Workshop.

To better round out this book, museums outside of the United States were added to the 12 selected American case studies. Though it would have been interesting and ideal to include projects from around the world, six recent and prominent European buildings were chosen to document and critique, and these were visited during the fall of 2011. While the six also respect the 2000 to 2010 time frame, their completion dates tend toward the end of the decade – an interesting and perhaps unique decade, not only because of the quantity of museums built, but also because many institutions and architects alike expressed a desire to reconsider the building type, to innovate, to make a mark, and to be the first great museum of the new millennium. It is this aspect that may set the decade apart. The period ended with economic recession, pessimism, and projections that the museum "bubble" had burst. Since at least the 1930s, writings on museums have portrayed each successive period as *the* period of unprecedented museum growth. With several important structures already opened since 2010 and more projects on the horizon from London to Los Angeles and from China to Abu Dhabi, the bubble may still be intact.

For a good while now the art museum has been established as a prominent and important building type. Museums are regularly described as the "cathedrals" of our time. They are places for collecting, exhibiting, and conserving. They are places for research, education, contemplation, introspection, and enlightenment. They are public forums and places for social interaction and outreach. They are also places for creation. They are places of leisure, pleasure, and entertainment. They are considered sacred spaces – a place for the preservation of memory and the transmission of the best of mankind. Conversely, they are also places of control and power – signs of a materialistic, consumer, capitalistic culture. Some are elitist and homogenize and dictate tastes. Others are places of Disneyland-like entertainment that have taken on the scale of shopping malls and airports. They are big business for cultural tourism.

Physically, museums have traditionally taken prominent sites within the city. They are now key components of urban, regional, or national transformations and a factor in economic development. They may be commissioned by individuals, private collectors, a board of trustees, or the government. They are seen as an opportunity to create a monument, a sign, an iconic presence. Visibility and recognition are important. Museum buildings should last. They often aspire to become strong symbols inspired by the "Eiffel Tower effect," the "Sydney

(Opera House) effect," or, more directly, the "Bilbao effect." Architecture becomes an attraction, and museums may become pilgrimage sites. The prestige of an important contemporary building is not unlike the earliest eighteenth- and nineteenth-century museums that projected national glory. In commissioning such projects, museums become patrons of architecture. There is an encouragement of the architect's personal expression and often a pursuit of the experimental and the unconventional. As most commissions are acquired through competition, "effect" is expected. Construction budgets are generally more generous than for other building types. For all of these reasons, museums are coveted commissions often making them a "global" affair. The designers of the buildings included in *The Architecture of Art Museums* hail from three continents and eight different countries, and many were also competitors for others of the 18 case studies. There is often an important geographical distance between the architect's office and the museum site, and in only four cases was the architect in the same country as the commission. Comparatively short distances separate Diller Scofidio + Renfro (New York) and their project in Boston or Sauerbruch Hutton (Berlin) and their project in Munich. Longer distances separate Japanese architects from their projects in the United States or Europe. In these circumstances, a response to context often has little to do with an intimate comprehension of place. Rather, projects rely conceptually on narrative and metaphor that includes water birds, aliens, ancient ruins, mountains, hats, or simply "flows." Though museum architecture is image oriented, these designs are generally not the isolated objects for which modernism has been criticized but are well nested in their sites and interact with existing public spaces or create new ones for everyday life.

Among the many writings on museums, a special issue of the magazine *L'Architecture D'Aujourd'hui* on *Muséographie* from 1938 was a particularly interesting find even if not exactly recent. It also examined newly completed buildings at that time in Europe and the United States and made apparent that even if there have been significant formal and technical evolutions over the last seven decades, many fundamental concerns and alternatives related to the conception and design of museums have remained the same. These involve such issues as the appropriate relationship between the building and the art it contains, circulation and how prescribed a visitor's path should be, natural and artificial lighting, dimensions, colors, and flexibility of gallery spaces, correlation between the décor of a gallery space and what it exhibits, museum fatigue and the integration of rest areas, multi-floor museums and vertical circulation, the relationship between inside and outside ... and so forth. Museum extensions and future growth, questions that remain pertinent today, were also mentioned, and Le Corbusier's then recently conceived "Museum of Unlimited Growth" was cited. The museum program of the twenty-first century had, for the most part, been set as well: gallery spaces, a library, a restaurant, administrative and curatorial offices, meeting rooms, conservation and photo labs, a loading dock, delivery and reception areas, art storage and general storage, a freight elevator, workshops, break rooms, and mechanical rooms. Though not listed, auditoriums have been part of the museum program since the early twentieth century. A museum gift shop was not yet mentioned. Today, education departments are often important elements programmatically and architecturally, as are large entries and atriums that may or may not include art works and often double as event spaces for museum functions or for hire for private parties. Similarly, some museums have integrated lease spaces to generate income. Special spaces for video and digital art have also been integrated. In the early 1990s virtual reality was a topic the English architect Ian Ritchie pondered in relation to the Museo Reina Sofía when he was involved in renovations there. Though initiatives for virtual museums exist today, any reflections on the subject by the architects or institutions presented here were rarely, if ever, shared. Art museums still communicate by presenting singular objects to a public that participates in person.

Design solutions for those spaces where visitors actually encounter works of art are virtually wide open. Other than the strict control of temperature, humidity, and light levels, there are really few set rules for museum design. There is little equivalent to more objective criteria for other types of art spaces such as acoustics in a concert hall, or even sight lines in a theater. Museums do not focus attention collectively like a space for performing arts, yet they should somehow provide an appropriate viewing environment. Though exhibition spaces are what a museum will largely be judged for, they may not be the principal motivator for the design. Also unlike other art spaces (the Sydney Opera House as an example), the inside and outside of a museum are rarely disassociated. The iconic qualities of exteriors generally translate directly into interior spaces. Of the buildings discussed here, it is the Centre Pompidou – Metz, with its rational tube galleries draped by an independent and visually striking tent structure, which is the clearest exception to the rule.

The appropriate relationship between the art of architecture and the visual arts is inevitably reconsidered by every design. Should museum architecture be highly visible or should it be a backdrop? Should it be an *oeuvre* in itself or more utilitarian: a simple "machine for exhibiting?" If the building is art, does it even need other art inside? Short of that, what is the best way to engage the visitor and reconcile the solitary experience of looking at art with the social activity of visiting a museum? How might spaces challenge curators as well as artists who create site-specific installations? How might the architecture accompany the art and accompany the visitor? In the end, however, the planning types of exhibition spaces are surprisingly few and can be resumed as the "room" where works are hung directly on permanent walls (the Museum Brandhorst), the "gallery" which is elongated (the MAXXI), the "loft" that is flexible and requires temporary exhibition walls (the Kunsthaus Graz), and perhaps the "hall" that combines exhibition with entry. Mies van der Rohe's New National Gallery in Berlin from 1968, more than any of the 18 case studies reviewed here, is an example of the hall.

Whatever the type, exhibition spaces may be entirely open to the exterior (the Toledo Glass Pavilion), they may offer framed views (Modern Art Museum of Fort Worth), they may provide spectacular, panoramic views from spaces outside the galleries (the de Young Museum), or they may be completely introverted (the Contemporary Art Center). A closed, calm, more edited environment would limit competition for the works and allow visitors to focus on them. A more open, stimulating environment would promote a general state of increased awareness resulting in a greater appreciation of the art. The path through the building largely determines the experience and can vary from one of "discovery" via interwoven galleries where multiple options are possible, to highly prescribed "circulation loops" that allow virtually no choice at all. In multistory museums elevators tend to disrupt the continuity of a visit, even more so when the floor plates are small (The New Museum). Escalators in museums are often equated with more commercial spaces, and as the Walker Art Center has interestingly pointed out, the museum and the department store came into being during the same period and "both were created for visual delectation and display ..." Escalators are used as a primary means of vertical circulation at the Museum of Modern Art and the Acropolis Museum; the Kunsthaus Graz uses low-slope travelators, and the Centre Pompidou – Metz uses only one escalator between the Ground Floor and the Gallery 1 Level to alleviate circulation congestion. The Reina Sofía has one escalator at the roof terrace level that was used instead of a stair so that visitors could better appreciate an unfolding view upon descending. All of the museums have public elevators except the Toledo Glass Pavilion. Many are discreet and utilitarian. Some such as at the ICA/Boston are playful and a major architectural element.

Museum lighting was also given special attention by *L'Architecture D'Aujourd'hui* and it was noted that good light quality makes a good museum. Though the original 1933 Nelson-Atkins in Kansas City (added to in 2007 by Steven Holl) was not included, many of the case studies examined were of a similar technology. In the 1930s electric light in museums was common as were luminous ceilings using exclusively artificial light in a cavity above a diffusing glass plane. Concerning naturally top-lit spaces, Sir John Soane's 1817 Dulwich Picture Gallery, an early, purpose-built exhibition space that employed a series of roof lanterns, remains an important touchstone for museum design. *L'Architecture D'Aujourd'hui* pointed out that a choice between natural or artificial lighting or a mixture of the two was influenced by heat gain as well as operation costs. The technical solutions described as a response at that time were resourceful. The goal was to admit as little light as possible and distribute it using prismatic glass, mirrors, heliostats, and the like in order to avoid excessive related heat. Today's full glass museum roofs such as those of the Nasher or the Brandhorst that provide pleasant and uniform natural light throughout the gallery space are feasible only because of the advent of air conditioning. Limiting top-lighting, be it natural or artificial, to only the center of a space, or inversely to only its perimeter, was already described as positioning the viewer and the art in different conditions which results in an overly theatrical effect. More recent and expressive formal strategies for capturing natural light such as the "nozzles" of the Kunsthaus Graz or the "lenses" of the Nelson-Atkins Bloch Building require the addition of artificial light. Cove lighting is sometimes used. The light track is ubiquitous. An entirely windowless and artificially lit space such as the "gallery box" of the Akron Art Museum is likewise an option. The integration of the actual light fixtures as well as other technical elements such as exit signs, sprinkler heads, cameras, fire extinguishers, smoke detectors, etc. also has a significant visual impact on any exhibition space.

Though the interior architecture of the Acropolis Museum, the de Young, or the Toledo Glass Pavilion is directly related to the collection, most of the 18 case studies use white walls for hanging. Spaces are generally large since many show modern and contemporary art that itself can be big in size. In some cases there is a subversion of the wall with the most extreme cases being the rounded shell of the Kunsthaus Graz and the sloped walls of the Denver Art Museum. The MAXXI offers vertical but curved walls. In the tradition of art spaces by Frederick Kiesler from the 1940s where works of art were detached from the wall using metal arms, or curatorial experiments in Mies van der Rohe's halls in Berlin and Houston where works were suspended from the ceiling using cables, the MAXXI has also integrated a system for suspending temporary walls or works themselves from the ceiling. Temporary walls are the norm. From a practical point of view, transforming galleries for each exhibition can be costly.

With all of the design diversity of these buildings, one commonality among many of the various structural solutions is the use of trusses. In some cases they serve to create exhibition spaces free of columns while in others they allow for a large expanse of unobstructed glass facade. They are used to dramatic ends to form large cantilevered elements or even more spectacularly when an entire building becomes a truss to make an inherently unstable form structurally possible.

More so than many buildings, Frank Lloyd Wright's Guggenheim in New York from 1959 is often referred to by architects and museums both positively and negatively. It too remains a touchstone and perhaps a limit case for exhibition spaces because of its sloped floor, its sole ramped itinerary, its curved walls, its introversion, its single open space, and its clear assertion of architecture as the dominant art. It is also an iconic form. The Guggenheim Bilbao opened little before the end of the twentieth century and was still causing a stir at the beginning of the twenty-first. It is referred to mostly for its iconic qualities and its "effect." Both projects, along with many other significant but less flamboyant buildings, can be seen as examples and counterexamples for these 18 museums that were completed in the first decade of the twenty-first century. Issues and alternatives in museum design are limited while the architectural responses to them are numerous and depend on the synergy between the design team and institution. In museum design the question remains of how and how much the building might act as a silent curator and even influence the mission of an institution.

Acknowledgements

I owe deep gratitude to Patricia Oliver, Dean, the Gerald D. Hines College of Architecture at the University of Houston for her support of this project, to the University of Houston Small Grants Program for funds for copyrights, to the Service de Coopération et d'Action Culturelle of the French Embassy in Washington D.C. for financial support for travel, and to Hilton Hotels & Resorts for accommodation support.

Special thanks go to Joelle Letessier, Chief Editor of Archicréé. Our working relationship over almost a decade contributed enormously to this project.

Great appreciation goes to Hung Pham and the University of Houston Provost's Undergraduate Research Scholarship. Hung conscientiously coordinated the drawings for the book and assisted with the graphic concept for the cover.

I want to thank Catherine Essinger and especially Chris Conway of the University of Houston Jenkins Architecture and Art Library for their help and Diane Lovejoy and Marty Stein of the Museum of Fine Arts, Houston for their many useful bits of advice.

I am indebted to all of the architects, associate architects, engineers, and consultants of the museums included in the book for their helpfulness, for information, and for providing drawings.

Very special thanks must also be given to all 18 museums for information and insights, and for organizing tours and allowing me to visit spaces in the buildings that are generally not accessible to the public.

I want to give a warm thanks to the photographers whose work illustrates the museums: Iwan Baan, Jan Bitter, Francesco Bolis, Joaquín Cortés/Roman Lores, Michel Denancé, Roland Halbe, Timothy Hursley, Annette Kisling, Haydar Koyupinar, Andreas Lechtape, Mitsuo Matsuoka, Paul Raftery, and Christian Richters.

I want to thank Fran Ford, Laura Williamson, Trudy Varcianna, Jennifer Birtill and everyone at Routledge for their professionalism and humanity, their prodding and encouragement, and for a very pleasant working relationship. I also want to thank Sarah Fish, the copyeditor.

A list of acknowledgements could not be complete without thanking my mother, Elsie Self, for her continued interest in my endeavors and her love.

Finally, I want to thank Bernard Bonnet, who visited most all of the museums with me, who has always loved and worked with books and museums, and is the very best critic of my work.

CHAPTER 1

Modern Art Museum of Fort Worth

Fort Worth, Texas

Tadao Ando Architect & Associates

2002

Figure 1.1 North facade and reflecting pool

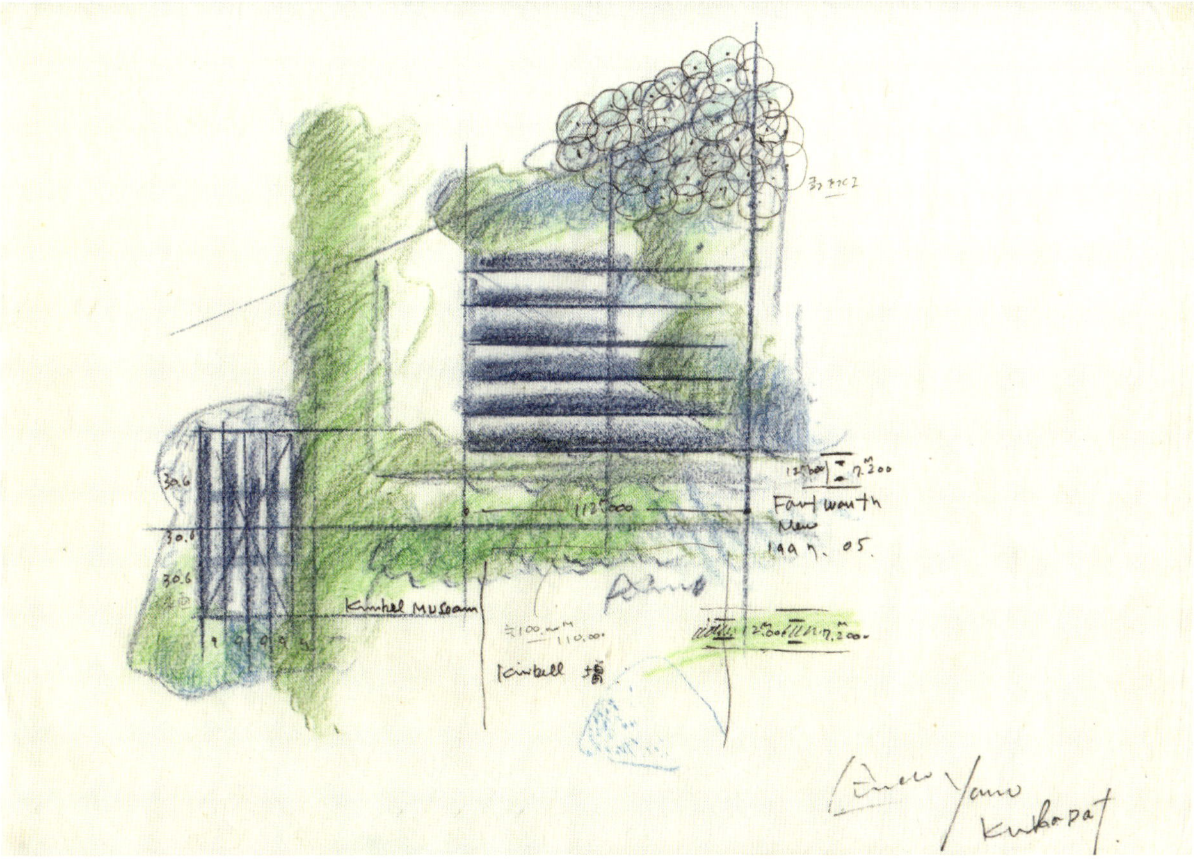

Figure 1.2 Sketch by Tadao Ando

Completely by coincidence, I made first visits to both the Guggenheim Bilbao and the Modern Art Museum of Fort Worth on the day after Christmas, shortly after the buildings were completed. Though the two museums opened five years apart (October 1997 for the Guggenheim and December 2002 for the Modern) and are obviously very different architecturally, the atmosphere was surprisingly similar. The buildings were packed with locals and visitors from far away, art-lovers, architects, and the curious. The atmosphere was festive after the holiday and the public was marveled. The architecture was on display as much as the works of art, and the buildings were explored, caressed, and photographed. The visitors in Fort Worth seemed as fascinated by the vast 6,070 m^2 (square meter; 1.5 acre) reflecting pond and the much-discussed concrete walls of Ando's building (Fig 1.1) as the Bilbao public was by Gehry's exuberant forms and titanium cladding. Ando's characteristic elements are once again employed at the Modern: concrete walls, the reflecting pond, circular or oval forms. His ongoing desire to create a contemplative architecture is not incompatible with a desire to attract visitors, and the Fort Worth Modern again proves that the museum, regardless of the architectural style, is the great public building type of our time.

It is said that the American West begins in Fort Worth. Since the completion of Louis Kahn's Kimbell Art Museum in 1972, this venerated architectural monument has made Fort Worth a pilgrimage site for architects from around the world. Any project for the Modern Art Museum of Fort Worth inevitably had to take into consideration the fact that the Kimbell is just across the street (Fig 1.2).

A work in the Modern's collection entitled *The Blind # 19* by the artist Sophie Calle is composed of three frames. One frame contains a frontal portrait of a young woman wearing sunglasses (we assume she is blind). A second frame contains a photograph of the back of a young man reclining on a sunlit bed wearing only boxer shorts. A third frame contains a text:

> The man I live with is the most beautiful thing I know. Even though he could be a few inches taller. I've never come across absolute perfection. I prefer well-built men. It's a question of size and shape. Facial features don't mean much to me. What pleases me aesthetically is a man's body, slim and muscular.

Ando's work, likewise, aspires to see beyond the simply visual and engage all of the senses through the interactions of "muscular" materials such as concrete and granite and the immaterial: light, sky, wind, and sound. In Fort Worth, Ando intertwines art, architecture, and nature. Much of the interest of his buildings comes from the fundamental and essential constructional parts, from refined proportions, volumes, and forms. Ando speaks of "approaching the space of the cosmos" through his buildings, and because of his express search for the metaphysical in architecture, his work might be held to a higher level of achievement for how it carries this quest to term. The Modern is a beautiful building, visually and experientially, even if it is not perfect.

As in many recent museums, Ando has devoted a substantial amount of space to the entry and circulation (Fig 1.11). Arriving visitors gaze through the glass-enclosed, double-height lobby to the reflecting pond and the garden beyond. On the ground floor (Fig 1.4) to the east of the lobby are a 250 seat auditorium and a corridor leading to the museum cafe which is defined by a 22.85 by 15.25 m (75 by 50 ft) elliptical roof slab that is held up by only two 90 cm (36 in.) diameter columns. Administrative offices are on the second floor above the auditorium. On the west side are ticket sales, the museum store, restrooms, and the passage to the galleries. A concrete bridge with glass handrails traverses the lobby space to link the second floor level of the two sides. After passing ticket control a grand stairway (Fig 1.12) and elevators lead to the second floor galleries. Farther ahead the outside curve of the 11.25 by 7.30 m (37 by 24 ft) elliptical gallery (Fig 1.13) guides visitors toward the ground floor galleries. Other offices and support spaces line the south facade on both floors. The building is 14,214 m^2 (153,000 ft^2; square foot) with 4,924 m^2 (53,000 ft^2) of gallery space.

The Modern's basement level houses separate art storage for photos, works on paper, and paintings with appropriate climate control for each. Boilers, chillers, air handlers, a backup generator and general storage are also located in the basement. An "L" shaped service corridor provides access to all spaces and borders a large mechanical area known as the "pit," a crawl space where the ductwork originates. From the pit, ducts enter into wall cavities to make their way to the first and second floors. Large trucks can enter inside the delivery area at ground level. Storage and a workshop are nearby, and an adjacent freight elevator links all floors. Concrete garden walls enclose a mechanical yard at the north/west corner of the building that contains the cooling towers as well as the mechanical equipment for the reflecting pond.

The Modern's galleries remain a powerful and memorable part of the experience of the building. They are simple, well-proportioned, white spaces that are strong but not in competition with the works of art. Multiple circulation paths give an impression of promenade and discovery rather than a predetermined exhibition itinerary. There are numerous places where visitors can step out of the exhibit, take a short break, and gaze at the landscape, the downtown skyline, or the sculpture garden. A dramatic linear stair that climbs the north side of the building links the upper and lower galleries and assures the continuity of the visit without backtracking (Fig 1.16).

Figure 1.3 Site plan

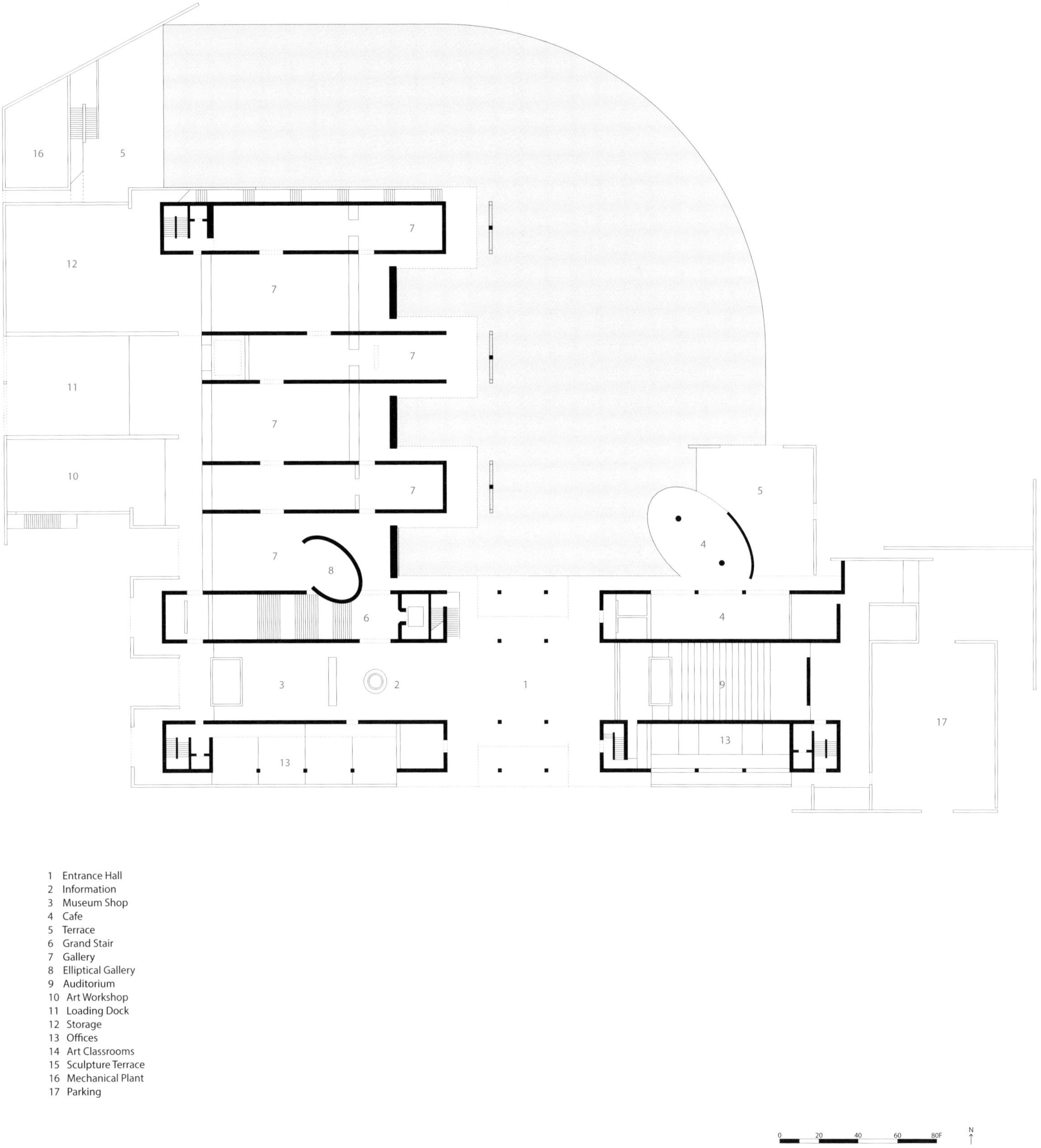

1 Entrance Hall
2 Information
3 Museum Shop
4 Cafe
5 Terrace
6 Grand Stair
7 Gallery
8 Elliptical Gallery
9 Auditorium
10 Art Workshop
11 Loading Dock
12 Storage
13 Offices
14 Art Classrooms
15 Sculpture Terrace
16 Mechanical Plant
17 Parking

Figure 1.4 First (ground) floor plan

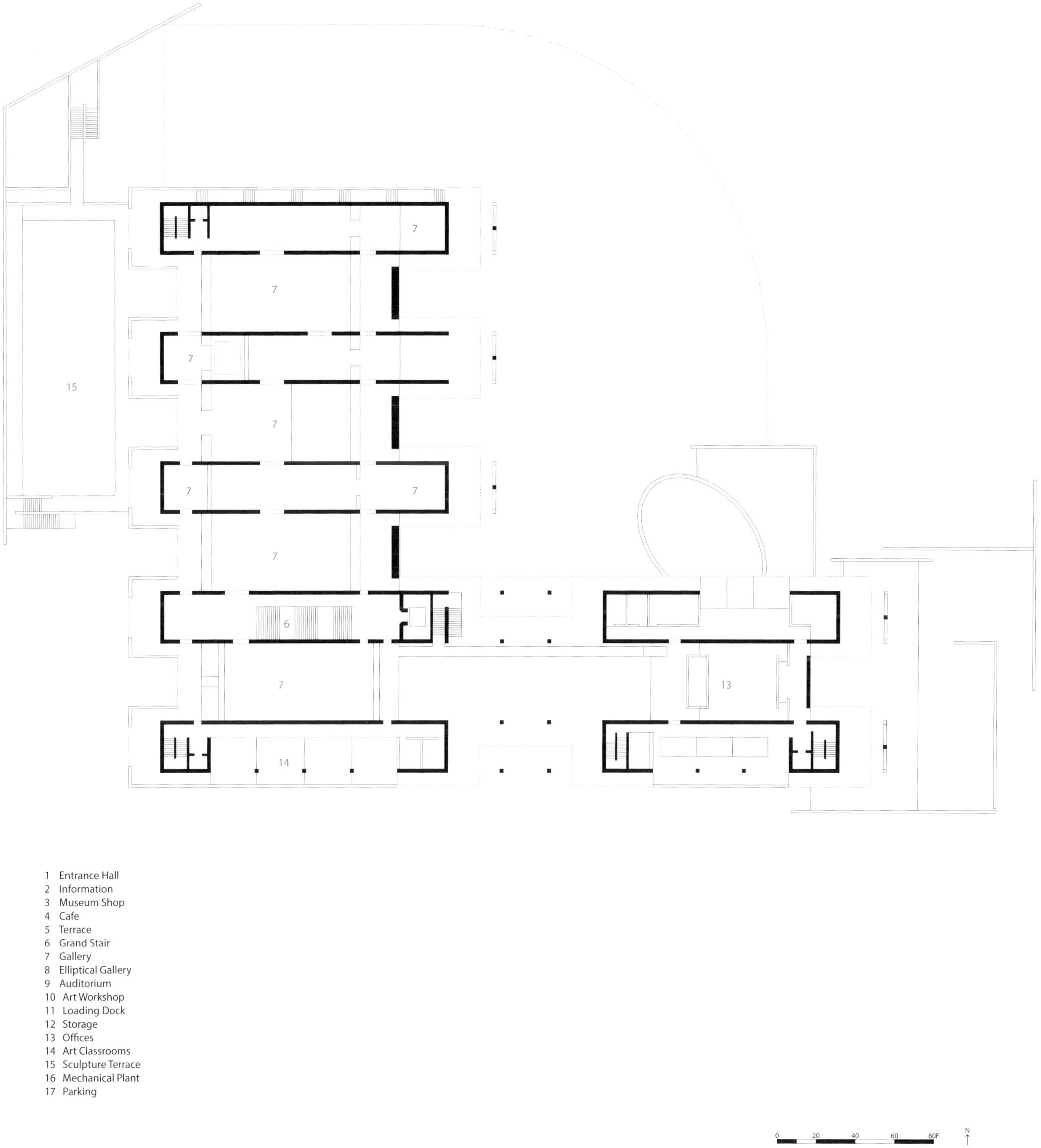

1 Entrance Hall
2 Information
3 Museum Shop
4 Cafe
5 Terrace
6 Grand Stair
7 Gallery
8 Elliptical Gallery
9 Auditorium
10 Art Workshop
11 Loading Dock
12 Storage
13 Offices
14 Art Classrooms
15 Sculpture Terrace
16 Mechanical Plant
17 Parking

Figure 1.5 Second floor plan

On the ground floor the labyrinth-like spaces between the concrete walls and the exterior glass walls are playful. The close spacing and the large size of the mullions compromise the impression of transparency of the facade, however. The aluminum mullions spaced every 1.5 m (5 ft) are 20 cm (8 in.) deep with the glass placed in the middle. They are reinforced by 20 cm (8 in.) wide-flange steel columns. The glass panels are 3.65 m (12 ft) high between horizontal mullions. Floor grills for air conditioning are integrated at the base of the facade. Small louvers at the top of the glass facade contain services such as sprinkler piping and motorized shades. These louvers also contribute to the heaviness of the facade.

Three double-height exhibition spaces are interesting architecturally, yet it is not obvious what the intended relationship is between the gallery spaces they link vertically (Fig 1.14). The first floor galleries have stone floors. Light tracks spaced every 1.5 m (5 ft) are recessed into the 4.60 m (15 ft) high gyp board ceiling. The second floor galleries have white oak floors and the natural top lighting is of two types: continuous, gabled skylights combined with suspended translucent ceiling panels in the 7.30 m (24 ft) wide galleries and 60 cm (2 ft) tall linear clerestory windows with an integrated exterior louver system in the 12.20 m (40 ft) wide galleries (Fig 1.15). The 7.30 m (24 ft) wide galleries have a ceiling height of 5.00 m (16 ft 4 in.), while the ceiling height of the 12.2 m (40 ft) wide galley is 4.30 m (14 ft). In both cases the light is homogenous and somewhat lifeless. The translucent ceiling panels offer little hint of the outside sky and light conditions, or the structure above. Generally, visitors are left with the unfortunate impression of artificially lit gallery spaces.

During my visit on December 26, I spoke to one of the many fellow visitors who had, in fact, participated in the construction of the concrete walls. It was his first visit to the building since completion, and his pride and regret that he might never again work on such a refined project were an indication of the importance of craft and workmanship in Ando's work. The concrete is impeccable. The reveal joint, for example, between the concrete walls and the plaster ceiling is well executed. The worker shared a "secret" though, that only approximately half of the expressed tie holes were necessary from a constructional point of view, and others were added for aesthetic reasons so that tie holes would appear systematically within the modules defined by the form work. He also remarked that the "concrete" ceiling in some parts of the building is not actually the structural slab, but a dropped ceiling made of glass-fiber reinforced concrete panels. Knowing the importance of concrete in Ando's work, it is also surprising that his trademark walls are used so sparingly as actual exhibition walls. The concrete walls toward the reflecting pond and the sculpture garden are like thick facades, or bookends perhaps, that hold white exhibition spaces at the core of the building. The dimensions of the building are based on the 2.40 by 1.2 m (8 by 4 ft) Finnish birch veneered plywood panels that were used as formwork. Several prototypes were made on the site, and the basement concrete walls were used as a final test for the walls that would be seen by the public. The freestanding interior walls are 60 cm (2 ft) thick, and they were hand scraped to acquire a very smooth finish.

Ando has mentioned that the interior of the building is its soul, and the attention given to the galleries and the quality of the interior spaces is evident. The exterior of the building is less successful though, and the project does not sit completely at ease on its 44,515 m^2 (11 acre) site (Fig 1.3). Having two delivery areas, the building's west elevation presents an unfriendly back side to its neighbor, Louis Kahn's Kimbell Art Museum located just across Van Cliburn Way, while its east elevation, particularly at ground level, gives a second less-than-friendly impression to University Drive. There is a certain logic that the Modern's main delivery would face the Kimbell's main delivery area. All delivery areas are not equal, however. Kahn very skillfully integrated this necessity into the concrete base of his building and aligned the loading dock door within one of the vaulted modules in a way that is compatible with the general order of his building. It hardly seems like a sacrificed side of the building. At the Modern the delivery area has no obvious relationship to the pavilions or the overall scheme. It seems more like the back of the building. On the north side, along Camp Bowie Boulevard, there is a concrete wall that denies physical access and extends little invitation to passing pedestrians or automobilists. Finally, the building's grand main entrance (Fig 1.8) and Richard Serra's remarkable sculpture seem a bit lost in the parking lot on the south side of the building. Ando's preliminary design called for an underground parking lot that unfortunately was abandoned as the project developed. The 130 car, on-grade parking lot that was realized is softening as the Cyprus trees planted among the cars mature.

Ando has spoken of the urban condition in Japanese cities that logically leads to walled projects and of his admiration for courtyard buildings such as the Alhambra in Granada, Spain. Yet in Fort Worth, the trade-off for a serene, introverted walled garden with its impressive horizontal reflecting pool (60 cm or 2 ft deep) is a divorce from the sub-urban context and an uneasy insertion into a site that was not all that flat and in fact slopes 7 m (23 ft) from one end to the other.

The total height of the building is 12.2 m (40 ft). The maximum height of the garden walls is 7.90 m (26 ft). Exterior materials are concrete, glass, and bead-blasted anodized, rainscreen aluminum wall panels that are 5 mm (0.19 in.) thick, 1.5 m (5 ft) wide, and up to 7.60 m (25 ft) high. The building should appear as a concrete building wrapped in glass.

Figure 1.6 East facade and reflecting pool at night

Figure 1.7 Competition model photo

Figure 1.8 South entrance facade

Seven Interviews with Tadao Ando, a small book produced by the Modern Art Museum of Fort Worth, offers interesting insights into the making of the building and into Ando's architecture in general. As for many modern architects, Ando feels that "for a building to be successful, the inside and the outside must relate closely." He admires the sense of architectural order of Louis Kahn's work and says that the pavilions at the Modern are partly inspired by the pavilions at the Kimbell. The organization of Ando's building is generally described as five parallel pavilions. Unlike Kahn's design, however, these pavilions are only understood as such from the outside. As the plans indicate, the spaces between the "pavilions" are actually the larger and more important areas. Even the entry hall and auditorium are located in a space between. This leaves the interior organization somewhat disorienting. At the Kimbell, the location of elements such as stairs, elevators, and restrooms can be predicted in relation to the gallery spaces, and they are found in Kahn's flat-roofed servant zones. At the Modern there is a reversal, and stairs, elevators, freight elevators, and restrooms are most often, but not always, located in spaces between parallel walls that from the outside appear as primary pavilions but from the inside seem secondary. The planning of the building seems casual. On arriving at the top of the grand stair, for example, an opening on the right allows the visitor to apprehend the layout of the galleries in enfilade, while an identical opening on the left leads to the restrooms (Fig 1.5).

The structural system of the roof is a very interesting engineering solution even if it lacks architectural clarity. It is a series of independent, "Y" shaped, concrete folded plates spaced at either 7.30 m or 12.20 m (24 ft or 40 ft) apart. In the 7.30 m (24 ft) galleries the skylight is simply and elegantly defined by the gap between the folded plates. (The translucent ceiling unfortunately masks this condition.) In the 12.20 m (40 ft) galleries the lower roof, a flat, post-tensioned, 17 cm (6.5 in.) thick concrete slab, is actually suspended by steel structural elements from the "Y" shaped folded plates above. This relatively complex roof structure clearly reveals itself in a section drawing (Fig 1.17) but remains concealed from inside the building. In the end it contributes little to the architectural expression. The arrangement does create a clerestory window that primarily provides light in the area of the longitudinal walls.

Because Ando is explicitly interested in meaning in architecture and because of his desire to minimize extraneous elements, his "Y" shaped exterior columns seem curious. Even though Ando has used such forms in previous projects, the Modern's columns made much more sense in earlier design drawings where they supported the two primary beams of what appeared to be a layered, steel-framed, translucent roof structure (Fig 1.7). In any project an architect has to make certain formal decisions, yet

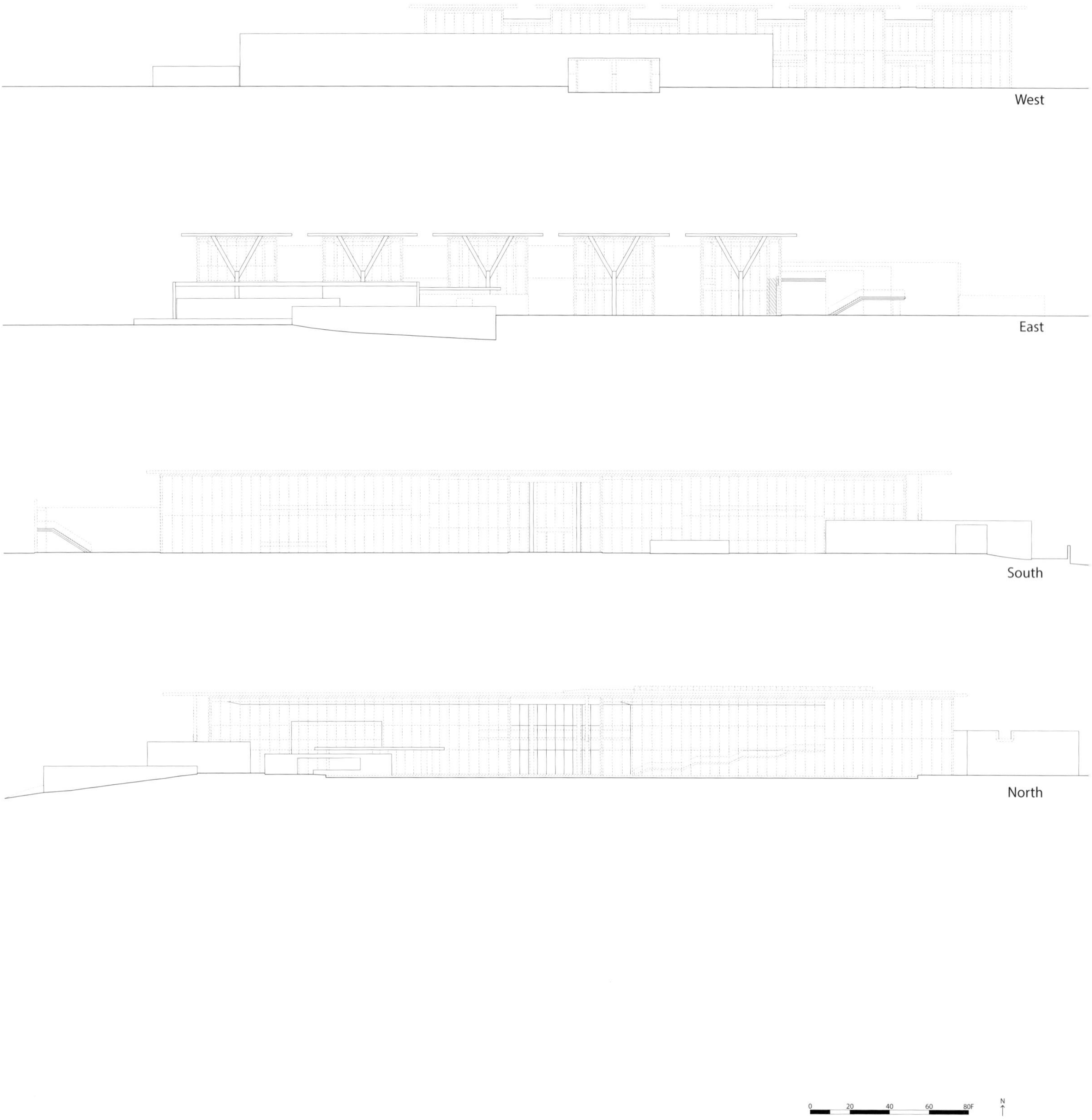

Figure 1.9 Elevations

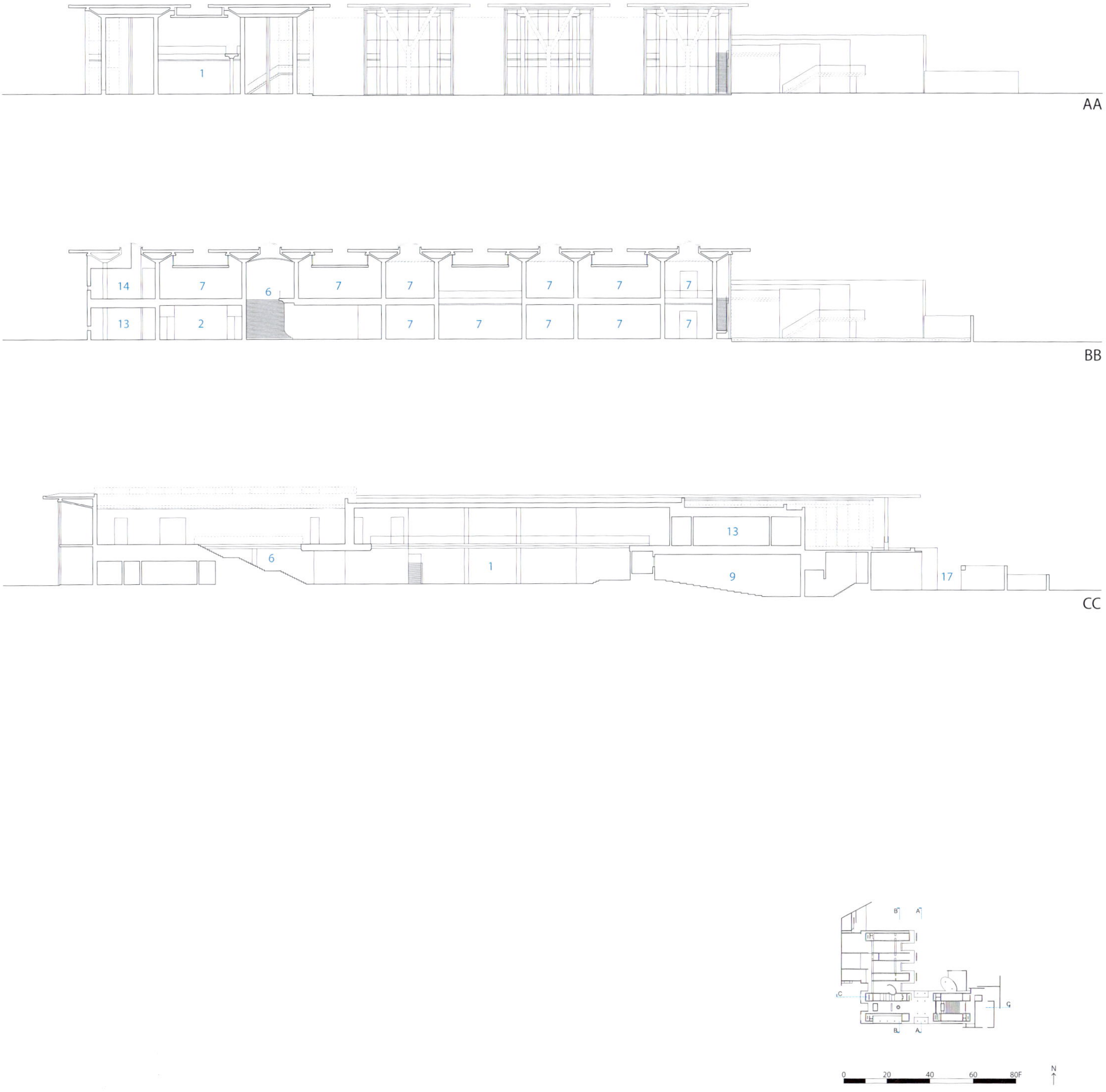

Figure 1.10 Sections

Figure 1.11 Double-height lobby

Figure 1.13 Elliptical gallery

Figure 1.12 Grand stair

Figure 1.14 A double-height exhibition space

Figure 1.15 A second floor gallery

Figure 1.16 North stair

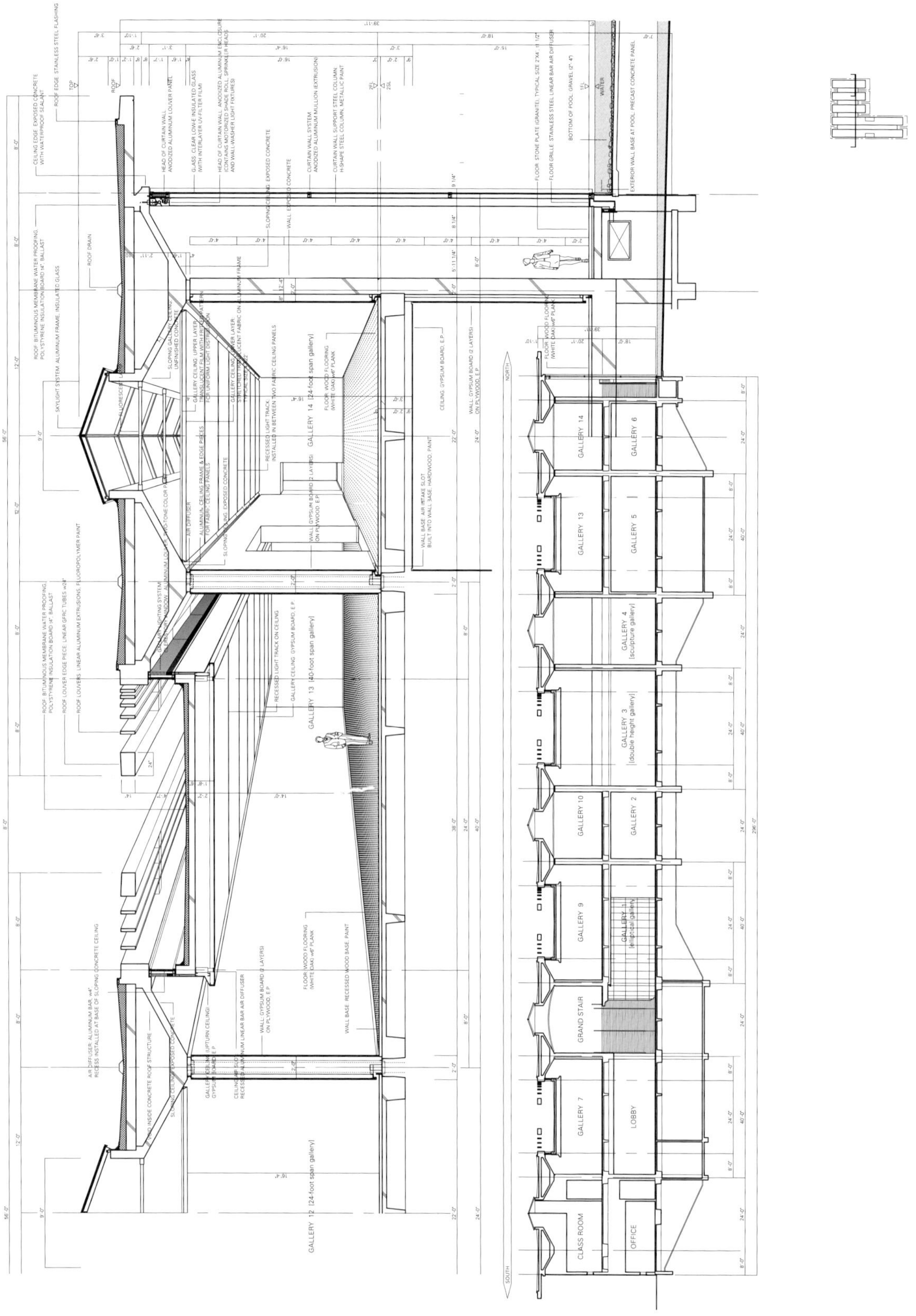

Figure 1.17 Detailed section perspective and section

these strongly iconic columns appear to be a vestige of an earlier scheme. With only a total of five of these seemingly important elements, it is surprising that two of them have been swallowed by the parking area and surrounded by PVC pipes at the eastern extremity of the building. It is also curious that the "Y" forms of the folded plates have little or nothing to do with the "Y" shape columns. The columns are 60 cm (2 ft) square and a total of 11.90 m (39 ft) high. They rise 6.70 m (22 ft) vertically before they fork to a width of 7.30 m (24 ft). Each fork piece was cast vertically on the ground and then lifted into place and attached with a cast in place "crotch" piece. The forks needed temporary bracing until they were loaded with the roof slab and became fully stable.

Though from the outside the Modern evokes more an office building than a "floating swan," which was Ando's metaphor for the project, the building does "come alive when someone enters it," just as the architect hoped. The whole may be more than the sum of the parts. Perhaps Ando's wish that the architecture be "seen together at a glance" and respond to a "larger rhythm and balance" is fulfilled even if, like Sophie Calle's "most beautiful thing," the building "could be a few inches taller" here and there.

CHAPTER 2

Contemporary Arts Center

Cincinnati, Ohio

Zaha Hadid Architects

2003

Figure 2.1 View from 6th Street

Figure 2.2 Study model

Figure 2.3 Painting by Zaha Hadid

From the exterior, the Lois & Richard Rosenthal Contemporary Arts Center (CAC) does not necessarily look like a museum. While its geometric, cantilevered forms and general boldness may hint at its function, it could be mistaken for an office building or a boutique. The building definitely stands out from its neighbors, yet it fits comfortably into its urban context (Fig 2.1). Pedestrians could walk by without even noticing it.

After well over a half century of existence, Hadid's building was the CAC's first freestanding home. Over the years the institution had declined proposals from other arts organizations to share space, and it resisted the temptation of moving out of the center of the city to areas that could offer bigger spaces for lower rents. With a new building, the CAC sought to express its autonomy as an institution and at the same time establish a stronger relationship with the community. Though in its own building, the CAC is surrounded by other cultural and entertainment venues located in the same area of downtown Cincinnati. For Zaha Hadid, the CAC was her largest realization when it opened in 2003, and though it may be less exuberant than what was suggested by the more abstract sketches, paintings, and models the architect was known for early in her career, the building has an undeniable vitality (Fig 2.2 and Fig 2.3).

The CAC began as the Cincinnati Modern Art Society in 1939, changing its name to the Contemporary Arts Center in 1952. Over the years and prior to moving into the current building it was housed in three different spaces, the last one only a few blocks away from its present location. The Center is recognized and respected for its ambitions and quality programming. Its most controversial show was likely a collection of photographs by the artist Robert Mapplethorpe that resulted in criminal charges of obscenity. The Center was acquitted in that case in 1990.

In 1995 Charles Desmarais was named director of the CAC, and the following year reflections began for a completely new space. From the outset ambitions were high, and an extraordinary structure was the goal. For Desmarais, a new building should be a sign in itself and foster experimentation and innovation. An architect of international renown was sought, and the list of 12 semi finalists resulting from a request for qualifications included Coop Himmelb(l)au, Diller & Scofidio, Zaha Hadid, Herzog & de

Meuron, Steven Holl, Toyo Ito, Rem Koolhaas, Daniel Libeskind, Eric Owen Moss, Jean Nouvel, Antoine Predock, and Bernard Tschumi. From that group, three finalists, Hadid, Libeskind, and Tschumi, were chosen, and in March 1998 Zaha Hadid was announced as the selected architect for a new building.

The choice of the busy, corner site at 6th and Walnut Streets offers high visibility and was in itself an important, positive point for the project (Fig 2.4). Hadid completed the urban alignment of the downtown block by neatly inserting her scheme between existing buildings dating from the early twentieth century. In the immediate vicinity there are high-rises alongside low, two-storied buildings. The CAC's long facade on 6th Street faces south and looks toward a parking garage that sits above ground floor retail. Hadid's project appears as staggered, horizontal blocks of metal, glass, and concrete stacked above a generally glazed ground floor (Fig 2.13). Glazed areas of the upper floors correspond to the administrative offices rather than gallery spaces, and the elevation is animated by the movements of the staff inside. From the street we are not able to see into the upper level exhibition spaces, however, and no visual connection was established between the two. There is a formal kinship with Hadid's later MAXXI in Rome. Though the opening dates of the two projects are separated by seven years, the competitions were roughly of the same period. Both buildings appear more as a thick facade – a sort of bas-relief – rather than freestanding, sculptural objects.

The short, east facade of the CAC is more compact, energized, and sculptural and can be better appreciated because of a small plaza across Walnut Street that provides more breathing room for the building (Fig 2.14). From a car or on foot, this facade provides the strongest image of the project (Fig 2.15). It appears complex, yet rigorous and, like the long facade, suggests the interior organization. A fourth floor corner terrace for the administrative offices offers a human presence and scale within this rather abstract composition that the architect compares to a three-dimensional jigsaw puzzle.

At ground level (Fig 2.6) the full height glazed facade is pushed in from the face of the building thereby opening the corner and creating a larger covered entry area. It also enhances the effect of a floating upper volume. The service entry and garage doors are at the west end of the building and are generally inconspicuous. The building's opaque exterior cladding is composed of panels of precast concrete or blackened aluminum plate. The aluminum originally had a matt finish. Early on, white markings developed on the panels and a subsequent coating gave a somewhat more shiny finish.

The CAC's site is 1,022 m^2 (square meter; 11,000 ft^2 (square foot)); the building is 8,083 m^2 (87,000 ft^2), and gallery spaces total 2,211 m^2 (23,800 ft^2). The basement level (Fig 2.5) contains a 214 m^2 (2,300 ft^2) black box performance space along with its own lobby. There are also mechanical spaces and a workshop located below grade. All upper levels (Fig 2.7, Fig 2.8, Fig 2.9, and Fig 2.10) are accessible to the public with gallery spaces above and below the third and fourth floor administrative offices. The top, seventh floor penthouse is a full mechanical level (Fig 2.12). It contributes to the overall exterior composition of the building much like the top mechanical level of the New Museum in New York by the Japanese architects SANAA. Special attention was also given to the roof in Cincinnati which was treated as an additional facade since it is visible from the taller buildings in the area.

The principal organizing element of the project is the "Urban Carpet" that was conceived to link the public to the art and the space of the street to the exhibition spaces at the upper levels. Conceptually, the public sidewalk along 6th Street enters the building as the concrete floor of the 6.40 m (21 ft) high, 465 m^2 (5,000 ft^2) entry hall where reception and a museum shop are located. After traversing the width of the lobby (Fig 2.22), the floor curves up to become a concrete wall that ascends the entire height of the north side of the building. A small portion of the Urban Carpet continues outside (Fig 2.16), past a glazed facade at the north/east corner of the Center, and this curved exterior portion is extremely tempting for skateboarders! However playful the curved or rolled portion of the Urban Carpet, it is a very literal, formal means of establishing continuity between the horizontal and the vertical. In detail there are differences of appearance between the floor with its precise finish layer, the rolled portion with its difficulties to form and pour, and the vertical wall that could be more easily controlled during execution. Self-compacting concrete that requires less vibration was used for the roll and the vertical portion of the Urban Carpet.

The 38 m (125 ft) tall, concrete wall is the defining element of the narrow, top-lit atrium and circulation space that contains a series of low-rise and long-run stairs known as stair-ramps. These long-span, narrow stair elements are made of deep, parallel steel beams that also act as railings. They are black in color and similar to the exterior aluminum cladding panels. Within the space, the stair elements appear as lines that crisscross the vertical slot making it the main spatial gesture of the project. The skylight at the very top provides abundant light as well as a place to lower the prefabricated stair-ramps into the building by crane during construction. Another intermediate glass ceiling just below the level of the third floor slab isolates the lobby from the spaces above and assures better temperature and humidity control in the galleries (Fig 2.24). The glass plane also provides a mixture of reflections and transparencies that further animates the space. Though we imagine that it is an element added for pragmatic reasons, the glass ceiling is a positive contribution to the overall effect.

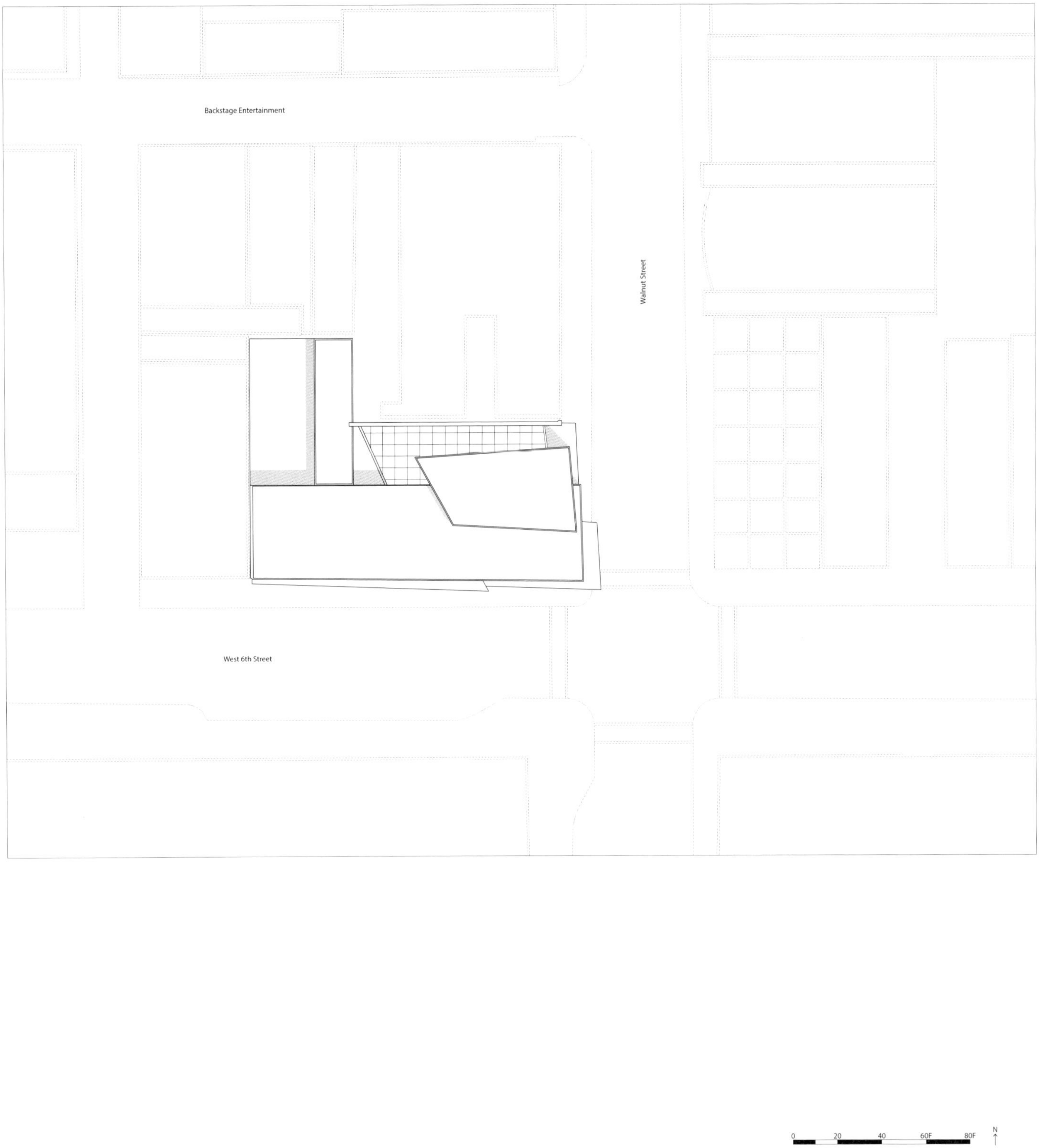

Figure 2.4 Site plan

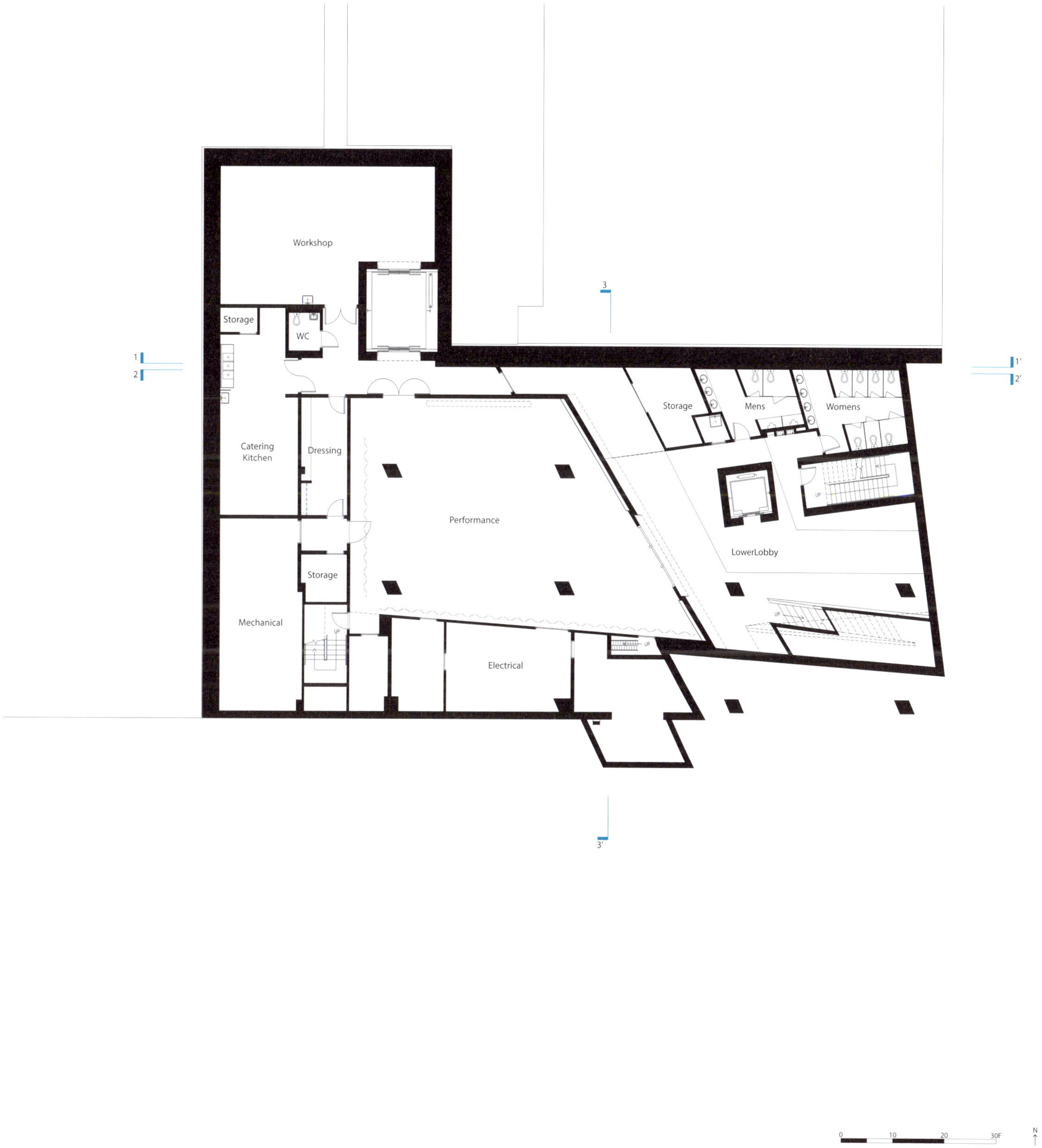

Figure 2.5 Lower level floor plan

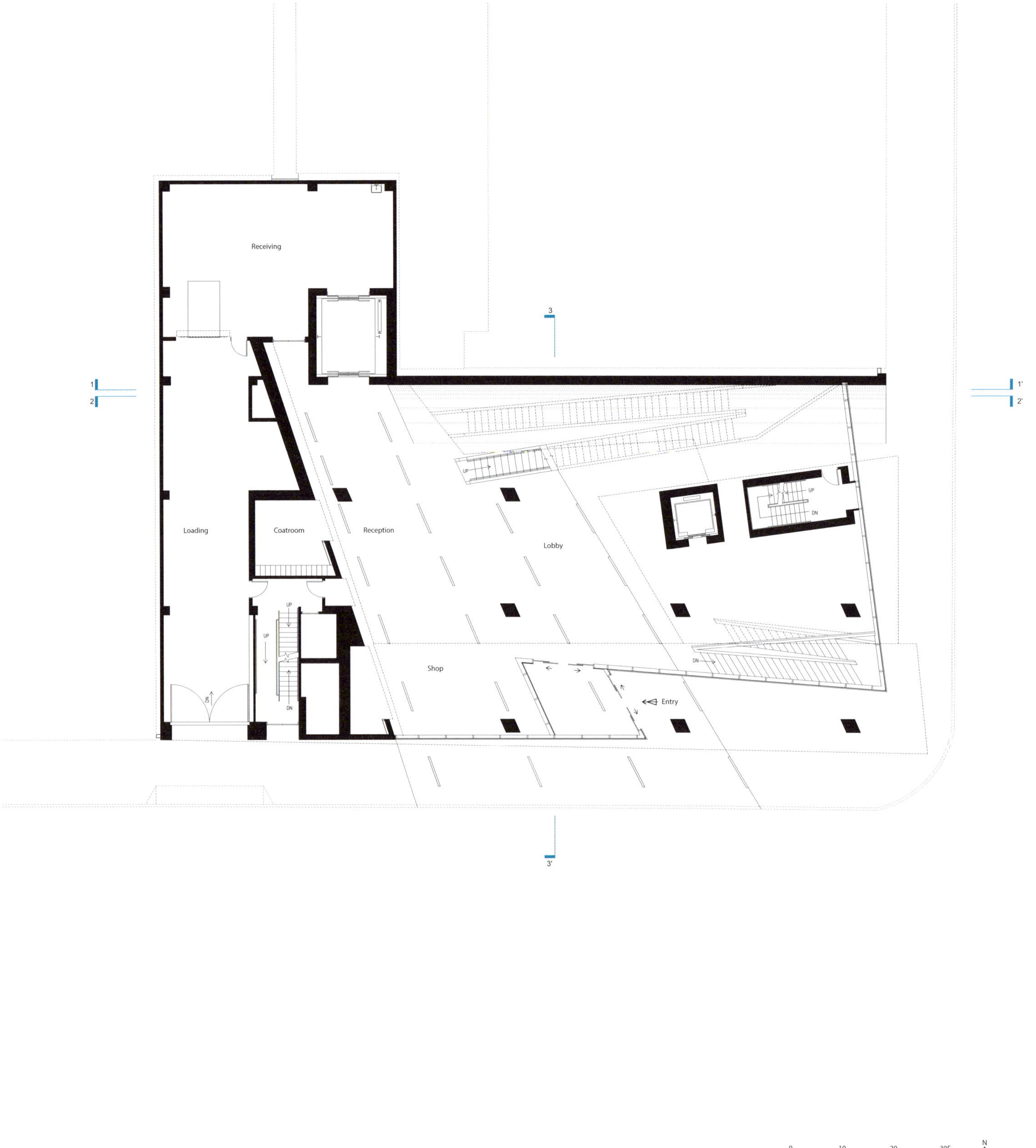

Figure 2.6 First (ground) floor plan

Figure 2.7 Second floor plan

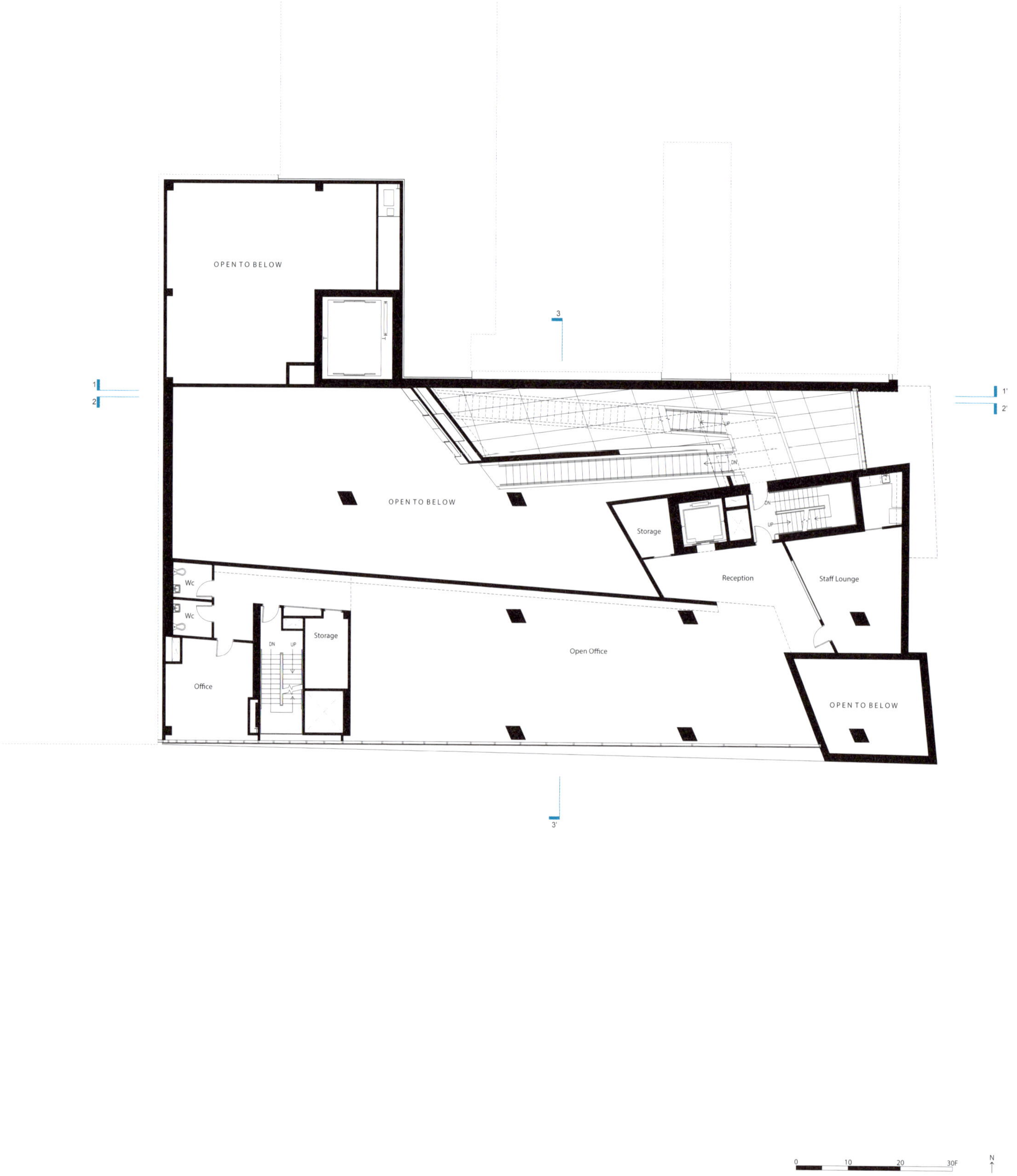

Figure 2.8 Third floor plan

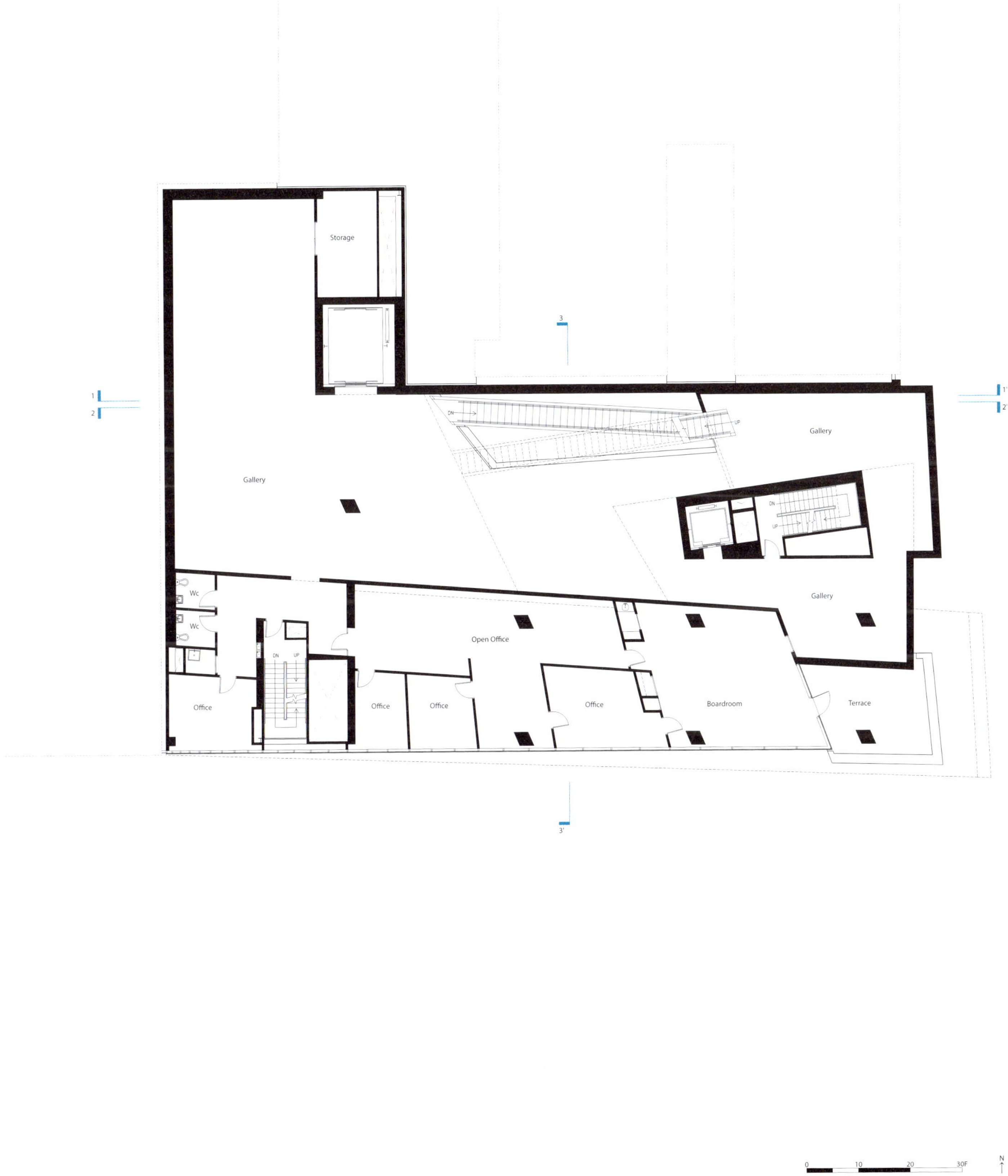

Figure 2.9 Fourth floor plan

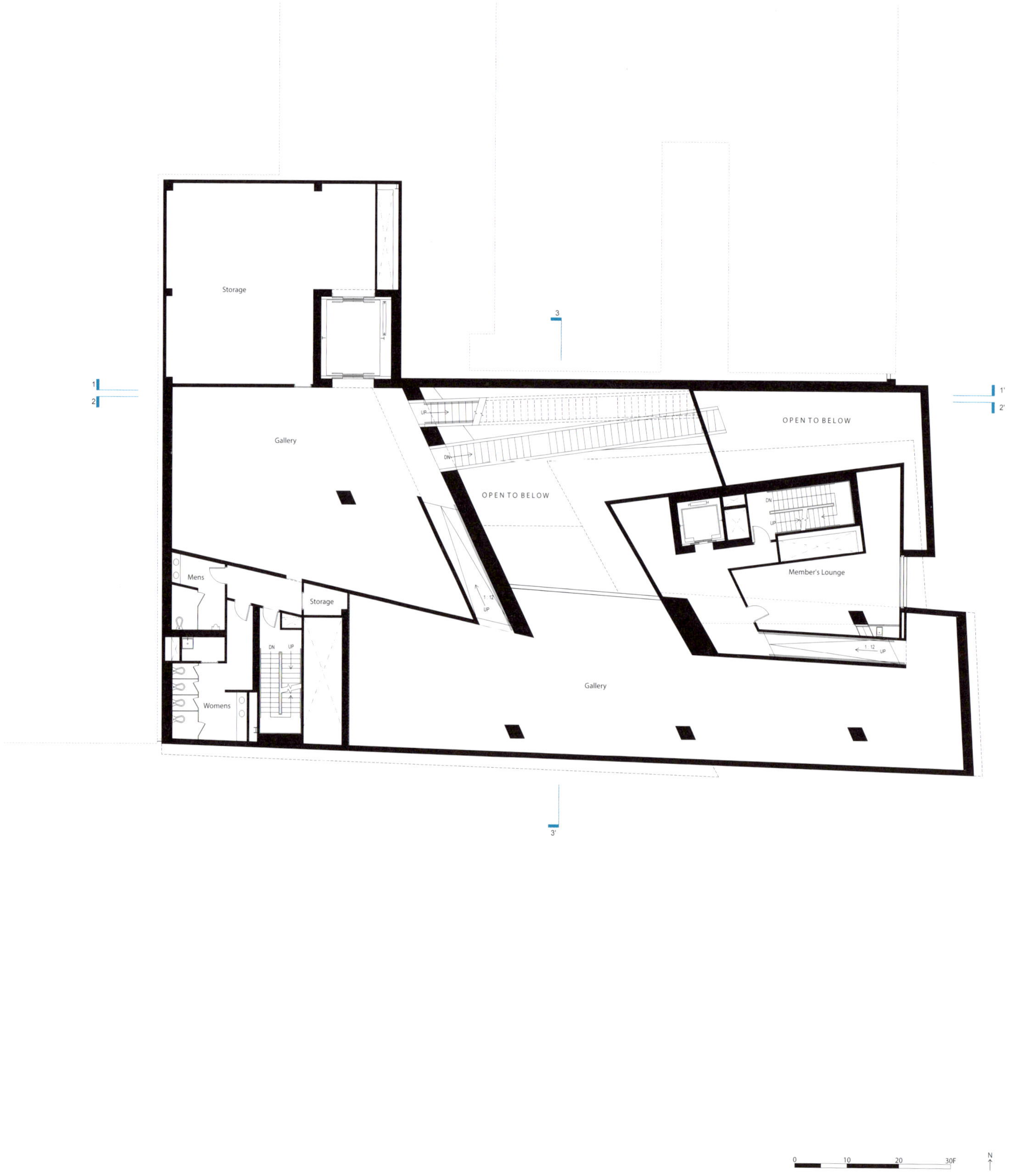

Figure 2.10 Fifth floor plan

Figure 2.11 Sixth floor plan

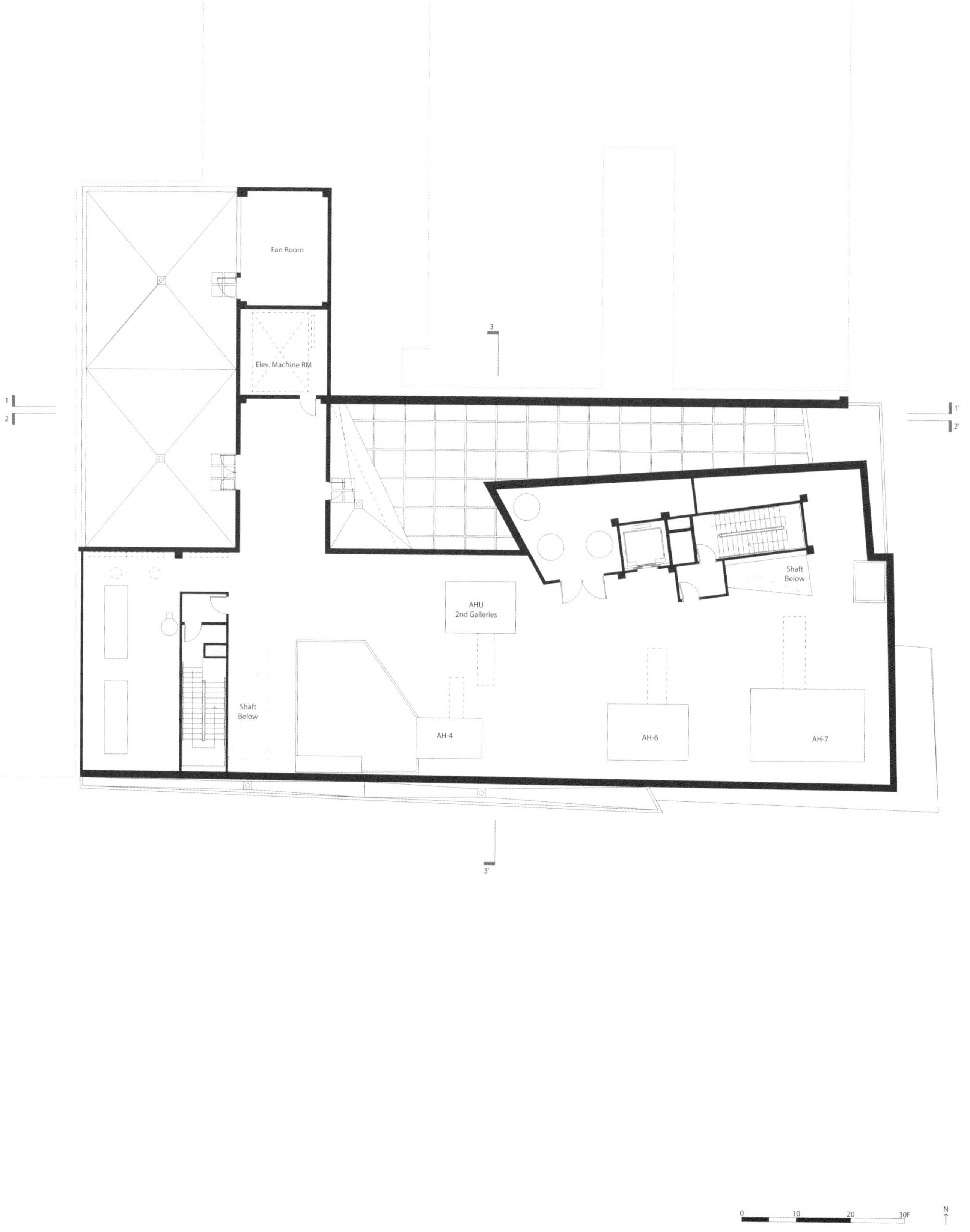

Figure 2.12 Seventh floor plan

Figure 2.13 South elevation

Figure 2.14 East elevation at night

Figure 2.15 View from Walnut Street

Figure 2.16 Urban Carpet from outside

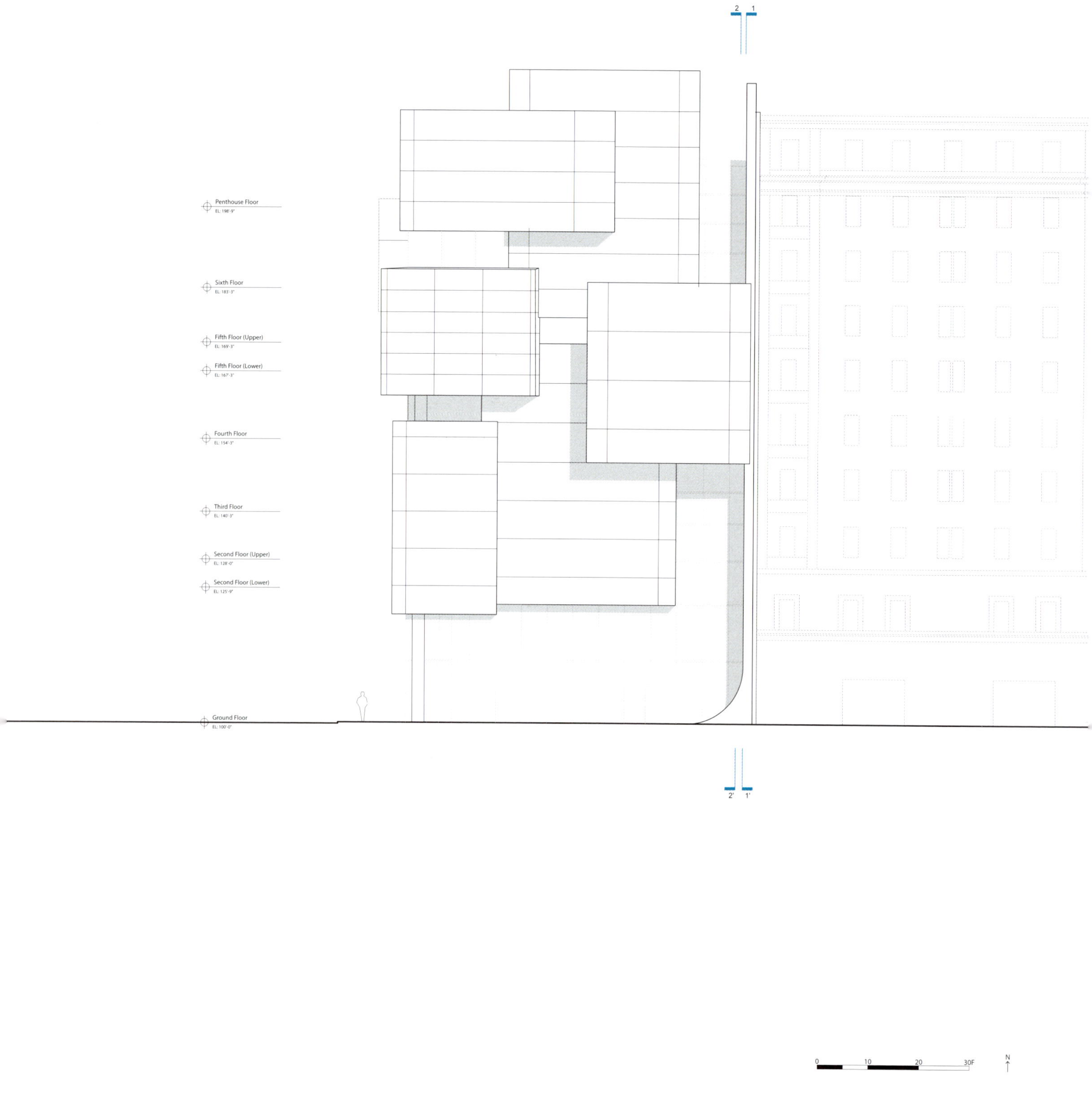

Figure 2.17 East elevation

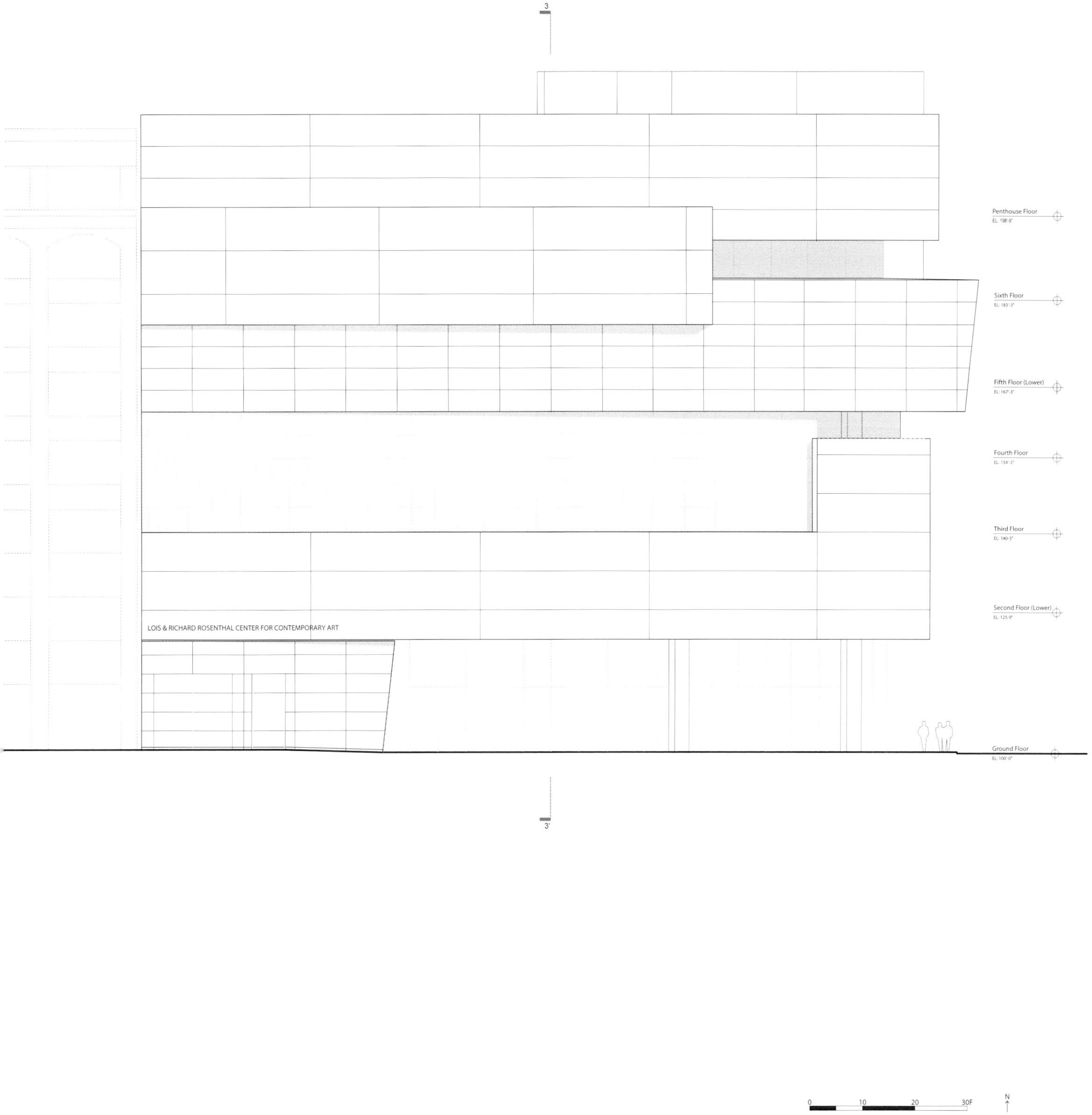

Figure 2.18 South elevation

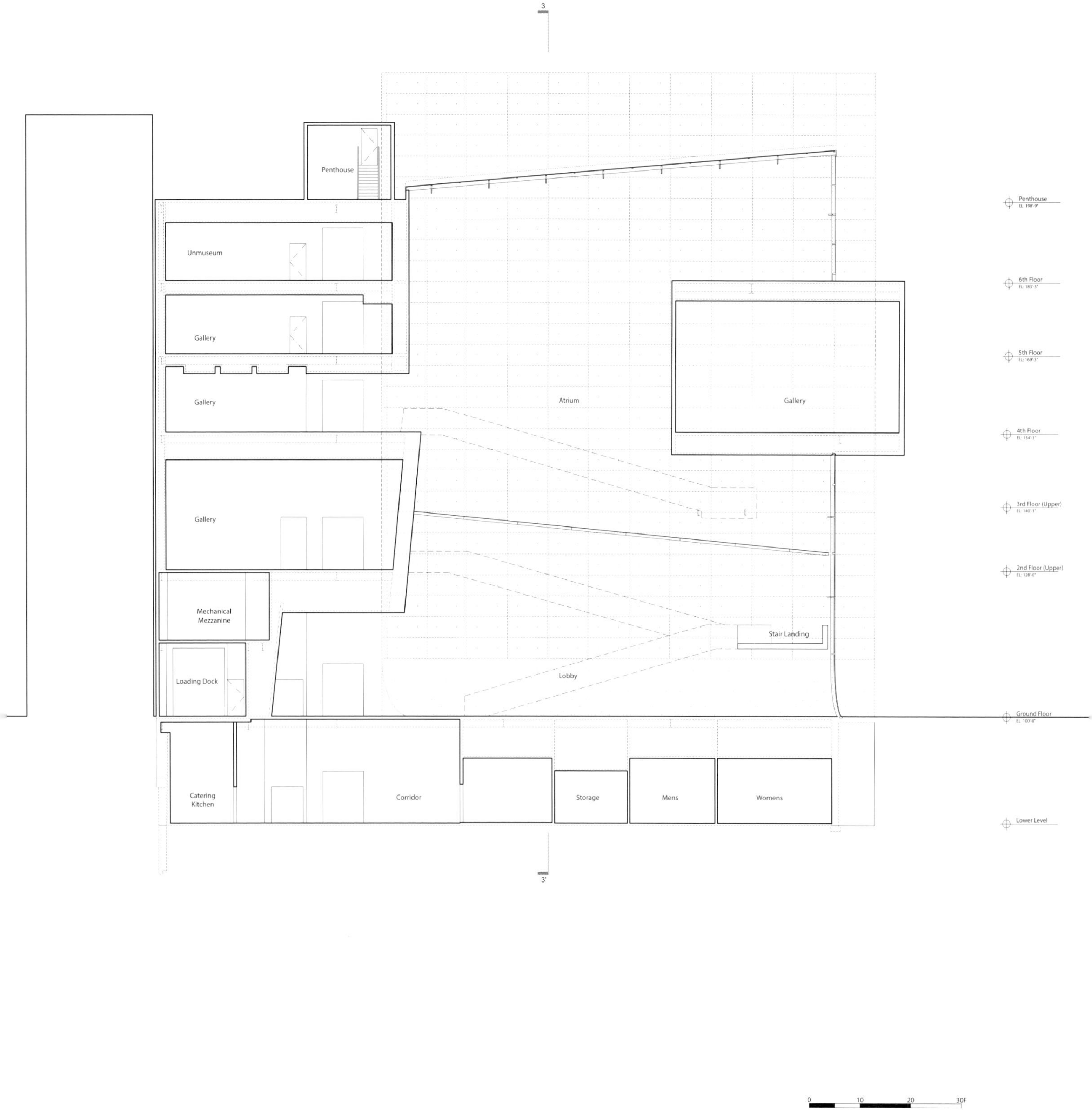

Figure 2.19 Long section 1

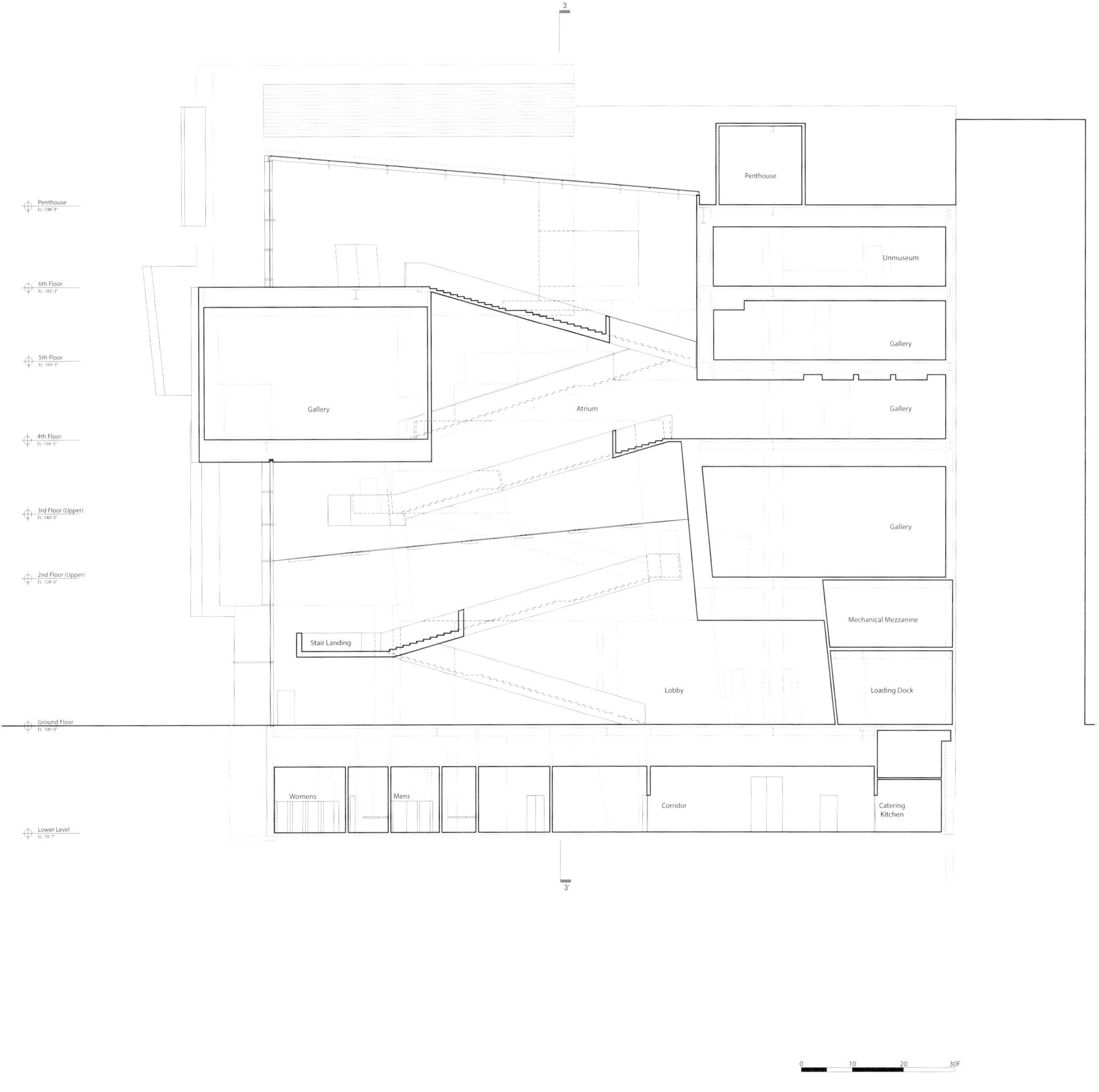

Figure 2.20: Long section 2

Figure 2.21 Cross section 3

Hadid imagined that visitors would take the passenger elevator or, even better, the large freight elevator that opens through the Urban Carpet directly to the top gallery spaces and meander down much like in Frank Lloyd Wright's Guggenheim. Most visitors, however, are attracted to the atrium space and the stair-ramp that provide a slower discovery of the building and changing views up and down and into the art spaces.

The jigsaw puzzle is likewise the reference for the interior where spaces of different shapes, sizes, and heights interlock. Since the Contemporary Arts Center possesses no collection, the gallery spaces should be flexible for temporary exhibitions. The architectural solution took into account, and perhaps prioritized, contemporary art types such as site-specific pieces and media or video installations. Throughout, more complex, labyrinth-like spaces were favored over simple lofts. Ceilings vary in height from single to double story to accommodate a range of works. Spaces remain generally open but weave around the building core or partition walls that contain and regroup the structural columns.

A vertical museum seems inevitable on the relatively small site. Galleries are located on the second (the largest exhibition level with 567 m^2 or 6,100 ft^2) (Fig 2.23), fourth (Fig 2.25), and fifth floors. At the top, the sixth floor is devoted to the UnMuseum (Fig 2.11 and Fig 2.26), a learning and exhibition space for children. There is little hierarchy in the galleries which gives a certain freedom to the visit. Movement is crucial for Hadid, and circulation and exhibition spaces merge and generally encourage or even incite motion rather than saunter. Stairs and ramps within the galleries link smaller, two-foot level changes that have the effect of displacing attention from the space of the art to the building elements themselves. With all its potential distractions, however, the interior architecture of the CAC can still recede at times, allowing works of art to advance, and then advance again itself as a strong spectacle.

The continuous movement and level changes were meant to make visitors more aware of other visitors and more aware of others looking at art. In this way a museum visit should become a more communal activity. High volumes are contrasted to low areas with ceiling heights of little more than 3.35 m (11 ft). Such smaller spaces appear as nooks or settings for artwork, highly framed and defined. Less successful spaces include awkward dead ends, no wider than an ordinary hallway. For a building with relatively small exhibition spaces, variety is abundant, even extreme. Practicality was not a prime goal for the client, and the galleries should challenge curators, artists, and visitors. While the architectural approach is meant to increase personal awareness and personal discovery it is obviously difficult to know if that is indeed the case.

Technical equipment in the exhibition spaces such as lighting, sprinkler heads, exit panels, air conditioning vents, etc. are treated in a straightforward manner. Though there was little attempt to reduce their visual impact, they are generally not bothersome in the overall scheme. Serene spaces were not the goal.

Natural light is present due to the atrium skylight, but unlike the later MAXXI in Rome, gallery spaces in Cincinnati are exclusively artificially lit. The exhibition spaces are a somewhat self-contained world, however, with little link to the outside save the conceptual link via the Urban Carpet. Glimpses into the curatorial and administrative offices from the vertical circulation slot give a pleasant hint of the inner workings of the Center.

The ideal space to show contemporary art, or most types of art for that matter, escapes consensus. Alternatives are determined on a case by case basis by museum directors, trustees, curators, politicians, architects, artists, etc. who represent by proxy the voice and supposed desires of the visitor. The CAC did not want neutral rooms or warehouse spaces that were seen as repetitious and monotonous.

By coincidence, along with the Contemporary Arts Center in Cincinnati, another important art space, the Dia:Beacon in the small town of Beacon, New York, opened in the same month of May 2003. In many ways it is the antithesis of the CAC. It houses a permanent collection of generally large-scale works dating from the 1960s to the present, and it was designed by the artist Robert Irwin and the relatively unknown architectural firm OpenOffice. It is housed in a brick factory building that was built for Nabisco in 1929. Though choosing an industrial building for an exhibition space may be a statement in itself, there is no architectural statement comparable to the CAC. In this case, the museum spaces remain utilitarian, discrete, and raw. The industrial architecture offers large spans and the majority of the 22,297 m^2 (240,000 ft^2) of exhibition space is naturally lit by north-facing shed skylights. Spaces are loft-like and vast. The Dia:Beacon is 97 kilometers (60 miles) from New York City, and most visitors go as a sort of pilgrimage.

Hadid's modernity has little to do with the functional, industrial architecture of the Nabisco factory. Her building should be more original and expressive and more like a work of abstract or conceptual art itself. Likely because of a limited budget for the CAC, the building is still comparatively straightforward. Early in the project structural solutions were sought that would be closely related to the organizational concept of the Urban Carpet with floor plates cantilevered from a primary structural concrete wall at the back of the building. Columns were added, however, and schemes were also explored using Hadid's preferred building

Figure 2.22 Lobby

Figure 2.24 Atrium at third floor level

Figure 2.23 Second floor gallery

Figure 2.25 Fourth floor gallery

Figure 2.26 Sixth floor UnMuseum

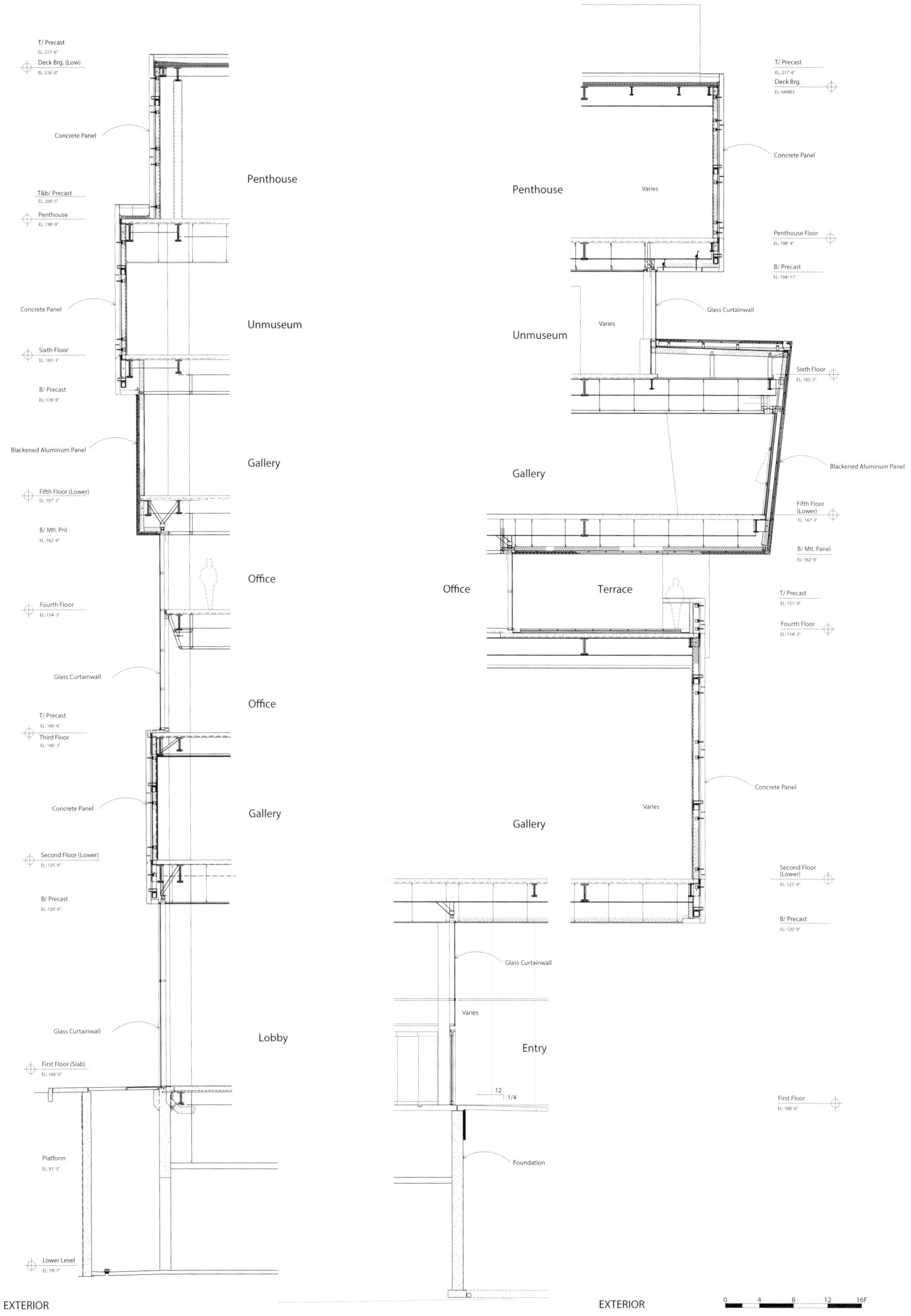

T/ Precast
EL: 217'-6"
Deck Brg. (Low)
EL: 216'-0"
Concrete Panel
Penthouse
T&b/ Precast
EL: 200'-5"
Penthouse
EL: 198'-9"
Concrete Panel
Unmuseum
Sixth Floor
EL: 183'-3"
B/ Precast
EL: 178'-9"
Blackened Aluminum Panel
Gallery
Fifth Floor (Lower)
EL: 167'-3"
B/ Mtl. Pnl.
EL: 162'-9"
Office
Fourth Floor
EL: 154'-3"
Glass Curtainwall
Office
T/ Precast
EL: 140'-6"
Third Floor
EL: 140'-3"
Concrete Panel
Gallery
Second Floor (Lower)
EL: 125'-9"
B/ Precast
EL: 120'-9"
Glass Curtainwall
Lobby
First Floor (Slab)
EL: 100'-0"
Platform
EL: 91'-3"
Lower Level
EL: 79'-7"
EXTERIOR
T/ Precast
EL: 217'-6"
Deck Brg.
EL: VARIES
Concrete Panel
Penthouse
Varies
Penthouse Floor
EL: 198'-9"
B/ Precast
EL: 194'-11"
Glass Curtainwall
Varies
Unmuseum
Sixth Floor
EL: 183'-3"
Gallery
Blackened Aluminum Panel
Fifth Floor (Lower)
EL: 167'-3"
B/ Mtl. Panel
EL: 162'-9"
Office
Terrace
T/ Precast
EL: 157'-9"
Fourth Floor
EL: 154'-3"
Concrete Panel
Varies
Gallery
Second Floor (Lower)
EL: 125'-9"
B/ Precast
EL: 120'-9"
Glass Curtainwall
Varies
Entry
12
1/4
First Floor
EL: 100'-0"
Foundation
EXTERIOR
0
4
8
12
16F

material: cast in place concrete. Eventually a steel moment frame structure was settled on (Fig 2.27) with only the Urban Carpet being site-cast concrete. When visible, the steel columns are encapsulated in concrete to give the appearance of a cast in place structure. They were also given a trapezoidal shape. Since spans are generally small and do not exceed 10 m (33 ft), the columns often appear oversized, especially in the lobby. The building's floor structure is a composite system using steel beams and metal decking with a concrete slab. Columns strictly follow a grid and are allowed to fall in awkward positions in the galleries or in the basement level performance space. There are few visible indications of how the building is actually constructed, though in the ground floor lobby the steel structure with its sprayed-on fireproofing can be seen through the metal grating of the dropped ceiling. Interior walls are generally made of plywood and gypsum board over metal studs.

The building is linked to a downtown steam and chilled water loop. Air handlers are all located in the penthouse mechanical room, and ducts are routed to the lower floors via chases integrated into the two vertical cores that also contain emergency stairs. The building was opened almost exactly two years after ground breaking.

In the 2004 book *Zaha Hadid: Space for Art*, Charles Desmarais, the then director of the Contemporary Arts Center, noted that the project began with discussions on how to create a great building. This was further explored in May 1997 with *In Search of Significance: A Symposium on Building Greatness*. Hadid's project is exceptional, perhaps even great in many ways: urbanistically, formally, and spatially. It is innovative without being overly eccentric. As in many spaces for art, it is the functional aspect and general qualities of the galleries that remain open for debate – whether innovation corresponds to improvement.

Apparently Hadid's approach must be more than merely acceptable since her second built project in the United States is also a museum. Hadid was chosen to build the Eli and Edythe Broad Art Museum on the Michigan State University campus in East Lansing. Though a completely freestanding structure, the building shares many of the qualities of the CAC including the concept of Urban Carpet. The same Broad couple also chose the very different Diller Scofidio + Renfro to do another museum for their private art collection in Los Angeles on a downtown site just next to Frank Gehry's Walt Disney Concert Hall. As Charles Desmarais points out, it is generally accepted that an architectural project can influence an institution's mission. As the Broads might agree, there are many different approaches for the contemporary art museum. That said, there is likely not a direct correlation between significant, even great, buildings and great spaces for art.

Figure 2.27 Wall sections (facing page)

CHAPTER 3

Kunsthaus Graz

Graz, Austria

Spacelab Cook/Fournier

2003

Figure 3.1 Aerial view from north-east

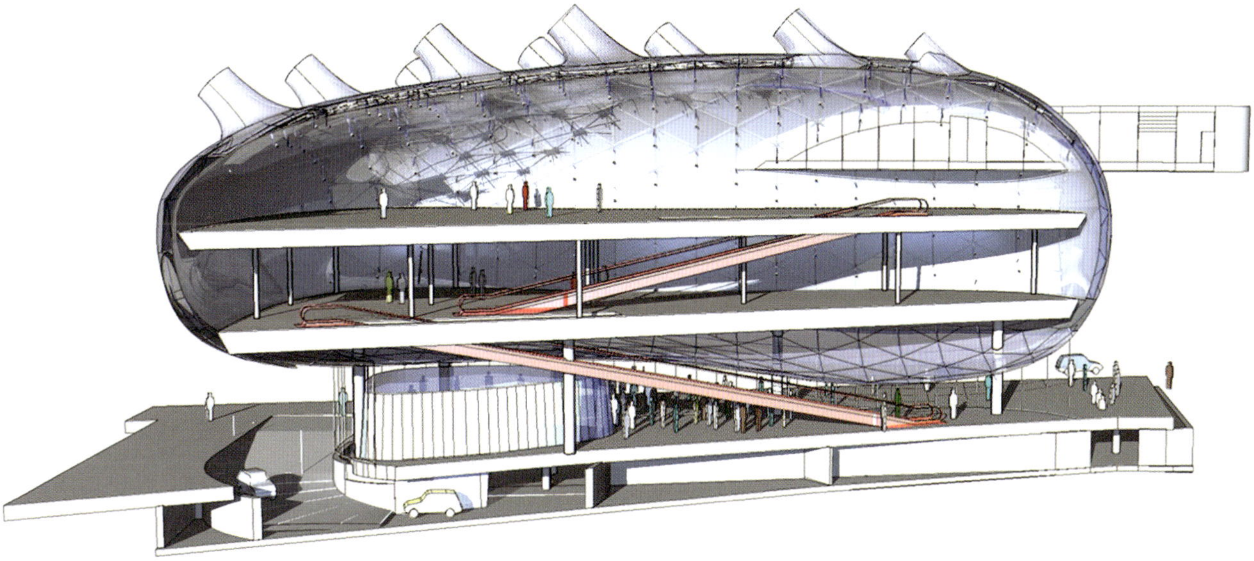

Figure 3.2 Section model

Peter Cook and Colin Fournier's biomorphic design for the Kunsthaus is not a predictable response to the architectural forms of the historical center of Graz. It does, however, resonate locally at a more general cultural level. Graz experienced an artistic and cultural high point during the 1960s and 1970s, and it was a defining period for the region still in the wake of World War II. There was a mood of open-mindedness, and affiliations beyond Austria's national borders were sought and forged especially with Italy and Yugoslavia. A close tie was established, for example, with the Italian artist Gianni Colombo, and his kinetic works and architectural environments are still a collective reference for Graz. The Austrian American architect Frederick Kiesler is also a local reference even though he had no strong link specifically to the city. Kiesler's *Endless House* project is a formal precedent for biomorphic structures, while his exhibition designs explored less conventional ways to present art works. Kiesler's designs include projects in Vienna in the 1920s and his *Art of This Century* project for Peggy Guggenheim's collection in New York in the 1940s. The work of architects such as Gunther Domenig who practices and teaches in Graz also paved the way for architecture somewhat outside of the traditions of modernism. (Domenig/Eisenkock/Peyker were also partner architects on the Kunsthaus.) Archigram would have been at home in the Graz of the 1960s and 1970s. A response to context may come in many forms and the Kunsthaus may be a belated landmark to the period and its values.

A new building for the exhibition of modern and contemporary art was long in coming for Graz. Cook and Fournier had participated in a previous competition for a building to be located at the foot of Graz's castle hill. That competition, like another one before it, did not result in a commission. In 1998 Graz was named as the European Cultural Capital for 2003 which provided a new opportunity for a new building. In 1999 a competition was launched, and from the outset it was known that the building should be an architectural event and should attract tourists. There were 102 competition entries in all, primarily by Austrian architects, but of varied architectural tendencies. Among the other high-profile firms that participated were Zaha Hadid Architects, Morphosis, and Coop Himmelb(l)au. Eight honorable mentions were awarded and the jury announced its unanimous decision for Cook and Fournier's project in April 2000. Construction began in July 2001 and the building opened in September 2003.

Also in 1999, Graz's well-preserved historic center was placed on the UNESCO World Heritage List. The Kunsthaus, located to the west and across the Mur River from the actual center, is within the listed area. Graz is Austria's second largest city with a population of 300,000. It has an impressive collection of museums and institutions of various types for the arts, sciences, and culture that are united and collectively known as the Joanneum Universal Museum, of which the Kunsthaus is part.

Though many locations were considered, a prominent, one-"block," right bank site just where the bridge, the Hautpbrucke, crosses the Mur River was chosen for the Kunsthaus (Fig 3.3). The river is well below street level, and its edges have been left natural in many places with trees growing in a haphazard pattern. The buildings on the northern part of the Kunsthaus block had been demolished previously, and when the competition was launched, this area was used as a surface parking lot. The Eisernes Haus, or Iron House, along the Sudtirolerplatz to the south dates from 1848 and was the first cast iron building in Austria. It is classified as an historical monument and was integrated into the Kunsthaus program. Two other buildings facing the Mariahilferstrasse to the west are also historical monuments and were conserved. Today some Kunsthaus offices and the "House of Architecture" are accommodated in one of the two buildings. Other structures on the block were demolished leaving a generally triangular site for the new Kunsthaus.

Neighboring buildings on winding streets are generally three to five stories tall, and the area is full of shops and cafes. Nearby, the Mursteg footbridge by Gunther Domenig provides access to the left bank, and a little farther to the north there is the Mur Island, a swirling, metallic artificial island that contains a cafe and an amphitheater. The structure was designed by the New York artist Vito Acconci and was also completed in 2003 for Graz's year as Cultural Capital of Europe.

The Kunsthaus was meant to be iconic (Fig 3.1). Its bubble form bulges to the site limits like a squeezed balloon with some invisible girdle holding it in. Its height generally conforms to that of surrounding buildings and seems diminished because of the curved forms. Nevertheless, the building most definitely stands out. Adjectives such as "friendly," "cuddly," and "chubby" have been used to describe it, and they all fit. The architects coined "friendly alien," and it has stuck. Comparisons have been made between the bulbous forms of the Kunsthaus and the numerous Baroque buildings in Graz.

For all of its visual exuberance, the project has few parts. The bubble, with its 16 protruding nozzles facing north, sits atop a glass enclosed ground floor. The generally orthogonal "needle" saddles the building and tames it somewhat (Fig 3.10). It is an intelligent and crucial element that visually links the Kunsthaus to the Eisernes Haus and thereby to the city fabric. The bubble seems to be tethered by the Eisernes Haus (as well as the other preexisting buildings on the block) which has been reworked, restored, and painted dark gray to be more compatible with the new building. The cast iron building makes the transition formally and chronologically between Graz's historical architecture and Cook and Fournier's building. Zaha Hadid used a similar strategy in Rome where she maintained existing buildings on the site to

Figure 3.3 Site plan

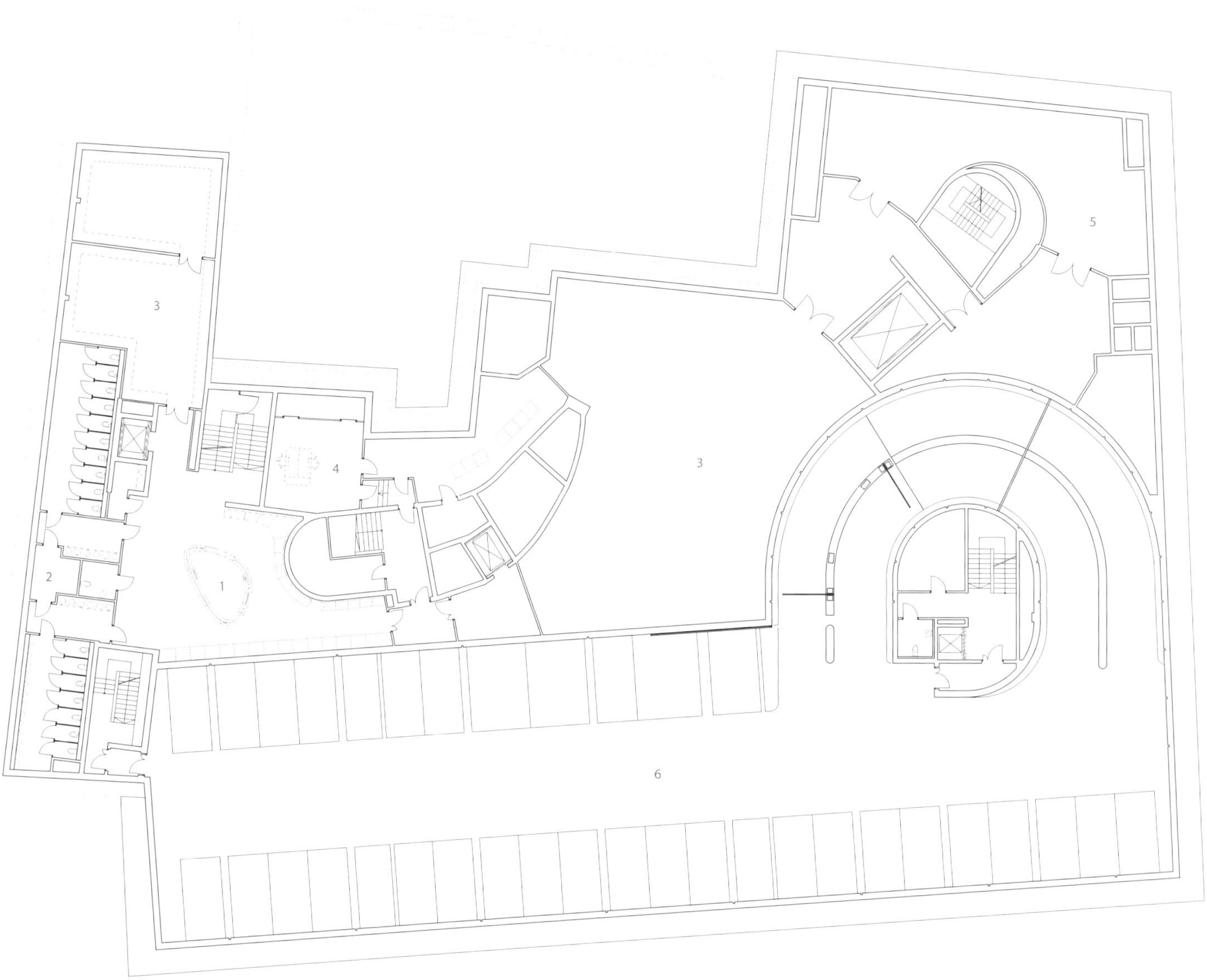

1 Check Room
2 Restrooms
3 Storage
4 Office
5 Conservation
6 Parking Garage

Figure 3.4 Lower level floor plan

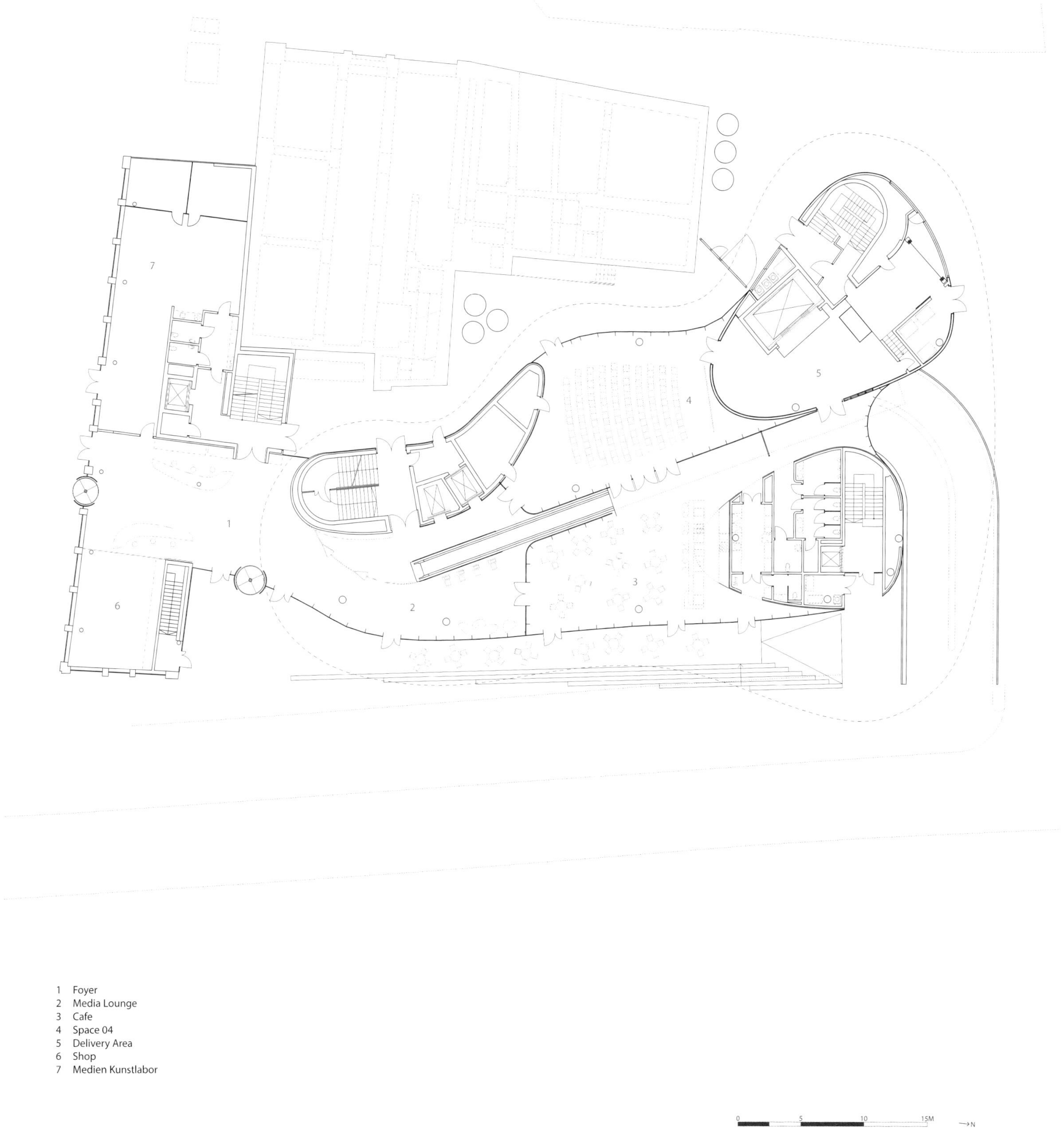

1 Foyer
2 Media Lounge
3 Cafe
4 Space 04
5 Delivery Area
6 Shop
7 Medien Kunstlabor

Figure 3.5 First (ground) floor plan

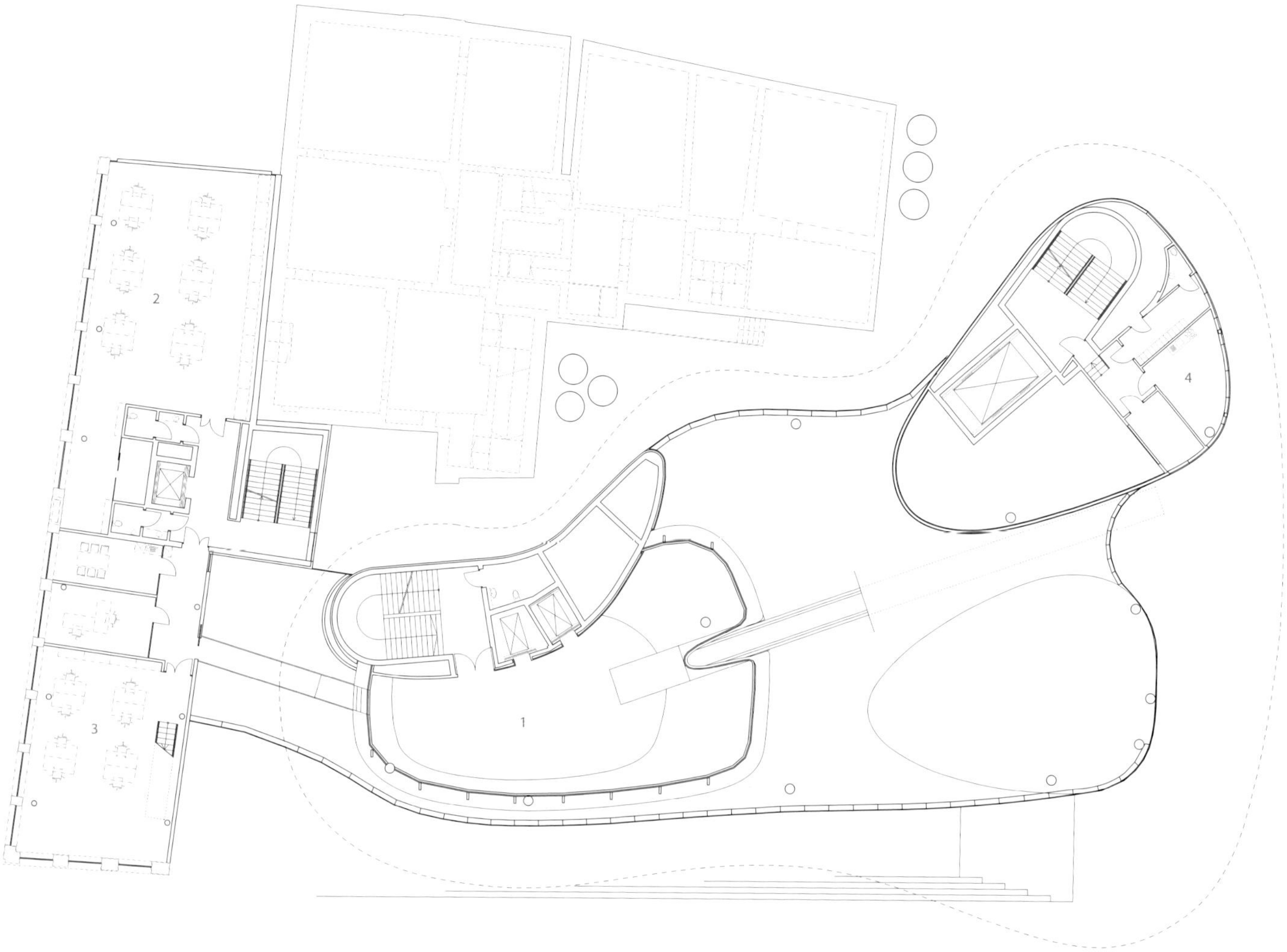

1 Space 03
2 Administration Kunsthaus
3 Administration Camera Austria
4 Office

0 5 10 15M →N

Figure 3.6 Second floor plan

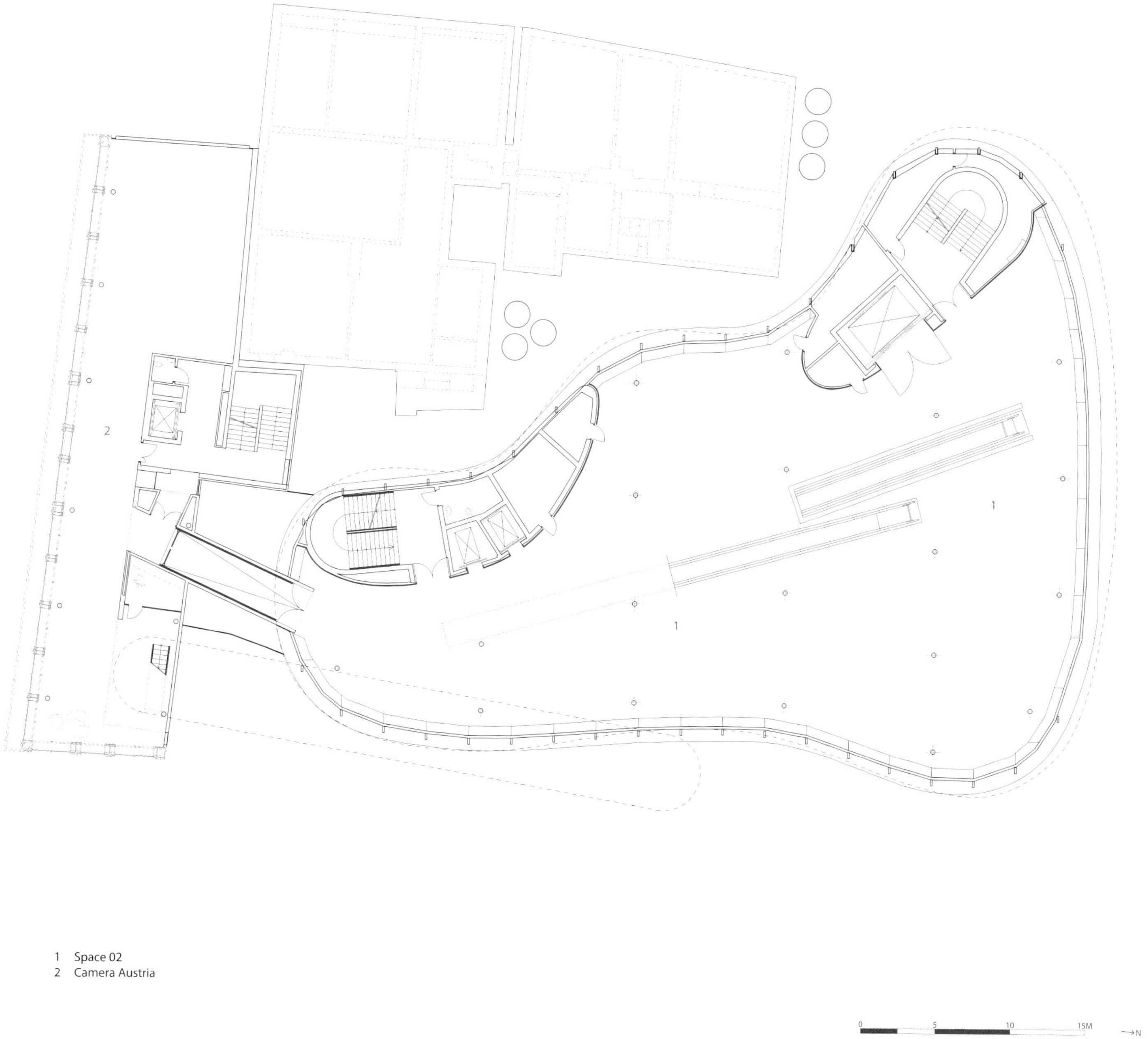

1 Space 02
2 Camera Austria

Figure 3.7 Third floor plan

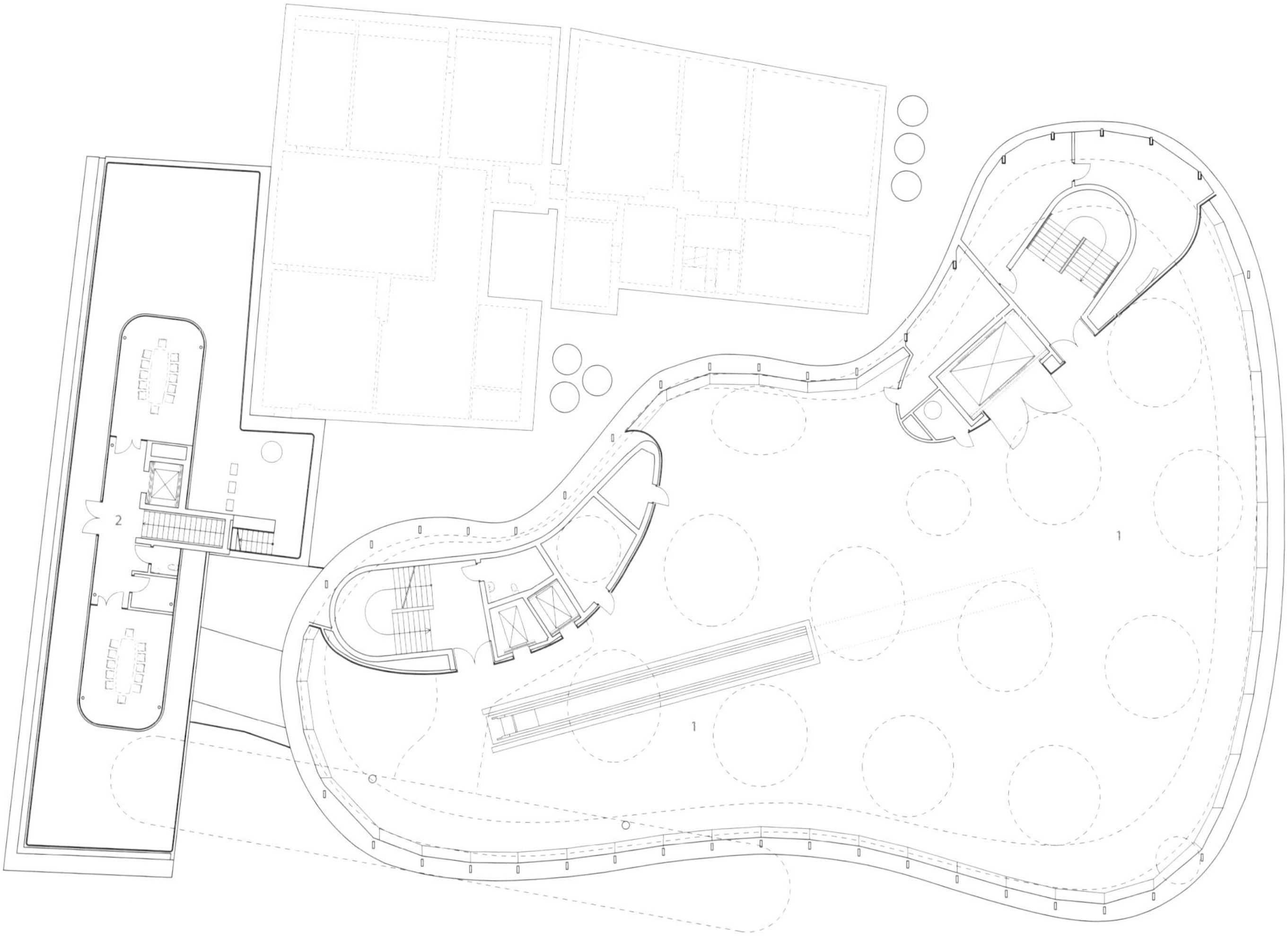

1 Space 01
2 Penthouse

Figure 3.8 Fourth floor plan

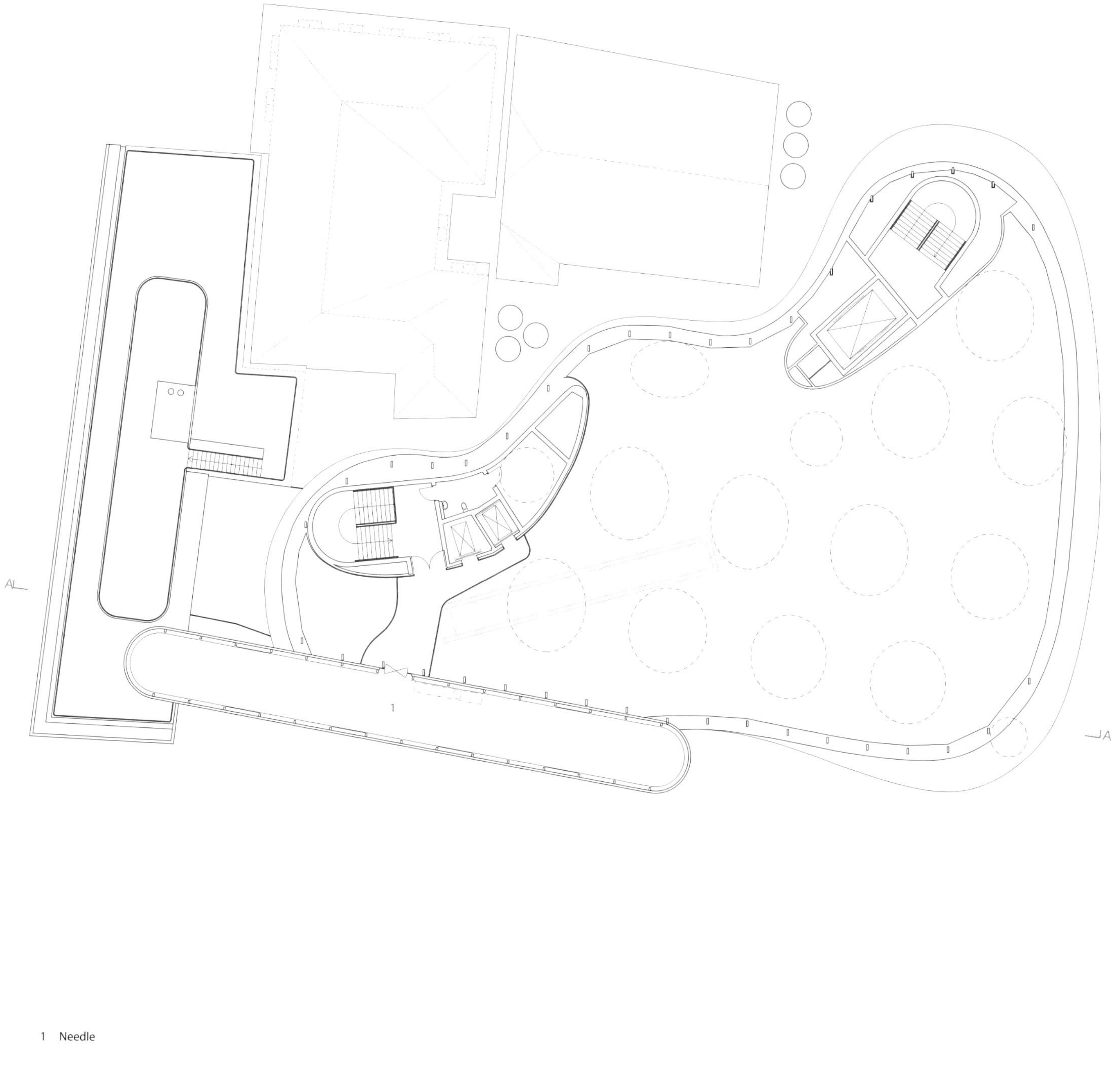

1 Needle

Figure 3.9 Fifth Needle floor plan

anchor the exuberant forms of the MAXXI that emerge out of more ordinary buildings.

The Kunsthaus is most noticeable from the Schlossberg Castle Hill when seen from above among Graz's typical red tiled roofs (Fig 3.1). For a pedestrian it is most visible on its east side, yet when the trees along the Mur are in leaf it is greatly masked from the other side of the river (Fig 3.11). To the north and west the streets are narrow and disallow long perspectives (Fig 3.12). On those two sides the ground floor wall is opaque, taller than elsewhere, and pushed outward in relation to the volume above. This compromises the effect of the bubble floating over a void. To the south, only the Eisernes Haus is visible, and the trams that pass frequently in the Sudtirolerplatz seem to form a family with the new glass penthouse on the Eisernes Haus and the cantilevered "needle" that hovers above.

The bubble also remains a polite distance from the other buildings on its block. It is linked to the Eisernes Haus by a glass volume, and the space between the Kunsthaus and the other two buildings is used as a sort of technical court with delivery, some mechanical equipment, and exhaust chimneys placed against the wall of the adjacent buildings.

Site planning in general is reasoned and well resolved. There are no neglected or sacrificed sides of the building. Main entry for visitors is through the Eisernes Haus on the south or from the Lendkai to the east. Delivery is through large doors concealed in the curved, metal cladding of the lower portion of the facade at the north-west corner. An automobile drop-off area is also located along the Lendkai as is access to the underground parking garage. Both are sympathetic to pedestrian circulation, though awkward changes in level, steps, and incongruous planter boxes near the facade make for a less than tidy cafe terrace.

Figure 3.10 View from south-east

Figure 3.11 View from across the Mur River

Figure 3.12 Street level view from the Mariahilferstrasse

Figure 3.13 Night View with BIX Media facade

The vertical ground floor facade is faceted rather than curved. The dark tint of the glass unfortunately reduces its transparency and diminishes the contrast with the bubble above. The competition images for the Kunsthaus suggested a sleek, uniform exterior skin for the bubble. The built solution, though complex geometrically, is relatively straightforward. Over 6,000 shiny spider connections support the exterior acrylic panels. These combined with the transparent, conical snow guards and exposed sprinkler heads give a freckled appearance to the "alien." The skin remains reflective, however, and provides interesting reflections from its underside of the tops of passing cars, buses, and pedestrians. It is not clear why the building is blue/blue-green, but from certain vantage points the rounded, tree-covered hills surrounding the city of Graz can be taken for other bubbles. For all its strangeness (alien), the building fits into its context surprisingly well (friendly).

At night the building becomes even more of a spectacle (Fig 3.13). Its "media facade" is more frontal that the building itself and is oriented toward the river and the historical center to the east. A high-resolution system with color capabilities was discarded early on in the development of the project for cost reasons and because of the quick obsolescence of such technologies. Instead, realities:united, an office from Berlin, developed the BIX (big + pixels) system using over 900 ordinary 40 watt circular fluorescent light tubes behind the acrylic outer skin. This solution gives a very low resolution, but one that is sufficient to display images and animations. Since media technologies become obsolete so quickly, the facade is "pre-aged" using techniques that seem already almost outdated. It becomes a sort of flip book equivalent for a media facade. The system can be programmed by artists, and it has been handed over to the public to control as well. The animated building at night is fascinating.

The Kunsthaus is 13,000 m^2 (square meter; 140,000 ft^2 (square foot)) with 2,500 m^2 (26,900 ft^2) of exhibition space. The basement levels are divided into two separate areas (Fig 3.4). An autonomous parking garage for 146 cars on four levels is to the east. The area to the west houses mechanical rooms, storage, and other services for the Kunsthaus on two or three levels depending on necessary ceiling heights. At ground level (Fig 3.5) an entry, a museum store, and ticket sales are within the rectangular footprint of the Eisernes Haus. A three-story glass-roofed volume makes the connection between the Eisernes Haus and the lobby space located under the bubble (Fig 3.15). Bridges in the volume connect the upper levels. A revolving door opens toward the river and doors on the opposite side allow a flow through the building to the offices in the historical buildings to the west. Stairs and two elevators are at the southern end of the lobby while restrooms and coat check are found on the first basement level. A cafe and an events space (Space04) for lectures, performances, films, etc. also occupy the ground floor. Though the spaces and volumes are not large, the ground floor feels generous since most exterior walls are transparent. Simple round concrete columns are distinct from the biomorphic forms of the project. They are set well inside the glass facade and support the bubble above. The facade stiffeners are visually present and compromise the immaterial effect of the glass and by consequence the continuity of the bubble form from inside to outside.

The Eisernes Haus is three full floors with a new glass penthouse on top. Offices are on the second floor, gallery spaces on the third, and the director's office is in the penthouse. Within the bubble itself there are two exhibition levels. There is also a partial, interstitial level for children's activities (Space03) at the lowest point of the bubble (Fig 3.6). It is a playful space with sloped floors generally following the curve of the architecture. It is the space where the exterior form is most directly experienced as interior space. It is a low, dark, introverted space, however. Portholes in the floor provide little light but do provide mischievous views down into the lobby and onto patrons in the cafe.

From the outside the building is a curiosity. Anticipation is high upon entering. From the generally open and transparent ground floor a slit in the bubble's belly along with a travelator give access to the galleries (Fig 3.16). As the architects describe it, visitors are led "up into the unknown." The narrow, single-width travelator gives a slow, pleasant ride. It is meant to suck the visitor into the building and makes for a passive transition into the galleries. At the top of the travelator the unknown becomes immediately known. In the name of flexibility, Space02 is one large loft (Fig 3.7 and Fig 3.17). The perimeter walls are clad with an "inner skin" (Fig 3.20) of gray woven metal and follow the double curve of the exterior form. Alignments of round columns structure the space. Alignments of round floor grills are recessed into the concrete slab and also provide access to electrical and information cables. Light tracks spaced at 1.25 m (4 ft) are recessed into the concrete ceiling while fluorescent fixtures are attached to the surface. The ceiling height is 4.7 m (15 ft 5 in.). There is no connection to the outside. Vertical, curved white walls enclose the service towers to the west and are marked by doors and air grills. A second travelator cuts through the space and leads to the top floor gallery: Space01 (Fig 3.8 and Fig 3.18).

Like below, Space01 is an open loft. Since the single bubble form outside has been divided into two levels inside, no interior volume fulfills the expectations the exterior suggests (Fig 3.2). Though it rises to a height of 8.5 m (27 ft 11 in.) in a clear span, Space01 is squat. The nozzles are also difficult to recognize inside, and natural light is eclipsed by the spiraling fluorescent tubes that have been inserted within. The interruption of the inner skin at the nozzles emphasizes their hexagonal shape and makes the domed envelope appear graphic with a distracting patchwork pattern.

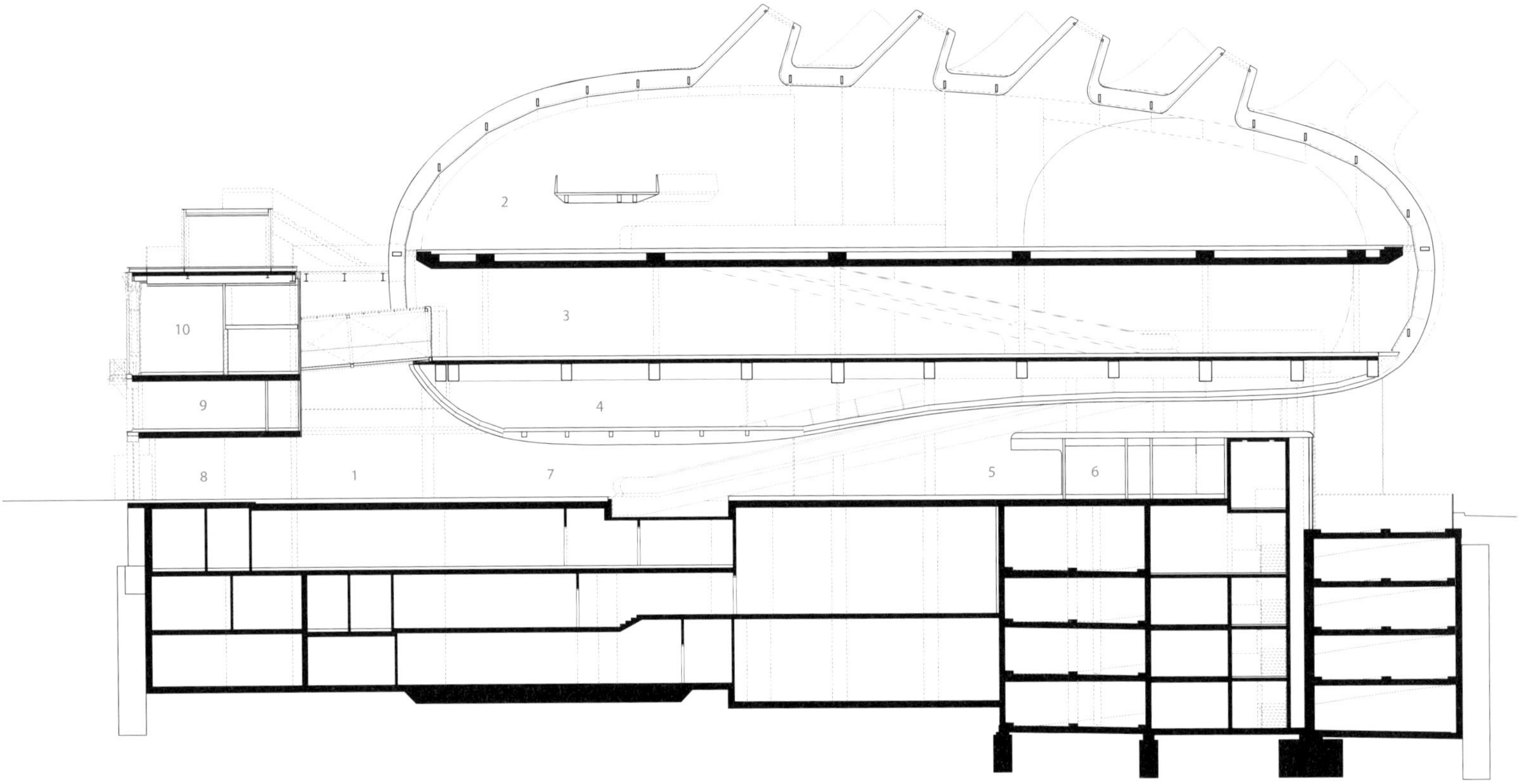

1 Foyer
2 Space 01
3 Space 02
4 Space 03
5 Space 04
6 Cafe
7 Media Lounge
8 Shop / Medien Kunstlabor
9 Administration
10 Camera Austria

Figure 3.14 Section

Panel joints of the inner skin provide straight lines for light tracks and additional artificial lighting (Fig 3.20). In Space01 there are the same white service tower walls and the same round floor grills as in the gallery below. The alignment of floor grills inevitably influences the position of temporary partitions in the space. Having the travelators within the galleries makes for circulation problems when one level is closed for an exhibition change.

The gallery spaces within the alien are not nearly as friendly as its exterior. They are at the same time overstimulating and somber. Though the white box gallery has been rejected, the architecture itself offers little as a substitute. The perimeter walls are little used, and temporary white (or other colored) walls must be erected for each exhibition. The galleries of the Kunsthaus are admittedly difficult to work with. Seemingly flexible, open spaces should allow unlimited possibilities, yet the architecture is not accommodating for all types of art. The spaces overwhelm small and subtle works, for example. At least since Cedric Price's Fun

Figure 3.15 Lobby

Figure 3.16 Lobby Travelator to exhibition spaces

Figure 3.17 Space 02

Figure 3.18 Space 01

Figure 3.19 View from the Needle looking north

Palace, there has been a common idea that the architecture of cultural institutions should constantly challenge the users. At the Kunsthaus the challenge has nudged the institution to focus the types of work it exhibits. The architecture may help to define (or warp) the character of the institution. From a practical point of view, transforming the galleries for each exhibition is costly. That said, multimedia works and video have been found to work well in Space02 while large sculptural and site-specific installations work well in Space01. The Kunsthaus generally exhibits works from the 1960s forward.

The Needle (Fig 3.9), the narrow, 40 m (131 ft) long, 4 m (13 ft) wide, all glass volume at the top of the building, should have been a luxury restaurant. For pragmatic reasons of delivery and odors in the galleries, it became an observation lounge and events space. The structure of the needle is basically two parallel trusses cantilevered from the structure of the bubble. It comes very close to the new, glass penthouse on top of the Eisernes Haus and from certain vantage points almost appears to sit on top of it. The needle offers extraordinary and liberating panoramic views of the city (Fig 3.19).

Columns, slabs, and the two rounded service towers on the west side of the building are all in concrete. The bubble is framed with parallel steel arches in the east/west direction with triangular bracing that is attached to the concrete. Once the building technique was defined, the final shape of the bubble was adapted accordingly. The nozzles are also part of the steel structure and were prefabricated as independent hexagonal elements (Fig 3.21), with one nozzle designated for smoke evacuation in case of fire. The competition proposed a translucent and transparent double-curved form that evolved, however, into a more conventional system of decking, rigid insulation applied in small blocks to approximate the curve, and membrane waterproofing (Fig 3.22). The structure and inner layers of the building are faceted polygons. Only the outer layer of 20 mm (3/4 in.) thick acrylic panels is double curved. All of the outer panels are of a different shape and each required its own mold for thermoforming. The panels reach a maximum dimension of approximately 3 m by 2 m (9 ft 10 in. by 6 ft 7 in.). Fireproofing of the structure is by intumescent paint and a sprinkler system on the outside of the building that can be seen peeking out between the panel joints.

The service towers contain large chase spaces for plumbing, electrical, and air supply ducts. They also serve as air return plenums. Public and emergency stairs, passenger elevators, and the freight elevator are located in the towers as well. Trucks can only partially enter into the loading area on the ground floor. There is also a gated area between the Kunsthaus and the adjacent buildings that allows delivery through the double-sided freight elevator that opens directly to the exterior. Information and electrical cables and ducts run in a plenum under the gallery floors. Approximately 30 percent of heating and cooling for the spaces comes from a radiant system in the floors while 70 percent comes from the forced air system.

Museum architecture at the beginning of the new century and millennium has often felt the obligation to somehow respond to a new era. Though the Kunsthaus exhibition spaces appear radical, it is unlikely that they will serve as a new model. They are fundamentally simple loft spaces based on a not so new idea of flexibility. Inventions are skin deep, and the way fundamental elements of circulation, lighting, materials, color, and surface are combined results in spaces that inhibit just as much as they enable, bringing the final balance back to the middle. The exterior forms and urban response seem to be the result of a much longer reflection and synthesis. There is certainly a dose of the brazenness of Archigram, but there is also a tolerance and even respect for tradition. The meeting is complex and rich ... and friendly. There is certainly a lesson here for architecture and urbanism of any shape and form. And by all accounts, Graz is very accepting and proud of its alien Kunsthaus.

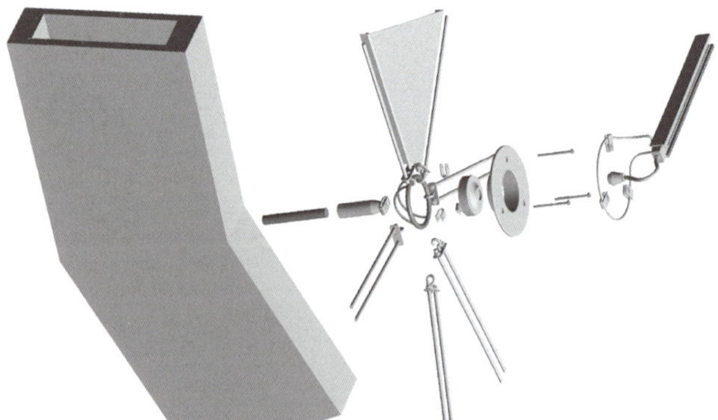

Figure 3.20 Inner skin detail

Figure 3.21 Nozzle detail

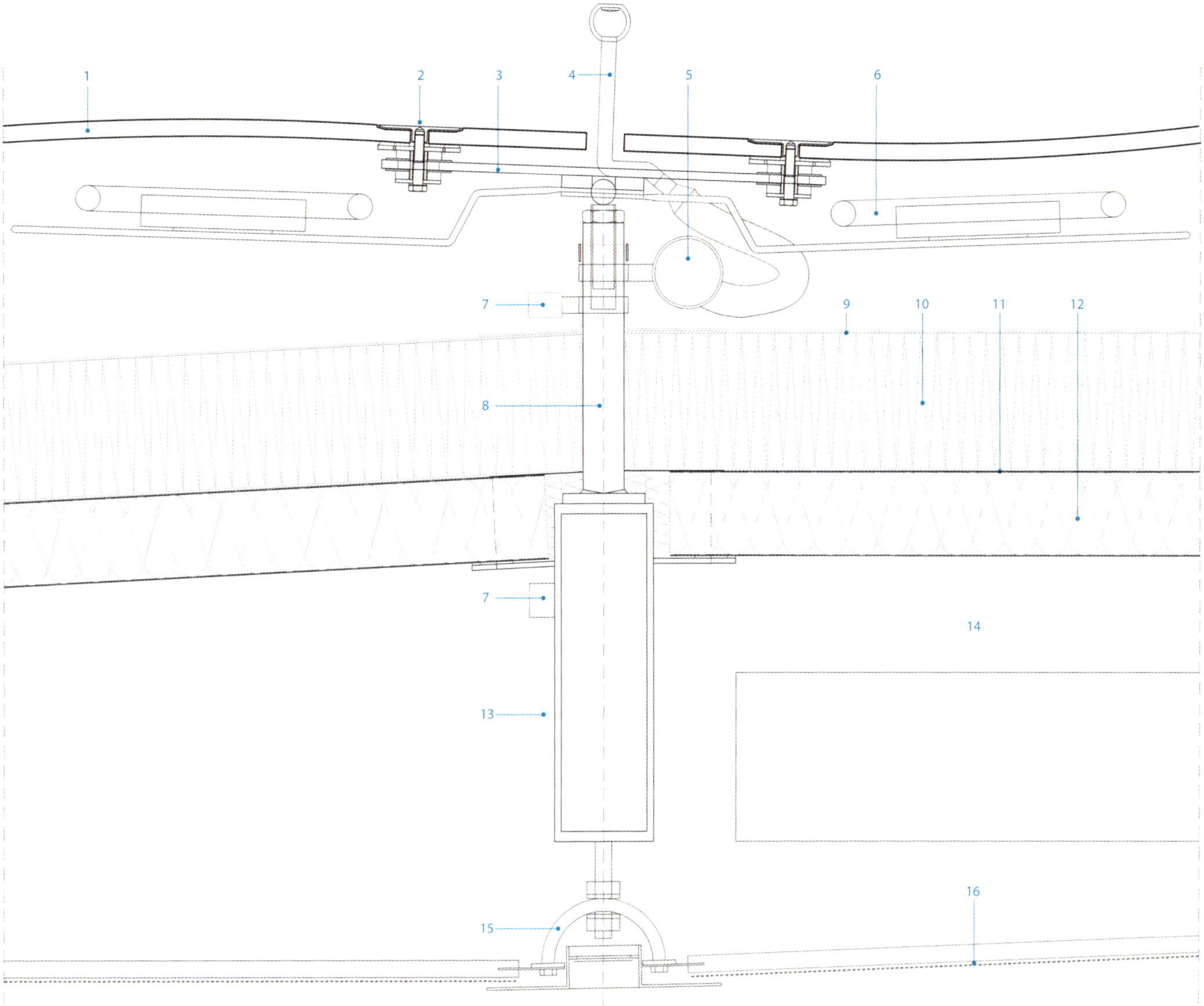

1 2cm Acrylic
2 Acrylic Connection Fitting
3 Connection Arms
4 Sprinker Head
5 Sprinker Pipe
6 Bix Media Light
7 Electrical Conduit
8 Stainless Steel Support Rod (3 Cm)
9 2mm Adhered Roofing Membrane
10 Ridgid Foam Insulation (16 Cm)
11 Bauphasendach Additional Waterproofing
12 Metal Decking With Rock Wool Insulation
13 Primary Steel Beam (12x40 Cm)
14 Cavity For Mechanical And Electrical Services
15 Fitting For Suspended Ceiling
16 Metal Mesh Inner Skin

Figure 3.22 Roof detail

CHAPTER 4

Nasher Sculpture Center

Dallas, Texas

Renzo Piano Building Workshop

2003

Figure 4.1 Aerial view from north

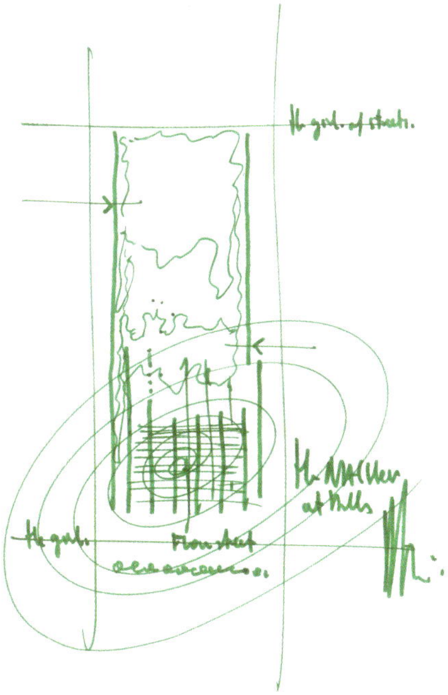

Figure 4.2 Plan sketch by Renzo Piano

Renzo Piano sometimes refers to the artist Piet Mondrian's *Composition* paintings – where black lines frame blocks of color – to exemplify his own approach of expressing the primary structure of a building and then attaching secondary elements such as cladding, blinds, brise-soleils, etc. expressed, in turn, as clearly applied pieces. Mondrian's studied repetition in painting also parallels Piano's method in museum design. Where Mondrian created singular paintings by employing again and again the same basic graphic vocabulary, Piano has designed a series of museums from Houston to Basel to Dallas, and beyond, derived from revisiting his own restrained palette of architectural elements that includes strongly expressed walls and, more importantly, a glass roof. As with each painting by Mondrian, each building by Piano – with the influence of the client, the location, and the collection – ultimately evolves into a unique museum.

Conceptually, the Nasher Sculpture Center is composed of few elements (Fig 4.1, 4.2, and 4.3). There is the garden with stone walls on three sides that enclose an entire city block. On the fourth side, to the south, there is a slightly elevated granite terrace with six parallel travertine walls that emerge out of it like vestiges of an ancient ruin – as described by the architect. Between these walls there is glass, inserted vertically and horizontally, to form walls and roof and enclose space (Fig 4.4). Perforated metal panels shade the glass roof. The solution of parallel walls brings to mind the smaller, more playful, and more frugal Sonsbeek Sculpture Pavilion by Aldo van Eyck that was built as a temporary structure and demolished in 1966. Van Eyck's parallel concrete block walls integrated semi-circular portions, and the ensemble was topped by a flat, steel-framed roof structure. The pavilion was reconstructed in 2005–2006 in the sculpture garden of the Kroller-Muller Museum in Otterlo in the Netherlands with a roof structure that is more transparent than that of the original project.

Piano has experimented several times with the concept of a "museum without a roof" or a glass-roofed museum. At the Menil Collection in Houston (1986) he devised a structure composed of two layers: an outer one of slightly sloped glass panels over an inner layer of ferro-cement "leaves" that diffuse and reflect sunlight. He experimented further with the Cy Twombly Gallery (1995) also in Houston and part of the Menil Foundation, where the roof is composed of four layers: (1) a horizontal exterior brise-soleil that shades (2) a sloped glass roof with (3) motorized interior louvers below that regulate sunlight which is then further diffused by (4) a fabric ceiling. Piano's roof for the Beyeler Foundation (1997) in Basel, Switzerland, is conceptually similar to the Twombly roof but adapted to the Swiss climate and is composed of five layers. First sketches for the Nasher's roof more resembled the Beyeler, but the final project is again composed of only two layers, and for the first time Piano used the glass as the ceiling material with no other diffusing or softening layer below. Several other projects have followed since the Nasher including the extensions to the High Museum in Atlanta, the Los Angeles County Museum, and The Art Institute in Chicago that continue the spirit of the "roofless museum" but adapt to place and climate.

Most all of the museums that Piano has designed include sculpture in the collection; however, two projects prior to the Nasher were devoted almost exclusively to the exhibition of three-dimensional works. The Atelier Constantin Brancusi (1997), for example, is a reconstruction of the Romanian sculptor's studio and is part of the National Museum of Modern Art at the Georges Pompidou Center in Paris. It houses all of the works that were in the artist's living and work spaces at the time of his death in 1957. The design was seen as an environment for a landscape or forest of Brancusi's sculptures. Before that, in 1982, Piano realized an exhibition of the work of Alexander Calder in the Palazzo a Vela in Turin. There, within the vast space of the arena, he worked with walls that radiated from a central point to define smaller spaces for the sculptures. Though only a temporary installation, there are similarities with the parallel walls that organize the Sculpture Center in Dallas.

Like both the Menil Collection and the Beyeler Foundation, the Nasher houses a private collection comprised of over 300 works from Rodin to Jeff Koons amassed by the Nasher couple, Raymond, a Dallas developer, and his wife Patsy. Most of the works had been displayed at the couple's home, and there was thought of converting their house and garden into a private museum. The downtown site in the Arts District, however, had the advantage of making the collection more accessible to the public. Thus the Nasher, along with its earlier neighbors, the Dallas Museum of Art (1984) by Edward Larrabee Barnes and the Meyerson Symphony Center (1989) by I. M. Pei, seems to have nudged other projects planned for the 18 city block District to move ahead. The High School for the Performing and Visual Arts by Brad Cloepfil/Allied Works was completed in 2008, and both the Wyly Theater by OMA/REX and the Winspear Opera House by Foster + Partners were completed in 2009. Though these additions have placed Dallas on the cultural tourism map, the Arts District still seems somewhat empty and underpopulated. This might change with the covering and transformation of the sunken Woodall Rodgers Freeway into a linear park immediately to the north of the Nasher. The area has continued to develop with a Museum of Nature and Science by Thom Mayne across the new park and a 42-story residential Museum Tower just across Olive Street from the Nasher. The site of the Sculpture Center has always been in the shadow of a high-rise to the south/east. It is now in the much more troublesome position of being in the reflection of the all glass Museum Tower to the north/east that

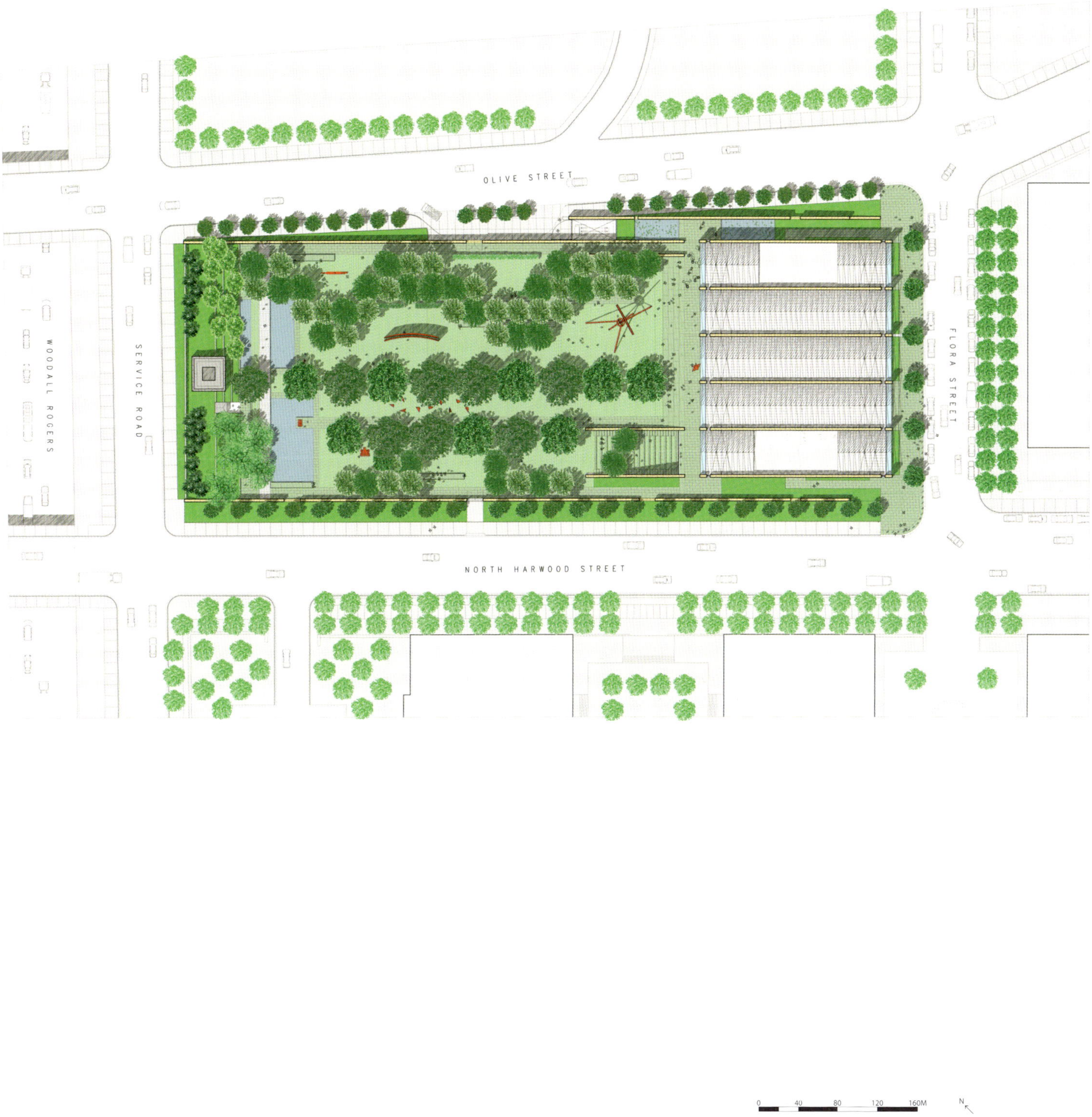

Figure 4.3 Site plan

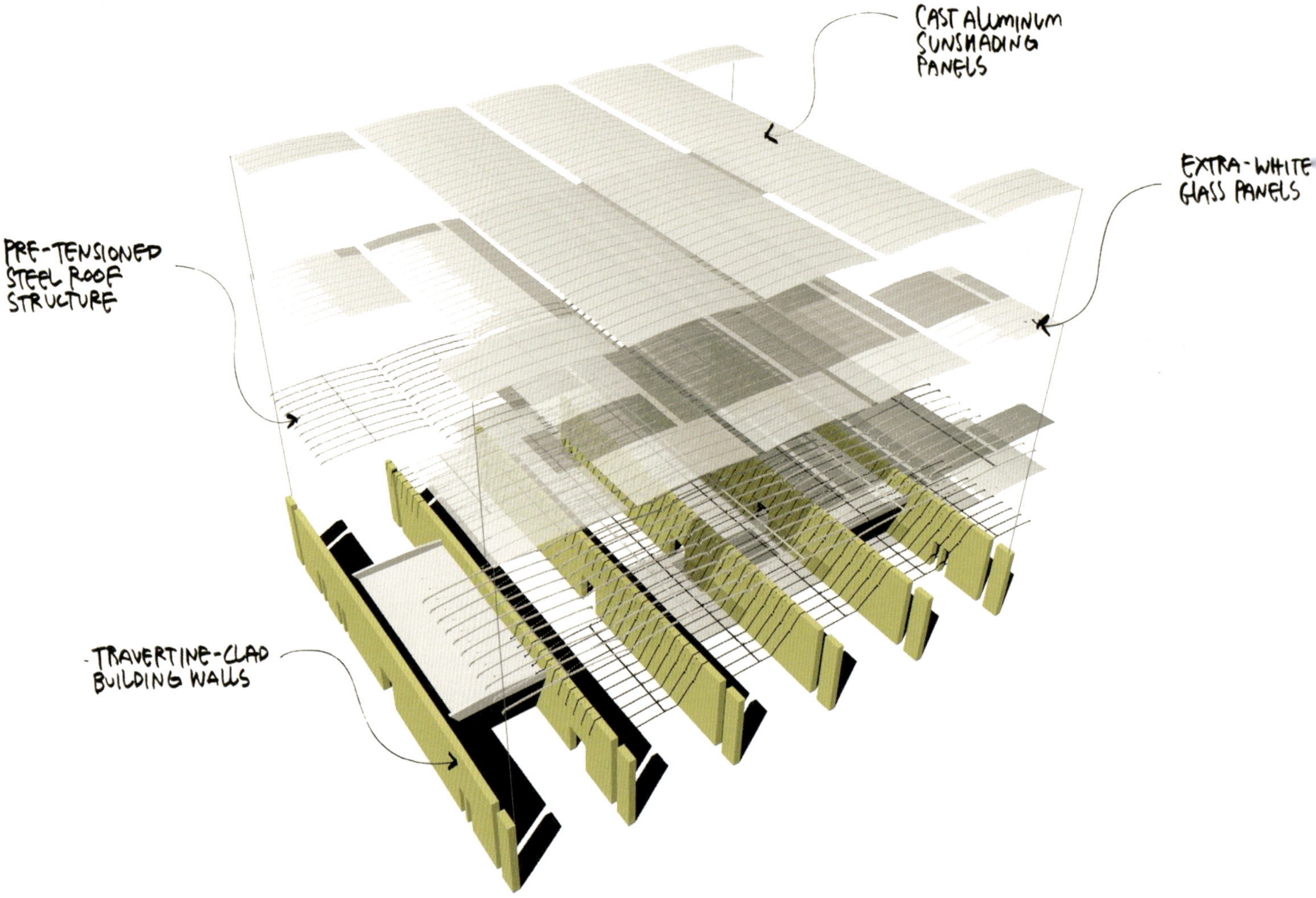

Figure 4.4 Axonometric

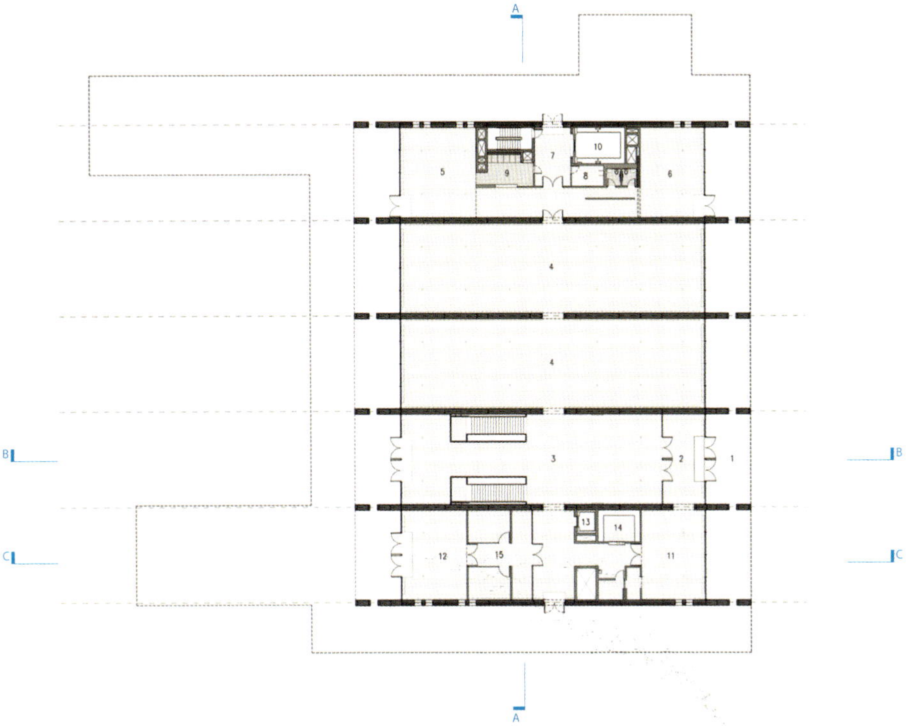

1 Main Entrance
2 Entry Vestibule
3 Entry Hall
4 Art Hall
5 Cafe
6 Multi-Purpose
7 Secondary Entrance
8 Security
9 Cafe Servery
10 Freight Elevator
11 Gift Shop
12 Boardroom
13 Passenger Elevator
14 Cloakroom
15 Offices
16 Classroom
17 Auditorium
18 Offices
19 General Storage
20 Art Storage
21 Conservation Storage
22 Workshop
23 Stage Area
24 Kitchen
25 Staff Break
26 Mechanical
27 Loading
28 Truck Lift
29 Terraced Garden

Figure 4.5 Lower and upper level floor plans

beams bothersome rays of afternoon light into the garden as well as through the sculpture center's roof and into the interior gallery spaces. While most projects cannot completely control what will surround them in the future, the New Museum in New York, for example, took a step in that direction by purchasing the low building to its south in order to better guarantee the preservation of the iconic image of SANAA's building in the future. Similar precautions were not imagined for the Nasher.

The Nasher is perhaps the museum project that has offered Piano the best occasion to realize a number of his ongoing architectural preoccupations. Since the building is small and narrow, transparency – a quest for many modern architects including Piano – was assured (Fig 4.6). Even from the street visitors see entirely through the building and glimpse the garden on the other side. Since sculpture is generally less sensitive to light

Figure 4.6 North elevation at night

Figure 4.7 View from south/west – Flora Street

Figure 4.8 North elevation

Figure 4.9 View from north/west

Figure 4.10 Roof detail

than are paintings, Piano conceived his simplest, lightest, and purest glass roof. Also, since the garden is integral to the project, Piano created a strong relationship between the interior space and nature outside (Fig 4.17) while at the same time reinforcing a more traditional urbanism by aligning the building along the street. The Nasher's location in the Arts District allowed Piano to participate in the development of a more dense and pedestrian urban structure in the heart of an automobile-dominated city.

The Nasher occupies an entire 9,700 m^2 (square meter; 2.4 acre) block that was previously a surface parking lot. The rectangular site is slightly sloped and at the time of construction was bordered to the north by an open, sunken freeway that has now been covered to become a linear park as mentioned above. The skyscrapers of downtown are to the south. A first proposal by Piano sketched two linear structures along the long edges of the site enclosing a narrowed garden in between. It also incorporated underground parking. A second scheme placed a single building at the bottom of the slope on the north edge of the site. The final scheme borders Flora Street, the principle axis of the Arts District, to the south and appears now as an inevitable solution. The built design is divided into five bays. It is compact with a total area of 5,110 m^2 (55,000 ft^2 (square foot)).

If the formula for many recent museum projects throughout the world is said to consist of a highly photogenic exterior combined with an impressive entry space, the Nasher does not follow the rule. The Sculpture Center, even if monumental for such a small building, remains discrete inside and out. From the street (Fig 4.7), the contrast is strong between the thick walls (the stone is a 5 cm (2") veneer over a steel frame) and the light, "immaterial" roof. The building is composed of repetitive bays with no emphasis given to the entry (Fig 4.8 and Fig 4.13). As in many of his designs, Piano "peels away" the structure at the perimeter in order to reveal the basic components. Here the stone walls break into pilasters and the glass roof is seen in its most simple condition without the perforated shading panel above providing a subtle transition between the exterior and the interior. Once inside the building, visitors are in the realm of the art. There is no hierarchy or differentiation of space. An ideal, general condition has been created for the sculptures and the viewer shares that space throughout the building. This approach is surely even more important in museums that exhibit paintings hung on walls such as the Menil and the Beyeler.

The entry bay traverses the building and connects the street directly to the garden (Fig 4.5 and Fig 4.14). A double stair leads to the basement level. The bay to the west of the entry contains the store, administrative offices behind glass walls, and an elevator. Two bays to the east of the entry contain the galleries. Beyond the galleries is the fifth bay that contains a cafe, a small banquet room, and offices for museum security. Openings in all of the walls are aligned and form a cross axis (Fig 4.15). Still, there is no set path for visits.

All of the bays are 34.15 m (112 ft) long, 9.75 m (32 ft) wide, and 4.90 m (16 ft) high. The stone walls continue another 4.90 m beyond the glass facade on both sides of the building for a total length of 43.90 m (144 ft).

The interior finishes are also discreet: travertine walls of 122 by 61 cm (4 by 2 ft) stones, white oak plank floors, and transparent glass facades (Fig 4.16). At the line of the facade, the floor finish changes from South African granite outside to wood inside. While continuing the stone inside the building would have established even more continuity between interior and exterior, the wood floor provides welcome warmth to the interior spaces. The travertine wall finish inside is smooth. Outside it has been water blasted to give it the more aged look of a "ruin."

The most prominent attribute of the interior is the light that floods the spaces and animates the galleries. The highly precise roof construction is composed of 1.22 by 4.90 m (4 by 16 ft) laminated, low iron glass, double-glazed panels supported by 15 cm (6 in.) deep beams at 1.22 m (4 ft) centers. Both are slightly curved with a rise of 30 cm (1 ft) from the sides to the center for a maximum height of 5.20 m (17 ft). Many of Piano's glass roofs are conceptually flat but are executed with slopes in order to evacuate water. At the Nasher the curve seems to be the desired form, and many comparisons have been made to Louis Kahn's Kimbell Art Museum in nearby Fort Worth. (An addition to the Kimbell by Renzo Piano opened in 2013.) The Nasher's roof directs rainwater into gutters concealed within the stone-clad walls (Fig 4.18). Overflow downspouts are integrated into the pilasters at the ends of each wall and terminate in small specially made outlets located at ground level. In certain areas such as the store, opaque roof panels replace the glass. In order to maintain the same structural equilibrium, steel plate was integrated to equal the same 544 kg (1,200 lb) of the glass. Curved light tracks follow the roof beams with every third track devoted to equipment other than lighting such as cameras and smoke detectors. Above, the roof beams are suspended at mid span by exterior stainless steel tensioned rods attached to the upper portion of the thick walls (Fig 4.18). The roof structure was reduced to a minimum depth and does not have a continuous thermal break. Instead electric heating has been integrated in order to minimize condensation.

Above the glass panels is an ingenious egg crate brise-soleil in cast aluminum that responds both to the building's geometry and the sun's orientation (Fig 4.10). At the Menil, for example, both the streets and the building are aligned with the cardinal

Section B

Section C

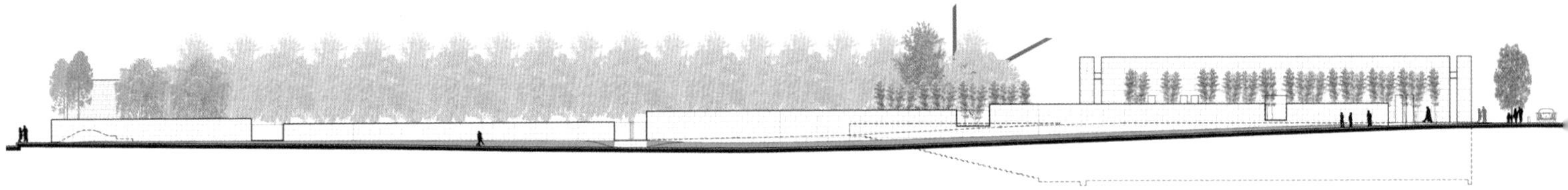

West Elevation

Figure 4.11 Long sections and elevation

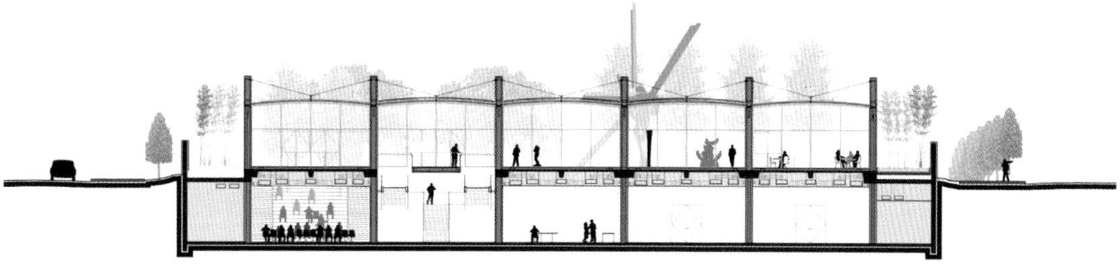

Section A

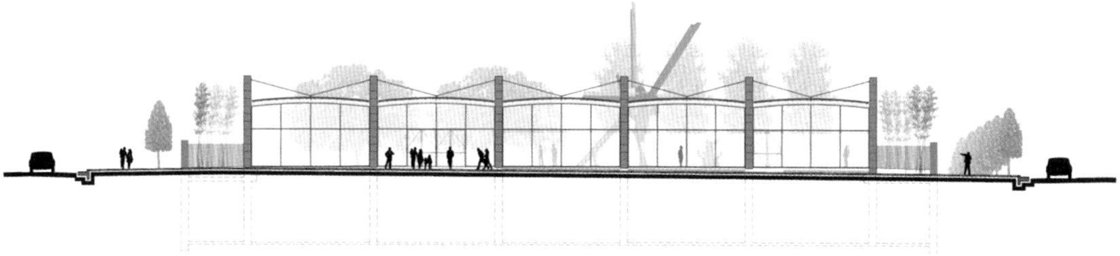

North Elevation

Figure 4.12 Short section and elevation

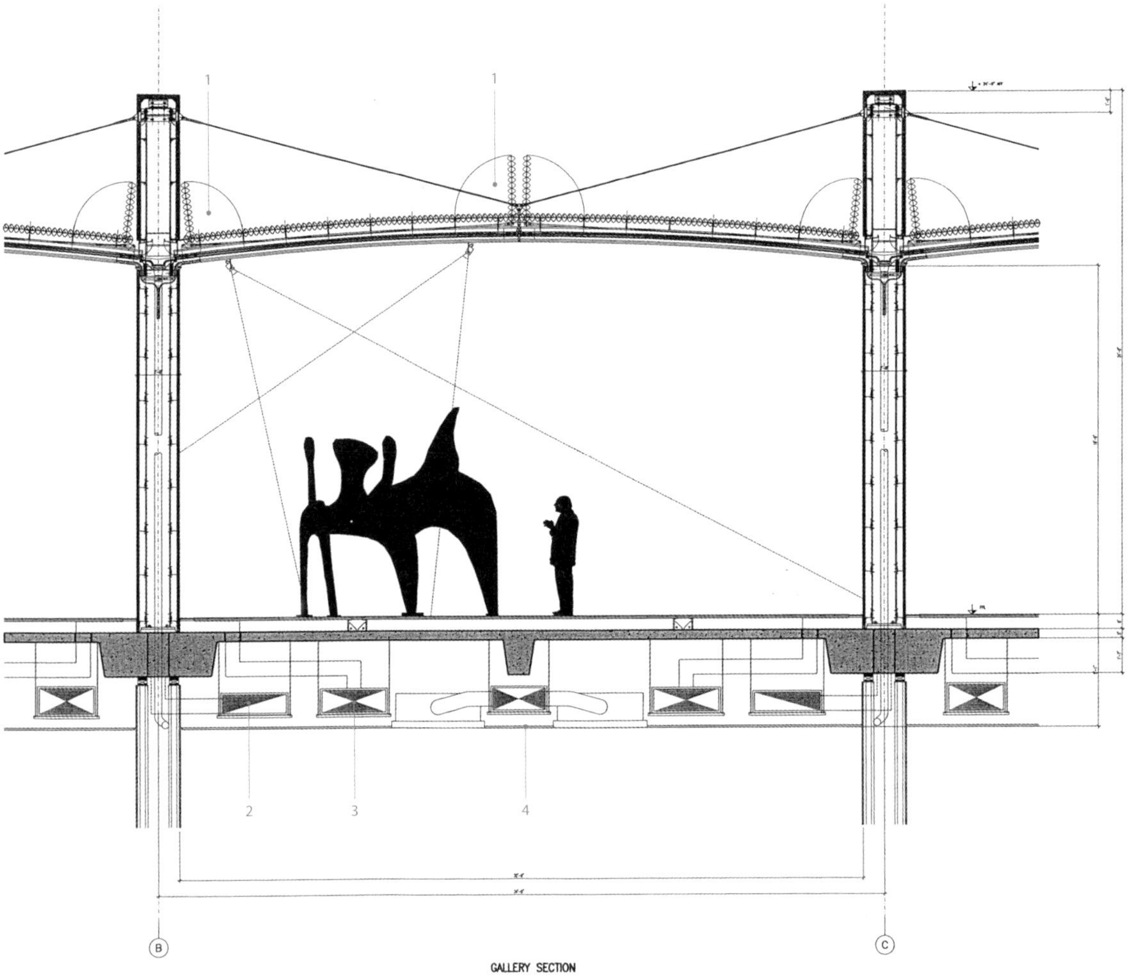

1 Automatic Smoke Vents
2 Return Air Duct Taking Air From Top Of Wall
3 Supply Air Duct Linked To Linear "Thoughs" And Sypply Grills At Bass Of Wall
4 Supply Air Duct For Basement

Figure 4.13 Partial section

Figure 4.14 Entry hall

Figure 4.15 Entry hall – looking east

points. At the Nasher, the 1.22 m (4 ft) square, white coated panel sections follow the orientation of the building and city grid while the small apertures are turned approximately 45 degrees and oriented to the north in order to capture a maximum amount of light while avoiding direct sun. The sunscreen itself resembles a kinetic sculpture that changes with the movement of the visitor. The screen of repetitive forms conjures multiple images such as tiny hoods, or eyelids, or sunflowers. The roof ensemble suggests infinite space and invites the visitor's eye to wander from sculpture to sculpture and beyond, outward to the garden and upward to the sky. The sky view now includes the neighboring museum tower.

Figure 4.16 Gallery – looking west

Figure 4.17 Gallery with view to garden

The structure of the building above ground is in steel. Ducts, rainwater pipes and electrical runs are integrated in the cavity of the walls. Both end bays have a flat roof area for mechanical equipment with the boilers located on the roof above the west bay and the chillers on the roof above the east bay. Instead of a full underfloor plenum, ducts are linked to linear troughs below the wooden air supply grills found at the base of the stone walls (Fig 4.13).

The structure below ground is in concrete. A full basement was incorporated in order to reduce the impact of the building at ground level (Fig 4.5). Below, public spaces include a small gallery for light-sensitive works or special exhibitions, restrooms, and an auditorium with movable chairs to seat approximately 200 spectators. Within the auditorium, a sliding glass facade (3.65 by 9.75 m or 12 by 32 ft) opens to a terraced, grass seating area that links the lower level auditorium to the garden above (Fig 4.9). There are also more administrative offices, a small library, conservation labs, delivery, a kitchen for the cafe above, a small amount of art storage, and mechanical spaces. In order to reduce the building's footprint above, some work spaces are below ground and windowless.

The lower level is actually bigger than the ground floor. Much of the mechanical equipment is located in a narrow "U" shaped space that brackets the basement and extends beyond the limits of the ground floor above. This space is isolated from the rest of the building by a double concrete block wall in order to avoid sound transmission of mechanical equipment into the building. Delivery for the building is also noteworthy. A long ramp to access the basement level was considered too disruptive to the streetscape. The alternative was a very large platform (4.55 by 9.75 m or 15 by 32 ft) adapted from lifts used in the aircraft industry that allows large objects and even vehicles to be lowered into the basement. Another 2.75 by 4.90 m (9 by 16 ft) freight elevator connects the basement back to the ground floor. This solution allows for a discreet delivery area at the ground level. Agreements were made to use parking facilities of neighboring buildings, and no on-site parking was provided.

The garden designed by the landscape architect Peter Walker is a large open space modulated primarily by vegetation rather than architectural elements. Initial schemes proposed a more informal design with winding paths, but these evolved to become more related to the layout of the building itself. Monumental works such as those by Mark di Suvero or Richard Serra occupy a large central lawn, a green carpet of grass developed to withstand heavy foot traffic. Less imposing pieces are found throughout the garden among hedges or in the shade of trees. The garden was conceived as an oasis in the city as well as an outdoor gallery that should not compete with the sculptures. While most of the pieces are meant to rotate, *Tending, (Blue)*, a *skyspace* by James Turrell was conceived as a permanent, site-specific piece located at the north end of the garden. It was deemed "destroyed" by the artist when the more recent, neighboring residential tower obstructed the clear view from within the work. Plant variety was intentionally limited, and main tree species include live oak, cedar elm, pine, crepe myrtle, weeping willow, holly, and magnolia. Plants were positioned for visual effect but also in relation to the constraints of the vehicles necessary to move the sculptures. The garden has matured nicely since the Sculpture Center opened.

Of all of the architects today confronted with the opportunity and difficulty of conceiving projects at the four corners of the earth, Renzo Piano is perhaps the only one to have developed a method, even a philosophy of architecture, to respond to this present situation. His approach is neither too cerebral nor linked to contemporary social trends. It is simply based on the "local" and the "universal." The application is physical and found in the construction itself. In his preface to Piano's "Logbook" the historian Kenneth Frampton employs the terms "placeform" and "produktform" to begin a reflection on this characteristic of Piano's work. As Piano elaborates in his book, an understanding of the local and the topos can be communicated directly through "the structure on which the building stands [which] is normally made out of materials from the place itself." At the same time he notes that the possibilities of communication and transportation in the modern, globalized, "universal" world allows an architect to take advantage of construction techniques and materials wherever they may be found. It is the appropriate dose, even if subjective, of local and universal that gives meaning to a project. For example, the Menil Collection is clad in cypress wood from the neighboring state of Louisiana which is the same wood used in many of the small traditional houses that surround it. In contrast, the "leaves" of the building in ferro-cement are inspired by the shipbuilding industry and are obviously not specifically of the place. The Beyeler Foundation follows the same rule. The glass roof tends toward the "universal" while the walls are clad in a stone close in appearance to the local red sandstone even if it actually comes from Patagonia. The Nasher is another notch removed from the method and approaches an imported building. All of the significant elements, the stone for the walls, the steel, the glass, the glass framing, the brise-soleil, the lights, the blinds ... are imported from Italy. We can easily imagine multiple pragmatic reasons that brought Piano to proceed in such a way, considering the difficulty of executing a building of such precision and sophistication. More than "place," the approach in this instance may speak more of the seductive pedigree of European luxury. The question may be asked if it is even important that an architect conform to his own philosophy if the end product is a success. There are numerous architects today for whom "place" is not a major concern. A realization in Atlanta can resemble another in Paris or elsewhere. Perhaps one exception is Glenn Murcutt who even with worldwide renown chooses by conviction not to work outside of his native Australia because of a profound respect and an intimate understanding of place. The beauty of Piano's approach is that it falls somewhere between the two extremes. His realizations such as the Menil Collection have shown a comprehension of place equal to or even superior to those of local buildings conceived by local architects. Dallas like Houston is a rapidly changing city and a city in the making. While the Nasher is a remarkable project and provides an appropriately pleasant environment for looking at sculpture, we could imagine that an architect such as Renzo Piano could scratch the topos a little more to better express a unique "placeform."

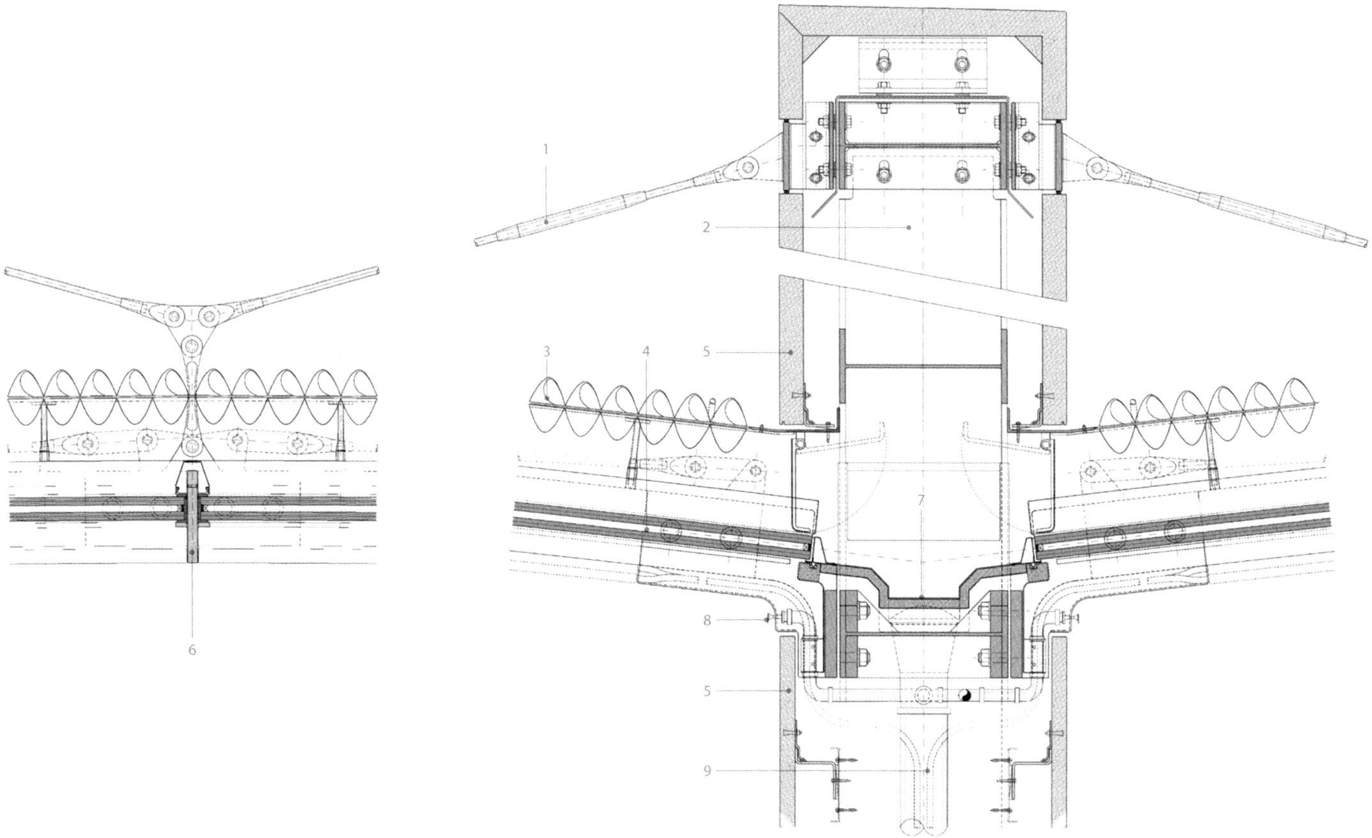

1 Stainless Steel Tension Rods
2 Steel Structure
3 Cast Aluminum Brise-soleil
4 Double Glazed Units
5 Travertine Cladding
6 Ridge Beam With Cover Strip
7 Gutter
8 Sprinkler Head
9 Rainwater Down Pipe

Figure 4.18 Roof details

CHAPTER 5

The Museum of Modern Art

New York

Yoshio Taniguchi and Associates

2004

Figure 5.1 54th Street facade looking west

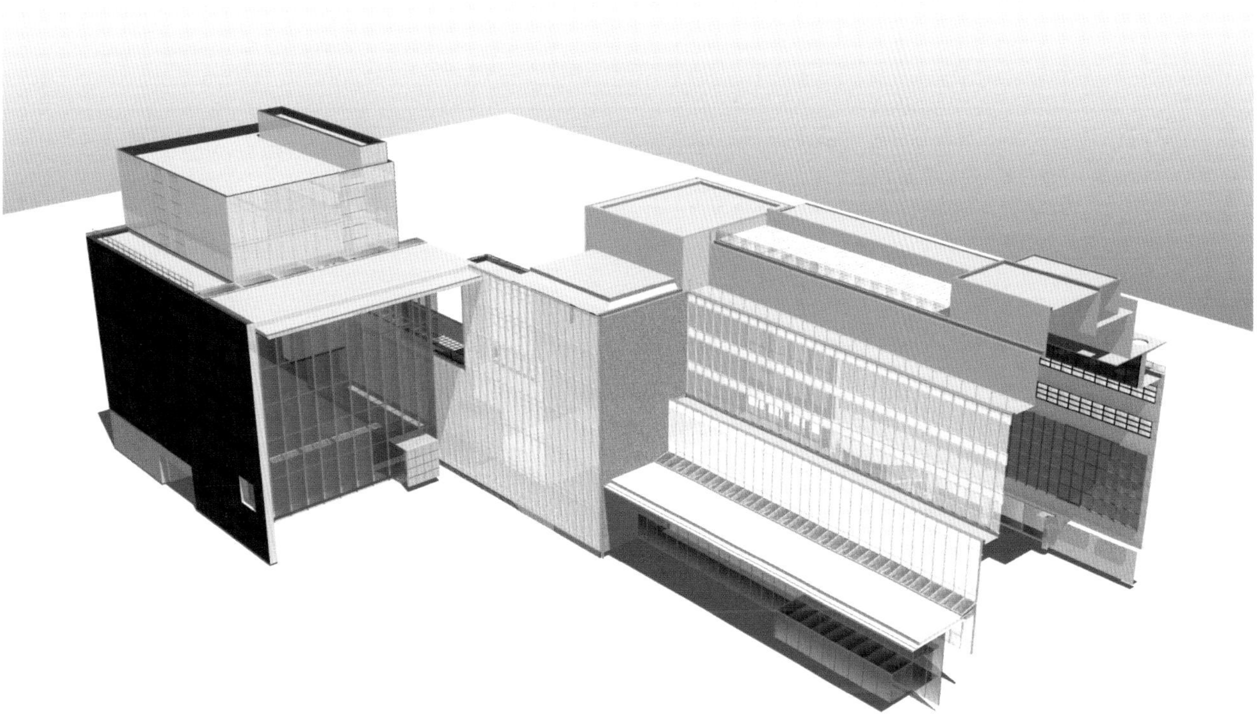

Figure 5.2 Model of the Education Center to the east of the Sculpture Garden with the office wing to the south

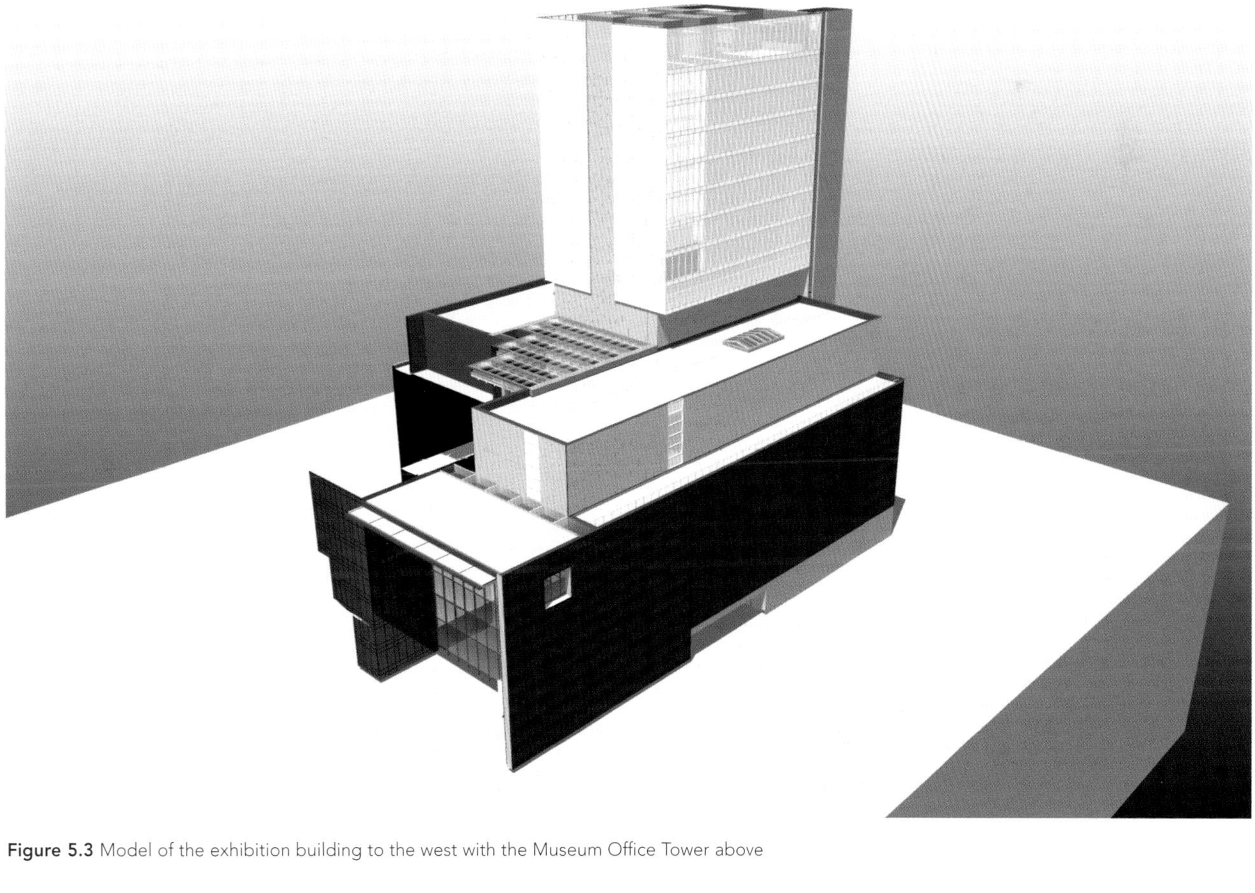

Figure 5.3 Model of the exhibition building to the west with the Museum Office Tower above

The selection of the Japanese architect Yoshio Taniguchi as the competition winner for the "new" Museum of Modern Art in 1997 concluded a long phase of research, discussion, and introspection in preparation for the project in midtown Manhattan. On the cusp of the new millennium, the MoMA invited artists, architects, curators, academics, writers, historians ... to participate in an exploration of aspirations and possibilities for the institution. Subsequently, it developed a building program and launched the architectural competition. The competition itself was also intended to help clarify the mission of the museum. A book entitled *Imagining the Future of The Museum of Modern Art* documents the full process leading to the choice of Taniguchi and makes evident the importance of the exercise for the institution. It is difficult, however, to see a direct influence of these efforts on the final project which shows no evident conceptual innovation for the museum as a building type. Apparently, the reputation, visitor-ship, and general success of the museum allowed it to resist any pressure for a more flamboyant architecture even as the highly celebrated Guggenheim Bilbao neared completion just as the MoMA embarked on its competition.

The architecture of the successive projects for the Museum of Modern Art has generally been restrained and in the modern tradition. The brownstone given by the Rockefellers that first housed the MoMA was demolished to make way for the 1939 building by Goodwin and Stone. This white, modern structure is handsome and continues to present a recognizable architectural image for the institution. Though the buildings by Philip Johnson from the 1950s and 1960s were generally undistinguished, it is his 1953 design for the sculpture garden that borders 54th Street that remains the most appreciated of his projects. Cesar Pelli's project for the museum from the 1980s was for the most part demolished to make way for Taniguchi's design. It included the 52-story Museum Tower fronting 53rd Street and situated at the western boundary of Pelli's own museum design. The tower is now embedded in Taniguchi's project. During one of the public "conversations" organized by the MoMA in 1996 and recorded in the publication mentioned above, Rem Koolhaas observed "that you can be a successful institution in mediocre architecture ..." Though not mediocre, the MoMA's architecture has rarely been truly inspiring.

The architects invited to participate in the two-phase competition for the MoMA are also generally of the modern tradition. Wiel Arets, Steven Holl, Toyo Ito, Rem Koolhaas, Dominique Perrault, Rafael Viñoly, and Tod Williams/Billie Tsien competed in the short charrette of the first phase. Herzog & de Meuron, Yoshio Taniguchi, and Bernard Tschumi continued on into a second phase to develop a more thorough design. The MoMA particularly appreciated Taniguchi's spirit of problem solving and the attention given to their collection in his architectural approach. Before the Museum of Modern Art, Taniguchi had never previously entered an architectural competition. He had, however, realized several museum commissions in Japan, though much smaller in size than the MoMA. For Taniguchi the goal as related in *Imagining the Future of The Museum of Modern Art* was "to create an ideal environment for art and people through the imaginative and disciplined use of light, materials and space."

The Museum of Modern Art was founded in 1929. Since 1932 it has been located on the north side of 53rd Street between Fifth and Sixth Avenues. It is, therefore, a "street museum" with less visibility than other important "avenue" museums in New York such as the Metropolitan Museum of Art and the Guggenheim Museum, both on Fifth Avenue, or the Whitney Museum of American Art on Madison Avenue. Its location, combined with its origins in a brownstone, instilled a sense of hospitality and intimacy in the institution. Its architecture has avoided monumentality.

The 1997 competition called for a much larger building on a larger site for an ever-growing institution. Unlike the Whitney, adjacent land acquisitions allowed the museum to avoid a move to an entirely different location. With the new project the MoMA increased in total area from 35,300 to 59,460 m^2 (square meter; 380,000 to 640,000 ft^2 (square foot)). Exhibition space increased from 7,900 to 11,600 m^2 (85,000 to 125,000 ft^2). The enlarged site boundary extended to the west, beyond Pelli's Museum Tower and also offered more frontage to 54th Street to the north (Fig 5.1). With a significantly enlarged site and program, the competition allowed for the design of virtually an entirely new museum with a unified vision. There were, however, considerable constraints to weave a project around and through existing buildings that made the process more akin to solving a complex puzzle than free-willed design.

The enlarged site allowed Taniguchi to create a lobby that traverses the block and physically links 53rd and 54th Streets (Fig 5.5 and Fig 5.15). This rectilinear space functions like a public passage and houses ticketing, information, coat check, and restrooms and provides access to the museum store. The entry space on 53rd Street is relatively low and straightforward. From 54th Street visitors immediately perceive the two spaces that allow for orientation in this vast program: to the left there is the sculpture garden viewed on its long, east/west axis (Fig 5.16), and ahead and above, there is the atrium that soars upward five floors and provides access to the galleries (Fig 5.17). With up to 20,000 visitors per day, the ground floor lobby is always well populated but accommodates crowds relatively well with only a few conflicts between the lines for ticket sales and the passage toward the galleries.

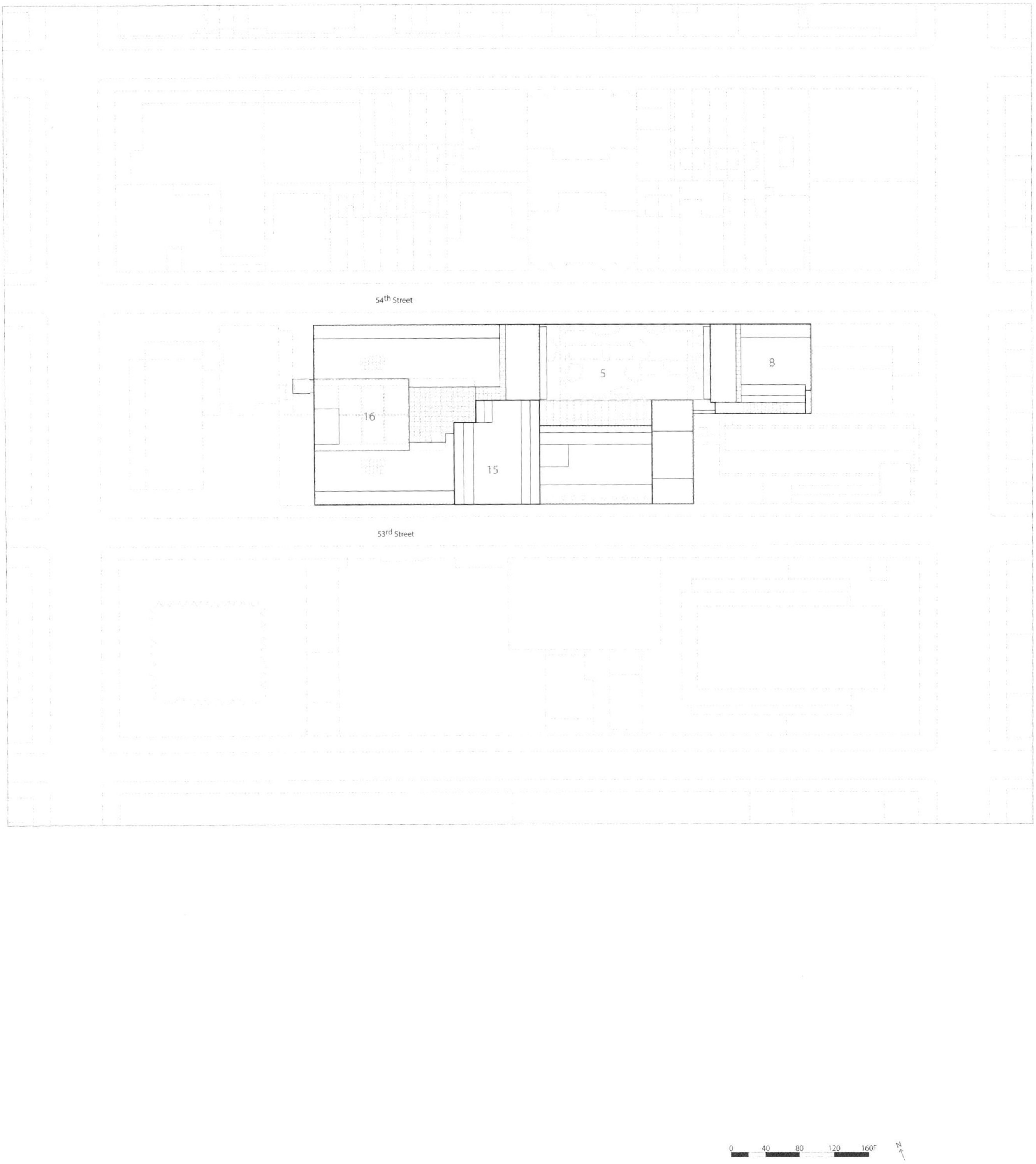

Figure 5.4 Site Plan

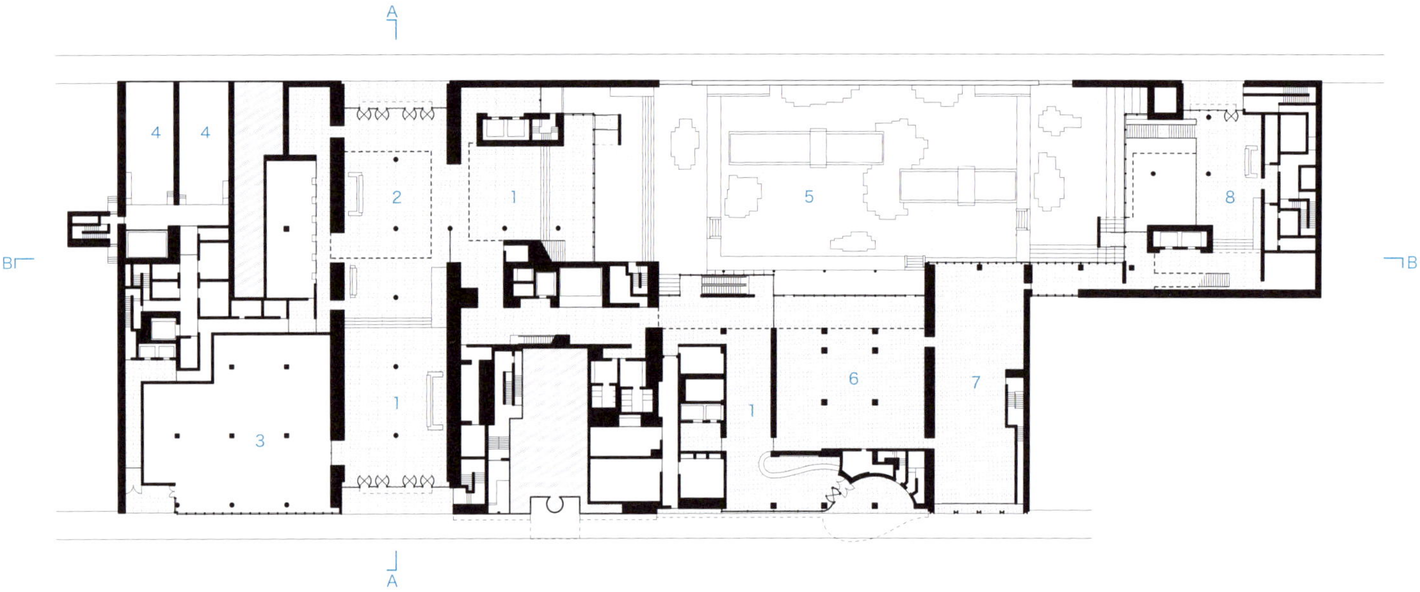

Figure 5.5 First (ground) floor plan

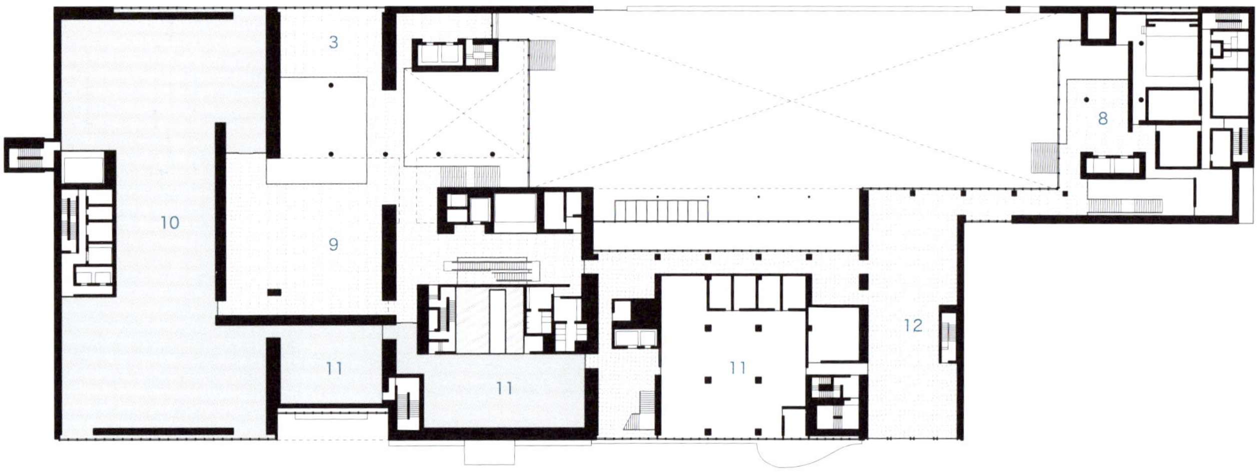

1 Lobby
2 Tickets
3 Museum Shop
4 Loading Dock
5 Sculpture Garden
6 Restaurant
7 Kitchen/services
8 Education Center
9 Atrium
10 Contemporary Gallery
11 Gallery (Prints & Books, Media, Architecture & Design, Photography, Drawing)
12 Cafe
13 Painting & Sculpture Gallery
14 Special Exhibitions
15 Museum Tower
16 Museum Office Tower

0 20 40 60 80F

Figure 5.6 Second floor plan

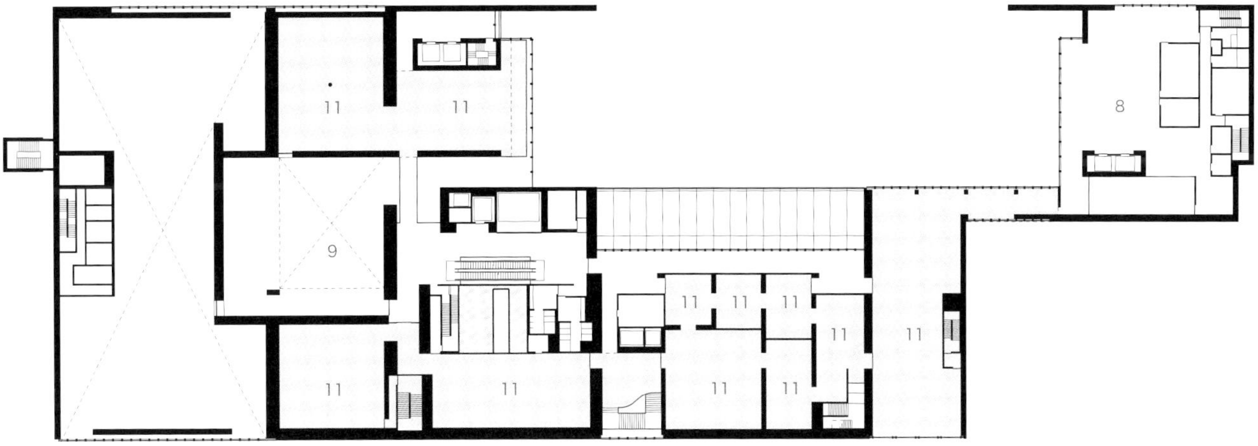

Figure 5.7 Third floor plan

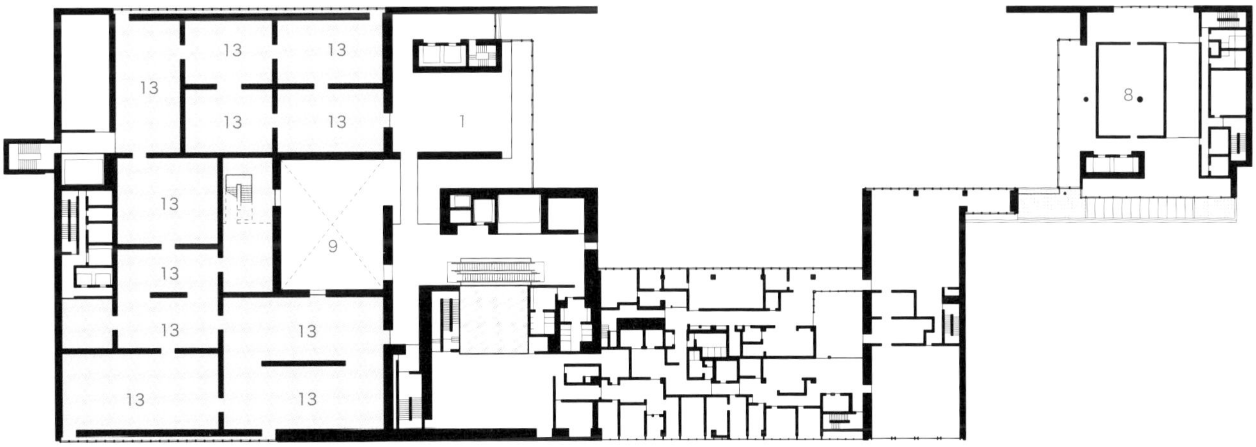

1 Lobby
2 Tickets
3 Museum Shop
4 Loading Dock
5 Sculpture Garden
6 Restaurant
7 Kitchen/services
8 Education Center
9 Atrium
10 Contemporary Gallery
11 Gallery (Prints & Books, Media, Architecture & Design, Photography, Drawing)
12 Cafe
13 Painting & Sculpture Gallery
14 Special Exhibitions
15 Museum Tower
16 Museum Office Tower

0 20 40 60 80F

Figure 5.8 Fourth floor plan

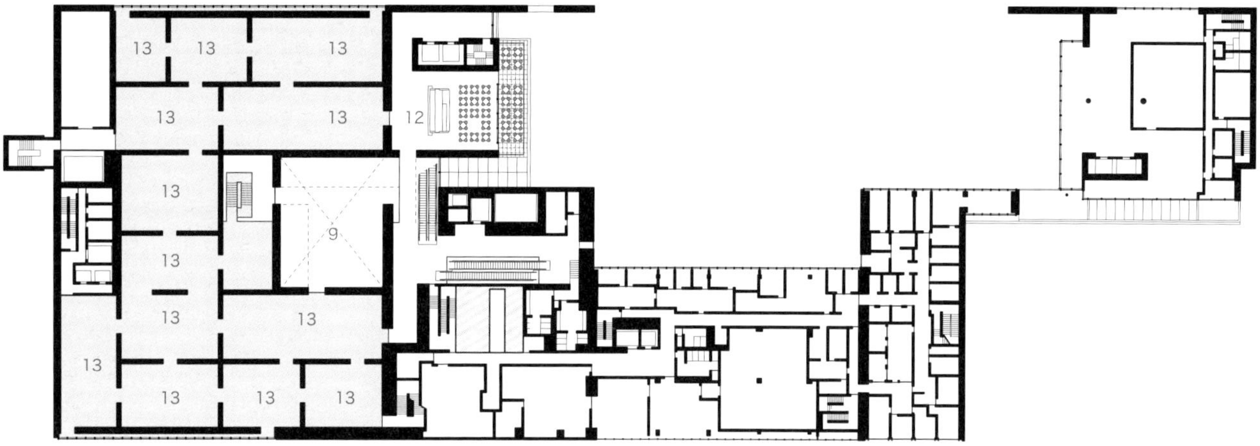

1 Lobby
2 Tickets
3 Museum Shop
4 Loading Dock
5 Sculpture Garden
6 Restaurant
7 Kitchen/services
8 Education Center
9 Atrium
10 Contemporary Gallery
11 Gallery (Prints & Books, Media, Architecture & Design, Photography, Drawing)
12 Cafe
13 Painting & Sculpture Gallery
14 Special Exhibitions
15 Museum Tower
16 Museum Office Tower

Figure 5.9 Fifth floor plan

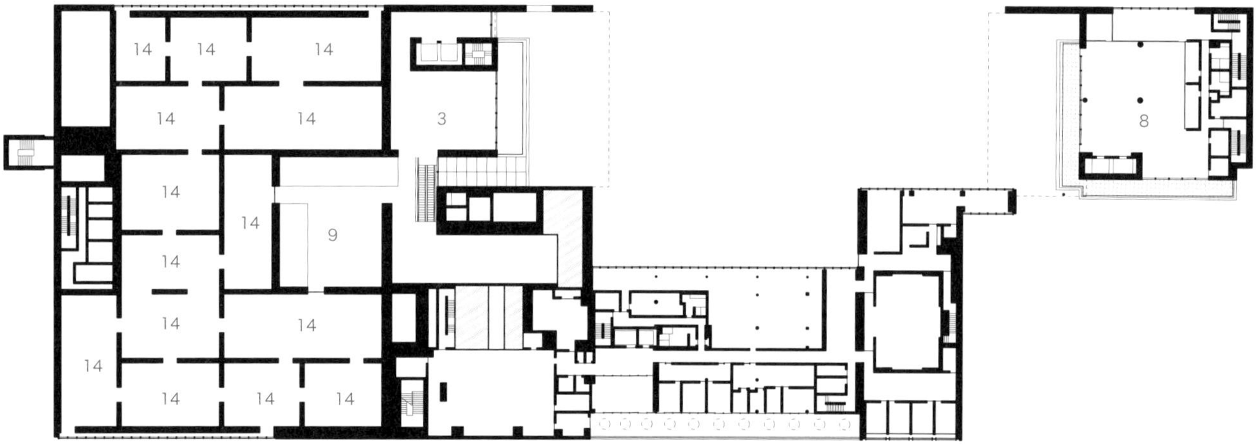

1 Lobby
2 Tickets
3 Museum Shop
4 Loading Dock
5 Sculpture Garden
6 Restaurant
7 Kitchen/services
8 Education Center
9 Atrium
10 Contemporary Gallery
11 Gallery (Prints & Books, Media, Architecture & Design, Photography, Drawing)
12 Cafe
13 Painting & Sculpture Gallery
14 Special Exhibitions
15 Museum Tower
16 Museum Office Tower

Figure 5.10 Sixth floor plan

The MoMA was inclined to maintain the sculpture garden even if the competition allowed for the exploration of other options. Its removal was suggested during the preliminary public conversations because, it was argued, it is poorly suited to contemporary sculpture. It is, however, highly appreciated by visitors and a welcome open space in this dense area of Manhattan. Taniguchi's interest in site in general as a point of departure for his designs led him to maintain the garden as a central and perhaps the most important element of his project (Fig 5.4). He even managed to slightly enlarge it. Taniguchi placed symmetrical pavilions on the east and west ends to accentuate it as a symbolic center for the museum (Fig 5.2 and Fig 5.3). This arrangement also projects a more coherent image to 54th Street and gives the museum a presence on its north side similar to that on 53rd Street to the south (Fig 5.11).

The composition of the 54th Street facade is dominated by the two simple cubic forms of the pavilions clad in black granite that frame the sculpture garden. To the east, the Education Center looks over the garden and toward the exhibition building to the west (Fig 5.12). Large canopies extend from both buildings and assure the transition between the interior and exterior. For Taniguchi, this architectural disposition symbolizes the double mission of the Museum of Modern Art: exhibition of collections and education of the public. Farther to the west, another ten-story cube sheathed in white frit glass, the Museum Office Tower, sits atop the lower volumes and houses offices, conservation, and lease office spaces. At ground level along 54th Street, a blank, somewhat inhospitable garden wall of granite and metal panels links the pavilions. In a second plane, beyond the garden, there is a glazed facade made of translucent and white frit glass. This facade masks both the Goodwin and Stone and the Philip Johnson buildings and presents a homogenous face to the sculpture garden. The facade is pleasantly uniform and milky white by day. At night, however, it becomes more transparent and less uniform when disparate functions, furniture, and lighting become visible. In contrast, the transparent facade of the exhibition pavilion takes life especially at night when larger pieces from the design collection such as the Bell-47D1 helicopter designed by Arthur Young become visible to passersby on 54th Street. The facade appears very light and is made of 6.4 by 17.8 cm (2½ by 7 in.) solid steel mullions. Interior floor plates are held off the facade to make it appear even more delicate, and only an alignment of a few small steel rods connect the 19.5 m (64 ft) high facade back to the floor slab of the third floor mezzanine to provide support (Fig 5.22).

Figure 5.12 Night view of Sculpture Garden looking west from the Education Building

Figure 5.11 53rd Street facade looking east

The institutional symmetry of exhibition and education expressed by the two main pavilions that bookend the garden may be more symbolic than real. The 8,360 m^2 (90,000 ft^2) Education Center inevitably appears empty compared to the bustling exhibition area. The main access into the Center is through a dedicated entrance on 54th Street, and access from the sculpture garden is not entirely obvious or inviting. An opening in the floor slab to the basement level just at the line of the glass facade negates any sense of continuity from outside to inside. Likewise, the connection between the two pavilions from within the building is through an awkward corridor on the second floor. In the end, the two pavilions seem detached one from the other. Both Herzog & de Meuron and Bernard Tschumi proposed placing galleries and public spaces around the three sides of the sculpture garden. Such a solution certainly would have established the primacy of the garden. In the end, Taniguchi's project shifts activity inside the building to his own atrium space.

On the 53rd Street side, Taniguchi and the associated architects Kohn Pedersen Fox took the opposite approach from the garden side, and this elevation allows the evolutions and successive buildings of the MoMA to remain visible. The existing facades of the Goodwin and Stone and the Philip Johnson buildings were renovated and remain distinct. Within this street facade, Taniguchi's addition conforms to the height of the earlier MoMA buildings while using a new palette of granite, aluminum panels, white frit glass, and gray tinted glass. Pelli's tower sits between Taniguchi's building and the Goodwin and Stone building. The Museum Tower appears to have been an important constraint for the interior space planning as well as the composition of the street facade. Taniguchi chose, however, to give the tower a prominent position in the sculpture garden.

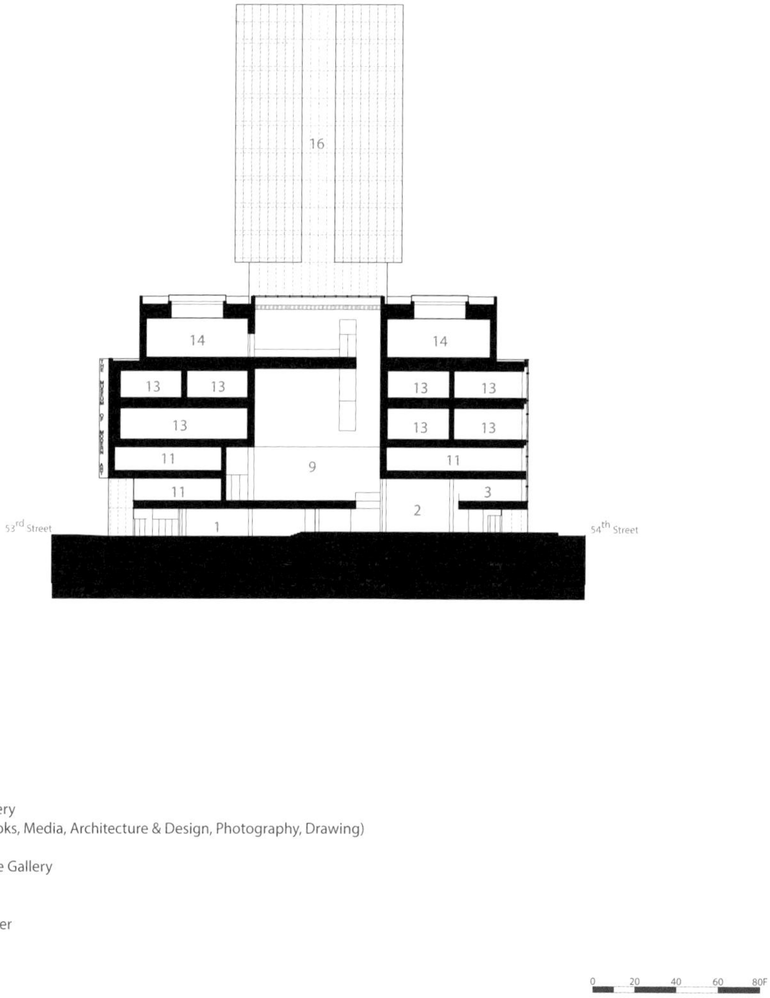

1 Lobby
2 Tickets
3 Museum Shop
4 Loading Dock
5 Sculpture Garden
6 Restaurant
7 Kitchen/services
8 Education Center
9 Atrium
10 Contemporary Gallery
11 Gallery (Prints & Books, Media, Architecture & Design, Photography, Drawing)
12 Cafe
13 Painting & Sculpture Gallery
14 Special Exhibitions
15 Museum Tower
16 Museum Office Tower

Figure 5.13 Transversal section A

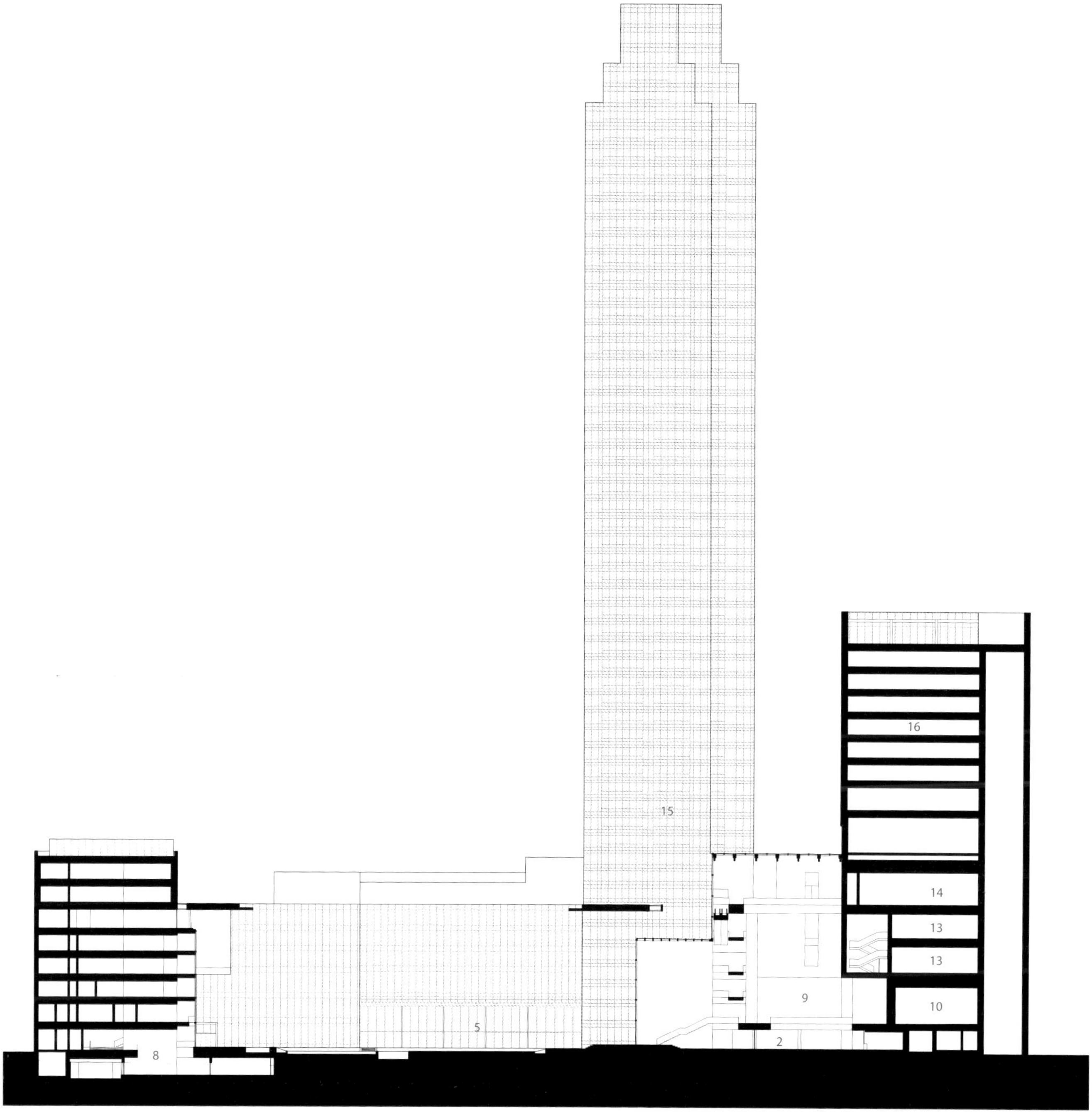

1 Lobby
2 Tickets
3 Museum Shop
4 Loading Dock
5 Sculpture Garden
6 Restaurant
7 Kitchen/services
8 Education Center
9 Atrium
10 Contemporary Gallery
11 Gallery (Prints & Books, Media, Architecture & Design, Photography, Drawing)
12 Cafe
13 Painting & Sculpture Gallery
14 Special Exhibitions
15 Museum Tower
16 Museum Office Tower

Figure 5.14 Longitudinal section B

To enter the galleries from the ground floor entry lobby, visitors turn to face the sculpture garden and pass through ticket control. Elevators are tucked behind a wall to the left and a relatively modest stair to the right doubles back and leads to the vast atrium on the second floor. Escalators are also available but are not apparent. The 465 m^2 (5,000 ft^2) atrium space is naturally lit by a glass roof 33.55 m (110 ft) above. It is bordered by "floating" walkways at upper levels. The commercial aspect of the former hall by Pelli has been replaced by a more discreet means of vertical circulation – escalators and elevators – conceived by Taniguchi. In a vertical museum, however, the vertical circulation could have been more systematic and clear. The escalators and elevators deliver visitors to different places on the various floor plates. From the atrium level upward the escalators are the privileged means of circulation while the less visible elevators open sometimes onto a lobby, sometimes onto a cafe, and sometimes onto a museum store.

The atrium functions as a spatial reference point and to a certain degree unifies the five levels of galleries. It becomes a second ground plane for the museum. The floor is green Vermont slate, the gypsum board walls are painted white, and handrails are glass. It is *the* architectural gesture of the project and seems an obvious response to a vertical museum with stacked exhibition spaces. It is a cloistered volume that provides a transition into the galleries. Like the sculpture garden, it allows for an encounter with artworks before entering into the more orchestrated spaces of the galleries.

For the opening in 2004, Broken Obelisk by Barnett Newman was the focus of the space and seemed for the most part at ease, though highly staged. Paintings, even very large ones, seem to be lost on the expansive walls of the very large space. The Water Lilies by Claude Monet, one of the major pieces of the collection, disappeared behind the constant flow and jam of visitors. As for any large museum, many visitors come to the MoMA not as a museum but as a tourist landmark. This is felt more keenly in the atrium. The museum is still experimenting with the space, and it has since been used for exhibitions that are less static as well as site-specific installations, and even performances. The lobby space directly under the glass roof on the sixth floor of the atrium leads to the special exhibitions galleries (Fig 5.20). It presents the same difficulty for the presentation of works of art and is essentially a circulation area.

The Contemporary Gallery is located on the second floor. For a visitor working through the building vertically, it would be the first exhibition space encountered. This was a symbolic gesture for Taniguchi in order to show the integral importance of contemporary art for the MoMA. From a pragmatic point of view, the second floor location offered higher ceilings because of the way it connects with the existing floor levels of Pelli's Museum Tower. The 6.70m (22 ft) high space is the combined height of the tower's second and third floors. The structure of the building is steel with floors of metal deck and concrete. The galleries remain flexible and virtually column free since the structure above is a system of large steel trusses and suspended structure. The Contemporary Gallery has gypsum board walls and a terrazzo floor.

A small portion of the second floor (Fig 5.6) is devoted to Prints and the exhibition of smaller works. The third floor (Fig 5.7) is devoted to Architecture and Design, Drawings and Photography. These spaces suffer the constraints of being housed within the base of the Museum Tower and the other preexisting buildings. Architecture and Design has the advantage of additional gallery spaces that overlook the sculpture garden. This seems a logical arrangement since many design pieces are less light-sensitive than prints, photographs, or paintings.

On the fourth and fifth floors (Fig 5.8, Fig 5.9, Fig 5.18, and Fig 5.19), the galleries for Painting and Sculpture are large but well proportioned. The floors are light oak, and ceiling heights are 4.10 m (13 ft 6 in.). The spaces are neither grand nor intimate. The galleries are somewhat like a maze with no apparent organizational system for the layout. Room sizes appear to be determined more by site constraints than any sort of architectural ordering device such as, for example, the repetitive pavilions Tadao Ando employed in his Modern Art Museum of Fort Worth. There is a stair within the galleries that links the fourth and fifth floors that would seemingly offer variety to a more prescribed visit. It appears little used, however. In such a large museum, opportunities for discovery are weighed against the risk of backtracking and missing entire gallery areas.

There is a visual calm in Taniguchi's spaces. Care was taken with the positioning of necessary equipment such as air conditioning grills, lighting, cameras, and other elements of the security system. Taniguchi accentuated the thickness of gallery walls and added aluminum doorframes to mark the passage between spaces. These frames are one of the few things that catch the eye in an architecture meant to disappear.

The sixth floor (Fig 5.10 and Fig 5.21) is devoted to two Special Exhibition galleries which are more generic spaces with 5.50 m (18 ft) ceiling heights. The larger of the two spaces is lit by two large skylights. Taniguchi had hoped to have more natural light entering into the Special Exhibition galleries by a series of shed roofs. His competition entry also showed a scheme for natural light in the Painting and Sculpture galleries on the fourth and fifth floors as well. These solutions presented certain technical problems linked, for example, with light control, but apparently the MoMA simply preferred to maintain the principle of artificially lit galleries. At all levels of Taniguchi's building there are links

Figure 5.15 Entry from 54th Street

Figure 5.16 Entry view with Sculpture Garden

Figure 5.17 Atrium looking east

Figure 5.18 View from fourth floor lobby toward Sculpture Garden and the Education Building

Figure 5.19 Fourth floor gallery space

Figure 5.20 Atrium at sixth floor level

Figure 5.21 Sixth floor gallery

with the cityscape outside via large gray-tinted windows. This allows orientation within the building and is a welcome pause in the museum visit.

Three basement levels house mechanical rooms, support spaces, and a small amount of art storage. The first underground level is the most important and connects all spaces. Three theaters are also located below ground including the refurbished 1939 theater designed by Goodwin and Stone. The escalator descending to the theater area is one of few elements of Cesar Pelli's project that remains. A loading dock is located on 54th Street. Of the three delivery bays, one is for the Museum Tower, one is exclusively reserved for art works, and the other is for everything else. A freight elevator links delivery to the basement levels, the galleries above, and conservation on the ninth and tenth floors of the Museum Office Tower. Other primary mechanical spaces, administration offices, and tenant lease space are also located in the Museum Office Tower.

When founded, the MoMA had no permanent collection. By the completion of Taniguchi's project in 2004 the collection numbered well over 100,000 works that are meticulously stored in ideal conservation conditions in a 7,430 m^2 (80,000 ft^2) industrial building in the borough of Queens. Few of the stored works are visible and most are in crates. The current storage facility served as a temporary exhibition space for the MoMA during the three-and-a-half years that construction was underway at the midtown Manhattan site. When Taniguchi's project was complete, 14 different storage facilities were consolidated into the single Queens site. Trucks go back and forth regularly between the storage space and the museum, and since there is limited storage space at the midtown location, empty crates are often sent back to Queens as well. The MoMA has approximately 35 gallery changes per year.

With the reopening of the MoMA, the United States discovered Yoshio Tanaguchi. The architect's second American building, a 2,800 m^2 (30,000 ft^2) cultural center for the Asia Society in Houston, Texas, opened in 2012. Taniguchi's project for the Museum of Modern Art is an attentive response to a complex problem rather than a grand gesture of architecture. It is not an intellectual exercise parallel to the program but gives priority to the exhibition of the works of art.

Goodwin and Stone's building for the MoMA was one of the first modern buildings in New York and was influential for that reason. Taniguchi's MoMA was anticipated as a significant new work of architecture in a city that at the time was lacking innovative projects. Since 2004, however, there has been a flurry of more audacious and inspiring projects by well-known architects that have upstaged the MoMA's architecture. Taniguchi's project for the Museum of Modern Art is not radical. It won't change the course of architecture, but its modesty may influence the strategies of other museums considering expansions. The project does not, however, seem to have "imagined" or addressed the question of the very large museum with large numbers of visitors, many of whom are sightseers. Though the MoMA is in the enviable position of having no shortage of museum goers, that situation may also be a burden. Visitors often appear to move through the spaces in a state of distraction. The very large, highly visited museum might be imagined and considered as a type apart.

Since 2004, the MoMA acquired more land between 53rd and 54th Streets to the west of Taniguchi's building. It also acquired the American Folk Art Museum designed by New York architects Tod Williams and Billie Tsien. That building, completed in 2001, has now been slated for demolition to make an even larger parcel for an ambitious mixed-use skyscraper project by the American developer Gerald Hines and the French architect Jean Nouvel. The MoMA will own upward of 3,700 m^2 (40,000 ft^2) in Nouvel's building and the new exhibition spaces that will connect to its existing second, fourth, and fifth floor galleries will be designed by Diller Scofidio + Renfro.

And yet another occasion to imagine the future of the Museum of Modern Art …

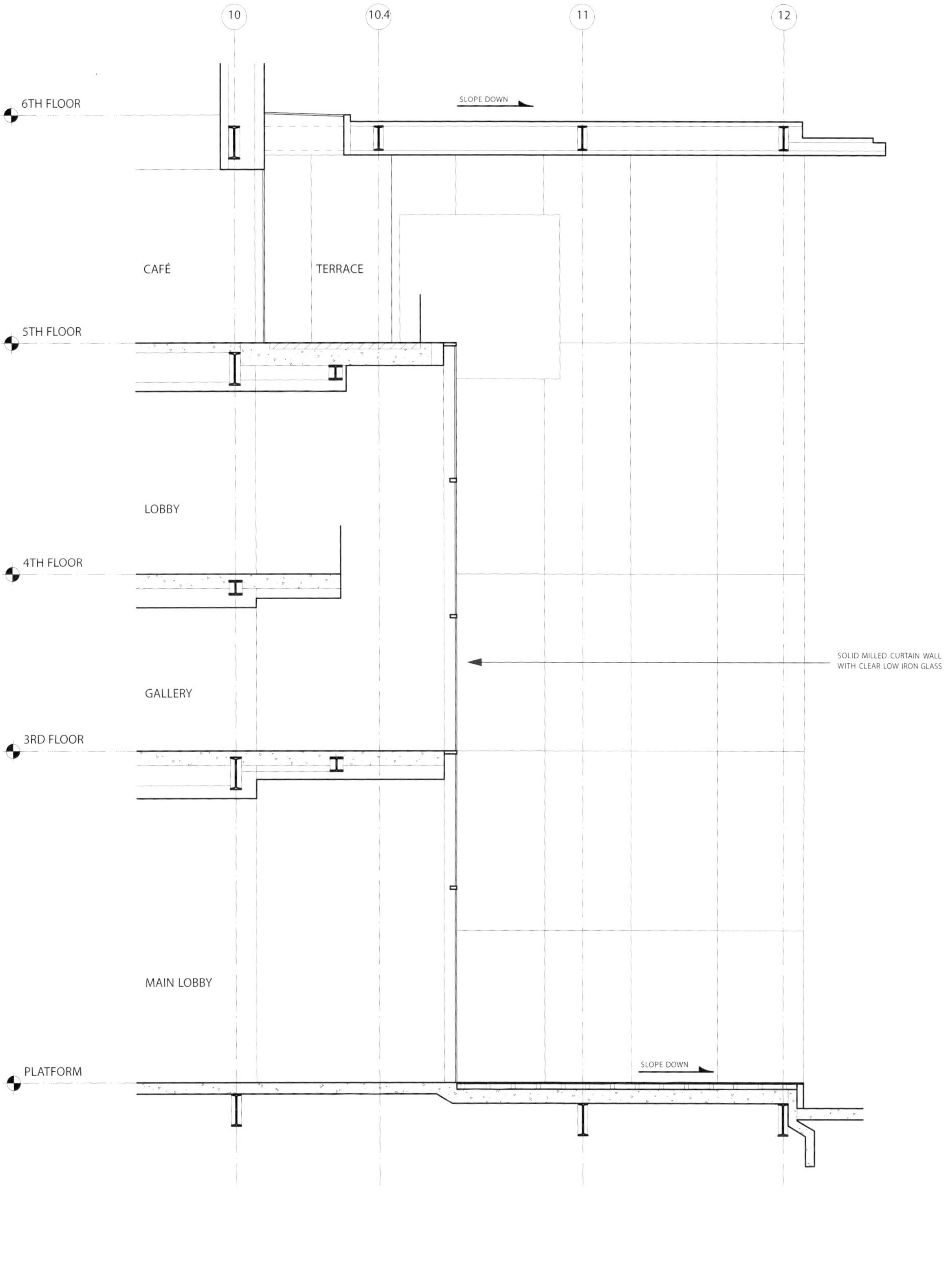

Figure 5.22 Facade detail

CHAPTER 6

Walker Art Center

Minneapolis, Minnesota

Herzog & de Meuron

2005

Figure 6.1 General view from north/east

From at least the 1970s until his death in 2004, Edward Larrabee Barnes was an important "museum architect." His body of work was such that in 1987 the Katonah Gallery in Katonah, New York organized an exhibition of several of his museum projects realized across the United States. The catalogue includes the Walker Art Center in Minneapolis that Barnes completed in 1971 and expanded in 1984. At the time of the building's opening the architecture was described as "minimal." It was considered innovative with white, flexible, loft-like gallery spaces that were designed to be a backdrop for the modern and contemporary art to be exhibited. Because of the small site available at the time, Barnes' building is a vertical museum. Rather than stacked, unconnected floors, however, gallery spaces are linked and step in a helical manner by half levels around a central core. Barnes gave priority to the interior spaces and the flow of visitors which resulted in an introverted building with a cubic, somewhat fortress-like exterior. Herzog & de Meuron described the solution as a pragmatic version of Frank Lloyd Wright's Guggenheim Museum.

In their first wave of museum projects in the United States, Herzog & de Meuron crossed paths with Edward Larrabee Barnes more than once. Besides being the original architect of the Walker Art Center, Barnes was also a trustee of the Museum of Modern Art in New York and served on the museum's Architect Selection Committee that chose Herzog & de Meuron, Yoshio Taniguchi, and Bernard Tschumi as finalists in the competition for the expansion of the MoMA. (Taniguchi was awarded the project.) Barnes was also commissioned by the Fine Arts Museums of San Francisco for renovations to the Legion of Honor and preliminary master planning for a portion of Golden Gate Park where Herzog & de Meuron's de Young Museum now stands. At the request of the museum, Barnes also established a first list of architects to be considered for the de Young project.

The Walker Art Center decided to forego an architectural competition for their expansion project and simply hired Herzog & de Meuron in the year 2000 shortly after the architects had won the de Young Museum competition. The Walker preferred commencing the design process with conversation rather than partially developed competition proposals. Like many museums, the Walker Art Center undertook a period of institutional reflection before hiring an architect, and much of those preparations as well as the development of the design and the actual construction of the addition are recounted in the book *Expanding the Center: Walker Art Center and Herzog & de Meuron*. As an art center, the Walker wanted to express more clearly its mission beyond that of a simple art gallery or museum and increase the public's awareness of its commitment to the performing arts, film, and media arts. The center identified four primary experiences that the expanded center should provide: a place for aesthetic contemplation of unique objects, an opportunity for learning, a space for social interaction, and a catalyst for introspection. The Walker was also inspired by the notion of "experience design" that would have affinities to more commercial strategies for developing consumer loyalty. The staging of a complete and memorable experience would go beyond the offer of a simple service or product and should establish relationships with individuals rather than a mass market. Noting that Minneapolis possesses the United States' largest indoor shopping mall, *Expanding the Center* also quoted the work of Mary Anne Staniszewski who noted that "both the museum and the department store arose in the nineteenth century. Both are institutions of modernity and modern capitalism. And both are created for visual delectation and display ... " In more physical terms, the Walker embraced the metaphor of the street and more specifically the town square rather than that of the shopping mall while keeping in mind that the social nature of the contemporary museum (or art center in this case) may be at odds with the contemplative nature of looking at art.

Figure 6.2 Site plan

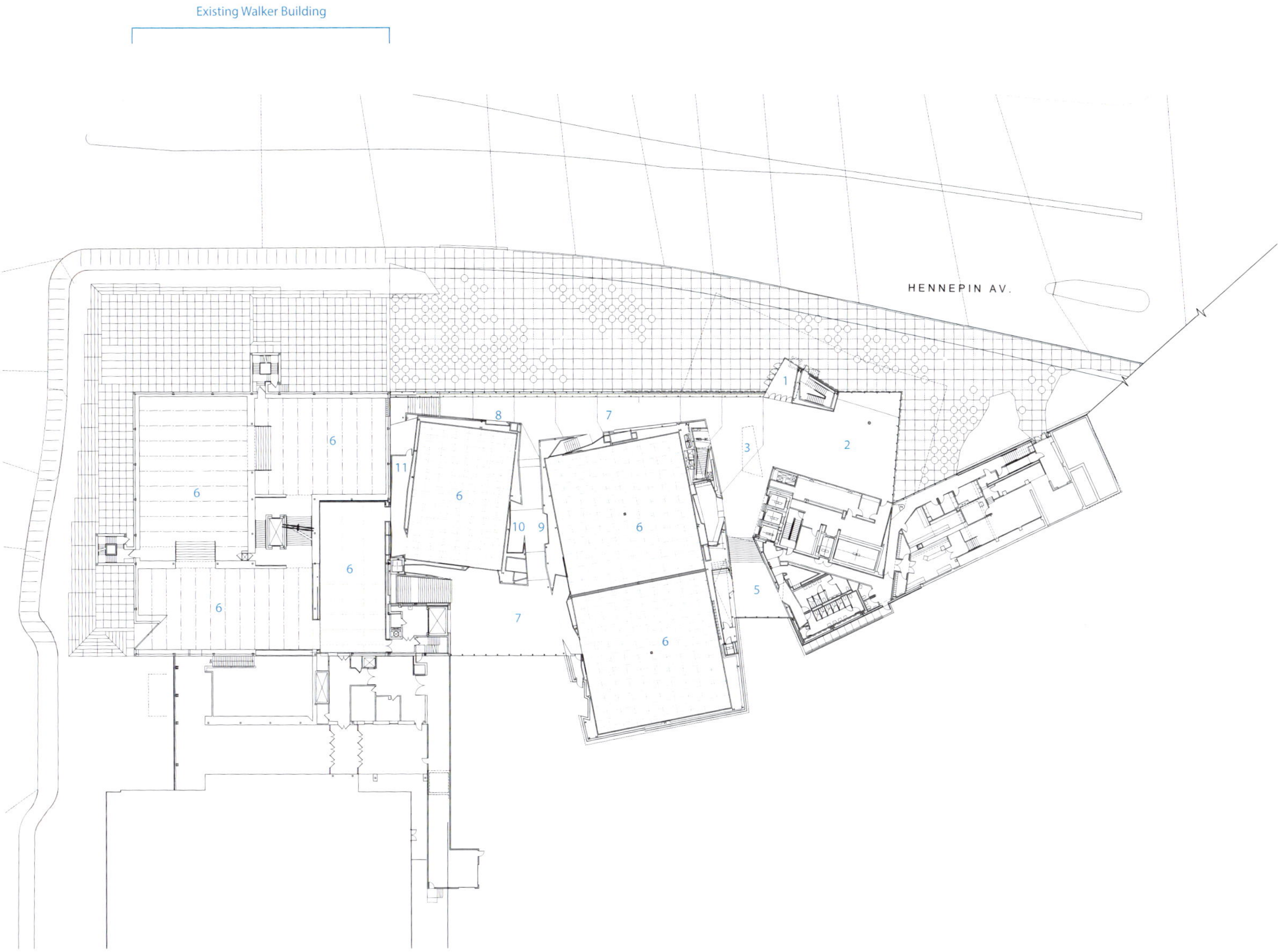

1 Entrance
2 Shop
3 Hennepin Lobby
4 Loading Docks
5 Garden Gallery
6 Gallery
7 Hennepin Lounge
8 Audio Bay
9 Film/video Bay
10 Info Lounge
11 Arcade
12 Restaurant
13 Offices
14 Theater
15 Special Event Space

Figure 6.3 Second and third floor plans entry level for extension

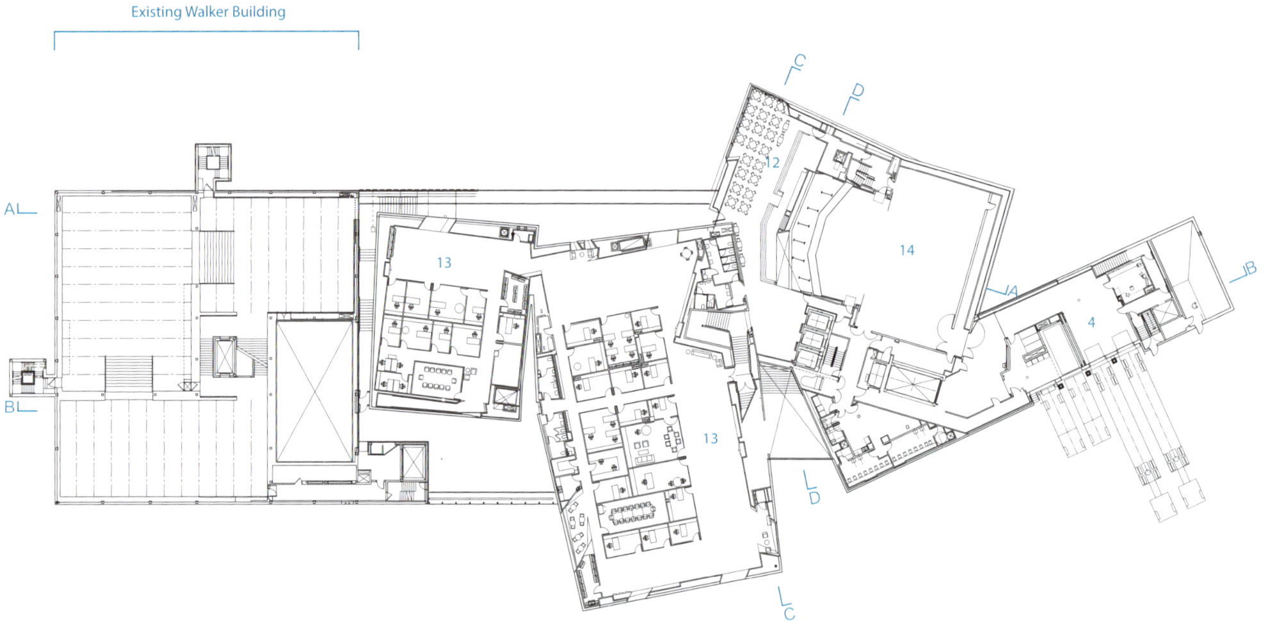

1 Entrance
2 Shop
3 Hennepin Lobby
4 Loading Docks
5 Garden Gallery
6 Gallery
7 Hennepin Lounge
8 Audio Bay
9 Film/video Bay
10 Info Lounge
11 Arcade
12 Restaurant
13 Offices
14 Theater
15 Special Event Space

Figure 6.4: Fourth Floor Plan

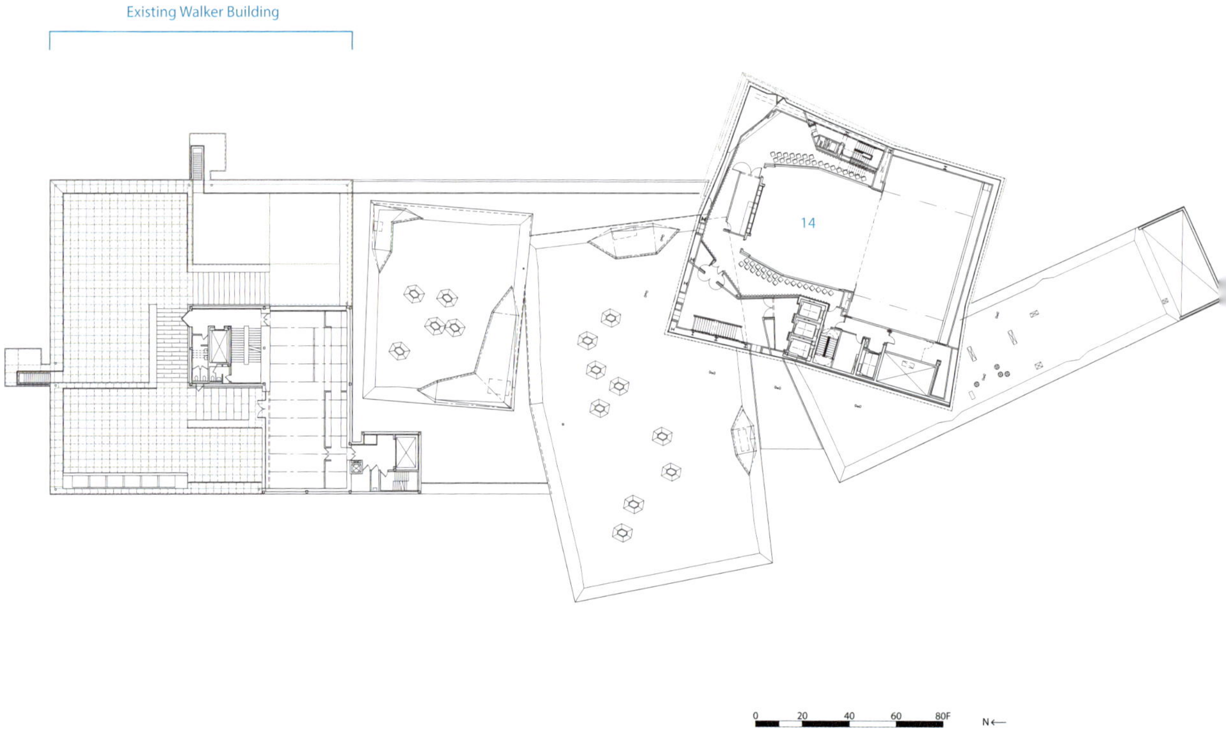

1 Entrance
2 Shop
3 Hennepin Lobby
4 Loading Docks
5 Garden Gallery
6 Gallery
7 Hennepin Lounge
8 Audio Bay
9 Film/video Bay
10 Info Lounge
11 Arcade
12 Restaurant
13 Offices
14 Theater
15 Special Event Space

Figure 6.5 Fifth floor plan (sixth and seventh floors similar)

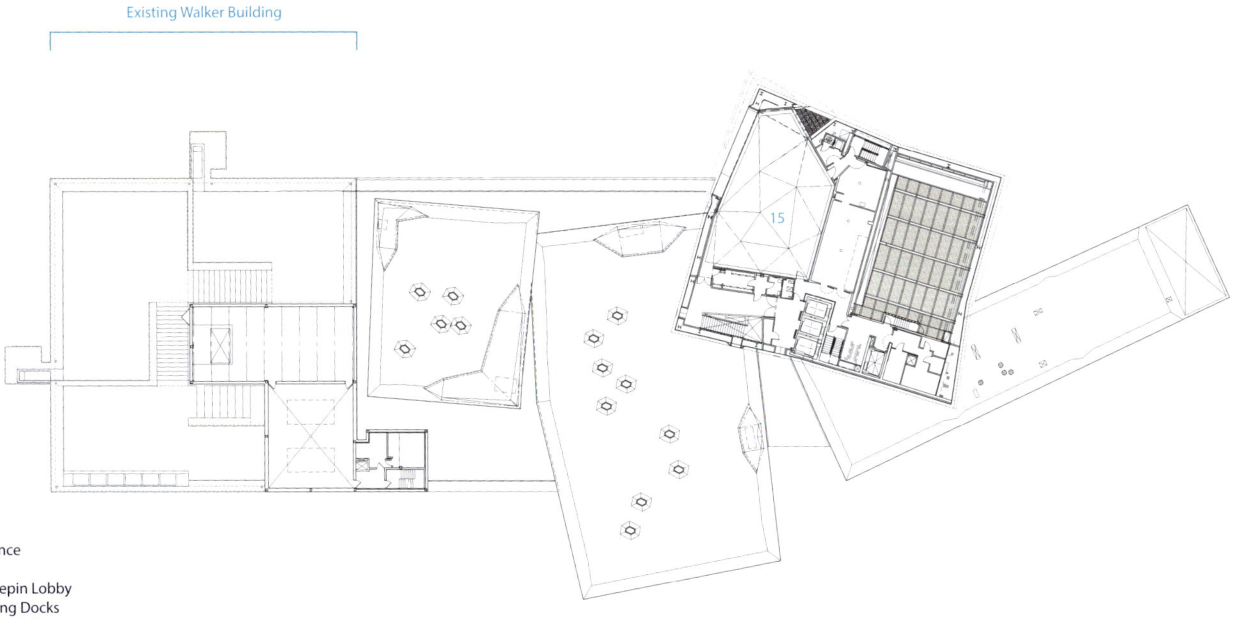

1 Entrance
2 Shop
3 Hennepin Lobby
4 Loading Docks
5 Garden Gallery
6 Gallery
7 Hennepin Lounge
8 Audio Bay
9 Film/video Bay
10 Info Lounge
11 Arcade
12 Restaurant
13 Offices
14 Theater
15 Special Event Space

Figure 6.6 Eighth floor plan

The Walker is located to the southwest of downtown Minneapolis. The Minneapolis Sculpture Garden is to the north; a sunken freeway separates it from Loring Park to the east; a residential neighborhood is to the west, and a mixed residential area is to the south beyond another freeway interchange. Barnes' building was previously hemmed in between the Allianz office building to the south and the Guthrie Theater, an important Minneapolis cultural institution, immediately to its west. The Walker and the Guthrie had even shared a glazed entry space opening onto Vineland Place to the north. In order to realize the expansion, the Walker acquired the Allianz building and razed it. The Guthrie Theater was razed after completion of Herzog & de Meuron's expansion and moved into a new building designed by Jean Nouvel on the banks of the Mississippi River. The expanded Walker now sits alone on its site and presents a face to the adjacent Hennepin Avenue to the east, and the overall structure, elongated in the north/south direction, presents another face to its own four-acre green space to the west (Fig 6.2).

Herzog & de Meuron's design responds to Barnes' brick-clad tower with a second cubic, metal-clad tower (Fig 6.1). The two are connected by a lower volume that aligns with a portion of the Barnes building and contains new galleries, offices, and service and delivery areas. To the south and west, the extension appears as white, smooth-surfaced masses projecting into the green space (Fig 6.7). To the east it appears as a 76 m (250 ft) long, glazed facade along Hennepin Avenue (Fig 6.8), behind which a parallel, ramped interior "street," the Hennepin Lounge, (Fig 6.14) provides a visual link between inside and outside. The newfound transparency, combined with a new pedestrian entrance from Hennepin Avenue, reorients the entire project to the avenue in order to better connect the Walker to the city. The glass facade itself is a double facade with a generous air space that is exploited for its thermal and acoustic properties (Fig 6.18). The structural steel, vertical mullions of the two facades are staggered, and the glass is transparent on the lower portion and translucent above. At night, the lit facade provides visibility for the center and the programs list is projected and streamed on the translucent glass which further animates the building. Access from Hennepin Avenue is located under the tower (Fig 6.9) and the entry space inside (Fig 6.13) contains a ticketing and information desk as well as the museum shop. There is a relatively small opening in the ceiling that connects to the floor above, but the entry is generally restrained and adheres to Herzog & de

Meuron's desire not to create spatial hierarchy in the form of large interior volumes such as a grand atrium.

Though it is primarily opaque, the new tower was also meant to symbolize the importance of the performing arts for the Walker, and the primary function housed within is a 385 seat theater. Glazed openings in the volume facing Hennepin Avenue correspond to other functions in the tower such as the restaurant that is located one level above the street level (Fig 6.4) and a 279 m^2 (square meter; 3,000 ft^2 (square foot)) special events space at the very top of the building (Fig 6.6) that offers a panoramic view of the downtown skyline. Another large window to the west provides light for the stairwell. If there is a rejection of spatial hierarchy inside, there is a desire to create a seductive form outside and an iconic presence in the city. Early proposals for the project explored alternatives more closely linked to

Figure 6.7 View from south/west

Figure 6.8 View from north

Figure 6.9 View from south

Figure 6.10 View from east

Barnes' building where an addition would sit atop and fill in the existing stepped structure. This approach was more akin to the architects' later designs for the CaixaForum in Madrid or the Hamburg Philharmonic where an existing building serves as the base for an addition. If Barnes' tower appears closed and somewhat indifferent to its surroundings and passersby, Herzog & de Meuron's tower as realized is more assertive. It appears ominous yet joyful at the same time. The tower, in itself, is a new sign for the Walker contributing, apparently, to the complete experience of experience design by shaping the perceptions of customers or visitors before a need of what is being offered is even understood.

A strong visual impact has been a constant in Herzog & de Meuron's work. A project such as the Goetz Art Gallery in Munich from 1992 derives its force from the horizontal glass strips that make the building's opaque portions seem to float. Here, image and purpose are fused since the glass strips also provide clerestory lighting for the exhibition spaces inside. Similarly, in the much larger Tate Modern in London from 2000 the architects placed a horizontal "light beam" atop the existing brick power station in order to create a new image for the museum. Though it contains functions unrelated to exhibition, the light beam was also conceived, in part, to bring natural light into some gallery spaces. In Minneapolis the strategy for creating a sign in the city is less synthesized with the purpose of the project. This is also the case for Herzog & de Meuron's de Young Museum in San Francisco.

The Walker tower is an articulated box that is lifted above the ground and cantilevers toward Hennepin Avenue (Fig 6.10). It measures approximately 30 m (100 ft) in both directions and its sloped top rises to a height of approximately 23 m (75 ft). The parapet extends well above the roof level to mask mechanical equipment. Initially the mass of the tower was conceived as a lantern, and backlit fabrics and membranes were explored as the outer finish. The cladding system as realized consists of expanded aluminum panels that are stamped to give a crumpled effect. Technically, this was achieved by rotating and stamping the material four times. The panels are actually 1.14 m (3 ft 9 in.) square boxes that are 15 cm (6 in.) deep. Though all panels are identical, they are turned in different directions to give more variety to the facade, and the combination of finish (brite dip clear anodized) and the apparently non-repetitive texture makes the facades shimmer. The panels, or boxes, are attached to a frame of aluminum tubes (generally 5 by 10 cm or 2 by 4 in.) that is in turn attached to an interior layer of insulated aluminum weatherproof panels. The crumpled, aluminum finish panels are also used for the exterior soffit and the interior ceiling of the entry space. Using the panels for the horizontal finish reinforces the impression of a unified mass. There are approximately 3,000 panels that were manufactured locally by M. G. McGrath who later also manufactured the expanded metal facade panels for SANAA's New Museum of Contemporary Art in New York. For Herzog & de Meuron, adopting local methods of production and available construction technologies is a way of responding to each place where they realize a project.

The irregular window shapes in the tower and in the lower, smooth-finished building masses appear willful even though Herzog & de Meuron describe such formal moves as "accidental." The windows seem at odds with the architects' desire to avoid "genius gestures" so that their designs might seem more objective and the author's hand less visible. Small, hexagonal openings in the metal skin are windows that connect to various points in the urban landscape. Many of the framed views are of churches.

Edward Larrabee Barnes' brick-clad building (12,075 m^2 or 130,000 ft^2) was constructed of concrete and precast concrete T-beams that are left exposed inside. Herzog & de Meuron's building (10,220 m^2 or 110,000 ft^2) is primarily a steel structure (Fig 6.19 and Fig 6.20). The cantilevers of the tower are achieved by using trusses sandwiched within the walls on three sides. These trusses are 18 m (60 ft) tall, virtually the full height of the structure, and cantilever up to 18 m as well. The structural engineer for the project was the Minneapolis office of Hammel, Green, and Abrahamson (HGA) who was also the architect of record.

The theater occupies the core of the tower. Lobbies are located on levels two and three above the ground level (with the restaurant in between on level one) and access is via three elevators and a modest but light-filled stairwell. Vertical circulation is generally downplayed and the stair takes a circuitous route at the lower level to then ascend more directly in the north/west corner of the tower. The vertical circulation has none of the "flow" and connection that interested Barnes, and this major program space seems detached from the center's other social spaces.

The horseshoe-shaped theater gives an impression of an experimental space and a classical theater at the same time (Fig 6.5 and Fig 6.15). The architects have mentioned Milan's Scala as an inspiration for this steeply sloped space where first row seats are at the same level as the stage. In Minneapolis the theater is dark and mysterious, and the black and aubergine palette of colors strongly contrasts with the generally white spaces in the rest of the building. Lighting is versatile and attached to exposed frames. Curtains cover the walls and function as decoration and acoustic control. The seats are upholstered in a gray fabric with a small floral pattern that was also designed by the architects. It is, however, the treatment of the wall surfaces – a vegetal pattern in relief that has been created by perforating and embossing black, steel panels – that is the most surprising and delightful feature

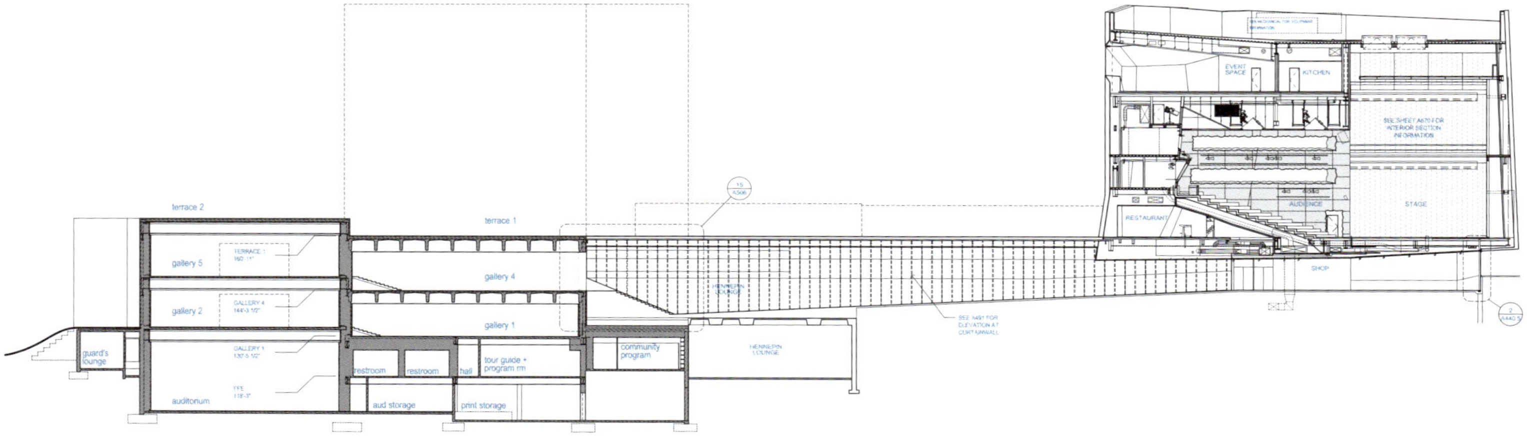

Section A

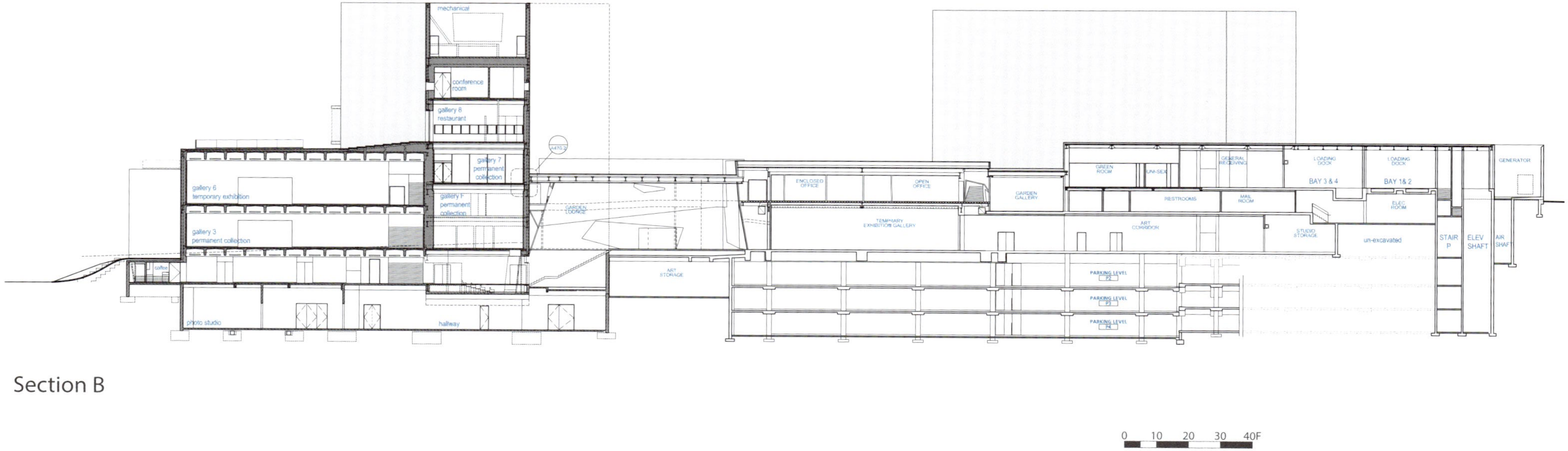

Section B

Figure 6.11 Section A and section B

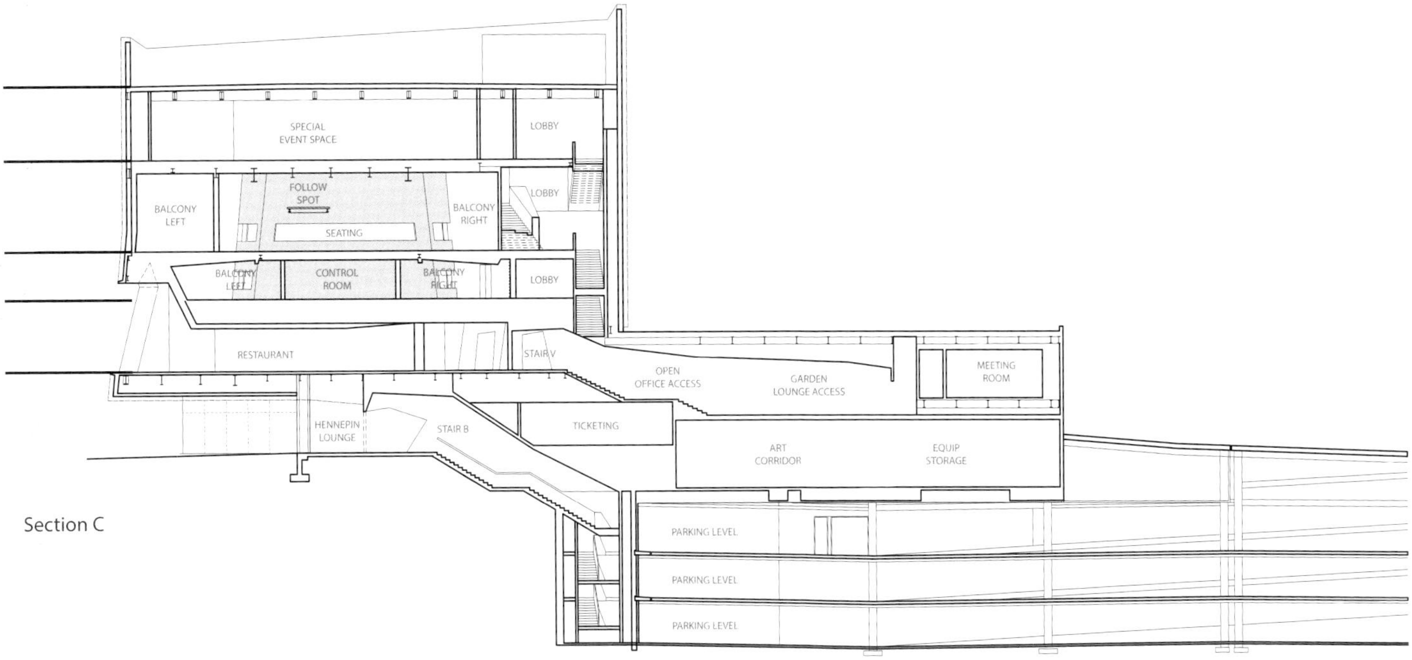

Section C

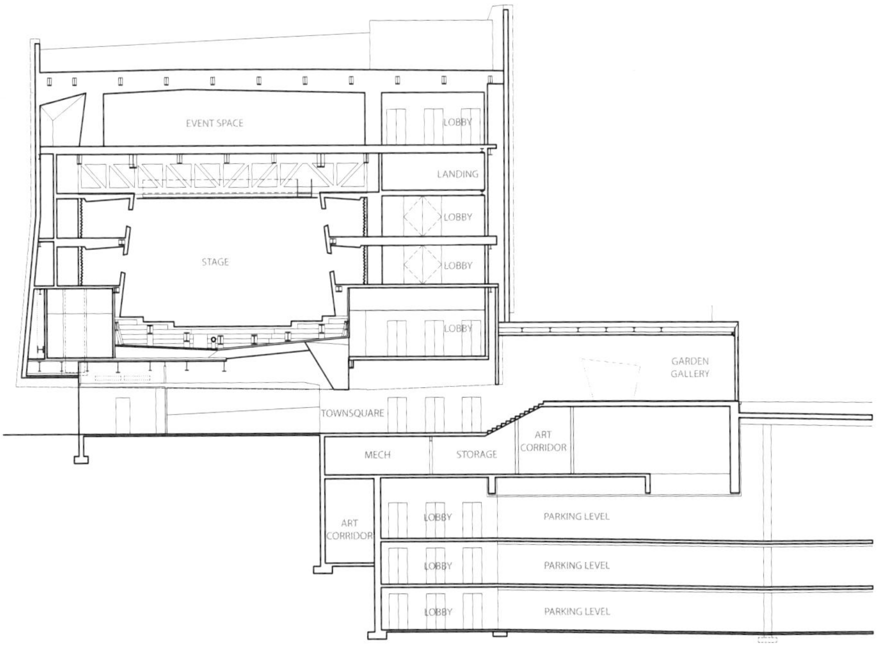

Section D

0 10 20 30 40F

Figure 6.12 Section C and section D

of the room. Acoustical materials are integrated behind the panels to reflect or absorb sound. The undulating handrails of the balconies are in black plaster and seem more inspired by Antoni Gaudi than any notion of minimal architecture – a preoccupation for Herzog & de Meuron's early work. With relatively modest means the décor oscillates between high performance design and irony and manages to marry gaiety and sobriety. The space is used for music, theater, dance, performance art, etc.

Figure 6.13 Interior – Hennepin Lobby

Figure 6.14 Interior – Hennepin Lounge

Figure 6.15 Interior – theater

Figure 6.16 Interior – gallery

Figure 6.17 Interior – gallery and gallery entry space

While Barnes' building remains larger in total area than the extension, the footprint of Herzog & de Meuron's project is almost two-and-a-half times bigger than the original. With the entrance to the original building located in the far north/west corner, the path between that entry point and Herzog & de Meuron's tower, theater, and new Hennepin entrance is drawn-out and circuitous in plan and in section (Fig 6.3). Since the elevation of the south end of the site is significantly higher than that of the north end, connection points between old and new were not evident, especially considering the stepping floor plates of Barnes' project. Nevertheless, multiple connections were made in order to facilitate links between the existing and new.

The circulation path through the extension is somewhat mazelike and can generally be described as a "Z." The floors are paved in brick similar to that of the exterior of Barnes' building and the walls are hand-rubbed plaster. The circulation is open to all visitors without the purchase of a ticket, and it is lined with gallery entrances (that do require tickets) and niches in the walls that are media bays that are meant to increase activity and enhance the quality of interior street and town square. The circulation spaces were purposely designed to be relatively small so as to seem lively even when there are only a few people. The urban metaphor remains somewhat symbolic, however, and internal to the center. The expansion project also included an underground parking garage for 650 cars that extends out from the building under the adjacent green space. Automobile access is from Vineland Place to the north and many visitors inevitably enter and leave the building through the garage using a stair that connects to Herzog & de Meuron's Hennepin Lobby space without ever encountering the outside of the project. Likewise, there is little urban activity immediately surrounding the Walker that would incite using the building's circulation as a short cut from one side to the other.

Herzog & de Meuron's conception of gallery space has been influenced by their collaborations with artists and an interest and knowledge of the spaces where they work. The exhibition spaces at the Walker are generally large rooms tending toward loft spaces which the architects believe are preferred by artists (Fig 6.16). Certain cues were also taken from Barnes' galleries that with time have generally been considered successful. The expansion doubled the Walker's exhibition space, and the three rectangular rooms Herzog & de Meuron added are simple and well proportioned. The rooms are defined and contained, and there is not a preoccupation for a constant unfolding of space within the galleries as was the case in Barnes' earlier solution. Unlike their own Goetz Gallery or the Tate Modern, however, Herzog & de Meuron did not introduce natural light into the spaces that are exclusively artificially lit with incandescent spots on light tracks. The general arrangement of the building did not allow for natural top lighting since office spaces are located above the galleries. Similar to Barnes' spaces, the new galleries have white walls and white terrazzo floors, and reflected light on the light-colored surfaces makes them generally luminous. Unlike Barnes' spaces, where large reveals at the top and bottom of the walls integrate air conditioning vents, there is no detail between floor and wall in the expansion. All of the services are located at the ceiling level in a multifunctional track that contains air supply grills and the fire suppression system as well as track lighting. These tracks are placed between boxed-out beam forms reminiscent of the precast concrete T-beams in the earlier galleries. When looking across the spaces perpendicular to the ceiling beams, the tracks and lights are little visible and the spaces appear especially calm.

If the galleries are generally sober and of a known typology, the entry spaces that connect them to the circulation "streets" are more exuberant (Fig 6.17). Pragmatically, these small volumes that vary in shape cleverly integrate the air return for the air conditioning system, and they also function as a transition zone for light levels and general atmosphere. The air return grills themselves, however, are the most striking elements of the small spaces. The grills look like large vegetal pattern stencils with a decorative motif similar to that used for the wall panels of the theater. The same pattern is used for sliding doors concealed within the wall thickness that are used to close the galleries. The design borders on kitsch but is joyful and enlivens the spaces.

Though Herzog & de Meuron's expansion is clearly distinct from the original building, a few nods to Edward Larrabee Barnes in relation to massing, alignments, circulation links, and certain materials establish a cordial relationship between the two. The projects are similar in that both are made with few gestures. Herzog & de Meuron's main gesture, the iconic tower, is primarily devoted to the theater, which enabled the architects to create a new sign – a sign to be used – in the city while avoiding the often difficult situation of a vertical museum with stacked exhibition spaces. Nevertheless, from the visitor's point of view the new tower is indeed organized as stacked functions and the theater remains less present within the ensemble than the exterior might suggest. Inside, the overall impression of the project remains that of an art gallery. The exhibition spaces, all at ground level, conform to a minimalism characteristic of the architects' early career. Most everything else veers in the direction of more exuberant shapes and forms that are meant to elude definition. There is also a substantial dose of surface ornament throughout, both inside and out, which introduces an informal, festive atmosphere into the project even if local press pointed out that Barnes' opaque building has never appeared particularly welcoming and Herzog & de Meuron's expansion, at a first glance, looks like the "Death Star."

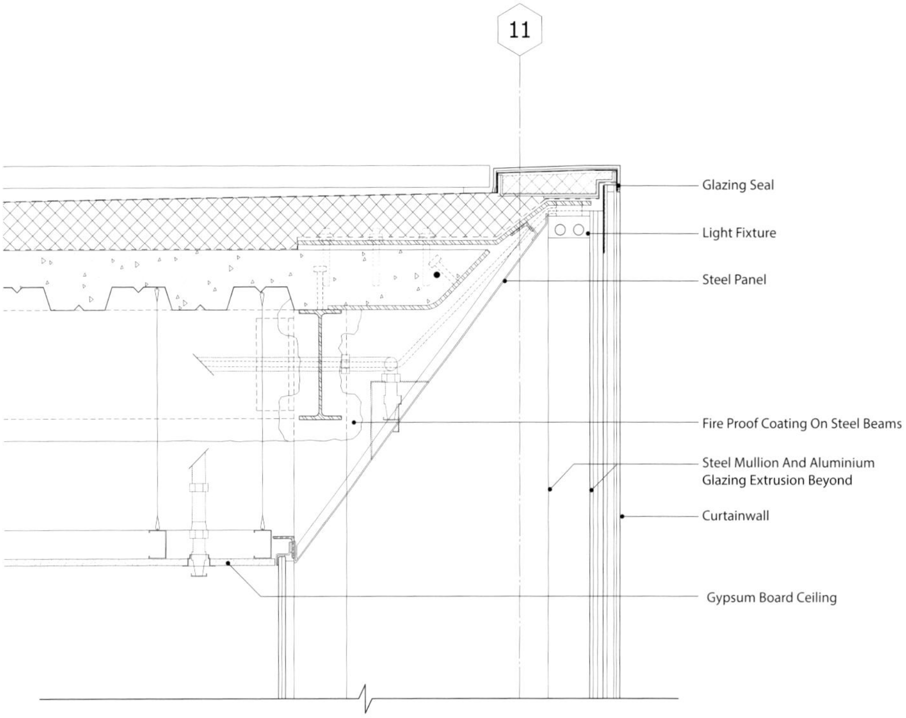

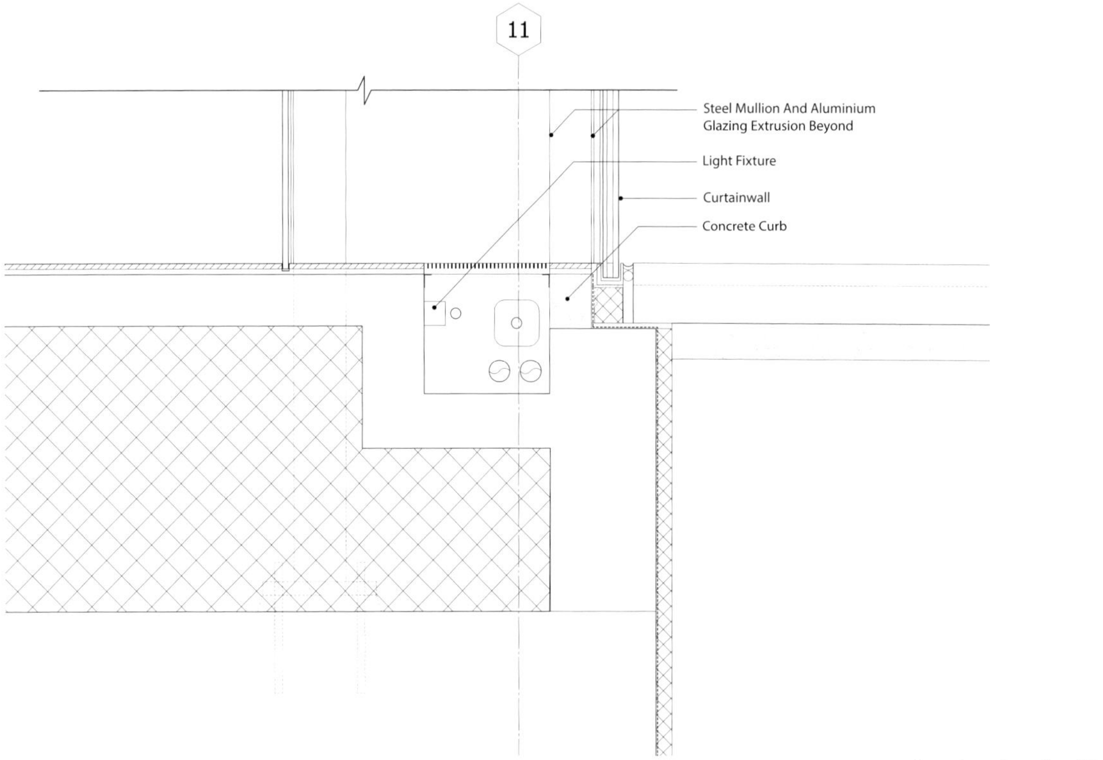

Figure 6.18 Hennepin Lounge detail

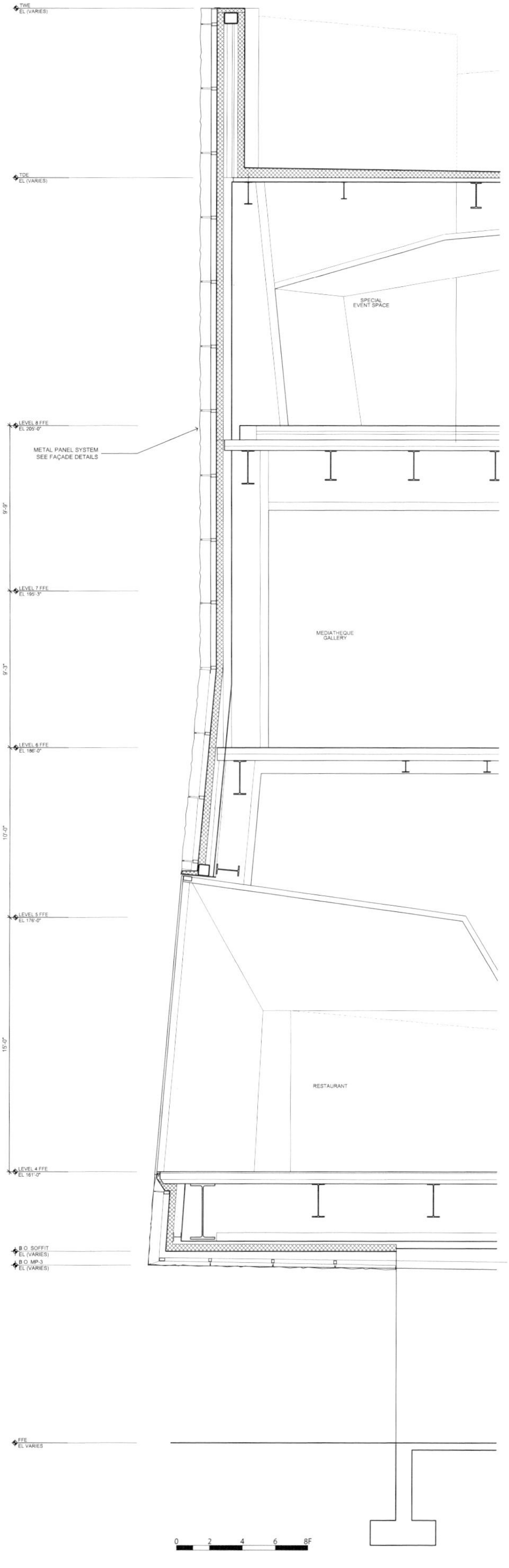

Figure 6.19 Wall detail

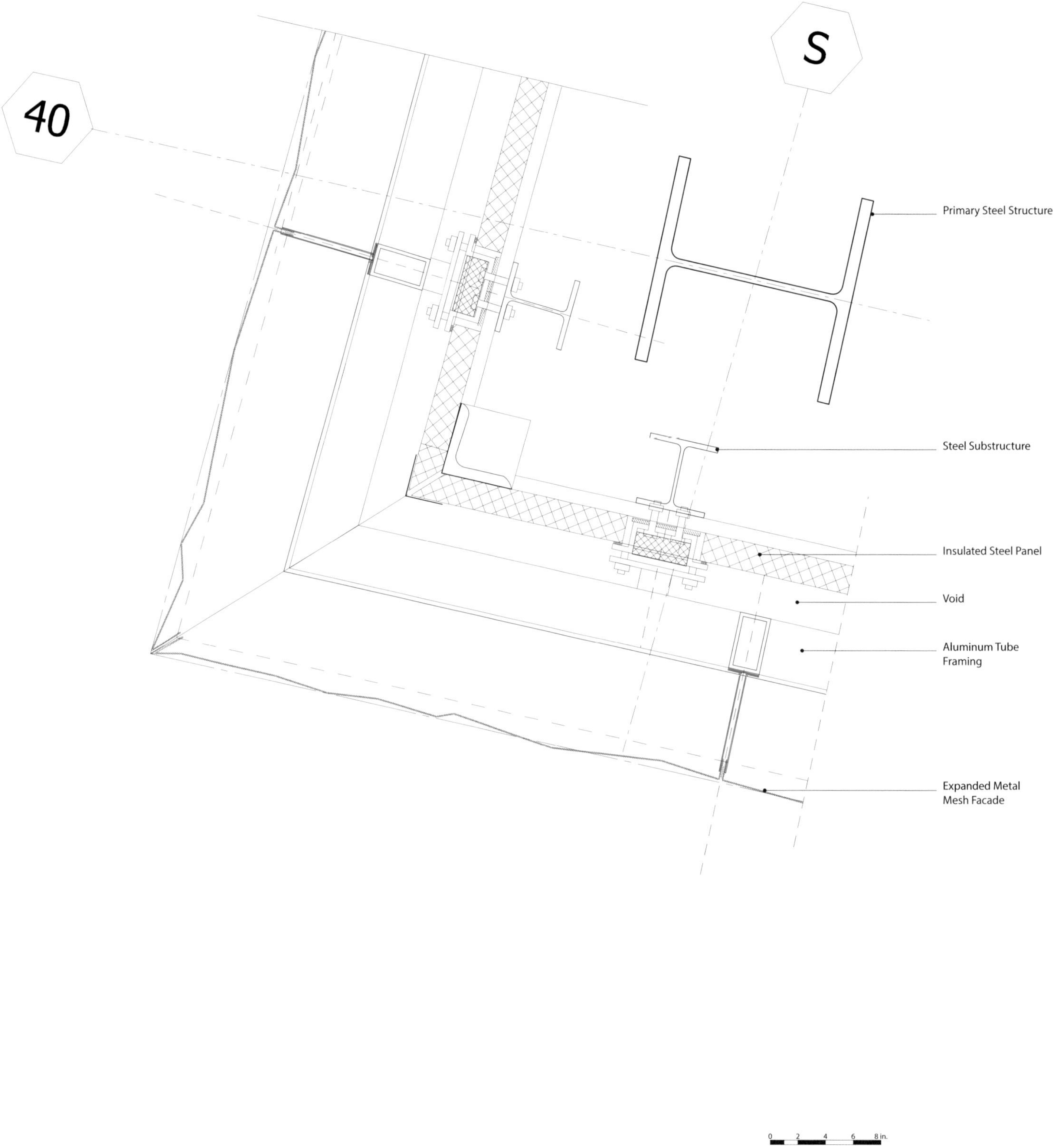

Figure 6.20 Detail 3

CHAPTER 7

Museo Nacional Centro de Arte Reina Sofía

Madrid, Spain

Ateliers Jean Nouvel

2005

Figure 7.1 View from south/east

Jean Nouvel's extension to Madrid's *Museo Nacional Centro de Arte Reina Sofía* is "everything else" in a museum. When we think of museums, we inevitably envision exhibition spaces and art-filled galleries. Nouvel's project is, for the most part, all the other program elements that make up most contemporary museums: a library, a bookstore, a cafe, auditoriums, administrative offices, meeting rooms, art storage, ticket sales – along with some exhibition space. Out of a program that can generally be considered "museum services," the architect nonetheless succeeded in making a monumental structure. Apparently the Reina Sofía expected as much when in 1999 it invited the likes of Dominique Perrault, Juan Navarro Baldeweg, Tadao Ando, Zaha Hadid, Enric Miralles, and Santiago Calatrava to present ideas for an extension. The Nouvel Building, as it is now called, collects three separate structures around a courtyard (the Patio Nouvel) and under one soaring roof (Fig 7.1). It abuts the south-west facade of the preexisting Sabatini Building (also named for its architect), an austere eighteenth-century edifice with a large interior courtyard originally built as a hospital and closed in 1969. After being left vacant for a time and with calls for its demolition, the Sabatini Building was instead protected and declared an historical monument in 1977. By 1986 the building was renovated and transformed into the Centro de Arte Reina Sofía, a space for temporary exhibitions. After subsequent renovations that began in the late 1980s, the Reina Sofía was inaugurated as a national museum in 1992 with a permanent collection of works dating from the late nineteenth century to the present. Nouvel's extension opened in September 2005. The architectural brief in itself underscores the importance of related, non-exhibition functions for the institution such as lectures, concerts, film, classes, seminars, programs for children, research, etc.

The beginnings of the Reina Sofía closely followed the death of the Spanish dictator Francisco Franco in 1975 and the establishment of the 1978 constitution. New-found freedoms allowed the museum to embrace international exchange, and a Spanish museum of modern art contributed to a new national identity. Pablo Picasso's famous *Guernica* painting was returned to Spain after a long stay at the Museum of Modern Art in New York during the Franco period. The painting has been exhibited at the Reina Sofía since 1992 and is undoubtedly the museum's best-known and biggest attraction. The Reina Sofía's mission statement says that its "program is based on a redefinition of the function of museums ..." "The museum is a place for debate and research ..." It is "conceived to be a place that generates opportunities for sociability and discussion in the public sphere..." The program of the Nouvel Building emphasized these intentions.

The lively, central location of the museum in the capital seems ideal – just off the Paseo del Prado, near the Botanic Garden, in sight of the Atocha train station, and surrounded by other important museums such as the Prado, the Thyssen-Bornemisza, and the CaixaForum (Fig 7.2). The Sabatini Building has stood out among the generally six-story neighboring structures by its size and mass rather than its height. Nouvel's project is slightly lower than Sabatini's. With this latest addition, the Reina Sofía now takes up an entire city "block," surrounded by streets on all sides. The triangular part of the site where the Nouvel project stands was previously occupied by several buildings that formed a small neighborhood around the hospital. When the site was turned over to the Reina Sofía, three buildings were occupied by Ministry of Education offices. Nouvel's division of the program into three independent structures was a reference to what had previously existed, and the project was thought of as a mutation of what had been there before.

The longest side of the extension faces the busy Ronda de Atocha to the south, and to the west there is a dense neighborhood with tree-lined streets. The main entrance to the museum, still through the Sabatini building, is off the Calle Santa Isabel and the large, paved plaza to the north-east that seems to be an integral part of the Reina Sofía. Though the plaza is not particularly polished architecturally, it is well used and very lively with children and adults, skateboarders, and Frisbee-playing dogs. Two all glass elevator towers flank the main entry of the Sabatini building and act as highly visible signs facing the urban space (Fig 7.8). The towers, controversial at the time, were designed by the British architect Ian Ritchie as part of the renovations executed by the architects José Luis Iñiguez de Onzoño and Antonio Vázquez that began in the late 1980s. Nouvel's outdoor space at the center of his project (Fig 7.9 and Fig 7.10) would seem to be conceptually in the same family, and somehow complementary, to the public entry plaza and the tree-filled courtyard at the center of the Sabatini Building. It lacks, however, the life of the first and the vegetation of the second. Though appearing to be related in plan, Nouvel's patio is not in dialogue with the other outdoor spaces and remains experientially disconnected. It is also unfortunate that the trees shown in the competition drawings were not maintained. Planters for four large trees were integrated into the patio's ground level structure. Trees could still be planted.

The immediate surroundings of the extension have less than friendly qualities. Just in front of Nouvel's project a dip of the Ronda de Atocha down into a tunnel creates a sort of separating moat. On the north-west side of the museum, along the Calle del Hospital, there is a long band of outdoor space devoted to delivery, services, temporary buildings, garbage bins, and on-grade parking. Trucks can enter into the building from this space providing easy access to well-organized and well-equipped underground art storage and handling spaces that extend below the patio. The outdoor space seems surprisingly underutilized

Figure 7.2 Site plan

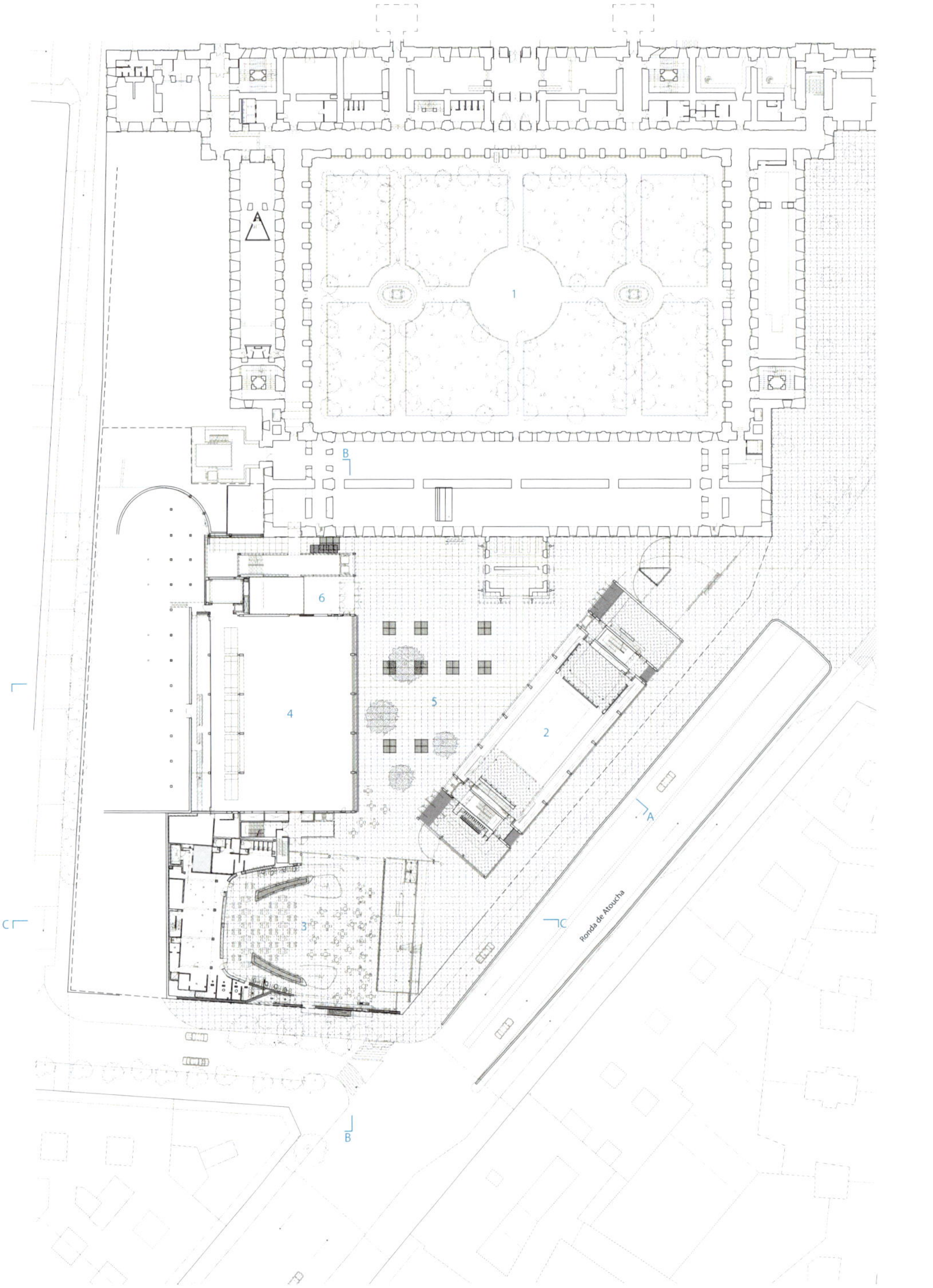

1 Building A - Sabatini Building & Coutyard
2 Buliding B - Library
3 Building C - Cafe
4 Buliding D - Gallery
5 Patio Nouvel
6 Entry

Figure 7.3 First (ground) floor plan – level 0.00 meters

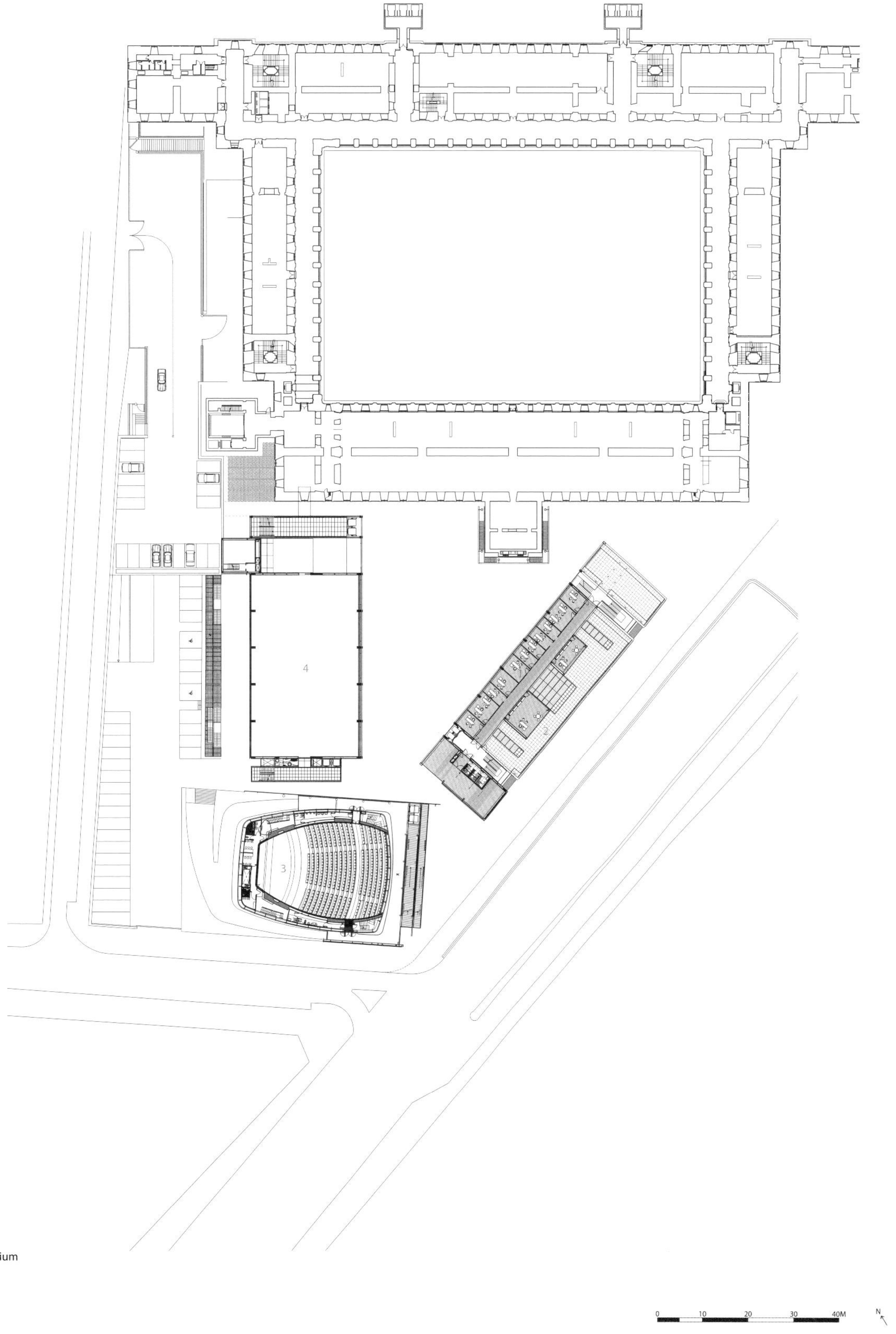

1 Offices
2 Terrace
3 Auditorium
4 Gallery

Figure 7.4 Floor plan – level 12.00 meters

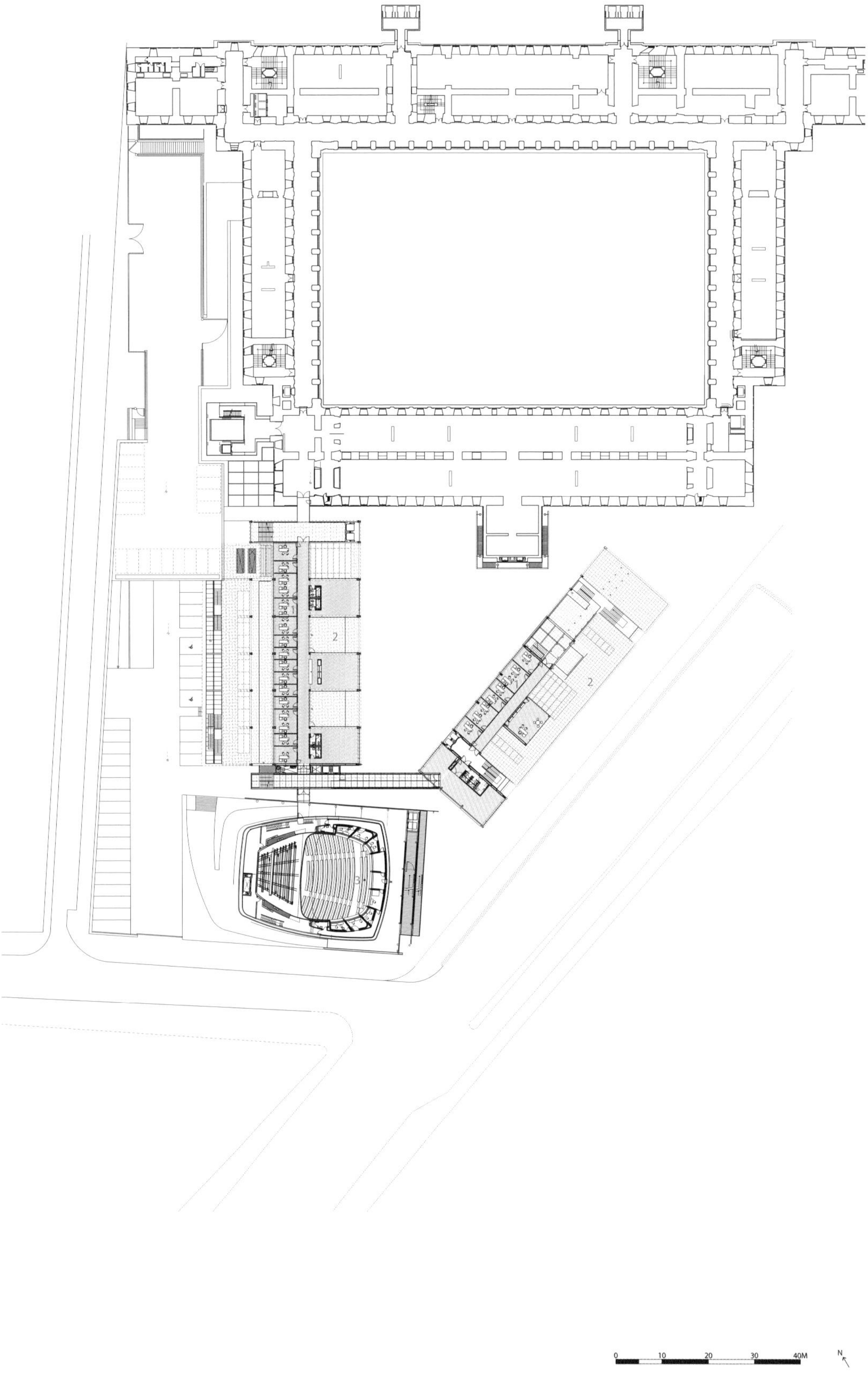

Figure 7.5 Floor plan – level 16.00 meters

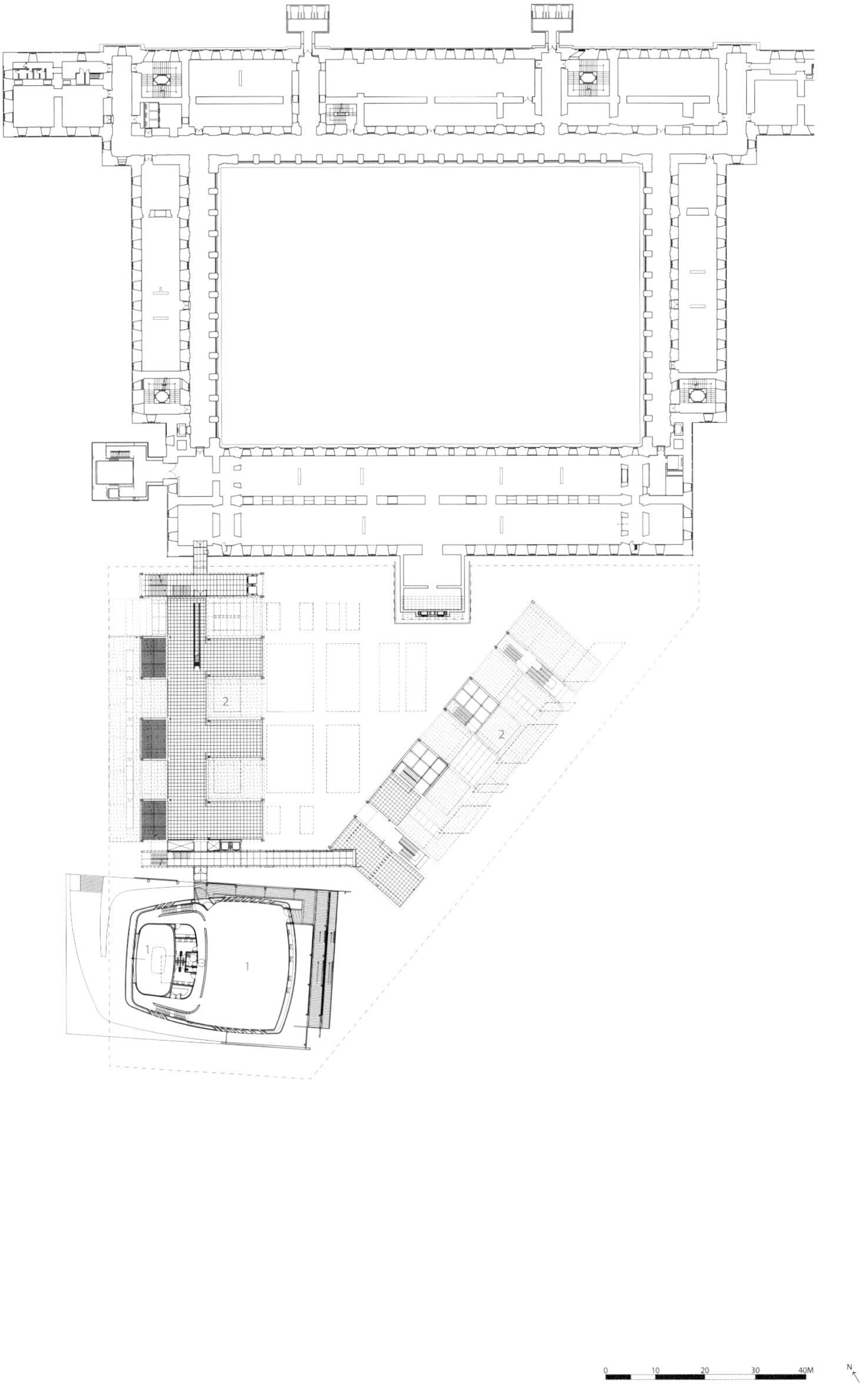

1 Meeting Rooms
2 Terrace

Figure 7.6 Floor plan – level 24.00 meters

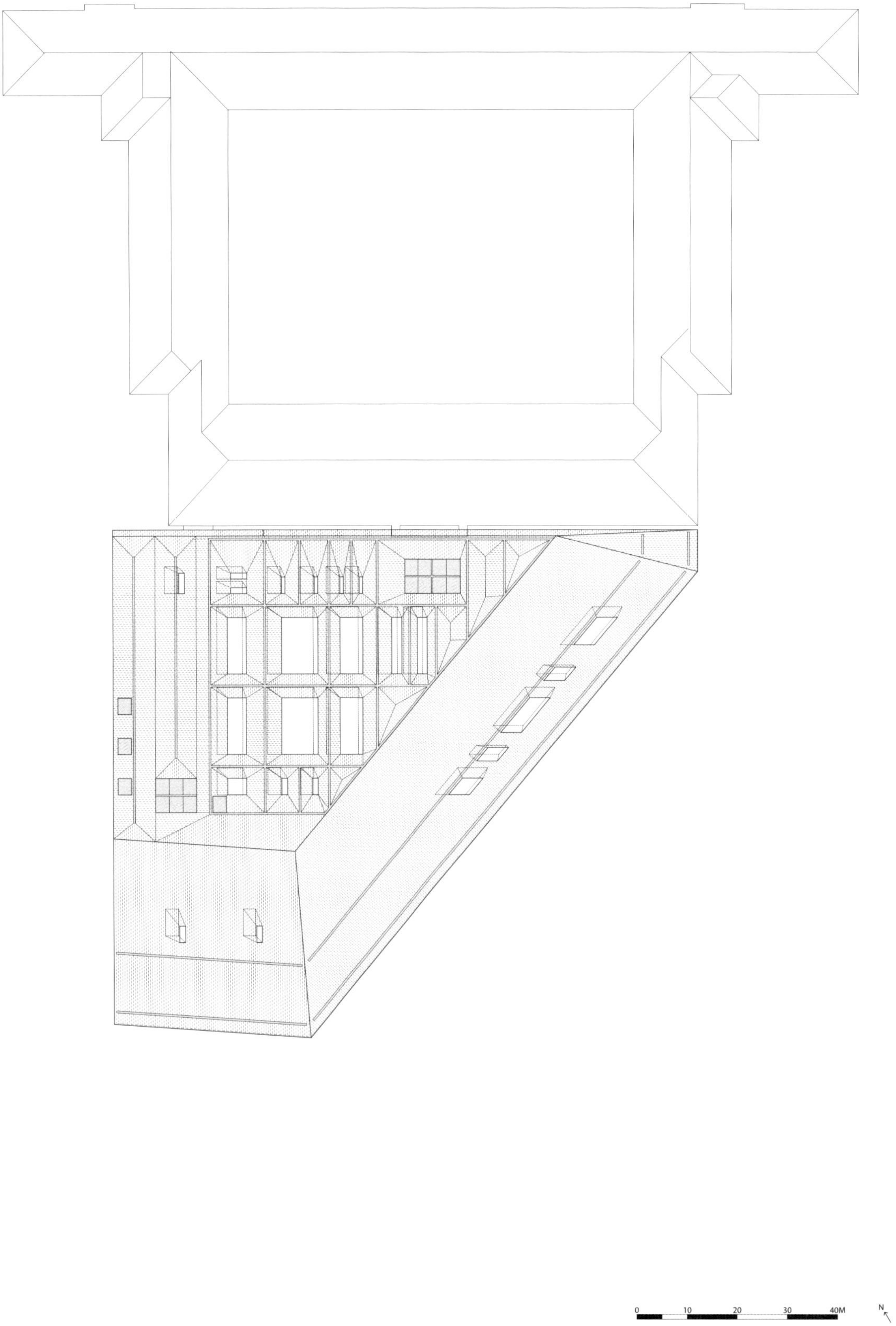

Figure 7.7 Roof Plan – level 33.00 meters

and not particularly civic minded in a city as dense as Madrid. A glass freight elevator, also by Ritchie, is equal in finish to his passenger elevators around the corner and keeps this facade from entirely appearing as a back side. We can imagine that the space is lying in wait for another extension in the future.

The almost 9,000 m^2 (square meter; 96,875 ft^2 (square foot)) wing-like roof structure hovering 30 m (98 ft) above the patio and cantilevering nearly 40 m (130 ft) in the area of the auditorium building is obviously the main gesture of the Reina Sofía. A prominent roof structure was also the main gesture of Nouvel's earlier Lucerne Culture and Congress Center that opened in 1998 and for his design for the Louvre Museum in Abu Dhabi which is conceptually similar even though the form of its roof is domed. In Madrid, the highly reflective red surface of the wing is meant to respond to the red tile roofs of neighboring buildings. Red, however, generally seems to be a preferred color for Nouvel. His 2010 all-red structure for the Serpentine Gallery in London, for example, is a veritable declaration of adoration for the color. The reflective surface is also one of Nouvel's preoccupations, as is covering large spaces with a single architectural element. A short text from the year 2000 entitled *Les objets singuliers* documents a public conversation between Jean Nouvel and the French philosopher Jean Baudrillard. Nouvel speaks of an evolution, a sort of architectural Darwinism that leads to mankind's attempt to cover the maximum space with a minimum amount of matter and in a way that makes it all appear effortless. Nouvel is interested in an idea of the immaterial, lightness, and emptiness. He is interested in transparency and the combination of transparency and reflection. He is less interested in form as such.

Figure 7.8 Sabatini Building entry facade with elevator towers

Figure 7.9 View of Nouvel courtyard looking south/west

Figure 7.10 View from roof terrace looking north/west with entry at right

Figure 7.11 View from north/west

The thin edge of the Reina Sofía's roof on two of the visible sides reinforces the effect of immateriality and effortlessness while the 3.7 m (12 ft) high back side, to the contrary, undermines it (Fig 7.11). The roof structure is in steel and is composed of solid beams and trusses. Contrary to most cantilevers, there are more, and more closely spaced elements at the extremity in order to assure a perfectly horizontal edge where the thickness is reduced to only 2 cm (¾ in.) (Fig 7.22). Primary mechanical equipment and elevator machinery are located within the cavity of the roof. Special attention was given to acoustics since venting is in the direction of residential buildings along the Calle del Hospital.

The surface of the roof is zinc over tapered rigid insulation and metal decking. Rainwater is channeled in carefully studied gutters sloped primarily toward the tower on the facade of the Sabatini building. Ninety percent of the rainwater from the roof is evacuated at this single location using a "full flow" drainage that relies on a syphon system rather than gravity which allows for smaller pipes and a more rapid evacuation. The pipes are visible from some vantage points and can be confused with structure. The roof, however, is structurally independent of the Sabatini tower, and is held away from the Sabatini facade by a 60 cm (2 ft) linear void, a sort of reveal joint, between the two. Nouvel's roof aligns with a cornice at the top floor level of the older building.

The roof plane (Fig 7.7) sits on 32 dark gray, painted H-shaped steel columns that emerge out of the buildings below. The eye is diverted by the red, mirrorlike, aluminum surface, the reflected movement of pedestrians and vehicles at ground level, and the oblique openings in the roof, known as "reflectors," that allow light in and glimpses out to the sky. The horizontal surface appears as a mirage and the blurred visual effect makes the vertical structure recede.

For the roof, the column grid is irregular. The vertical structure is spaced according to the logic of the buildings below and simply projected upward to support the roof. Though the columns appear the same, they are all different. Overall sizes and steel plate thicknesses (the maximum thickness going to 6 cm or 2¼ in.) change depending on location and loads. What appears to be H sections masks a cavity that is filled with concrete for structural reasons and for fireproofing. Twelve of the columns supporting the largest loads are filled with a special glass-fiber reinforced concrete that is four times stronger than the conventional concrete used for the others. The sum of the area of all of the columns touching the roof is only 8.5 m^2 (91 ft^2). All of the technical efforts and refinement of details contribute to the overall effect of effortlessness that the architect seeks.

The overall effect of the roof is striking. The gesture, however, doesn't seem to correspond to another of Nouvel's preoccupations which is to create "specificity" – a singular, specific architectural object for each place and site that would combat the banality of a globalized architecture. As noted above, the hovering roof appears to be a recurring architectural response for Nouvel from Switzerland, to Madrid to Abu Dhabi.

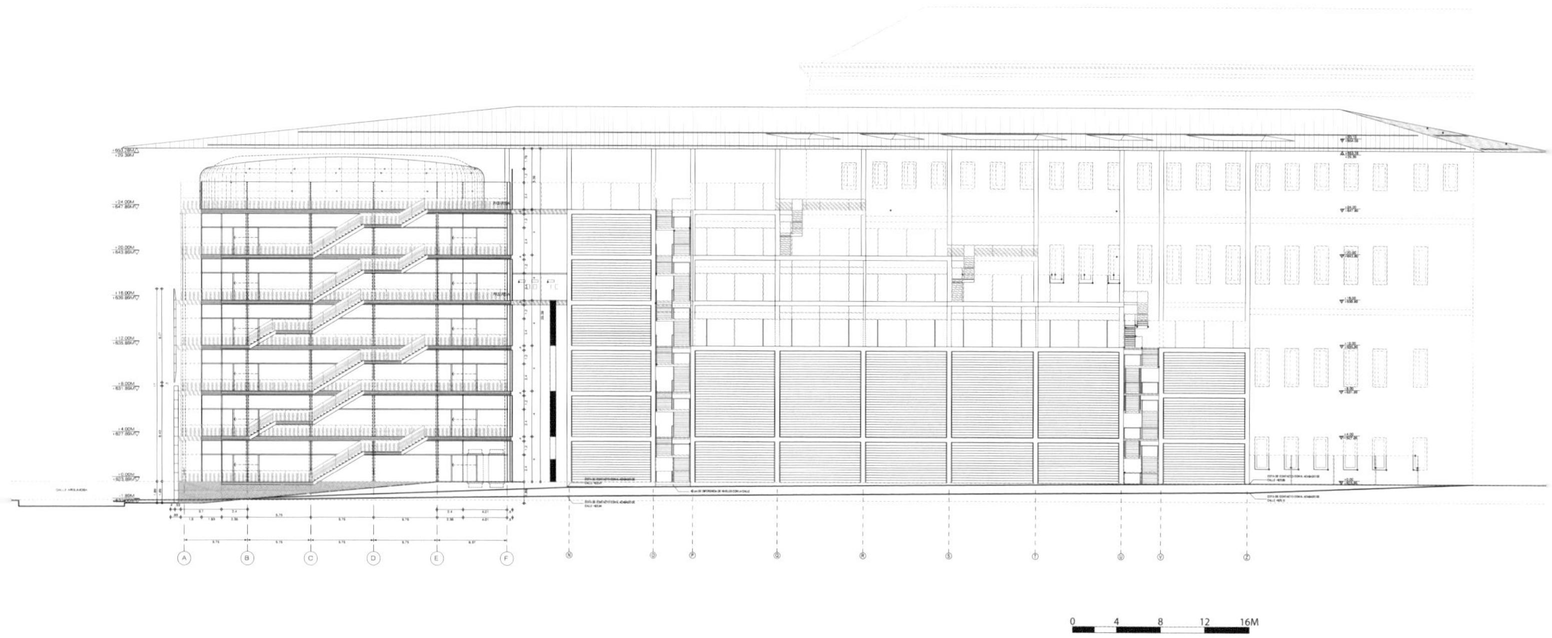

Figure 7.12 South elevation

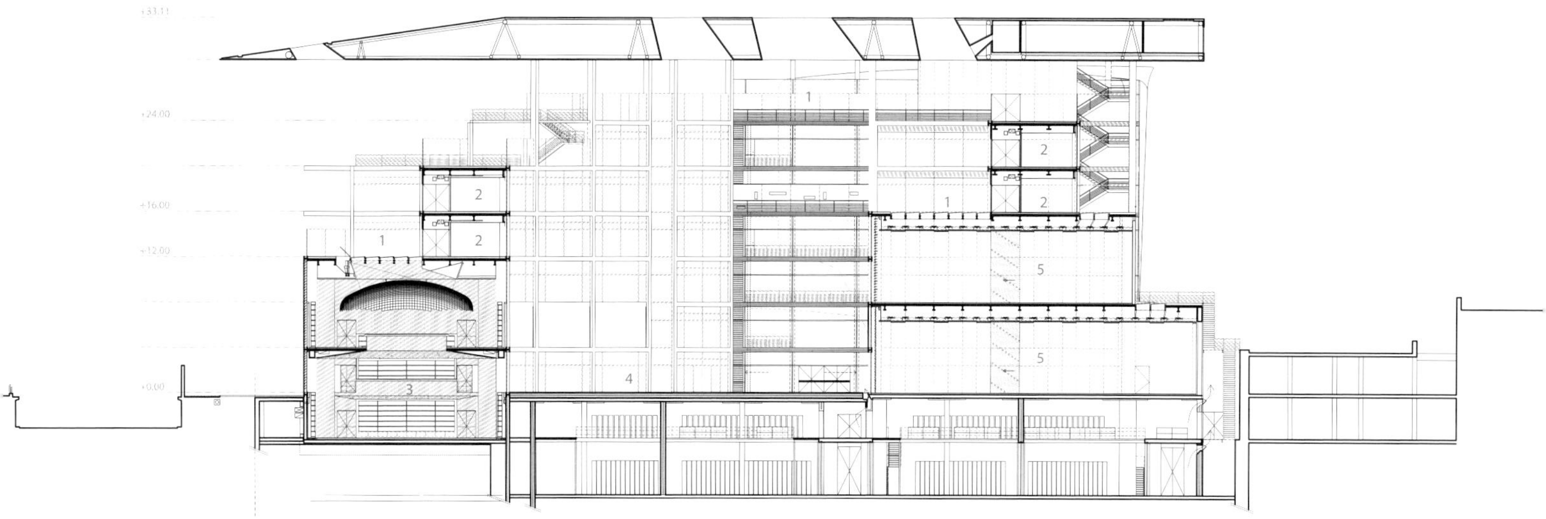

1 Terrace
2 Offices
3 Library
4 Patio Nouvel
5 Gallery

0 4 8 12 14M

Figure 7.13 Section AA

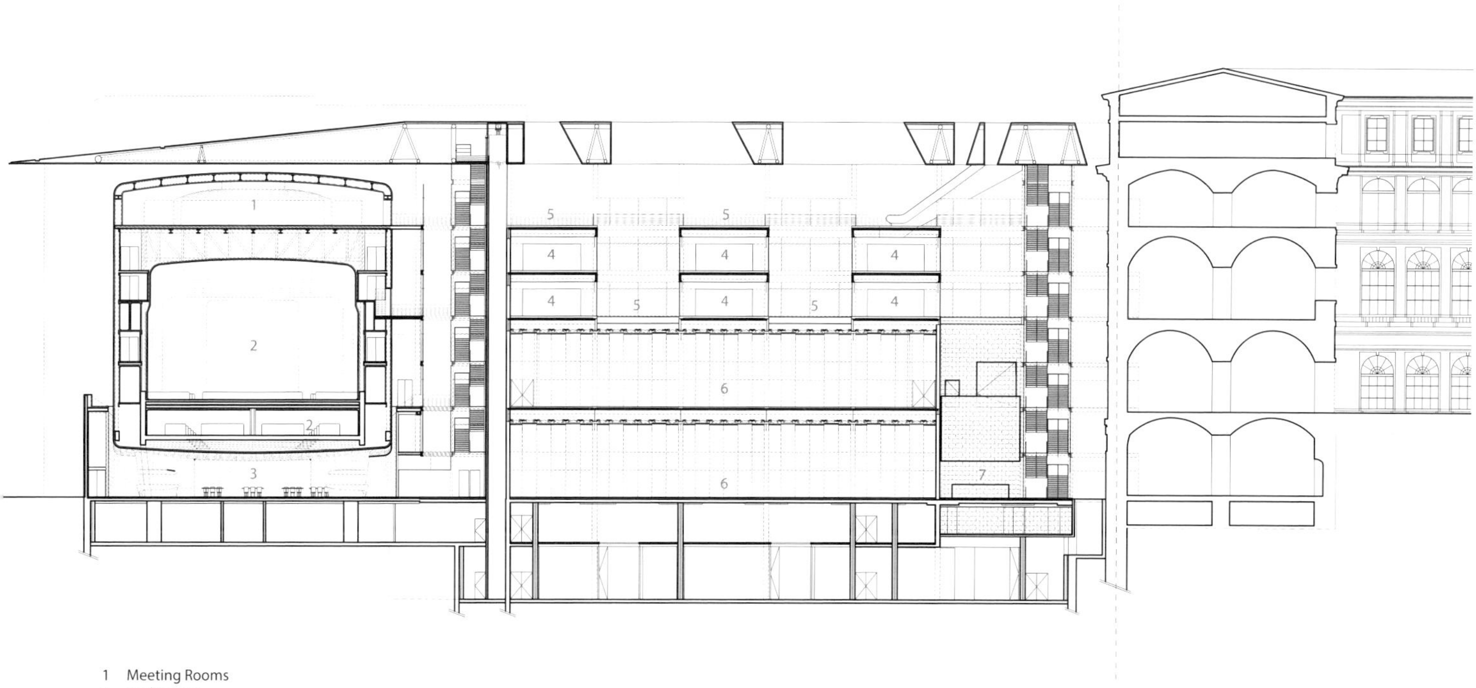

1 Meeting Rooms
2 Auditorium
3 Cafe
4 Offices
5 Terrace
6 Gallery
7 Entry

0 4 8 12 16M

Figure 7.14 Section BB

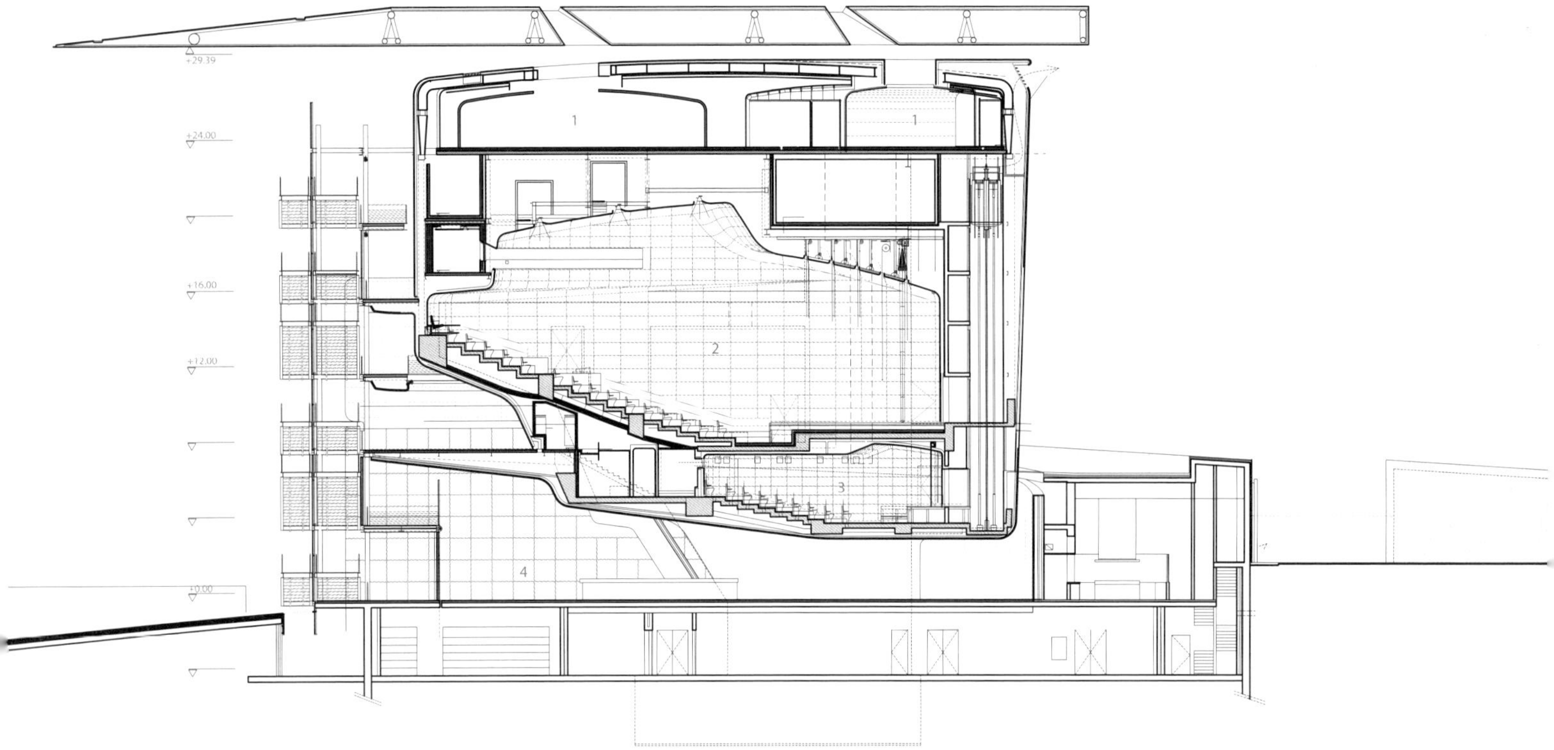

1 Meeting Rooms
2 Auditorium - 400 seats
3 Auditorium - 200 seats
4 Cafe

Figure 7.15 Section CC

Though the tectonics of the structure communicate lightness, the building seems solemn and somber, which perhaps is in keeping with the Sabatini Building. From the street, colors are dark and the ensemble appears opaque. Deep shadows were sought. The scale of the patio is vast and inevitably seems underpopulated. The tower-like structure of the Sabatini Building juts into the patio and houses ticket sales at the ground level. There is little continuity between inside and outside at the patio level and the cafe and bookstore are insufficient to animate the space. Additionally, even large sculptures such as Roy Lichtenstein's *Brushstroke* seem lost. The multiple terrace levels above and the stairs attached to the facade of the auditorium building (Fig 7.12) also appear as unoccupied spaces in daily goings on and contribute to an impression of emptiness. The granite paving and especially the roof plane reflect sound and the patio is loud with traffic noise. The reverberation of a single helicopter passing overhead seeds a sense of near panic in the space. On the other hand, seeing it pass from one roof opening to the next is visually thrilling. It is not a space to linger in.

To facilitate visitor orientation the buildings of the Reina Sofía have been identified by letters. The Sabatini Building is Building A; Nouvel's three buildings are B, C, and D. The building D is situated at the back of the Patio Nouvel and provides a public entrance (primarily for groups), passages to the Sabatini Building, exhibition spaces on Level 0 (1,120 m^2 or 12,055 ft^2) (Fig 7.3) and Level 1 (950 m^2 or 10,225 ft^2) (Fig 7.4), and two floors of offices above (Fig 7.5). Glass elevators, mini versions of Ian Ritchie's, are located behind the facade of the entry space and connect all floors. A link to the Sabatini Building was created on Level 1 but not on Level 0 of the patio. Though this is understandable because of the difficulty or even the impossibility of such a link, the connection between the two buildings remains awkward and timid. Another link on the second floor connects the Sabatini galleries to the locked door of Nouvel's private office spaces, and visitors must go up or down to reach other public areas (Fig 7.5). Circulation is not intuitive and the museum in its entirety would certainly have benefited if the scope of the project had extended farther into the Sabatini Building.

Nouvel's galleries (Fig 7.16) were conceived as temporary exhibition spaces following the architectural brief but are now used for the permanent collection. They are approximately 5 m (16 ft 6 in.) high and align with the floor levels of the older building. They are generally loft-like and are articulated by temporary walls. The louvered windows facing the patio that were meant to provide views in and out as well as natural light to the galleries were blocked soon after the building was occupied. Drawings also show skylights integrated into the office level terrace spaces. They were omitted, but a band of skylights was realized on the Calle del Hospital side of the upper level galleries. The louvers below the skylights are normally kept in the fully closed position, making for completely artificially lit gallery spaces. Similarly, the granite floors were covered with a more uniform screed. Any "specificity" of the space has been exchanged for neutrality.

Figure 7.16 Interior – gallery

Figure 7.17 Interior – cafe below auditorium

Figure 7.18 Interior – 400 seat auditorium

Figure 7.19 Interior – library looking east

Figure 7.20 Roof terrace looking south/east

Figure 7.21 Roof terrace looking north/east with escalator

In the early 1990s, an architect such as Ian Ritchie envisioned the near future of art. In an interview related to the renovations of the Reina Sofía at that time and published by Architectural Design in *New Museums* (1991), Ritchie spoke of the coming of telematics art, cybernetics, electronic space, and virtual reality and the manipulation of virtual images by visitors. Stored data would replace the collection of physical objects. What the influence might be on the space of museums was not elucidated. For now it seems that the art museum is instead a stronghold of more traditionally produced works, and its gallery spaces are still conceived accordingly.

Above Nouvel's galleries, two stories of administrative offices leave an impression of rich wood finishes, large expanses of glass opening onto terraces, and the ever-present roof structure. From the patio level below, the offices look like true work spaces with piles of files, papers, books, etc. visible behind the windows.

From the Calle del Hospital and the Calle de Argumosa the Building C appears as a shiny, rounded, red box (approximately 33 m high by 26 m wide or 108 by 85 ft) (Fig 7.11) sitting atop a granite base and stopping just shy of the floating roof. The red polyester panels borrow from techniques used in the construction of boat hulls. They are powder coated to give a more metal-like finish. The granite wall is made of open-jointed square panels both inside and out. At the southern tip of the building, the concrete structural wall along with the thin stone cladding and the metal attachments are revealed as in a section cut. It is a detail that stands out for pedestrians partly because of its departure from the general smoothness of the building. It does not appear particularly meaningful, however.

Seen from the patio and the Ronda de Atocha, the red, projecting auditorium box is veiled by exterior emergency stairs that also act as a brise-soleil for the full height, south-facing, glass facade behind. The stairs and facade are independent of the post-tensioned concrete structure of the auditorium building. A cafe is inserted under the cantilevered slope that suggests the rake of the 200 seat auditorium overhead (Fig 7.15 and Fig 7.17). Above that there is another 400 seat auditorium (Fig 7.18) and yet above that two meeting rooms at the very top. Entry to the cafe is primarily from the patio but also through a small door from the Calle de Argumosa. The color red is present throughout.

The Building B along the Ronda de Atocha houses a library, a bookstore (accessible from the street and the patio), and offices above. The library (Fig 7.19) appears to be a space given particular design attention, and it is very pleasant. It is the full width of the Building B and has large windows to both sides. With the main level of the reading room located one story below grade, there is a peculiar relationship, however, with the ground level and pedestrians looking down into the space. Nevertheless, the space seems grand. The three-level library has 100 reading desks surrounded by book stacks. It is inserted into a volume 16 m (52 ft) high that corresponds to four floor levels. The height provides generous space for the suspension of a large, eye-shaped chandelier/light diffuser made of 20 cm (8 in.) glass cubes hung below skylights that are integrated into the outdoor terraces above. The "lens" mixes artificial and natural light. Its glass cubes were manufactured by the Royal Glass Factory of La Granja (Segovia). The primary finish material in the library is a Brazilian cherry wood known as Jatoba. It was chosen for its durability and its red tint.

Like the Building D, the Building B is an expressed, gray-painted, steel structure with what appears as an infill of red corrugated panels. The panels are generally perforated, folded metal louvers, shading large glass panels behind. The operable, though seldom changed, louvers have a surprisingly long span. The extrusions, approximately 30 cm (12 in.) wide and 6 m (20 ft) long, approached the maximum fabrication sizes possible in Europe at the time. Near the Sabatini Building the Building B is only three stories high but rises to six stories toward the higher volume of the auditorium building (Building C).

The space under the roof that crowns the building provokes curiosity and exerts a strong attraction from below (Fig 7.20). The architects had always meant for the space to be public. It was privatized for some time, however, and used for special events only. Visitors can now go there without paying for entry or visiting the museum. The terrace inevitably does not meet expectations. With an area of over 600 m^2 (6,460 ft^2) above Buildings B and D, it is not a particularly good space for exhibiting sculpture, and it is not high enough to offer commanding views over the city. Ian Ritchie's glass elevators were meant to reconnect museum goers back to the world outside during the visit. Nouvel's roof terrace does something similar though it is less integrated into the museum itinerary. Like the patio below, it is noisy, generally appears empty, and as such is not a place to linger. The cafe bar is not always open. Visitors meander, take pictures, and sit for short periods on the benches and chairs scattered throughout the space before moving on.

It is possible to ascend another level into the mysterious space of the actual roof cavity. We anticipate something perhaps akin to the interstitial spaces of a Renaissance dome where the technique and magic of Nouvel's spectacularly cantilevered roof might be revealed. Instead we enter into a small, empty room clad in corrugated metal with an escalator leading back down to the terrace (Fig 7.21). Visitors can't help imagining that something was missed. Something is, in fact, missing. The space is a vestige of an earlier design idea and was meant to be the point of connection with the galleries of the uppermost floor of the Sabatini Building. Visitors were meant to come out of Sabatini through this small, transitional space and then descend by escalator toward the roof terrace. An escalator was used so that the view would unfold slowly.

At night the buildings simply go dark. The roof structure also fades into dimness though the undersurface reflects surrounding city lights and car lights. Large gates close the patio to the public.

There is an atmosphere of seriousness in Jean Nouvel's Reina Sofía. Even with its architectural exuberance, it is never a "fun palace." It is physically prominent but does not establish itself as a hub of spontaneous, public activity. The intention was for the Sabatini Building to remain dominant. There is a disconnect, however, between the subordinate position of the extension and its monumentality. It is neither sufficiently linked to the Sabatini, nor sufficiently independent. For visitors to the galleries it is off the beaten path and functions as a sort of back door. Its large-scaled public spaces seem ceremonial and they crave hefty crowds such as those that fill the auditoriums. The Nouvel Building appears rational, but in many ways – from the extravagant gesture of the roof to the scale of its patio, and partly because of omitted design elements – it often and oddly does not seem well reasoned.

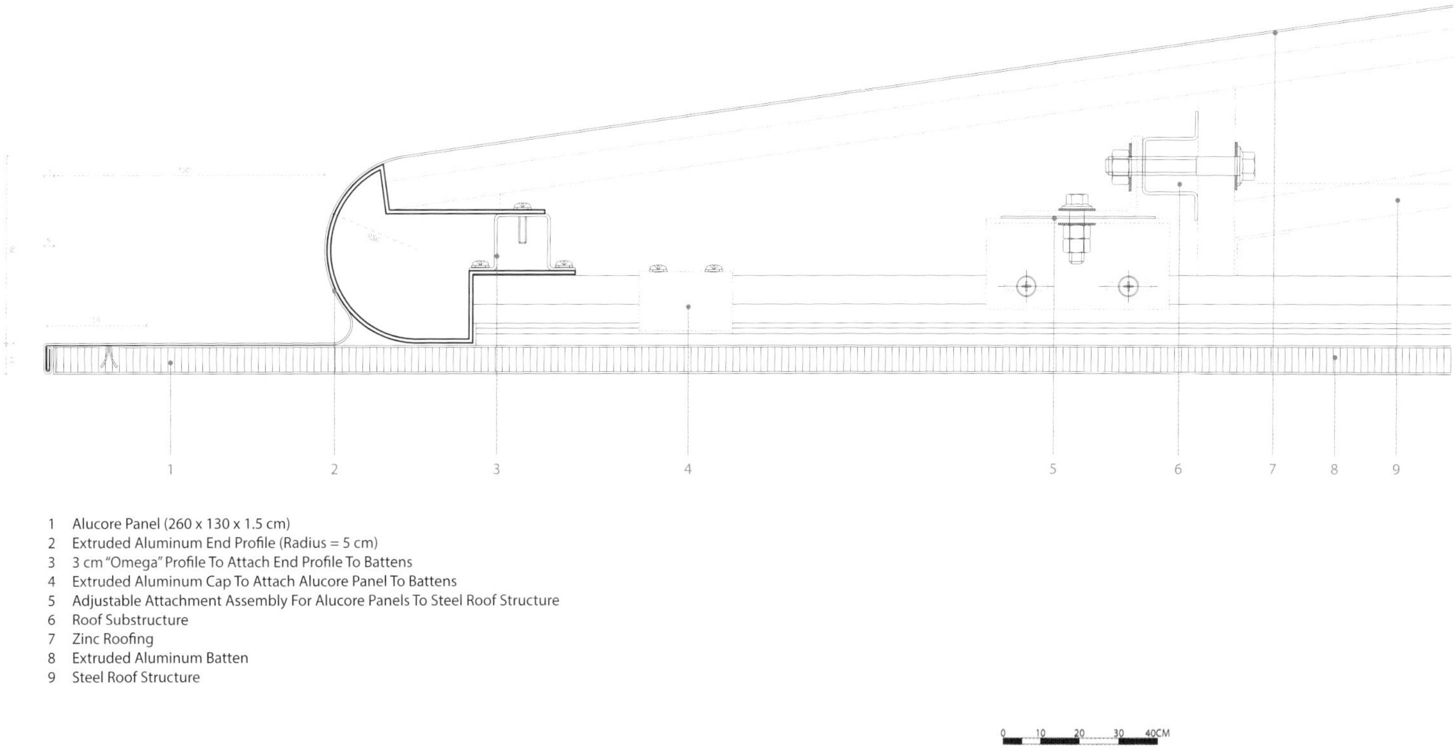

1 Alucore Panel (260 x 130 x 1.5 cm)
2 Extruded Aluminum End Profile (Radius = 5 cm)
3 3 cm "Omega" Profile To Attach End Profile To Battens
4 Extruded Aluminum Cap To Attach Alucore Panel To Battens
5 Adjustable Attachment Assembly For Alucore Panels To Steel Roof Structure
6 Roof Substructure
7 Zinc Roofing
8 Extruded Aluminum Batten
9 Steel Roof Structure

Figure 7.22 Roof detail

CHAPTER 8

de Young Museum

San Francisco, California

Herzog & de Meuron

2005

Figure 8.1 General view from south/east

Only six months after the inauguration of the Walker Art Center in Minneapolis, Herzog & de Meuron opened their second American museum in San Francisco. The de Young Museum was founded in 1895, and today, along with the Legion of Honor which is located in Lincoln Park and housed in a 1924 replica of an eighteenth-century Parisian *palais* of the same name, it comprises the city-owned *Fine Arts Museums of San Francisco*. Undertaking an entirely new building for the de Young a century after its founding was made possible and necessary because of the Loma Prieta earthquake that shook San Francisco in 1989 and damaged the earlier compound of museum buildings beyond repair. Measures were taken to stabilize the ensemble of the structures after the earthquake, but by the mid-1990s the decision was taken to raze the existing and rebuild at the same location in Golden Gate Park, a 400 hectare (1,000 acre), rectangular park to the west of the city center. The de Young was initially housed in a neo-Egyptian style structure built for the 1894 California Midwinter International Exposition. Over the years buildings were added and others were demolished. A 1921 addition included a tower that became a symbol for the de Young and a source of inspiration for Herzog & de Meuron's design.

As a city museum, public financing for a new project was twice sought by referendum and twice refused by voters. It is generally acknowledged that turning to private donors allowed the de Young to ignore the supposed taste of the public for a more nostalgic, postmodern architecture and seek out more innovative architects. In 1999, Tadao Ando, Herzog & de Meuron, and Antoine Predock were asked to compete for the project. Herzog & de Meuron's design was chosen and they elaborated the project between 2000 and 2002 with the assistance of Fong and Chan Architects of San Francisco. Groundbreaking was in June 2002, and the building opened to the public in October 2005. An earlier short list of architects for the project included Norman Foster, Ricardo Legoretta, Pei Cobb Freed, Cesar Pelli, and Rafael Viñoly.

The de Young's neighbor located just to the south within the park, the California Academy of Sciences, suffered a similar fate in the 1989 earthquake, and its damaged buildings were also razed and replaced by a new structure designed by Renzo Piano Building Workshop. The de Young and the Academy of Sciences that opened in 2008 both face the opened landscaped area of the Music Concourse which has underground parking below.

The de Young Museum possesses a varied collection that includes paintings from the seventeenth century onward, decorative arts, arts from Africa, Oceania, and the Americas, textiles, photography, and works on paper. Herzog & de Meuron initially proposed a scheme where separate, independent pavilions sprinkled in the park each focused on one type of art in the collection. This approach was similar to their initial proposal for the later Parrish Art Museum (2012) in Water Mill, New York where "anchor spaces" meant to emulate the studio spaces of selected artists of the collection were expressed as autonomous units, even though physically connected. In both cases the initial, dispersed pavilion concept evolved into one structure marked by a unifying roof. Something of the original concept combined with the architects' preference for smaller, pavilion-like exhibition spaces did carry forward, however, and the project in San Francisco was planned as three parallel elements each containing a distinct portion of the collection. This arrangement was meant to unify rather than separate and to demonstrate a concept of the coexistence of cultures. The parallel elements are physically connected in a manner that diminishes their autonomy, allows the flow of visitors from one to another, and allows for the park to enter into the building via narrow, finger-like, outdoor gardens (Fig 8.2). Interestingly, the London power station designed by Giles Gilbert Scott and redesigned as the Tate Modern by Herzog & de Meuron (their first major museum project) was also organized in three parallel spaces: one containing the boiler house, one the turbines, and one the switch house.

The 27,000 m^2 (square meter; 292,000 ft^2 (square foot)) of the de Young project are organized on three levels – one below ground and two above. The building form is most visible from the south (Fig 8.1) and is generally a rectangular mass with a tower rising from the north-east corner that is counterbalanced by a cantilevered roof projection to the west. Both the tower and the interior courtyards of the design are a nod to the earlier museum compound. Herzog & de Meuron's building is relatively compact, with a footprint of only 60 percent its predecessor, and actually returned approximately 8,094 m^2 (2 acres) of land to the park space. (The building footprint is 8,500 m^2 or 91,000 ft^2.) Nonetheless, the appearance of the design was criticized, and the project encountered strong public opposition. At first view the building appears aggressive – a sort of beached aircraft carrier with mirador. The overall form of the building is said to have been derived from the necessities of the interior spaces, yet certain refinements and features – such as the slightly sloped roof in the structure's length, the transparency of the twisting tower, the cantilever at the western extremity, slight variations in the alignment of the facade, and, more importantly, the patterned copper panels of the outer skin – temper the initial gesture and produce an overall impression and form that tends to elude definition which is generally the goal of the architects.

Herzog & de Meuron's first choice for the exterior cladding was wood, but this material was abandoned because of concerns for its longevity and its appropriateness for a public building. The desire for a natural material remained and led to the choice of copper. Different possibilities were explored before deciding on a rainscreen system with over 8,000 perforated and embossed panels suspended in front of the waterproof wall.

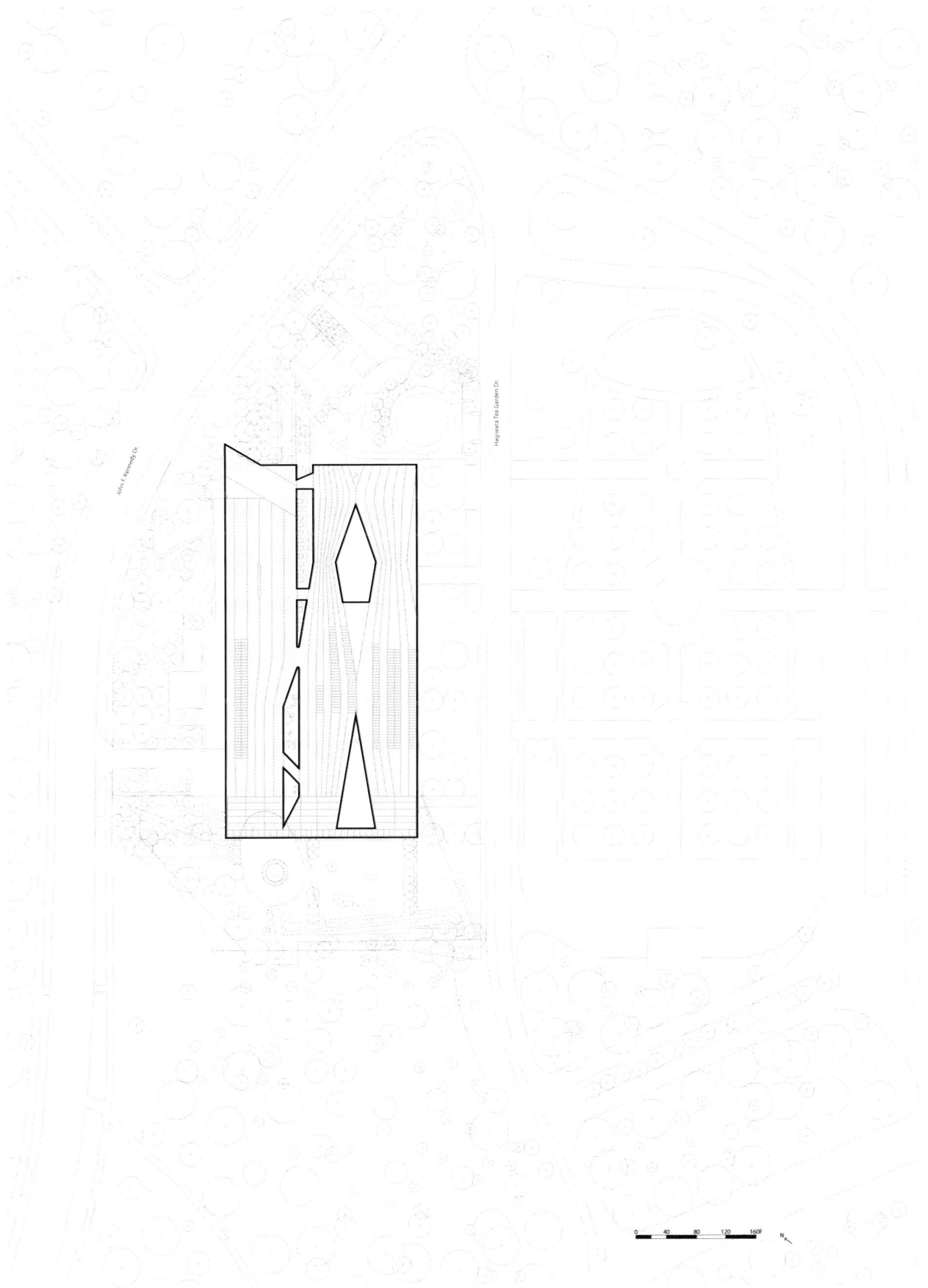

Figure 8.2 Site plan

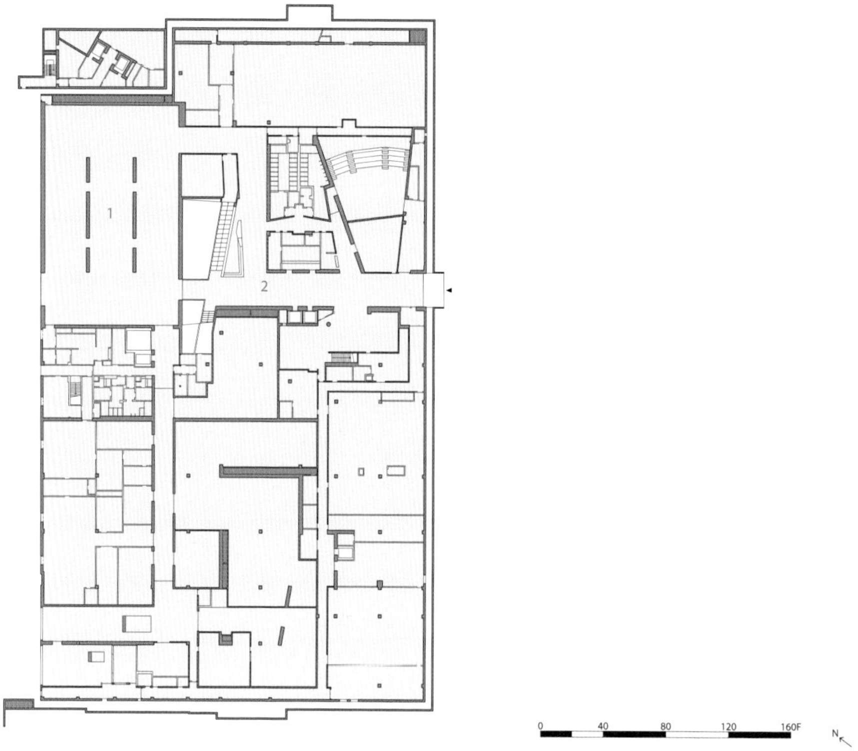

1 Special Exhibitions
2 Lower Lobby

Figure 8.3 Lower level floor plan

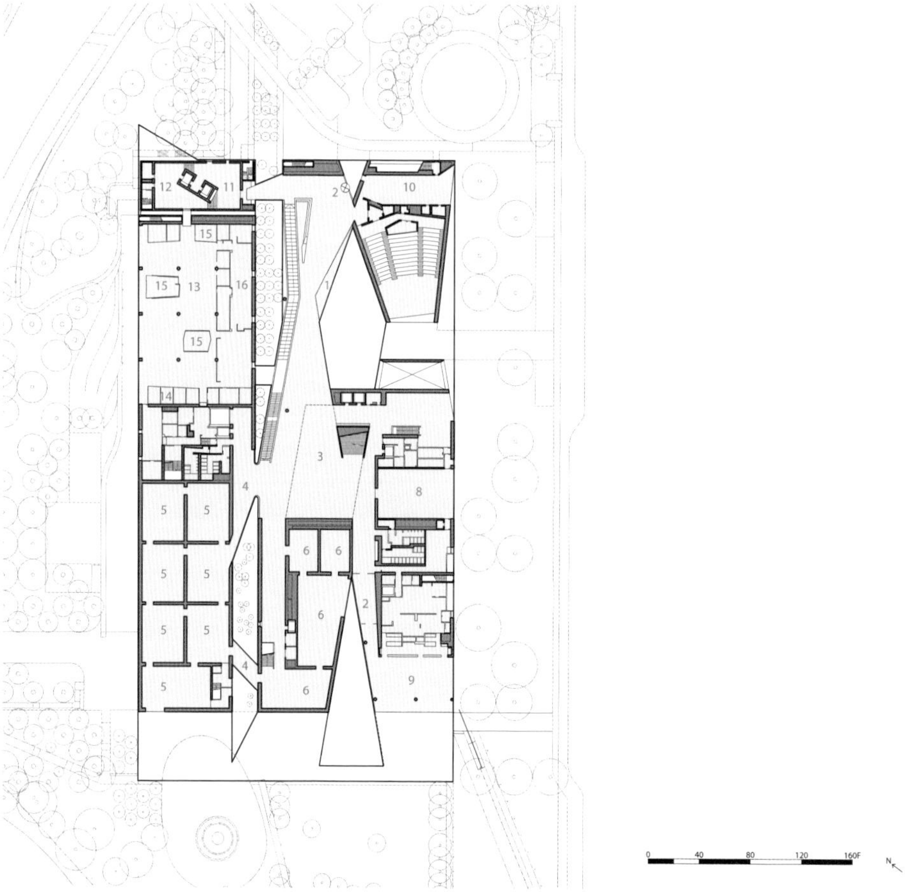

1 Main Entry
2 Entry
3 Main Lobby

Collection
4 20th Century Interstitial
5 American Art / 20th Century
6 Native Art / American
7 Native Art Interstitial
8 Museum Family Room

9 Cafe
10 Children's Gallery
11 Tower Lobby
12 Membership & Info Center
13 Open Office
14 Office
15 Conference
16 Library

Figure 8.4 First (ground) floor plan

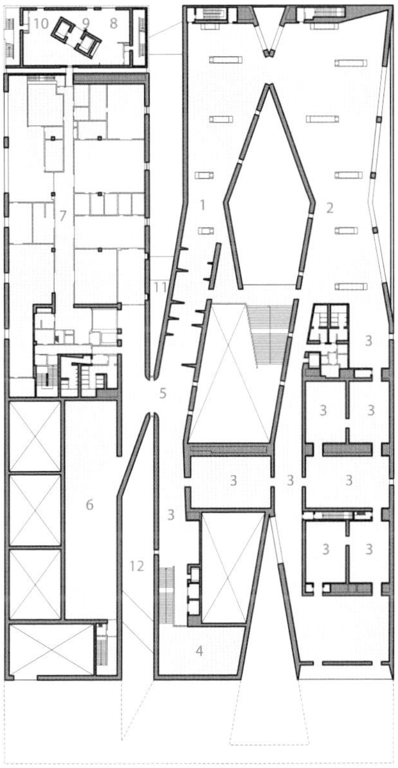

Collection
1 Art Africa
2 Pacific Art Gallery
3 American Art 19th
4 Native Art American
5 Interstitial Gallery
6 Textile Gallery
7 Storage
8 American Art Curatorial
9 Lobby
10 American Art Study Center

11 Fern Court B
12 Eucalyptus Court

Figure 8.5 Second floor plan

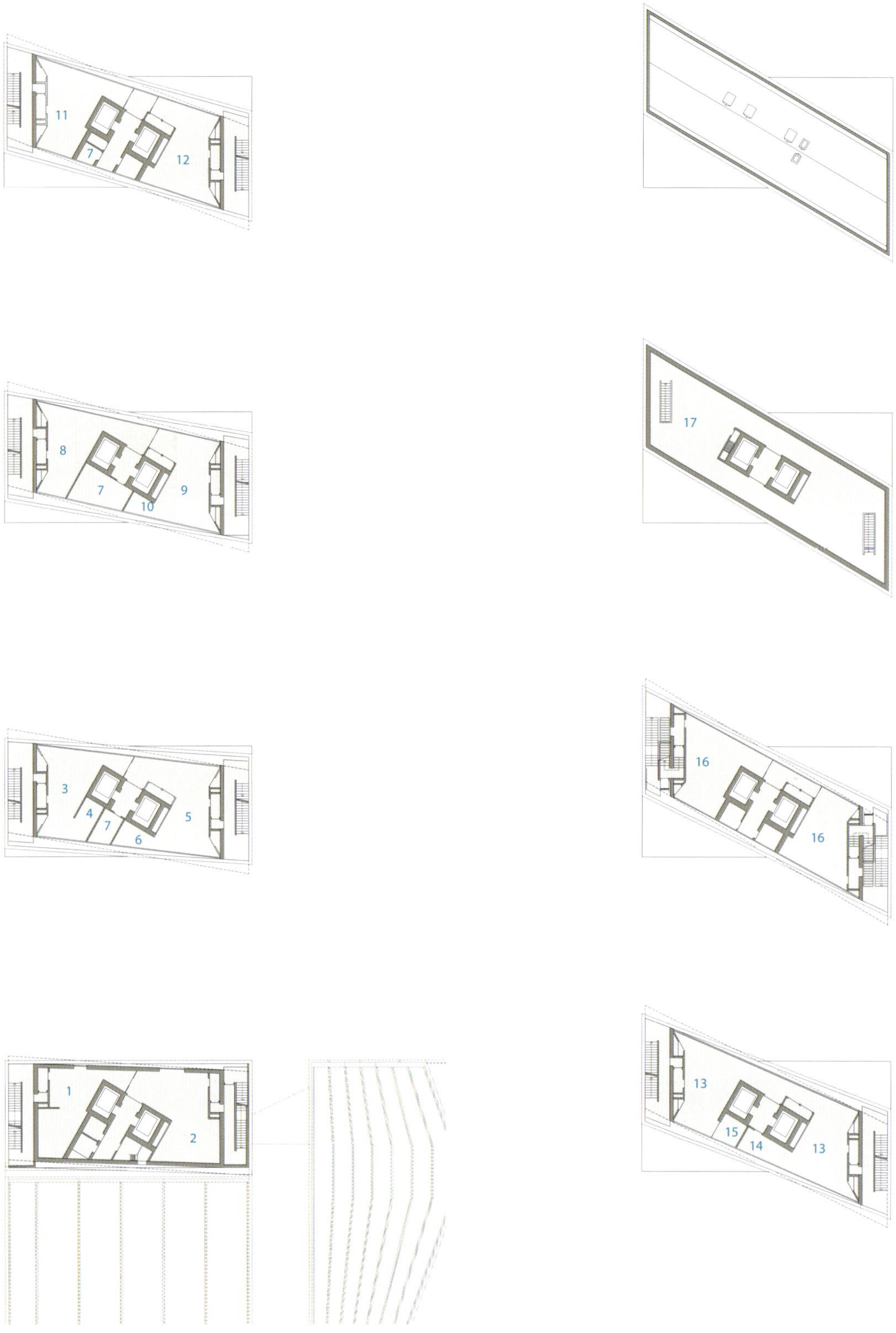

1 Aoa Study Curatorial Center
2 Public Reading
3 Publications
4 Publications Staff
5 Volunteer Center
6 Volunteer Center Manager
7 Storage
8 Education Resource Center
9 Docent Center
10 Manger
11 Artist's Studio
12 Classroom
13 Education Center
14 Work Room
15 Office
16 Classroom
17 Observation

Figure 8.6 Tower floor plans

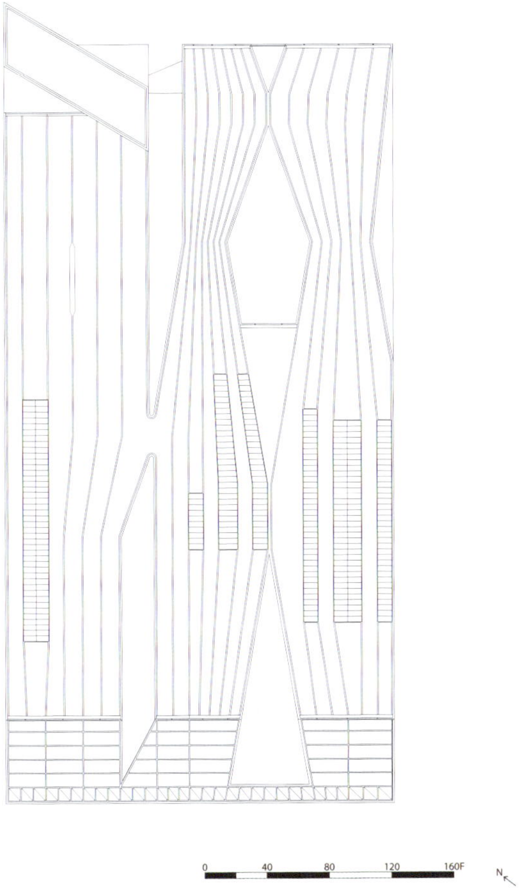

Figure 8.7 Roof plan

Figure 8.9 View from tower looking south/west

Figure 8.8 General view from north/west

Figure 8.10 View from south/east – entry and tower

Figure 8.11 View of entry court and tower

The pattern of the panels was inspired by the trees in the park and a photograph taken from the ground looking up to the sky through branches and foliage. The photo was abstracted, and the general image was transferred to the copper panels using a technique of embossed circles of a constant dimension and spacing combined with circular perforations of different sizes and spacing. The two patterns overlap to give a vegetation-inspired configuration that appears quasi natural. From near, without a complete view, the design of the panels appears abstract. Within a certain range of distances, the concept of the facade becomes evident and the overall form appears almost camouflaged with the effect enhanced by the region's famous fog. From farther away the texture of the panels is lost with only the more ominous silhouette of the structure remaining. That effect is likewise heightened by the fog. The copper was meant to have a natural patina and to turn green but with variations depending on orientation and placement. The panels, all different, were fabricated by the company Zahner in Kansas City, Missouri who also fabricated the exterior panels for Tadao Ando in Fort Worth and Zaha Hadid in Cincinnati.

The other exterior material is the black glazing that homogenizes the ensemble but contributes to the general lack of transparency and the monolithic aspect to the project.

The de Young tower (Fig 8.6 and Fig 8.8) was a controversial and contentious piece of the design. As for the Walker Art Center, a tower for the de Young was meant to give visibility to the project. The sign in San Francisco is less synthesized with the purpose of the project than in Minneapolis, however, even though it does project a strong importance for the 1,858 m^2 (20,000 ft^2) education department housed within. Several solutions were proposed for the form of the vertical element during the elaboration of the project and the final geometry is parallel to the rest of the building at the base, with the stacked floors twisting as they rise to become parallel with the city street grid at the top. The elevator core that links all levels is parallel to the uppermost floor. The twisting play of geometry was meant to link the museum to the city, and the gesture is playful rather than cerebral – innocent and mischievous at the same time. The form is dynamic and seems to advance or recede depending on the point of view. The exterior escape stairs, visible behind the screen of copper, give depth and lightness to the tower. After responding to height restrictions in the park and to public opinion, the tower was shortened from its desired height by 4.9 m (16 ft), and as built, its nine stories reach a height of 43.9 m (144 ft). Access to the top level observation deck (232 m^2 or 2,500 ft^2) is free of charge and offers an extraordinary panoramic view of the city and the surroundings. The roof of the main building below is also very visible (Fig 8.7 and Fig 8.9). It is clad in copper as well and is treated as a fifth facade with all exhaust vents, gutters, etc. integrated into the roof's overall pattern.

The structure of the tower is in concrete while that of the rest of the building is in steel. Concealed, large-span steel trusses are used in certain places such as above the continuous glazed areas that border the landscaped fingers so that these facades may remain unobstructed by structural columns. The superstructure of the building is isolated from the foundations, and a "moat" or trough filled with polystyrene and topped with earth encircles the building so that in the case of an earthquake the structure is able to move up to 90 cm (3 ft) horizontally and approximately 10 cm (4 in.) vertically.

Though there are several points of access into the building, the primary entry (Fig 8.10) is from the Music Concourse through a covered passage where the museum's 288 seat auditorium can be glimpsed to the right from behind and above the stage. The view is through a thick, double-glazed opening where the two layers of fritted glass of a pattern similar to the façade panels set up a moiré effect as it is moved past. Looking out from inside the auditorium, entering visitors appear, disappear, and appear again as the superimposed patterns become more or less dense.

The passage opens into a pentagonal courtyard (Fig 8.11) where there is an immediate contact with a work of art: *Drawn Stone* by

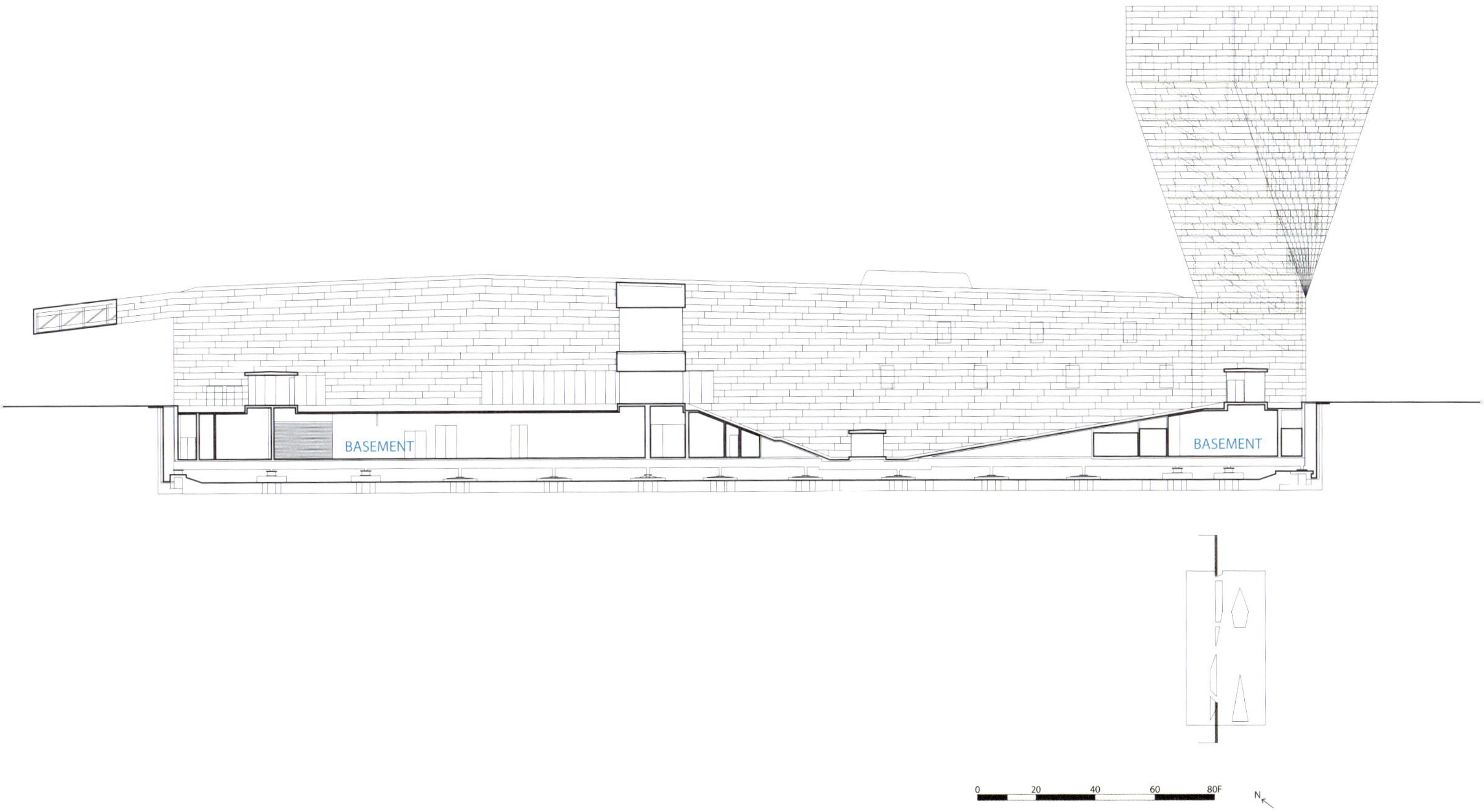

Figure 8.12 Longitudinal section AA

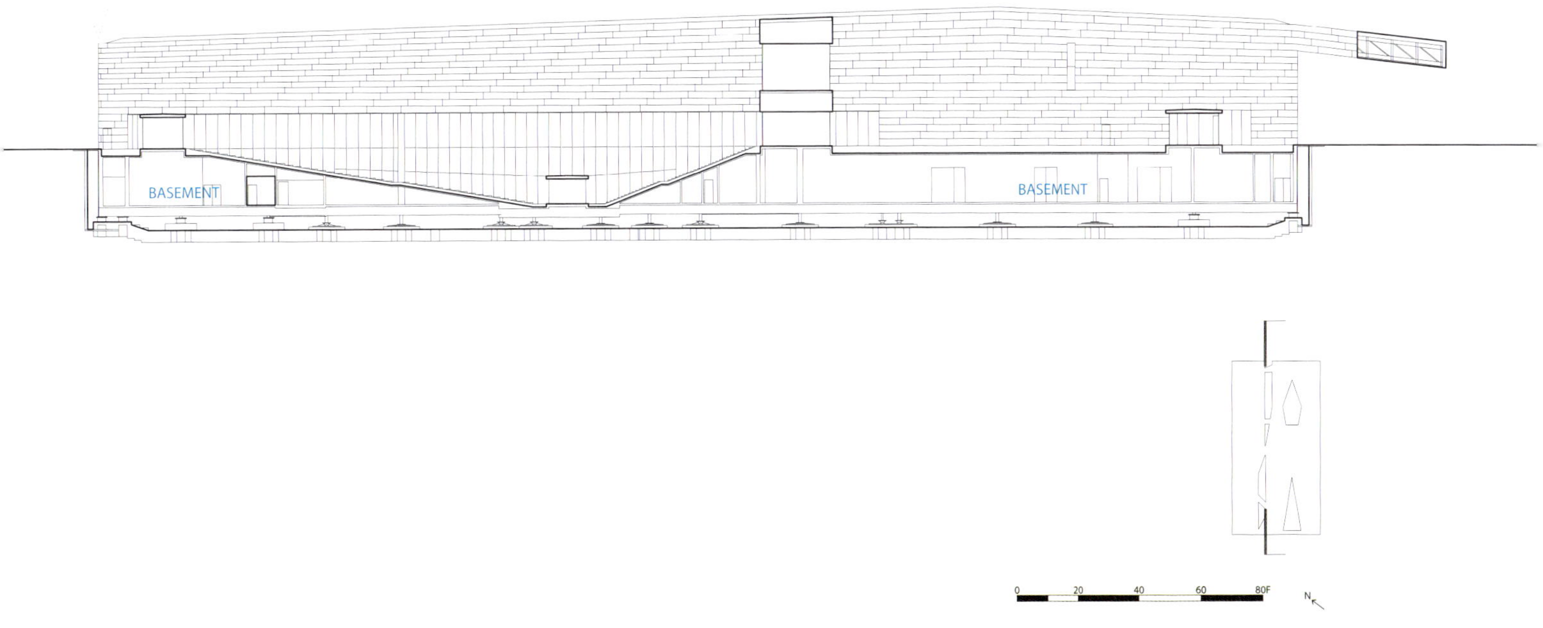

Figure 8.13 Longitudinal section BB

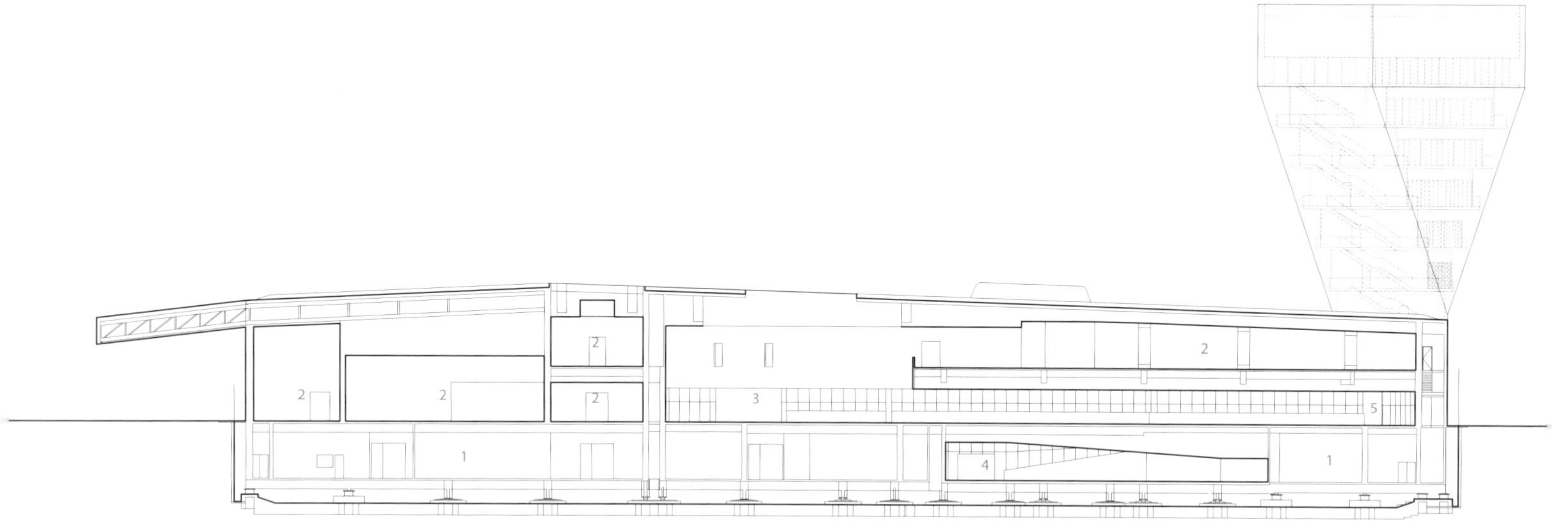

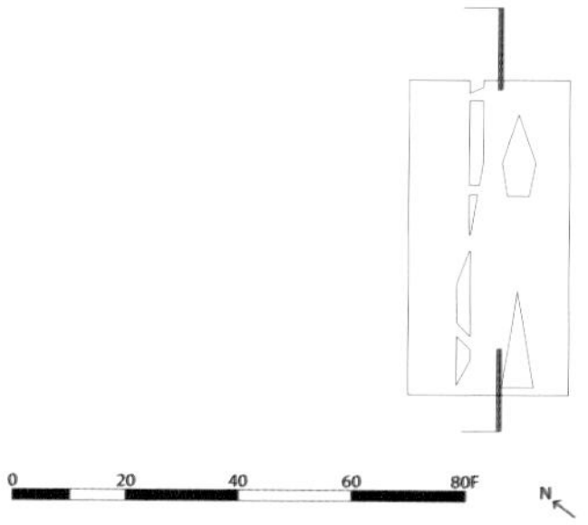

1 Basement
2 Gallery
3 Main Lobby
4 Lower Lobby
5 Entry

Figure 8.14 Longitudinal section CC

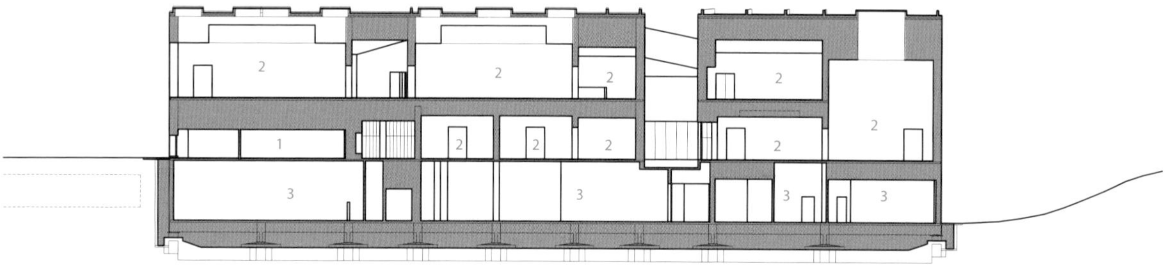

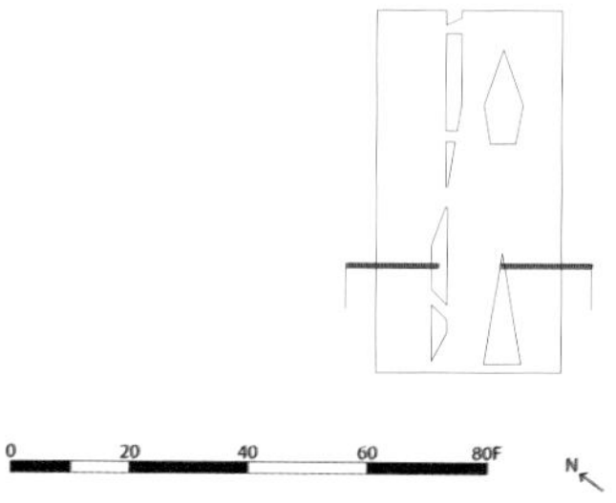

1 Services
2 Gallery
3 Basement

Figure 8.15 Cross section DD

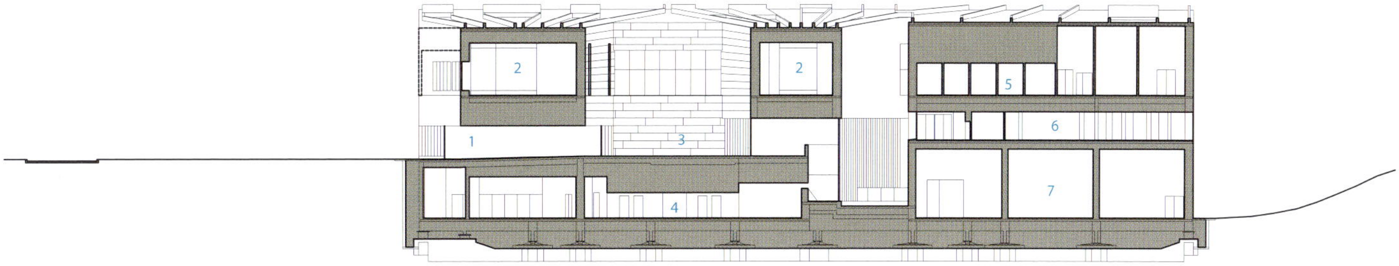

1 Entry Passage
2 Gallery
3 Entry Court
4 Lower Lobby
5 Storage
6 Office
7 Special Exhibitions

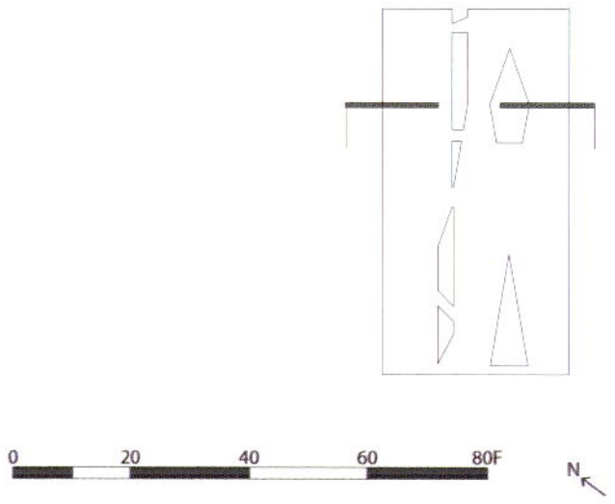

Figure 8.16 Cross section EE

Andy Goldsworthy. *Drawn Stone* is a permanent piece conceived specifically for the space. It is inspired by the tectonic fault lines of the region, and a crack in the ground pavers runs from the Music Concourse, through the passage, and then through large, rough-hewn stone slabs located in the courtyard. The crack ultimately leads to the entrance.

From the court, arrival is into the center band (Fig 8.17) of the project facing a narrow, sloping, finger garden. Stairs descend (Fig 8.18) along a 20 cm (8 in.) thick, double-glazed garden wall where the glass has been placed at both faces of the mullions in order to maintain the facade's planar quality both outside and in. The stairs lead to a lower lobby and a flexible and intentionally neutral temporary exhibition space (111 m^2 or 12,000 ft^2) at the basement level (Fig 8.3). Visitors who have parked in the garage under the Music Concourse also arrive via the lower lobby and, much like at the Walker Art Center, may come and go without ever actually seeing the building's exterior.

At ground level (Fig 8.4), visitors move to the left upon entering the building and into a double-height main lobby where another, grander staircase ascends to the main exhibition spaces above (Fig 8.5). The logic and form of this stair is graphic in plan rather than being directly linked to the real circulation of visitors. Elevators linking the lower lobby and the main lobby are located under the grand stair. Another elevator located to the south of the lobby stair links the ground and second floors. Other elevators toward the western extremity of the building are somewhat awkwardly embedded within the gallery spaces. A freight elevator on the north side of the building directly connects all three levels.

Figure 8.17 Interior/lobby with stair to second level

Figure 8.18 Interior – stair to lower level

Figure 8.20 Interior – gallery

Figure 8.19 Interior – gallery

Figure 8.21 Interior – gallery

The floor finish of the entry and lobby spaces is 15 cm (6 in.) wide stone pavers of Italian Porphyry. The walls are white gypsum board, and the lighting is primarily recessed fluorescent tubes. Galleries at the ground level are devoted to American Art, Twentieth Century Art, and Native American Art. At ground level there is also office space to the north, a 279 m^2 (3,000 ft^2) cafe that opens onto a terrace to the west, a museum store near the lobby, and, near the east museum entry, the entry to the auditorium. The auditorium, with its light-brown leather seats, aubergine-colored walls, and purple carpet, is pleasant and more staid than that of the Walker Art Center in Minneapolis.

Compared to the Walker, the interior spaces in San Francisco are generally more staid and also more hierarchical. There is the double-height main lobby and the grand stair (Fig 8.17) that leads to what is basically the museum's *piano nobile*. Herzog & de Meuron's preferred type for gallery spaces – the artist's studio or loft – is applicable, at best, for only a portion of the de Young's collection: twentieth-century art. Since the de Young collection is varied, the architecture was meant to demonstrate the coexistence and equality of cultures. In most all cases there is an attempt to establish a correlation between the contained and the container. The spaces become somewhat themed in relation to what is exhibited, and the décor is a sign of what the gallery is to be used for. Twentieth-century art is shown in rational, white spaces (Fig 8.19). More historical Western art is shown in rational, colored, enfilade spaces (Fig 8.20). African and Pacific arts are shown in non-orthogonal spaces, freer in form, with predominantly wood finishes (Fig 8.21). Textiles are shown in simple, dimly lit spaces where the design is driven by a necessity to assure their conservation. For the architects, the diversity of the de Young's collection and the cultures it represents should be demonstrated through the diversity of the spaces themselves and should preclude a *white cube* approach. There was no search, however, for some architectural common denominator for the diversity, and the architects categorized the works primarily by those created in the context of Western understanding and those that were not. This approach seemingly does not allow for more nuanced classifications, and African art and Oceanic art are placed together in the same architectural space and décor. The link pieces between the three parallel elements are meant to be "switches," and they should join and separate the various parts and collections.

The organization of the museum allows for multiple paths that permit a variety of logical visits of the collection. It is easy to remain oriented within the 6,782 m^2 (73,000 ft^2) of permanent exhibition spaces due to views to the outside and openings onto the main lobby space. Ground floor galleries have the same stone floors as the entry and lobby with metal grills integrated for air conditioning. On the second floor, Sydney Blue Eucalyptus wood is used for floor, wall, and ceiling finishes as well as for the display vitrines. The vitrines in the African and Pacific art galleries also contain columns that are designed for vertical as well as seismic loads. Walls throughout are often gypsum board over plywood on metal studs within the steel structure. Conservation facilities are located in the north-east corner of the second floor in the area above the ground floor offices.

Though Herzog & de Meuron have expressed a preference for fluorescent lighting, American museums in the first decade of the twenty-first century have favored incandescent spotlights on tracks. This was also the de Young's preference. In several of the more classical museum gallery spaces, natural top lighting is mixed with fluorescent light and diffused by a stretched synthetic fabric at ceiling level. The result is a light that is constant, generally perfect, and visually striking, though lacking the more lively qualities of fluctuating daylighting. The same lighting strategy in the form of two parallel bands is used in the main lobby, and they appear as a form of light-art themselves.

An interesting aspect of the top lit galleries for paintings is the lack of correspondence between interior space and exterior form. A tight fit between inside and outside has sometimes made for challenging gallery spaces such as those of the Kunsthaus Graz by Cook and Fournier or the Denver Art Museum by Daniel Libeskind. In San Francisco Herzog & de Meuron have integrated a generous, accessible poché space above their galleries that contains shades for modulating the natural light, artificial light fixtures, and catwalks for maintenance. The poché space also allows the roof skylight and the ceiling skylight not to be aligned, and each responds to its own logic. While dissociating the interior from the exterior could allow for a perfect proportioning of the exhibition spaces, the tallest "classical" galleries at the de Young feel too tall and well-like. All said, the treatment of natural light in the galleries of the de Young is not nearly as ingenious as the treatment of the nature-inspired facades.

In relation to the Walker Art Center in Minneapolis, the de Young gives the impression of a greater sobriety that is likely explained by the inclinations and history of the institution, the locale, and the nature of the collection itself. Even if somewhat sober, the project is still removed from the architects' earlier, more minimal design approach. In their 2001 Pritzker Prize acceptance speech Herzog & de Meuron expressed their doubts concerning a continued dominance of the rectangle in their designs. A newfound liberty allowed for more expressive and gestural forms and spaces. At the de Young the geometry of the exterior form does indeed elude definition, just as the architects hoped, while the interior galleries, to the contrary of their intentions, show the mark of the hand as well as the mind of the architects. Nevertheless, the de Young Museum, in total, remains an example of Herzog & de Meuron's gift to create a building of great rigor that is also capable of generating strong emotion.

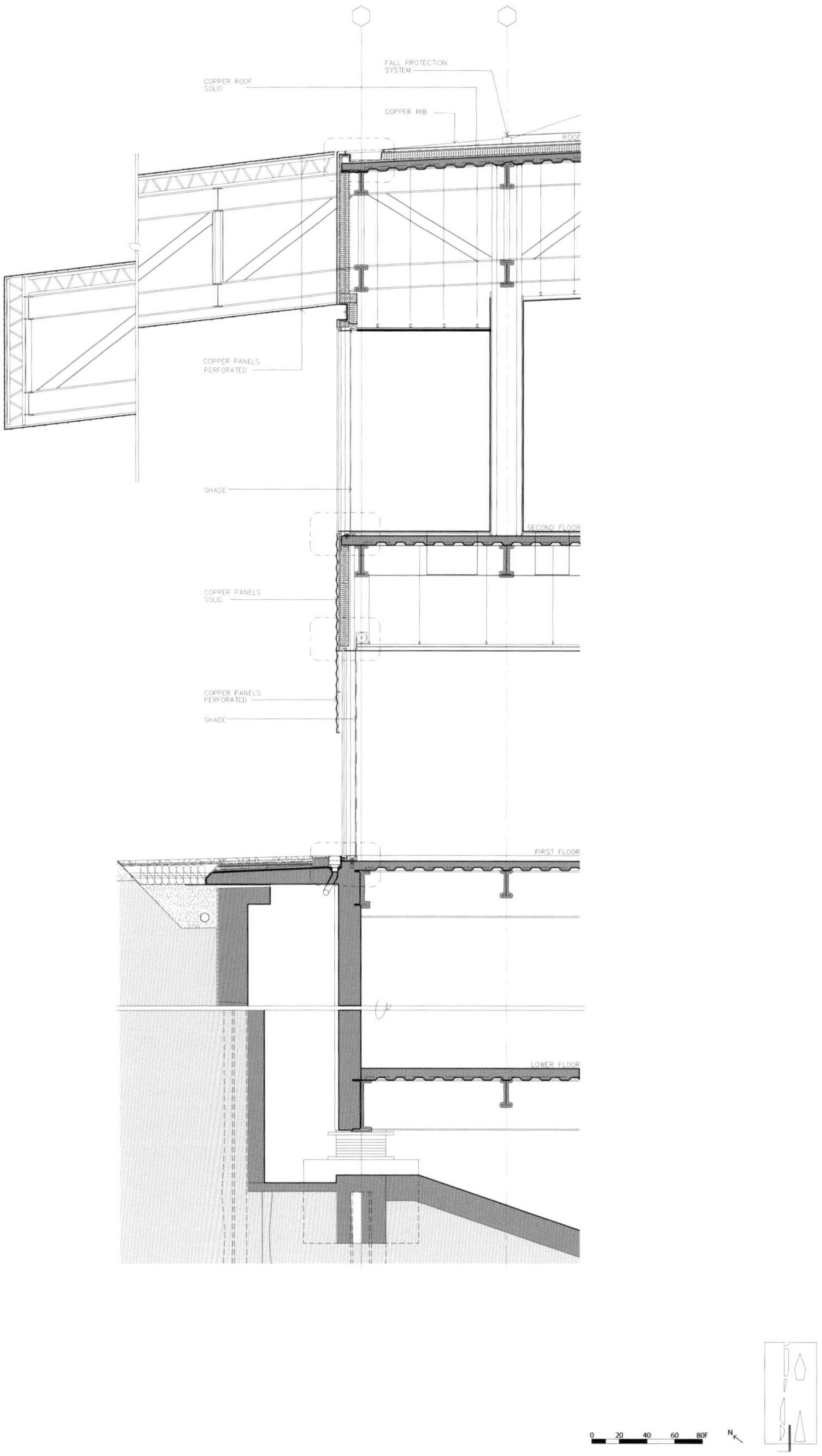

Figure 8.22 Wall detail

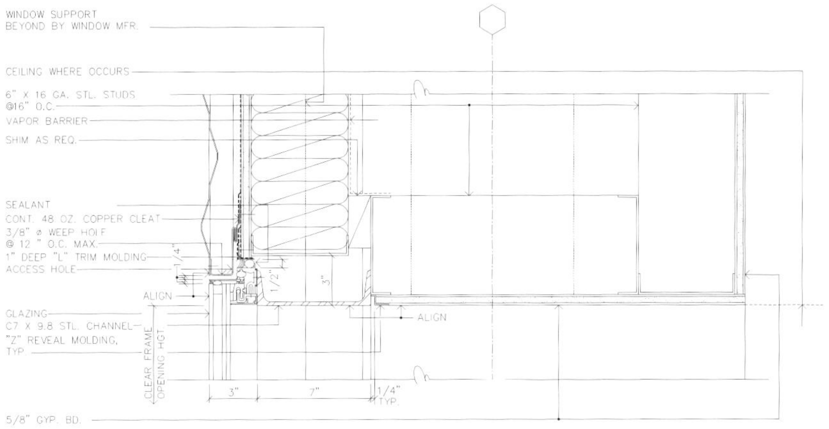

TYPICAL WINDOW HEAD

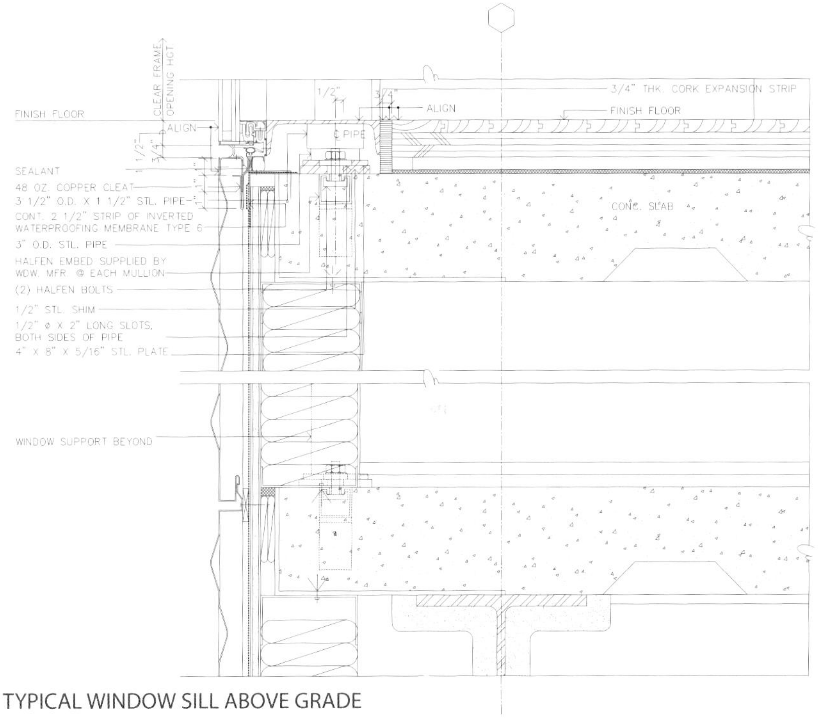

TYPICAL WINDOW SILL ABOVE GRADE

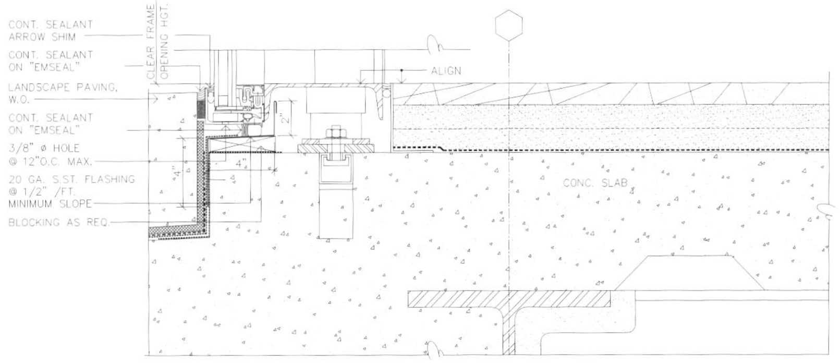

TYPICAL WINDOW SILL AT GRADE

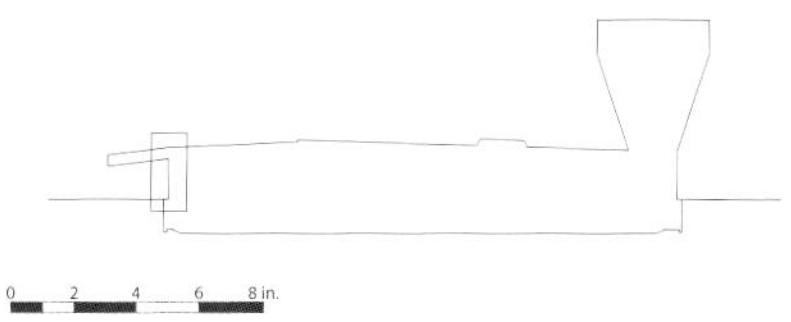

Figure 8.23 Details

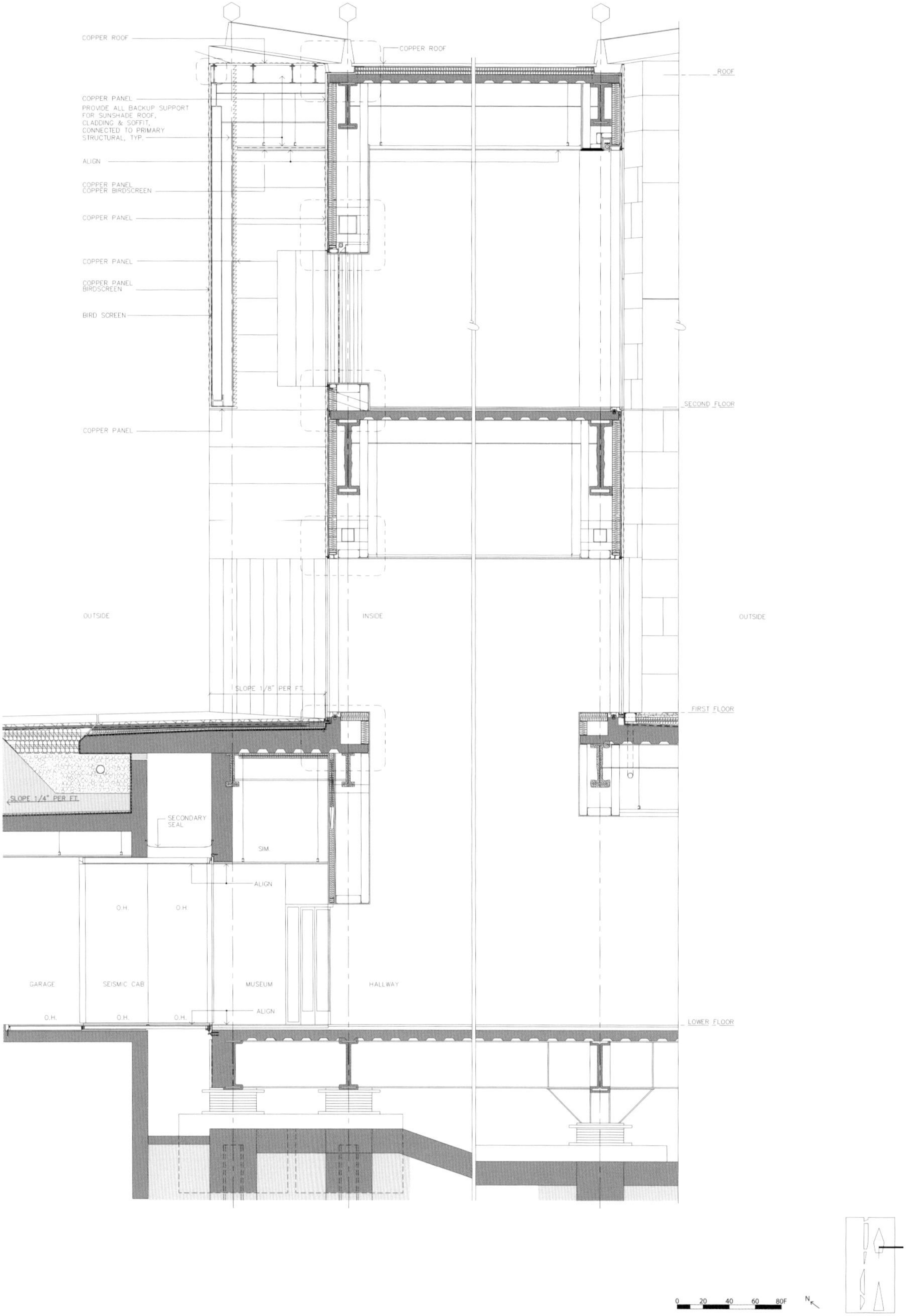

Figure 8.24 Facade detail

CHAPTER 9

Toledo Museum of Art Glass Pavilion

Toledo, Ohio

Kazuyo Sejima + Ryue Nishizawa / SANAA

2006

Figure 9.1 View from south

The Glass Pavilion is an intriguing blend of the serious and the playful. Outside (Fig 9.1) it appears restrained and serene, but also fanciful – more like a garden folly set within its treed site than an addition to the existing architecture of the Toledo Museum of Art (TMA). Inside it evokes reason and rigor combined with the sensations of a fun house or a house of mirrors. The plan (Fig 9.3) is reasoned but appears diagrammatic. The construction demands extreme precision and integration yet it appears effortless. There are few opportunities to design all glass buildings and even fewer to design all glass museums – with curved walls no less – but to house the TMA's extensive glass collection, it seemed almost to be an obligation. Kazuyo Sejima and Ryue Nishizawa – SANAA – fulfilled the obligation.

Toledo, Ohio is known as the "Glass City." In 1888 Edward Drummond Libby opened the Libby Glass Company there. Many of the names equated with glass in the United States such as Owens and Corning are still based in Toledo. Libby was also a major benefactor of the Toledo Museum of Art which was begun in 1901 and moved into its first newly constructed building in 1912. When few others were interested, Libby began to collect American glass as well as objects from around the world. His efforts provided a foundation for the TMA's renowned collection of glass art that is exhibited in the Glass Pavilion today.

Perhaps the principal advocate of glass architecture in modern architecture was the German writer Paul Sheerbart who published a book of that title in 1914 near the end of his life. Sheerbart dreamed of all glass buildings. He already spoke of double glass walls for climatic reasons with lighting integrated into the cavity and heating through the floor. A glass building's structure should be in iron. They would be sparkling jewels in gardens, and at night a glass building would be an illumination element in itself. Glass architecture would transform mankind. For Sheerbart, however, the glass would be multicolored. Much of what Sheerbart dreamed of is found in the Glass Pavilion – even if its glass is extra white rather than colored.

SANAA's earlier 21st Century Museum of Contemporary Art in Kanazawa, Japan appears to be a precedent for Toledo. In the United States the Glass Pavilion brings to mind Mies van der Rohe's Farnsworth House (1951) and Philip Johnson's Glass House (1949). It may share kinship with certain of Norman Foster's projects such as the Pilot Head Office for IBM completed in 1971 in Hampshire, England. Like SANAA's pavilion, this low, very repetitive, relatively inexpensive all glass building appears like a mirage in the landscape. Another Foster building, the Willis Faber and Dumas Headquarters building in Ipswich, has an undulating, all glass facade that, like the pavilion, is technically sophisticated. Since Foster's buildings use reflective or tinted glass, their main effect is through reflection rather than transparency – at least during the day. The Glass Pavilion is a refined response to an ongoing architectural quest for glass architecture.

SANAA's solution manipulates the same visual effects of these earlier buildings but even more so. Since there are multiple layers of glass – and curved glass – there are even more reflections. Surprisingly, there are also multiple planes of transparency. Views weave through the building rather than being bared all at once. The layers emphasize the material quality of the glass without compromising its transparent quality (Fig 9.10). The smaller glass-skinned houses mentioned above offer a more singular effect. The composition of glass planes in Sejima and Nishizawa's much larger, 62 by 57 m (202 ft 8 in. by 186 ft 8 in.), building offers multiple effects.

The Toledo Museum of Art is located in the Old West End, an affluent residential neighborhood with large Victorian and Edwardian style homes. The Glass Pavilion is placed in the middle of its site and parallel to the generally horizontal, neoclassical, white marble main building that it faces across Monroe Street (Fig 9.2). Though the pavilion is not centered on the earlier building, the two entrances are aligned (Fig 9.4). A second entrance on the southeast side leads toward an automobile drop-off area and a parking lot across Parkwood Avenue. Both of the pavilion's entrances are protected by 4.9 m (16 ft) wide canopies, only 16 cm (6¼ in.) thick. A ramp descending to the basement delivery area is also located to the south-east while a straight run emergency stair from the basement is located to the north-west. The site is flat and somewhat irregular since it is located at a shift of the grid of the city streets. Several mature trees were conserved, and many others were planted and are now reflected in the glass walls of the building. Frank Gehry's University of Toledo Center for the Visual Arts (1992) is to the south across Monroe Street.

From outside, the building couldn't be simpler. Everything has been reduced to a minimum and the elevation can virtually be drawn with five lines (Fig 9.6). The structure is 4.6 m (15 ft) tall. Panels of glass 2.4 m (8 ft) wide and 3.96 m (13 ft) high are capped by a 61 cm (2 ft) anodized aluminum fascia with panel joints every 4.9 m (16 ft) (Fig 9.15). The curved glass corners contribute to the immaterial effect and the seeming weightlessness of the structure. The exterior is animated by the activity of the two glassblowing studios – hot shops – inside the building where glass objects are actually made (Fig 9.8). The pavilion is even more striking at night when, as Paul Sheerbart imagined, glass architecture becomes an illumination element in itself.

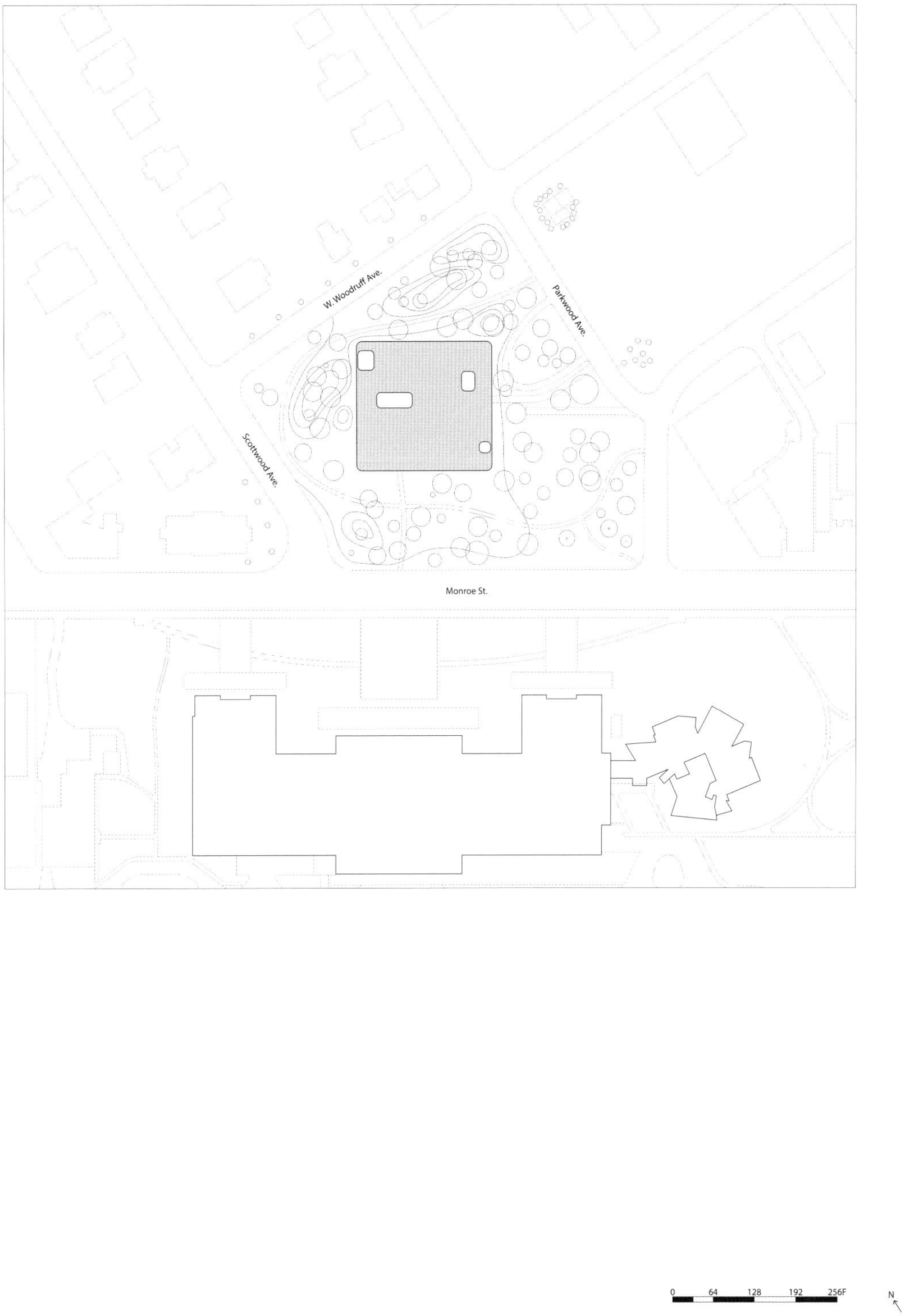

Figure 9.2 Site plan

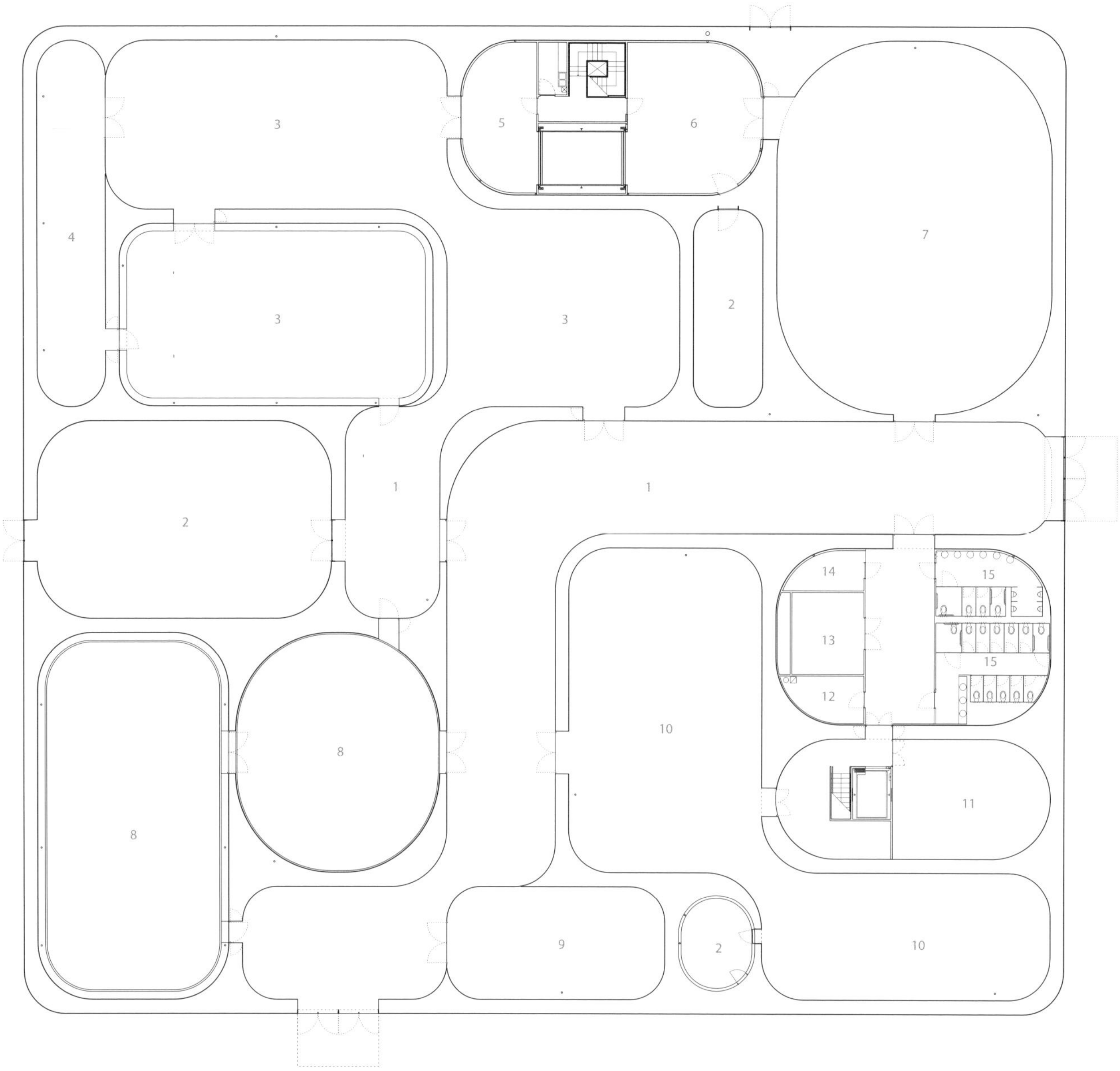

1 Foyer
2 Courtyard
3 Primary Exhibition
4 Rest
5 Art Holding
6 Food Holding
7 Multipurpose
8 Open Storage
9 Food
10 Hotshop
11 Lampwork
12 Technician Room
13 Coat
14 First Aid
15 Toilet

Figure 9.3 Floor plan

Figure 9.4 Monroe Street entry – south/west facade

Figure 9.5 Detail of north/west facade – courtyard

Figure 9.6 Elevations

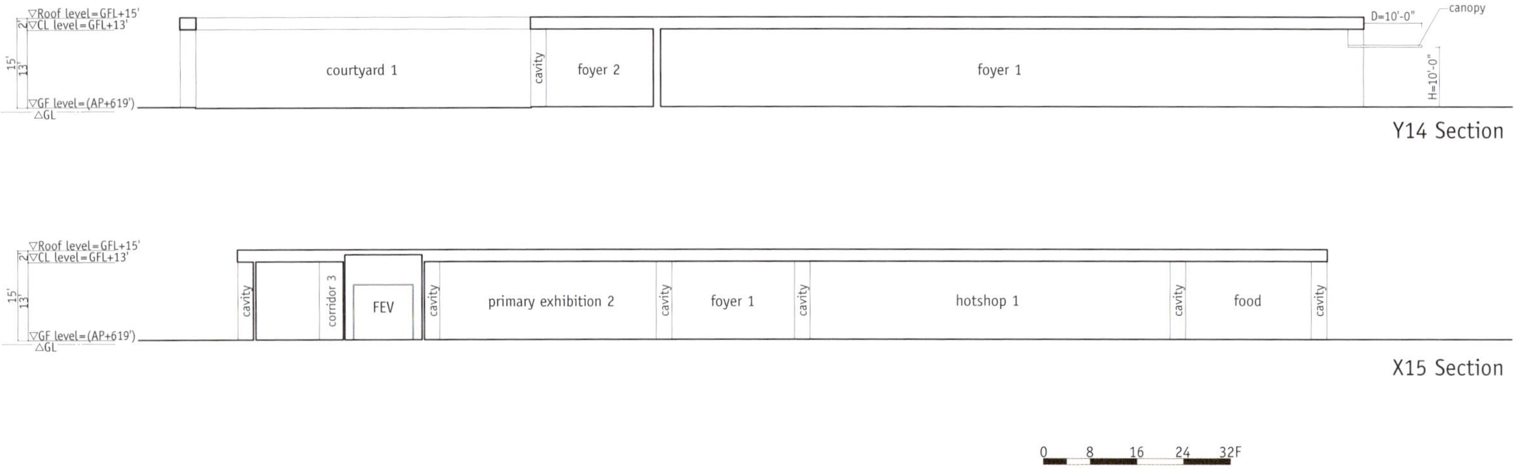

Figure 9.7 Sections

The impression upon entering the 7,060 m^2 (square meter; 76,000 ft^2 (square foot)) pavilion is of whiteness, fluidity, transparency, and reflections. A suspended, colorless glass sculpture, *Campiello del Remer Chandelier #2*, by the American artist Dale Chihuly greets the visitor in the Monroe Street lobby. The entry space squeezes into an L-shaped "Crystal Corridor" that passes through the building and connects with the second entrance toward Parkwood Avenue (Fig 9.9). This passage allows a first glimpse of all of the spaces and provides access to the galleries (Fig 9.11), hot shops, cafe, and a multipurpose room. Like SANAA's earlier 21st Century Museum of Contemporary Art, the Glass Pavilion is conceived as distinct volumes – or bubbles – encircled by the exterior glass wall. The corridor is perhaps the most interesting space architecturally since it passes through the center of the building where the effect of the individual bubbles, multiple layers, and veiled views to the outside is most pronounced. The curved glass not only produces a visual effect that makes the building itself seem to move as it is moved through but, at certain points, focuses sound as well. The white, opaque volumes (three service areas, two gallery spaces, and one courtyard) keep the entirety of the pavilion from being revealed all at once. Two interior courtyards bring natural light to the center of the structure, and the smaller of the two has a 2.9 m (9 ft 6 in.) diameter domed glass skylight at ground level that lights the conservation area in the basement (Fig 9.5 and Fig 9.12). A third (opaque) courtyard allows a basement level shop to be ventilated. Simple, sheer, full height curtains provide another layer and more animation to the composition.

The Glass Pavilion was conceived as a working glass studio for demonstrations and classes as well as an art museum. The hot shops are an attraction and spectacle for visitors. The exhibition spaces are either glass enclosed or opaque. The all glass galleries are coherent with the overall concept of the building. The opaque galleries such as the Glass Study Room, however, appear detached from the rest and clinical in comparison. Here, art pieces are displayed in cases, the whiteness becomes very present, and lighting becomes uniquely artificial. All exhibition spaces have track lighting while other spaces have recessed spots. Ceilings are gypsum board and, like the glass panels, are 3.96 m (13 ft) high. Walls are either gypsum board or 22 mm (¾ in.) steel plate. The floors are light-colored concrete. The courtyards have 75 mm (3 in.) thick precast pavers on pedestals.

The Glass Pavilion is striking in general. It best presents itself in areas with few program requirements such as the long, narrow rest area in the north/west corner of the building (Fig 9.13), the multipurpose room to the north/east, and the "Crystal Corridor."

Figure 9.8 Interior – Hot Shop

Figure 9.9 Parkwood Avenue entry seen from interior

Figure 9.10 Interior – general view looking south-east

Figure 9.11 Interior – general view looking south-west

Figure 9.12 Courtyard with domed skylight to basement

Figure 9.13 Interior – rest area at north/west corner

Figure 9.14 View from within glass wall cavity

The basement houses the loading dock, mechanical rooms, support spaces, storage, offices, conservation, and a kitchen for events related to the multipurpose room above. The partial basement of early schemes evolved into a full basement, and at completion of construction there was also significant undesignated expansion space for future use. Trucks can enter the basement and unload with the dock doors closed. A north/south service corridor links the dock to the freight elevator on the north side of the building that at ground level arrives into one of the opaque "bubbles." Another passenger elevator and two stairs also link the two floors. Dividing walls in the basement are orthogonal, and columns are generally aligned but are not on a grid. The depth of the basement excavation was minimized for budget reasons and to reduce the length of the ramp that descends to the loading dock. Still, high ceilings were required. The floor to floor height between the two levels is 4.6 m (15 ft). In order to reduce the depth of the cast in place concrete structure, the number of columns was increased and spans, as well as beam depth and slab thickness, were reduced. Spans do not exceed 7.3 m (24 ft). Wide and flat beams are approximately 61 cm (24 in.) in depth, and slabs are 28 cm (11 in.) thick.

The relationship between space and structure in the pavilion is interesting. Space – the bubbles – were determined first and column locations followed. A regular grid was eliminated in order to downplay the column pattern and make the building appear even lighter (Fig 9.16). Columns are concealed within hollow walls or replaced by 22 mm (¾ in.) steel plate walls when possible. The steel plate lampworking room in the south/east corner of the building is the primary element for lateral stiffness in the structure. There are three other braced frames in the building. The one in the multipurpose room is freestanding and also provides a place to conceal the sliding curtains. Columns are 89 mm (3½ in.) or 114 mm (4¼ in.) steel round bar. The building is on a 2.4 m (8 ft) module with a 1.62 m (5 ft 4 in.) module at the corners. Spaces are related to the building module but not to the actual structure.

The thickness of the roof was kept to a minimum. In general there are six crooked structural lines of girders in the east/west direction. The layout of the girders is determined by the optimal position of the columns below. In the north/south direction joists are regularly spaced every 2.4 m (8 ft). Joists are offset from the building module, however, so as not to interfere with lighting and other services that strictly adhere to the building module. Though the depth of both structural elements varies depending on spans, girders are generally 30 cm (12 in.) deep and up to 12.19 m (40 ft) apart and joists are generally 25 cm (10 in.) deep. Girders have a common bottom elevation. Deeper girders encroach into the space of the rigid roof insulation above. Special girders were fabricated for certain locations in order to maintain minimum necessary insulation. The joists have a common top elevation but, whatever their depth, never descend below the bottom of the girders. There is only 15 cm (6 in.) available between the bottom of the structure and the ceiling. Since drainage pipes, sprinkler pipes, electrical runs, and ductwork cannot all fit in this limited space, they were very closely coordinated and often pass through the structural elements themselves. The building is sprinkled and the steel structure required no additional fire protection.

The roof of the pavilion can be seen from the entry of the main building across the street. The roof is a gray single-ply membrane on tapered insulation on 38 mm (1½ in.) metal decking. Depressed pits were created in the roof to hide exhaust fans. Linear, louvered hoods for heat exhaust from the hot shops project 51 cm (20 in.) above the level of the fascia. Roof slopes are generally 3 mm (⅛ in.) in 30 cm (12 in.).

The 4.88 m (16 ft) wide by 4.27 m (14 ft) deep entrance canopies were also reduced to a minimum. They are supported by four interior elements: two 4.76 by 22.86 cm (1⅞ by 9 in.) stainless steel columns integrated with the door stiles, and two 4.76 cm stainless steel tubes that tie it back at its interior edge. The canopy is only 15.88 cm (6¼ in.) high. It has integrated snow melting heat cables.

Preliminary design explorations for the pavilion included structural glass columns to make even more of glass as a material and a roof in welded steel plate borrowed from the ship building industry to minimize the thickness of the roof.

In his book *The Architecture of the Well-tempered Environment,* Reyner Banham spoke of Le Corbusier's use of the brise-soleil as a "masterly invention" that allows transparency and view, while limiting heat gain. The brise-soleil, however, also deals with an architectural study of enclosure when "transparent glass membranes" replace massive walls. Banham also described a double wall scheme called the *mur neutralisant* (neutralizing wall) that Le Corbusier proposed and later tested with the French glass manufacturer Saint Gobain. His goal was to control a building's climate regardless of its geographical location. This was to be achieved by the creation of a "neutralizing" double membrane surrounding the building into which would be blown "scorching" air in cold climates and cold air in hot climates. Banham briefly relates Saint Gobain's seemingly skeptical conclusion at that time "that the use of hot air between double glazing needed a third layer of glass, trapping a second layer of (still) air, to make it a workable proposition!"

The Glass Pavilion does not use the brise-soleil. It does, however, employ a version of the "neutralizing wall" in the form of an active system cavity between two planes of glass 61 cm (2 ft)

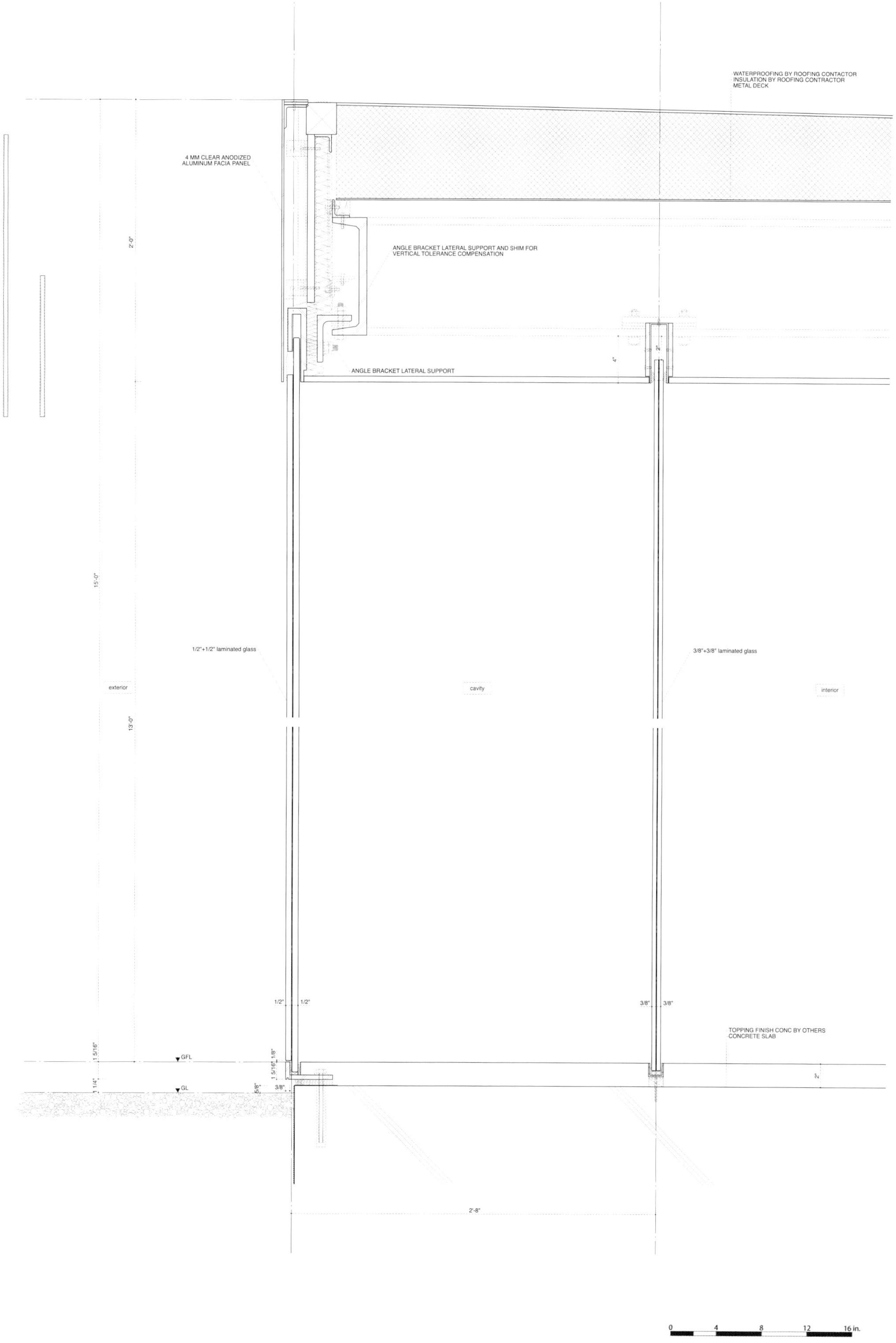

Figure 9.15 Wall section

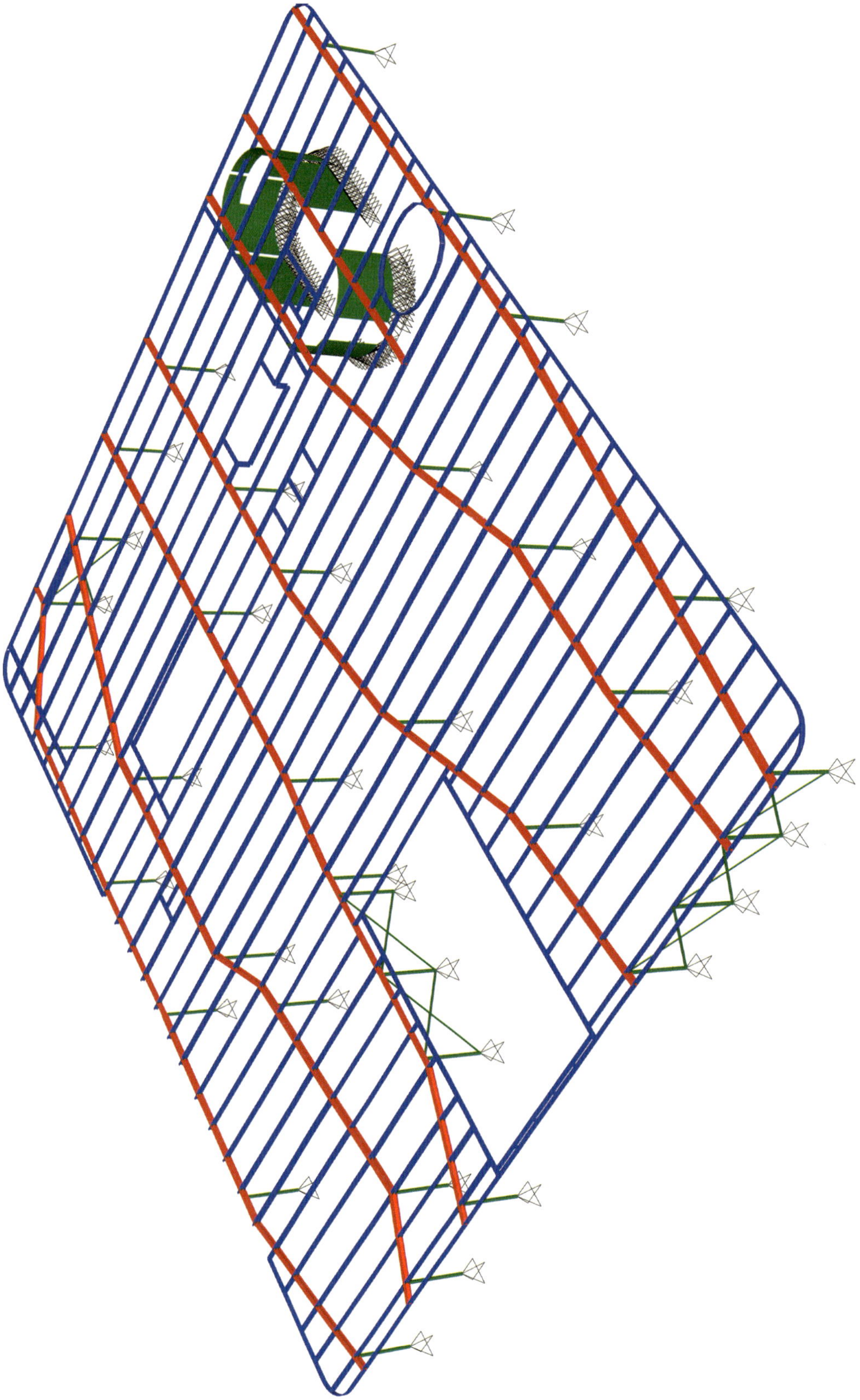

Figure 9.16 Structural diagram

apart at the perimeter of the building (Fig 9.14). (The 61 cm space also allows for cleaning within the cavity.) Double glazing was not excluded from the outset for the project; however, for technical reasons related to the glass dimensions, lamination, and bending, a solution using only single glazing was retained. This was also more compatible with the architects' research for transparency and lightness. Since the single glazing has virtually no insulation value, the climatic solution was found within the glass enclosed cavity. Here, hot or chilled water is circulated in a radiant system located above the ceiling and in the slab at the perimeter of the building and around the courtyards. Design in Toledo's climate is primarily for winter cold. Fortunately the pavilion has its own source of heat in the kilns of the hot shops that is captured and recirculated. Air is also pumped into all of the cavities. At the perimeter, circular, anodized aluminum floor grills are spaced every 4.88 m (16 ft) to pressurize the cavity against infiltration. Solar gain is a seasonal problem and is reduced by the manual curtains which also reduce light quantity and glare. The mesh at the top and bottom of the curtains allows for air flow. Early studies for motorized curtains would have allowed for daily adjustments. The manual curtains are adjusted seasonally.

The building is conceived as three climatic zones: the hot shops, all other inhabited spaces, and the cavity spaces between the glass panels. The building is organized so that galleries are generally to the north where they receive less sun, and the hot shops are located to the south. Mature, existing trees help to shade the south side of the building. Mechanical equipment including boilers, chillers, and air handlers are located in the basement. Supply air for all spaces is via floor grills. The limited space above the ceiling is used as a return air plenum. There are few opaque partitions for vertical ductwork to connect between the ceiling and the basement. Freestanding "air towers" are located in the two entry areas and the rest area for additional return air. In some areas of the building sunlight entering through the all glass walls hit temperature sensors and produced false readings. Small metal shrouds were designed to rectify the problem.

The low iron glass for the pavilion was manufactured by Pilkington in a plant in Austria. Cutting, bending, and laminating were done in Shenzhen, China. Exterior walls are composed of two 13 mm (½ in.) thick laminated glass sheets while interior walls use two 10 mm (⅜ in.) glass sheets. There is a 10 mm joint between glass panels filled with a transparent silicone gasket and sealant. At the sill, the glass is flush with the stainless steel angle that supports it. At the head, a recessed channel accommodates vertical movement and the aluminum fascia is slightly in front of the glass. The glass facades are precise with very small tolerances. The details are well resolved and call little attention to themselves.

The Glass Pavilion is conceptually simple, experientially rich, and technically refined. It is an unselfconscious building that carries forward the dream of glass architecture.

CHAPTER 10

Denver Art Museum

Denver, Colorado

Studio Daniel Libeskind

2006

Figure 10.1 View from east

Figure 10.2 Watercolor sketch by Daniel Libeskind

Before the Guggenheim Bilbao by Frank Gehry there was the Sydney Opera House by Jorn Utzon. The iconic Australian building opened in 1973 and quickly became an emblem for the city and, no less, all of Australia. Like the Guggenheim before them, the city of Denver and the Denver Art Museum had the "Sydney effect" in mind when they embarked on an ambitious building expansion that, like others at the time, was envisioned as the first great museum building of the twenty-first century (Fig 10.1).

The Denver museum has a prominent location not far from downtown and just to the south of Civic Center Park where the domed Colorado State Capitol and the neoclassical City and County Building face each other across the landscaped green space. Other government buildings and museums are also in the area, and the Denver Art Museum and the Denver Central Library are located along a cross axis just outside the park and beyond a neoclassical colonnade and amphitheater. Though the museum's site is significant in the city, it cannot rival the drama and extreme visibility of Sydney's Bennelong Point where the opera is located or even that of the Bilbao site along the Nervión River.

The Denver Art Museum established a list of some 40 architects potentially capable of conceiving the iconic museum they hoped for. The list was narrowed to five, and then, after a first round of interviews that resulted in the elimination of Steven Holl and Robert Venturi, the three remaining competitors were Arata Isozaki, Daniel Libeskind, and Thom Mayne. A very informative and interesting three-part documentary film by Amie Knox and Jocelyn Childs entitled *Defying Gravity* traces the interviews, presentations, and selection process of the architect, the design phase, and the construction of the building. Through the film we learn, among many other things, that the competition jury found Isozaki contemplative and refined, and many members were tempted by Thom Mayne's dynamism. The jury was actually two juries: one group composed of museum trustees and another of city officials. All of the members were seduced by Daniel Libeskind's energy and optimism. They liked his collaborative spirit and his taste for dialogue. They also felt he had good political instincts and that as a rising star he would bring even more attention to the Denver Art Museum in the future. Libeskind's expressed admiration for the city of Denver, a true American city in his eyes, was appreciated as well. Rather than the immediate urban context of the city, however, the principle reference for his design was metaphorical in nature and inspired by the vision of the Rocky Mountains from the air upon arriving in Denver. Crystal forms are a general interest for Libeskind, and, similarly, the building in the Mile High City should be more akin to a geological formation – more like the Rocky Mountains themselves. This allusion, along with a more abstract notion of "two lines going for a walk," would guide the conceptual, formal, and spatial framework for the project. Similarly, Libeskind's earlier Jewish Museum in Berlin was described by the architect as "between the lines," where the relationship of two lines, one straight and the other tortuous, forms the conceptual basis for the design.

The DAM was founded in 1893. In 1971 the museum moved into a 19,510 m^2 (square meter; 210,000 ft^2 (square foot)) building by the Italian architect Gio Ponti that borders the south side of Civic Center Park. At the time of the Ponti project the museum had decided to remain in the center of the city, and the relatively small site obtained led to a seven-story building. Ponti was associated with a Denver architect for the museum and was mainly responsible for the exterior of the "castle" as the building was immediately called because of its massive, double-tower design with slot windows of various shapes and dimensions that pierce the gray tiled facades in a haphazard manner. From the outside, the building is peculiar and somewhat daunting.

The Central Denver Public Library is across a pedestrian mall from Ponti's building and also borders the park. The low, restrained, modern building by the architect Burnham Hoyt was completed in 1956. A larger addition from 1995 by Michael Graves more than tripled the facility and is equivalent in height and mass to Ponti's project. The Graves design is typical of the architect; it is monumental, uses forms derived from premodern architecture, and is colorful.

The intersection of the north/south pedestrian mall and 13th Avenue defines the heart of a cultural arts district. Ponti's building (now known as the North Building) and the library occupy the two north quadrants. Two projects by Libeskind occupy the two south quadrants (Fig 10.3 and Fig 10.9). To the west, facing Ponti, is the 13,565 m^2 (146,000 ft^2) museum extension (the Hamilton Building) and to the east, facing Graves, is a multi-level, 1,000 car parking garage wrapped on two sides by luxury condominiums and some offices and retail spaces. Libeskind also organized his buildings along the pedestrian mall that is also a link to the neighborhoods south of the arts district.

The mixture of architectural types is surprising. For Libeskind, architecture is generally resistant to change; yet, the buildings of the cultural arts district are a sampling of fluctuating architectural evolutions over several decades. Improbably and ironically, in this immediate context Libeskind's own parking garage comes closest to the neutral, well-mannered box building that he adamantly rejects. The buildings in the area remain individual objects. The various architectures do not exactly battle, nor are they exactly antagonistic, but they do not make for a greater urban whole either. Oddly, when placed side by side, these various overt efforts at creating meaning through references, symbolism, metaphor, etc. seem to neutralize,

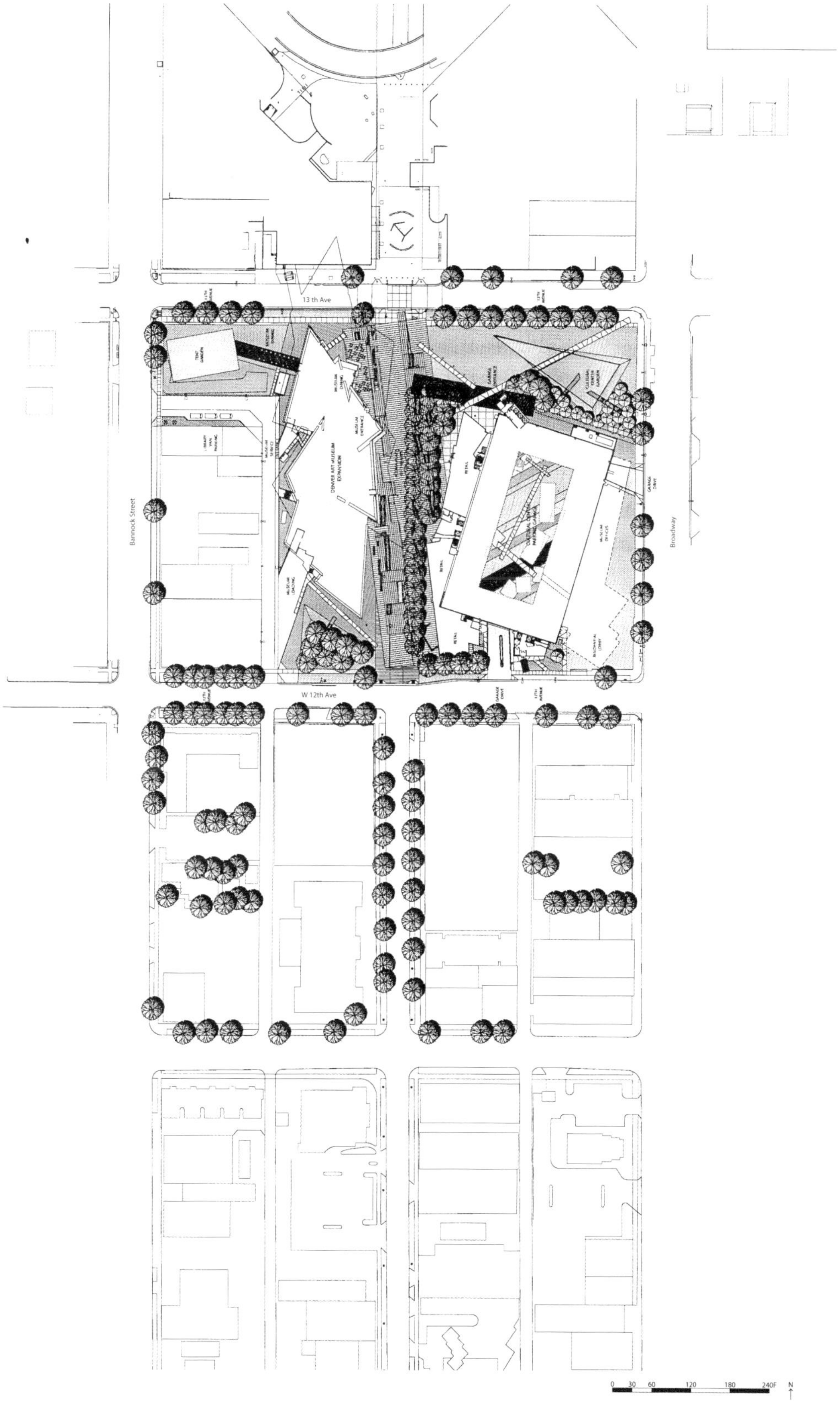

Figure 10.3 Site plan

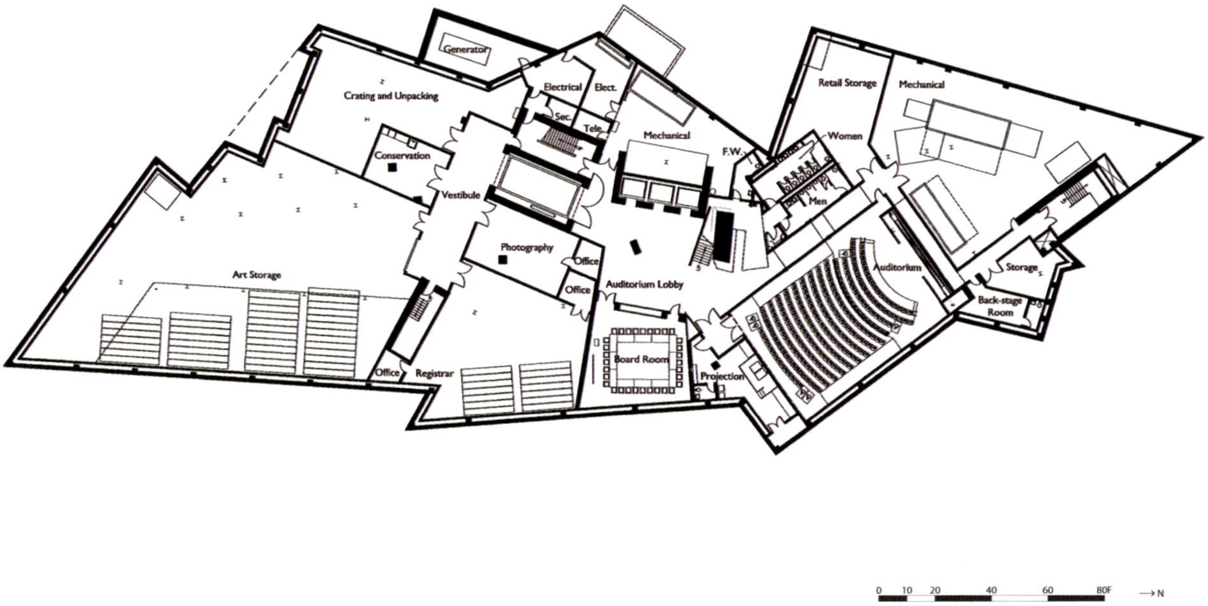

Figure 10.4 Lower floor plan

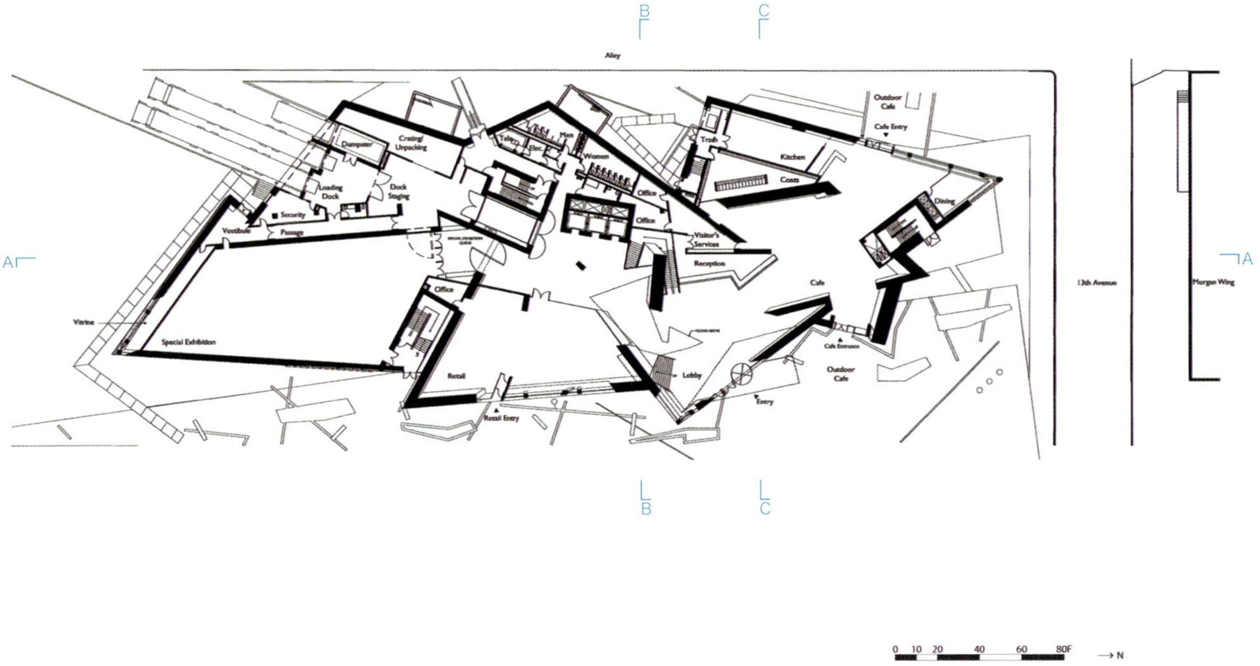

Figure 10.5 First (ground) floor plan

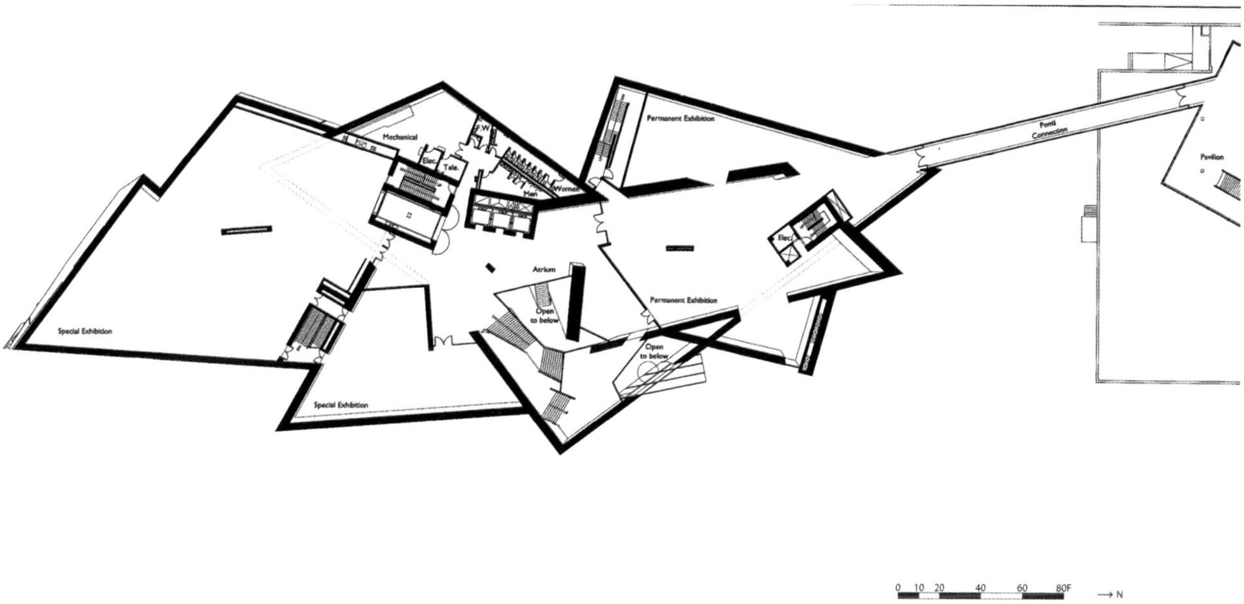

Figure 10.6 Second floor plan

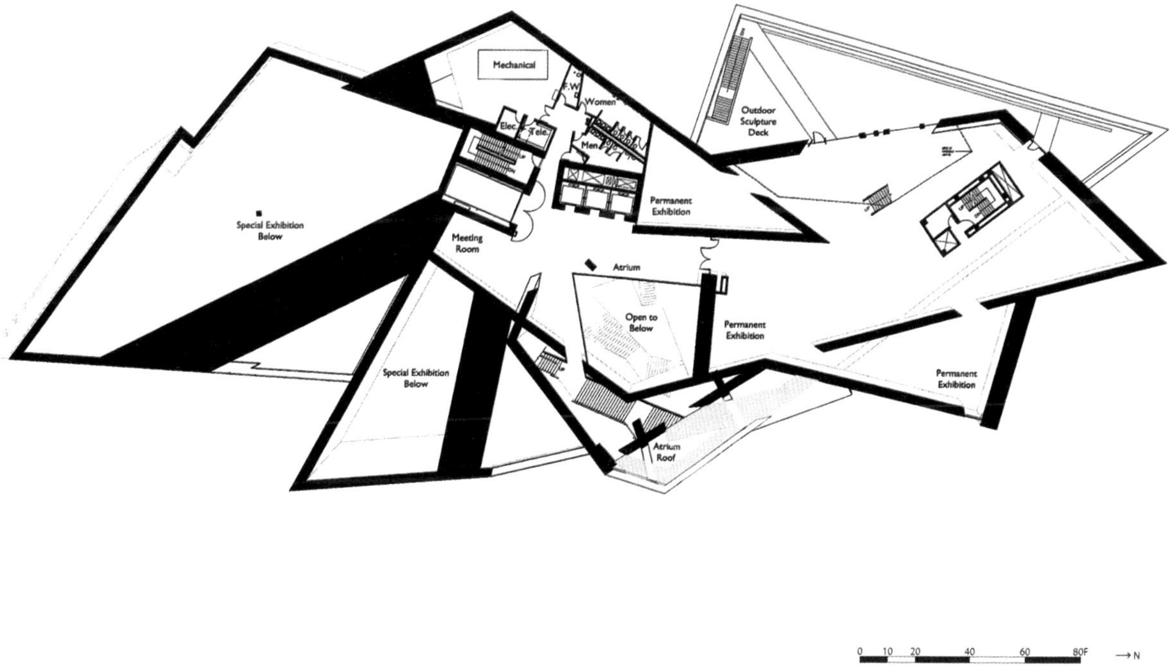

Figure 10.7 Third floor plan

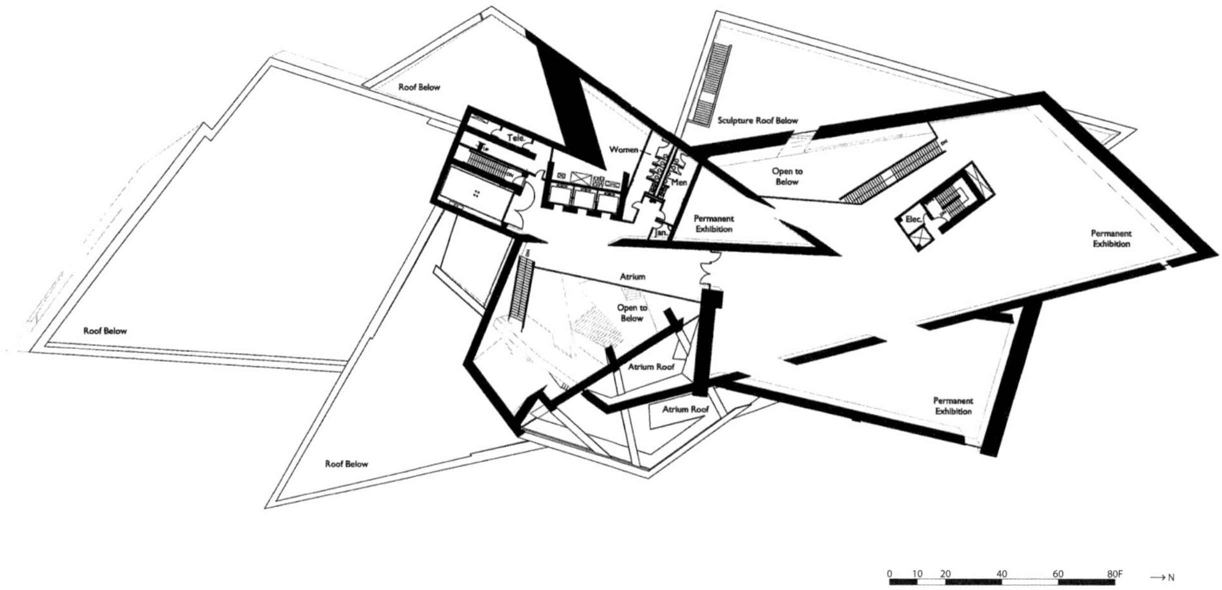

Figure 10.8 Fourth floor plan

cancel, or counteract each other intellectually and formally like architectural antidotes one of the other. This is especially the case between Libeskind's museum and Graves' library. Since late 2011 the most recent addition to the cultural arts district that neighbors the Hamilton Building to the west is the calm, rectangular Clyfford Still Museum by Allied Works Architecture. Presumably, this building would meet Libeskind's criteria for a well-mannered box.

Rather than fluid, curved forms, Daniel Libeskind prefers angular and pointed shapes. In Denver there is a strong pointed form that projects over 13th Avenue and is directed toward the Ponti building (Fig 10.10 and Fig 10.13). The gesture is meant to connect the two structures, and Libeskind equates the effect to the almost touching fingers of God and Adam in Michelangelo's famous Sistine Chapel painting *The Creation of Adam*. The tension and impact are somewhat compromised, however, by the glass pedestrian bridge that crosses the street at a lower lever like an angular umbilical cord to link the two buildings.

The exterior of the Hamilton Building is abstract, sculptural, and very photogenic (Fig 10.11). Because of its urban situation, the building is more animated on its east and north sides toward the pedestrian mall and Ponti's building. For Libeskind there is no reason to be constrained by the right angle, the horizontal, or the vertical. From the ground level, forms lean outward like inverted pyramids, and the main "prow" of the building is an impressive, sharp cantilever. The ensemble generally appears unstable. Openings and windows are few, and the exterior gives little indication of what might be found inside. Ponti's earlier building set the example. The Italian architect felt that if a museum is meant to protect works of art, then it should be a castle. The addition carries the same torch and appears opaque and impenetrable. All of the exterior surfaces are covered with titanium panels which was a response to the reflective gray tile finish of Ponti's building. The titanium was provided by the same Denver company that also provided the materials for the Guggenheim Bilbao.

The main entrance to the museum is now through Libeskind's building (Fig 10.12). Tickets are sold across the pedestrian mall in a space on the ground floor of the parking/condominium building, and from the plaza outside, with ticket in hand, visitors arrive into an impressive atrium of irregular forms, 36.60 m (120 ft) high and lit from above (Fig 10.16 and Fig 10.17). The DAM requested a grand entry space as a key part of the project. Here, floors in black granite meet angled walls, and a monumental stair runs along the inclined surfaces and links all of the levels. Eighty shiny discs with integrated LED lights counting from one to nine, forward and backward, are located on the walls throughout the space. They make the site-specific work *ENGI*, by the Japanese artist Tatsuo Miyajima. Relief strips on the floor are necessary in places to indicate where certain of the inclined planes in the atrium do not provide sufficient ceiling height and visitors might bump their heads on the building.

Figure 10.9 View from north/pedestrian mall

Figure 10.11 Exterior view

Figure 10.10 Exterior view with Ponti Building

Figure 10.12 Main entrance

Figure 10.13 East elevation

Figure 10.14 Section

AA

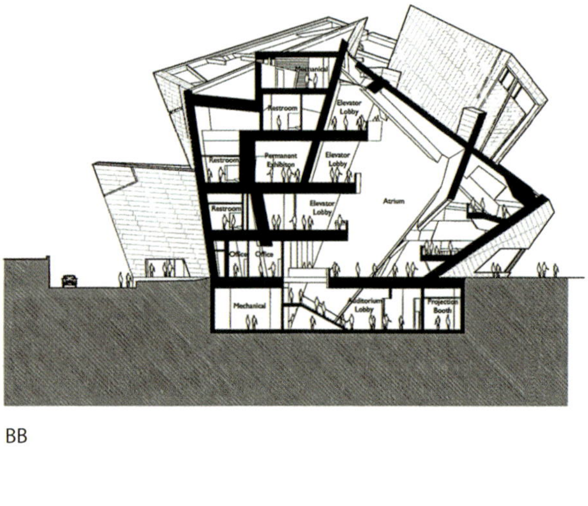

BB

CC

Figure 10.15 Section AA, BB, CC

The basic layout of the museum is simple. Within the elongated plan, temporary galleries are to the south of the atrium and permanent galleries are to the north toward the Ponti building. The atrium is the central focus point. The main delivery and dock area is also located at the south/west corner of the Hamilton building providing easy access to the temporary galleries (Fig 10.5). The DAM had lacked space for large traveling exhibitions making it a central concern for the new project. At basement level there are private areas such as storage, conservation, mechanical rooms, workshops, etc. as well as a meeting room and a 280 seat auditorium (Fig 10.4). At ground level, along with temporary exhibition spaces, there is a museum store and cafe. More temporary exhibition space is located on the second floor (Fig 10.6) and permanent galleries are located on the second, third, and fourth floors with the bridge link to Ponti's building at the second floor level (Fig 10.7 and 10.8). There is approximately 1,858 m^2 (20,000 ft^2) of temporary exhibition space and 2,787 m^2 (30,000 ft^2) of permanent galleries in the Hamilton Building. The size of the Denver Art Museum with the two buildings is 33,073 m^2 (356,000 ft^2).

The volume of the gallery spaces generally follows the exterior form which makes for inclined and angled walls and ceilings

Figure 10.17 Atrium from above

Figure 10.16 Atrium and grand stair

Figure 10.18 Interior – second floor gallery

Figure 10.19 Interior – fourth floor gallery looking north

Figure 10.20 Interior – fourth floor gallery looking south

inside (Fig 10.18). Throughout the building, floors remain horizontal which results in horizontal ceilings as well at the lower levels. The temporary galleries are a notch more restrained than the others while the fourth floor permanent gallery is the most dramatic space with a ceiling sloping up to a height of 9 m (30 ft) within the cantilevered point of the building (Fig 10.19 and Fig 10.20). Walls throughout are generally in gypsum board and floors are wood (Douglas fir). Galleries are generally loft spaces with exhibition walls stopping shy of the ceiling. They are artificially lit since there are few windows, and natural top lighting was reserved for the atrium. The interior is self-contained and can be disorienting – likely a quality appreciated and even sought by Libeskind. There is a stair within the galleries linking the third and fourth floors, and an outdoor sculpture terrace on the west side of the third floor offers an opportunity to step outside to views of the downtown skyline and glimpses of the surrounding mountains.

The DAM did not want traditional exhibition spaces, and as is the case for other museums with more expressive galleries, architect and curator prefer to describe them as an "opportunity" rather than a challenge. The irregular spaces should create new relationships between art and architecture, and they should incite curators to abandon conventional methods of installing exhibitions. That said, many temporary, vertical exhibition walls are installed within the spaces and occasionally just in front of the building's own inclined walls. Paintings are sometimes suspended by cables, but there is no secondary or complementary system within the architectural envelope designed to assist in the use of the spaces. Zaha Hadid, for example, integrated rails into the ceiling of her atypical galleries at the MAXXI in Rome so that works of art might be suspended or temporary exhibition walls might be positioned and stabilized. Louis Kahn's Kimbell Art Museum in Fort Worth that Libeskind praises in his book *Breaking Ground* also integrates a refined and discreet system for attaching temporary walls within the galleries, and the architect also designed the movable walls themselves to form a sort of kit. This type of integration was not done at the DAM, and little was offered to mediate between the architectural space and the presentation of artwork. In this context, very large works may hold their own, but smaller works and more traditional paintings are often overshadowed by the secondary exhibition installations necessary to simply hang them. Artwork and even added exhibition supports often seem adrift in the space. The approach taken for the galleries generally seems misguided.

While the exterior of the building appears as a sculptural object, the interior, divided by floor plates, reads less like the corresponding outside volume and more like a collection of distinct surfaces: wood floor, gypsum board walls, and a dropped ceiling. The ceiling, with its strong grid and lines of light tracks, hovers over the space and exhibition walls and is very present. It appears more as a catalogue product than a true architectural surface designed for the project. Spotlights, air conditioning grills, exit panels, etc. are numerous and distracting. The result is visually overwhelming – rigid and chaotic at the same time.

In order to realize his iconic building in Sydney, Utzon used geometry to derive and describe the structure, and developed a scheme with all of the shell shapes coming from a same hypothetical sphere. Though the forms of Libeskind's building are

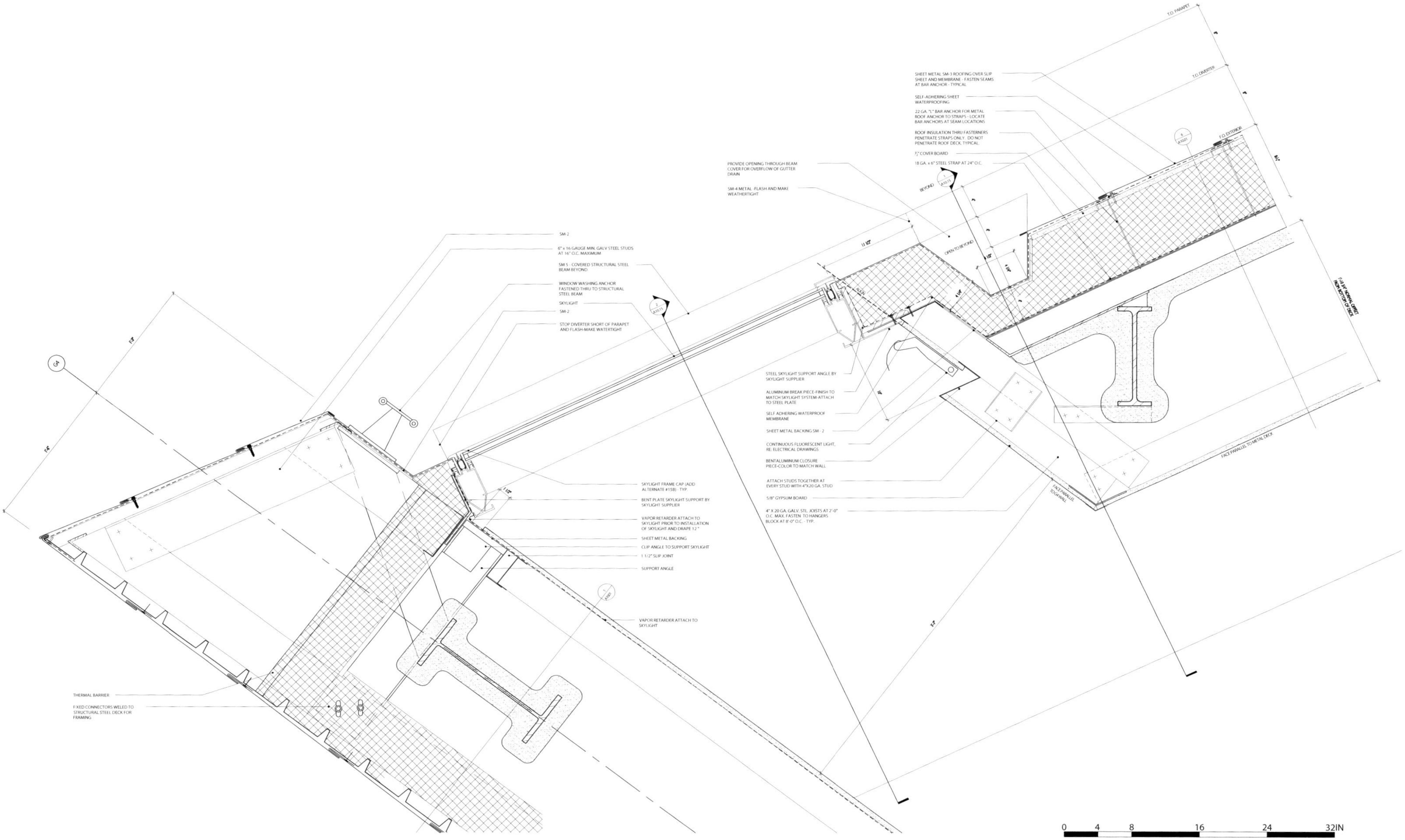

Figure 10.21 Skylight detail

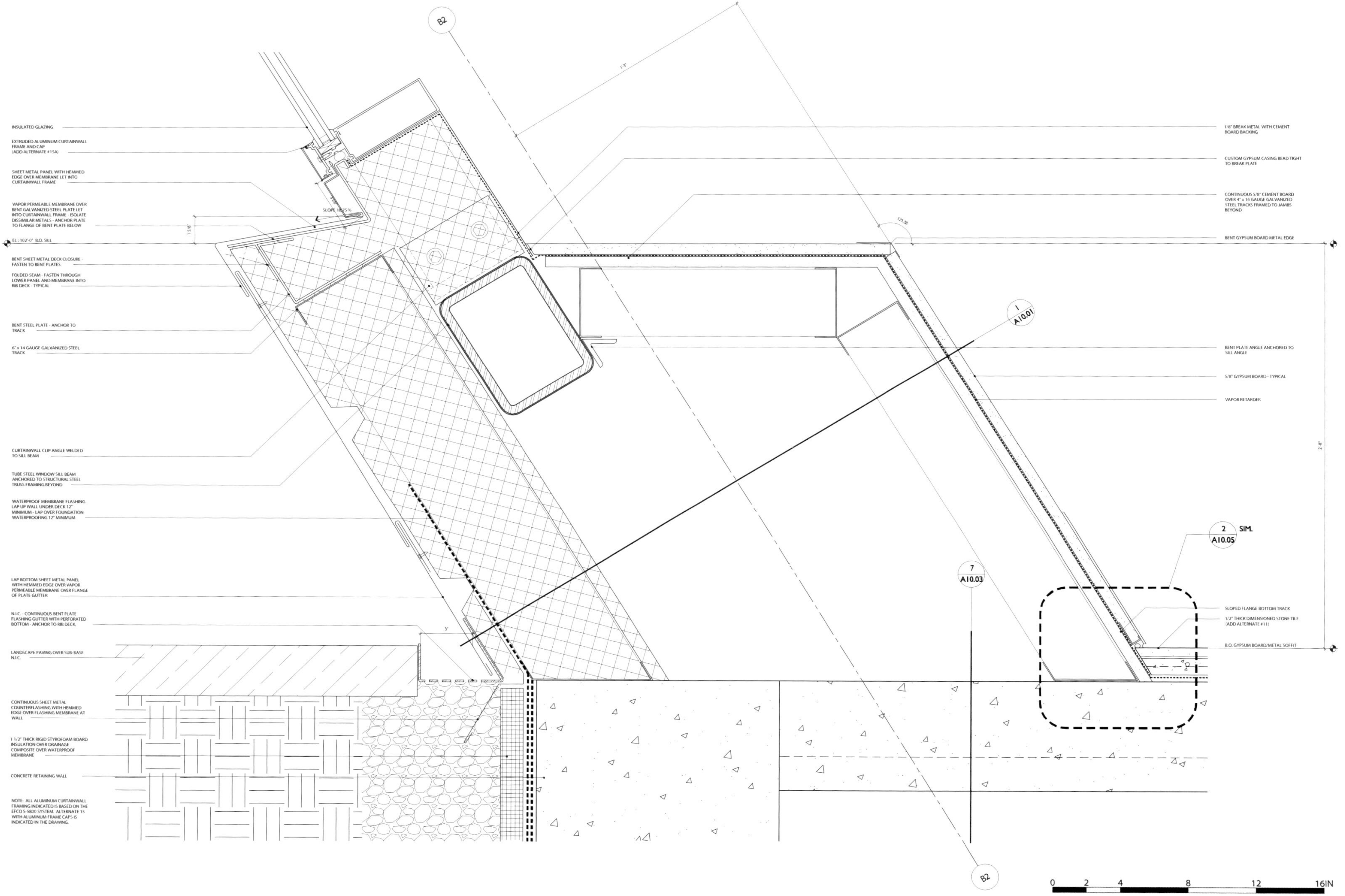

Figure 10.22 Exterior wall and window details

described as crystal-like, the reference remains metaphorical and was apparently not used as a structural inspiration. In Denver, crystals would be interpreted as solid, architectural geometries, and structure was concealed within the walls. The engineering solution for the DAM was a question of finding the structure that would make the form – and those forms not only appear unstable architecturally, but, interestingly, are inherently unstable structurally. The entire steel frame of the building generally functions as a truss but only when complete. During construction it was held in place by approximately 50 shoring towers. Vertical structure in the museum is for the most part limited to the elevator and emergency stair towers. The structure of the horizontal floors as well as the sloped roof (all composed of steel beams, metal decking, and concrete slabs) acts as diaphragms to distribute lateral loads and also function as tension ties to hold the outwardly leaning walls in place. Steel connections were complex with multiple elements of various orientations converging at single points. Structural efficiencies inspired by crystals apparently did not guide the architectural design, and the Hamilton Building is said to have used five to six times more steel than a more ordinary building with smaller spans.

Coordinating structure and mechanical systems was also a feat. Ducts are generally placed in thickened structural walls in order to move from one floor to another and then routed in dropped ceilings. Main mechanical rooms are located in the basement, a second floor volume, and a penthouse space at the top of the building. The museum is connected to a city steam and chilled water system that made boilers and chillers unnecessary, leaving more usable space in the building. Within the galleries there is a 6 by 6 m (20 by 20 ft) grid of air diffusers in the ceiling. Flexible ducts can tap into the hard ducts to provide temporary diffusers in a case where exhibition walls would obstruct air flow if built to the ceiling.

The design and execution of the structure and mechanical systems and the coordination between them relied heavily on 3-D modeling and visualization, which was also exploited to organize the complex yet rich construction process. Davis Partnership Architects in Denver were the local architects for the project. The Los Angeles office of Arup was the structural and mechanical engineer. The general contractor, Mortenson Construction, also built Frank Gehry's Walt Disney Concert Hall in Los Angeles.

There are actually few rules for the contemporary art museum, yet the DAM seems to have stretched them even farther. Museums must meet objective requirements for lighting levels, temperature, and humidity, but solutions are wide open for the spaces where visitors actually encounter and view works of art. Museum professionals often seek, or at least accept, more radical solutions. There is little that might be considered the equivalent of more objective criteria such as acoustics in a concert hall or even sight lines in a theater. The museum does not focus attention like a space for performing arts, yet it should somehow provide an appropriate viewing environment. Though proposals for exhibition spaces have been varied, museums over the past few decades have generally shared an attitude that such institutions should not be intimidating, and intimidating has often been synonymous with elitist and a bygone era of museums. The DAM does not seem elitist, but in interviews in the film *Defying Gravity* the users of the building do describe it as "intimidating." If this sentiment is shared by visitors, the solution could not be seen as a step forward in museum design.

Libeskind's spectrum of interests in architecture includes the complex, the divine, and even the universal. While the aspirations of everyone involved – the architect, the museum, and the city – were high for the new Hamilton Building, the structure has not produced an architectural shock wave like that of the Guggenheim Bilbao. Compared to the Spanish building it appears self-conscious. Architecture as a mirror of complexity can take many forms; however, the pointed shapes in Denver often simply appear unfriendly rather than complex. In the multiverse of museum architecture, the universal is a tall order.

CHAPTER 11

The Institute of Contemporary Art/Boston

Boston, Massachusetts

Diller Scofidio + Renfro

2006

Figure 11.1 View from north/east

South Boston's Seaport District was reconnected to the center of the city with the completion of the *Big Dig*, an important highway and infrastructure project that placed an imposing elevated freeway in an underground tunnel thereby making the former maritime industrial area along the harbor a prime area for revitalization. A new convention center designed by Rafael Viñoly was located in the redeveloping district and completed in 2004. A 80,940 m^2 (square meter; 20 acre) parcel known as Fan Pier sits to the east of downtown. It was owned by the Pritzker family from Chicago (of the Pritzker Prize) and was designated for offices, hotels, apartments, etc. A site within the more commercial development was reserved for a cultural building. Thus, the Institute of Contemporary Art/ Boston found its centrally located, waterfront home.

The ICA is among the oldest museums in the United States devoted exclusively to contemporary art. It began as The Boston Museum of Modern Art in 1936 but changed names 12 years later. It also changed locations several times over the years. Though not previously a collecting museum, with its new, permanent home the ICA also began a permanent collection of late twentieth- and twenty-first-century art.

The search for an architect for its first purpose-built building was narrowed to four candidates: Peter Zumthor from Switzerland, Studio Granda from Iceland, and Office d'A and Diller Scofidio + Renfro, both from the United States. Though Zumthor was seen as the favorite, D S + R were confirmed as the choice for the project after the various teams made public presentations of their work in March 2001. The ICA was the first entirely new museum to be built in Boston in almost a century, and it was also the first major building project for the office of Diller Scofidio + Renfro. Construction began in the fall of 2004 and the building opened in December 2006 (Fig 11.1).

The site where the Institute of Contemporary Art now stands is remarkable for its panoramic views of the downtown skyline and especially the Boston harbor (Fig 11.2). The architects responded to the project's unique situation, and the relationship between the building and the water is spectacular. D S + R seek to work with individual site circumstances, context, and project particularities and avoid what they call a *tabula rasa* approach. At the time of the museum's opening, however, it was one of the first new buildings in the area and it sat in a barren, blank-slate area of empty sites and surface parking which provided an extreme visibility for the museum. Several years after the ICA's opening, the immediate context continues to develop and has also been envisioned as part of an "Innovation District" that would attract entrepreneurs and startups.

Seen from the exterior, the four-story building appears as a composition of stacked cubic forms. On the east and west facades, the two side walls, there is a ribbon form that follows the floor slabs and suggests vertical continuity of interior space and potentially the visitors' path of movement (Fig 11.7, Fig 11.9, and Fig 11.12). At the top of the building, a cantilevered, all glass box houses 1,580 m^2 (17,000 ft^2 (square foot)) of galleries and is understood as the *piano nobile*. The building was organized as a progression from the ground level upward with very public spaces below and a more intimate museum above.

The cantilevered scheme was developed in order to respond to the client's desire to have all of the gallery spaces on one floor on a site too small to accommodate them if setbacks were respected. A deal was struck with the planning authorities that allowed the top floor gallery box to advance to the water's edge in exchange for a larger than required public space/setback at ground level. This space becomes an activated node along the 76 km (47 mile) long harbor walk that passes under the building.

The organization and structural system of the ensemble of the 6,040 m^2 (65,000 ft^2) project are determined in large part by the top floor. Four parallel, 7.3 m (24 ft) deep trusses, along with the eight "mega-columns" they sit on, constitute the fundamental structure, allow for the 22.9 m (75 ft) cantilever, and also define three building bays. The interior organization that results is clear and rational.

The middle bay of the building is the smallest and is devoted primarily to vertical circulation – a public stair, an elevator, a large glass freight elevator also used by the public, and an emergency stair – and the mediatheque. The mediatheque is accessed from the gallery level. It is modest in size but impressive and vertiginous because it hangs below the main volume like an open luggage bin on an airplane. Stepped platforms with computer stations descend to a 6.4 by 2.9 m (21 by 9.5 ft) window that frames only water below. The view is pleasingly disconcerting (Fig 11.19).

On the fourth floor gallery level, the two outside bays are equivalent in size and house the permanent collection along with some special exhibitions on the east side and only special exhibitions on the west side (Fig 11.6). Since the structure of the roof is a space frame, no intermediate vertical structure between the trusses was necessary. Though the space is generally an open loft and highly flexible, the galleries have been subdivided and articulated as distinct rooms that are well proportioned and provide a good viewing environment for works of most all types (Fig 11.18 and Fig 11.20). The partitions can be modified from one exhibition to another. The floor is concrete and the walls, including the exterior walls, are gypsum board generally painted white. In preliminary phases of the project, the exterior translucent glass panels were also to be visible inside and allow

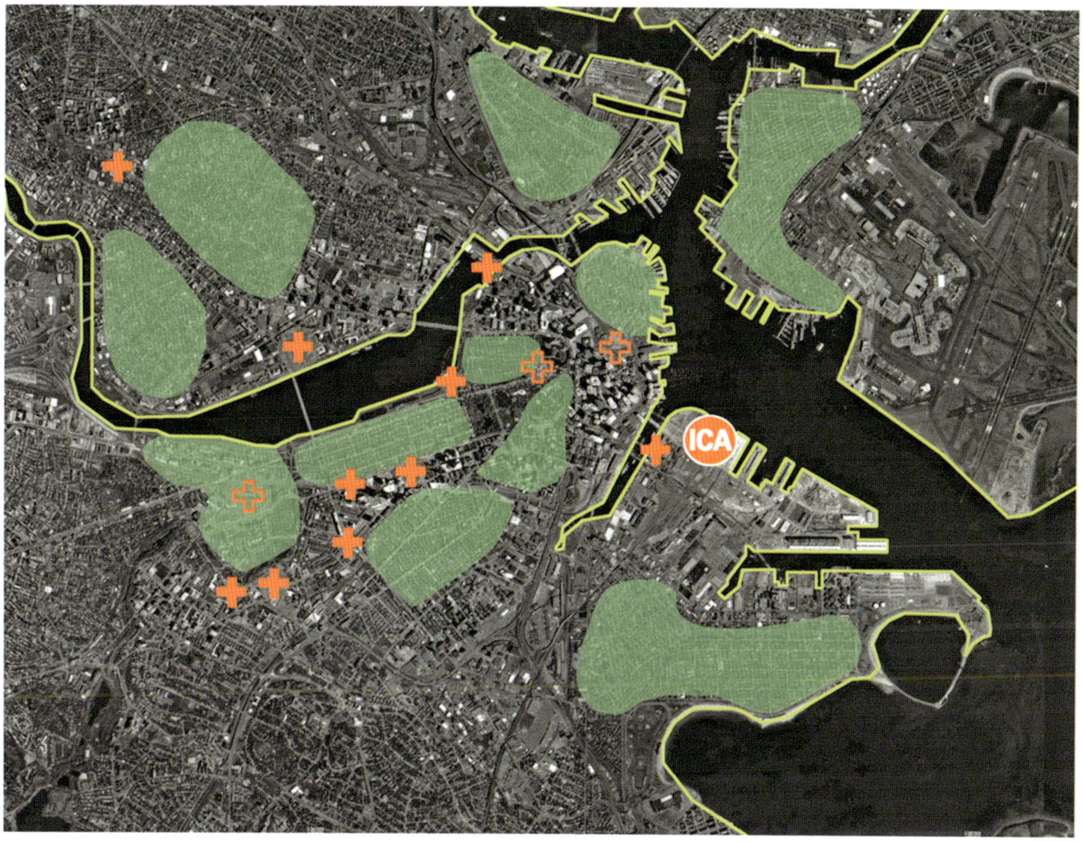

Figure 11.2 Site plans

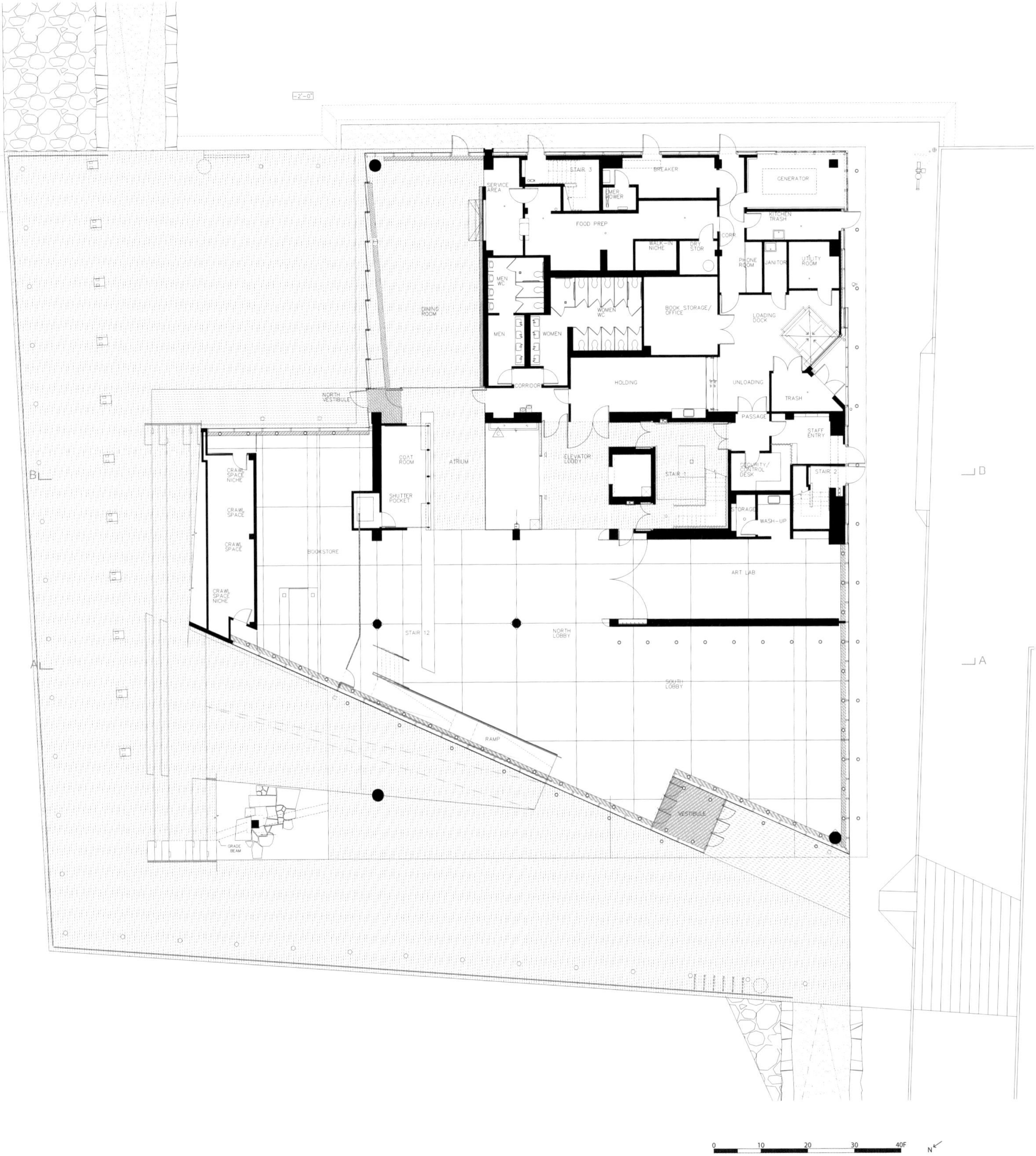

Figure 11.3: First (ground) floor plan

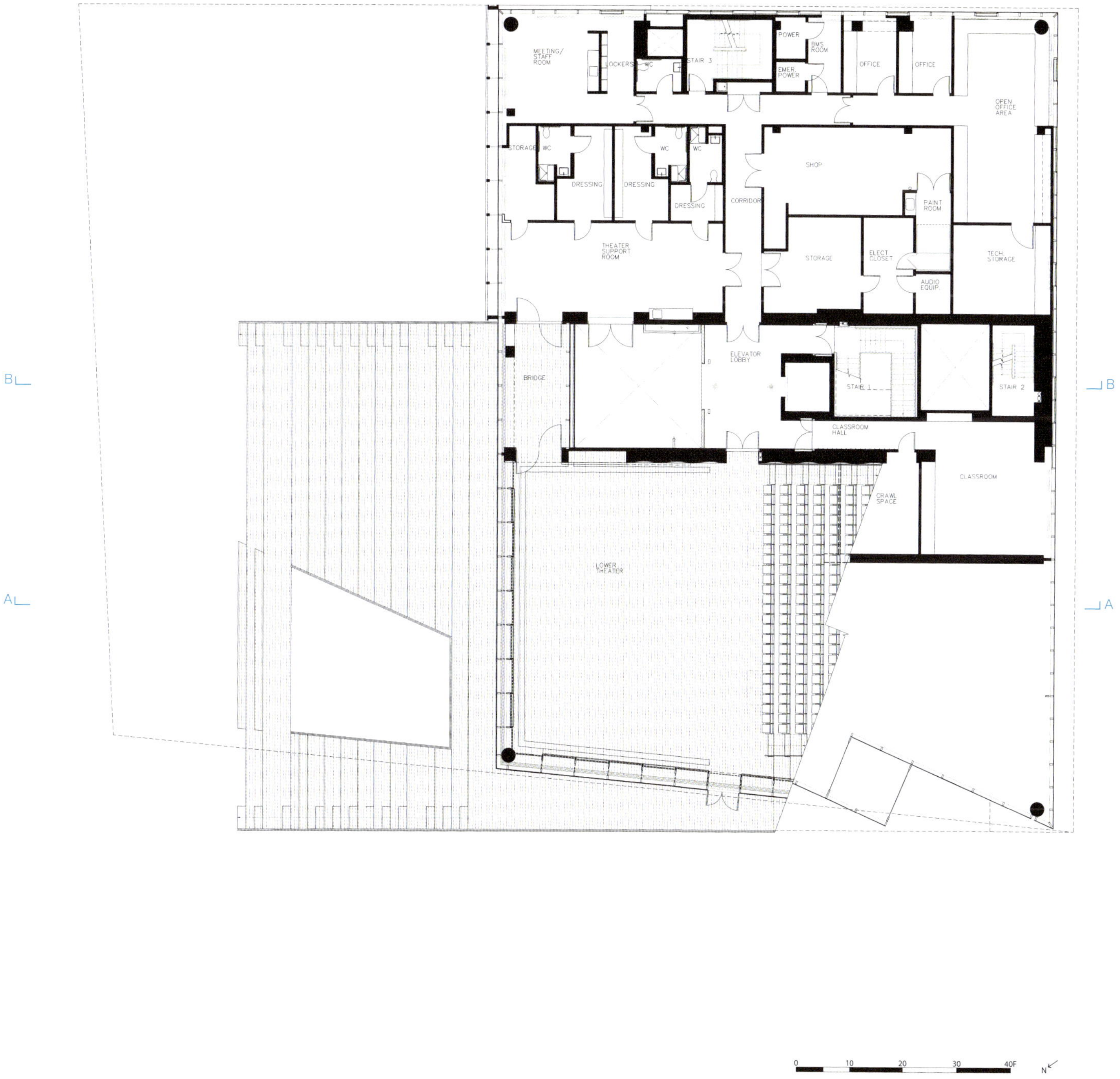

Figure 11.4 Second floor plan

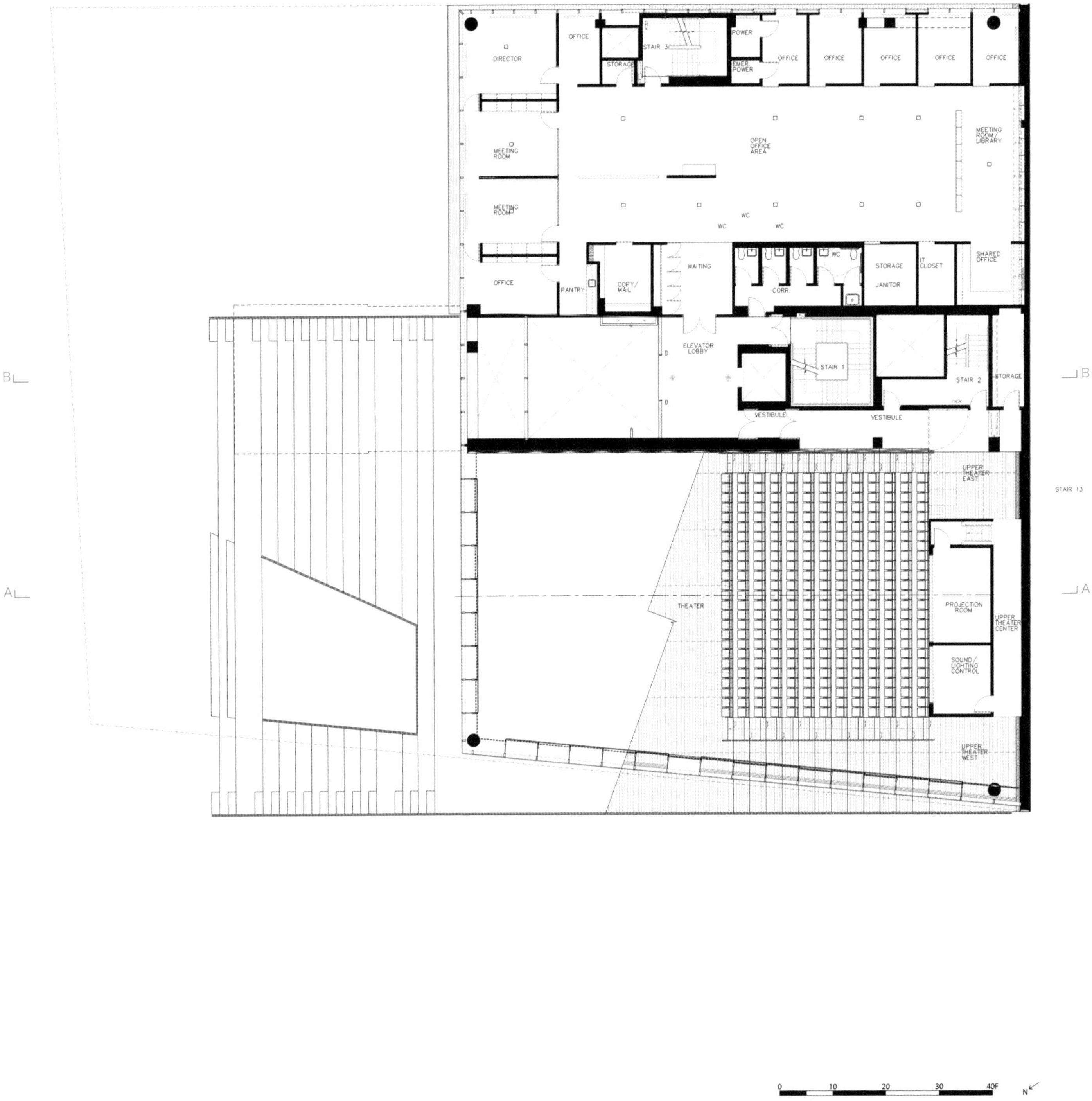

Figure 11.5 Third floor plan

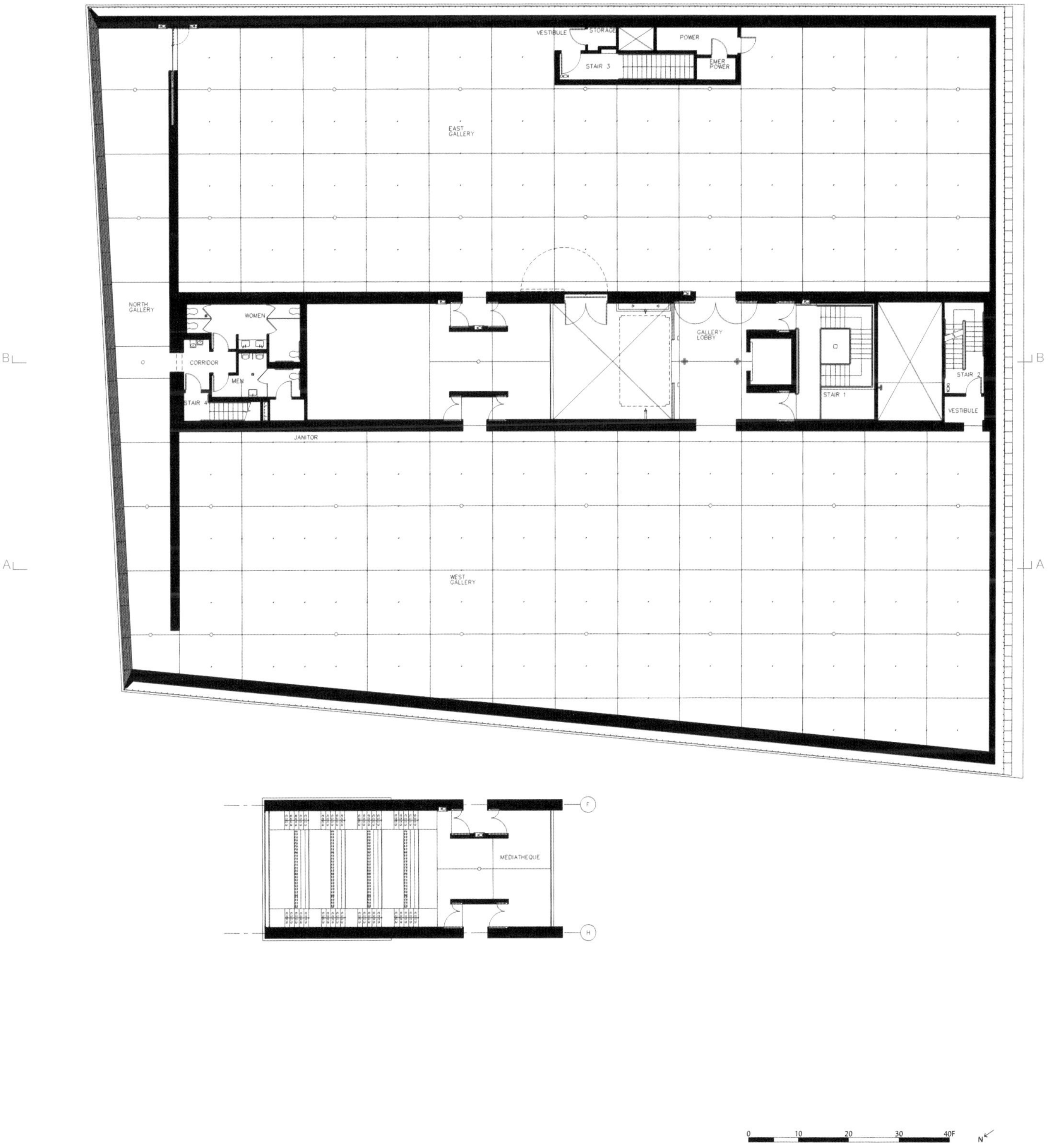

Figure 11.6 Fourth floor plan

Figure 11.7 View from south/east

Figure 11.8 Night view from north/west

light to enter into the galleries from all sides. As constructed, 33 cm (13 in.) wide, vertical glass planks are the outer layer of a rainscreen type wall composition with waterproofing assured by a PVC membrane on an opaque wall behind. The cavity of the double skin is approximately 46 cm (18 in.) thick and was conceived primarily for its aesthetic qualities. The fixtures for nighttime lighting, for example, are located within; however, the cavity was not conceived or truly exploited for its potential benefits for the thermal performance of the building.

All of the top floor gallery spaces are, nonetheless, naturally lit by 26 skylights in the form of north-facing sheds (Fig 11.22). Inside, the ceiling is at a height of 4.9 m (16 ft) and is composed of an extruded aluminum frame with integrated light tracks and sprinkler heads. The frame holds panels of stretched trevira fabric that diffuses the natural light. Roller blinds were also integrated at the level of the sheds to control or completely black out the light. Ducts run within the structure above the fabric ceiling, and air conditioning grills are integrated into the ceiling frame or in a reveal joint between the walls and the ceiling. Surfaces above the stretched fabric ceiling are reflective in order to diffuse the natural light, and artificial uplighting was also integrated within the cavity.

Natural top lighting in all of the exhibition spaces was at the request of the client. It was a fortunate choice and somewhat surprising for the temporary exhibition galleries since such spaces are often of a more generic nature and artificially lit. The lighting is uniform and a technical success. There is little hint of the outside sky, however, just as there are no windows that would allow views out of the galleries making the exhibition spaces introverted. At the ICA, the galleries should be contemplative spaces. They should not compete with the works of art, nor, at the other extreme, should they be neutral backgrounds. They are restrained spatially, in finish and material choice, and in the resolution of details. The space is homogenous and the atmosphere is generally calm and pleasant. Diller and Scofidio's relation to a museum space seemed more conflicted when their own work was displayed during a retrospective at the Whitney Museum of American Art in New York in 2003. The exhibition was entitled *Scanning: The Aberrant Architectures of Diller + Scofidio*. Among more conventional presentations of architectural projects and installations that dealt with surveillance, tourism, and home chores, there was a robotically controlled drill that could be heard throughout the gallery space and randomly bored away at the exhibition wall itself, one hole at a time, during the run of the show.

When visitors arrive on the fourth floor gallery level of the ICA they have the choice of entering the east or the west galleries. Spatially and architecturally the two are virtually the same though the west gallery is slightly larger and has an angled west wall that is hardly noticeable from within the space, and the east gallery has a block that contains mechanical, storage, and an emergency stair that creates a "bump" along the east wall. The path through both galleries is prescribed. At a certain point visitors make a turn around and through exhibition walls and unexpectedly find themselves walking the plank 15 m (50 ft) above the water level. The narrow North Gallery or Founders' Gallery most assuredly provides a surprise in the museum visit (Fig 11.21). Few if any works are exhibited there and its primary function is to provide a stunning view of the harbor and city. It also functions as a passage between the two gallery bays. An entry to restrooms is located at the middle of the space. Within the architectural promenade of the building it is literally the highpoint. The entire north wall at the end of the cantilever is mullion-less glass. The insulated units are divided vertically into three panels and held in place by a system of suspended glass fins and stainless steel fittings. Joints between the glass panels are silicone. D S + R specified a lenticular film for the glass facade that would allow views out when viewed perpendicularly and mask the view when viewed obliquely. They had previously used a similar film for

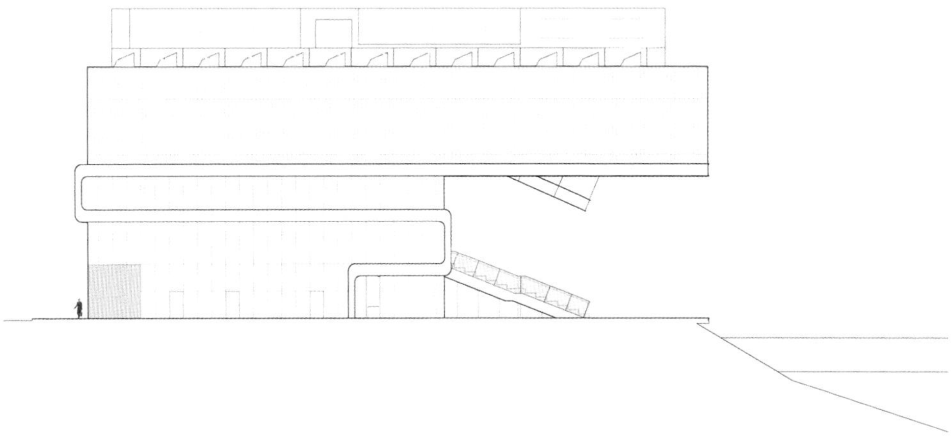

Figure 11.9 Elevation 1

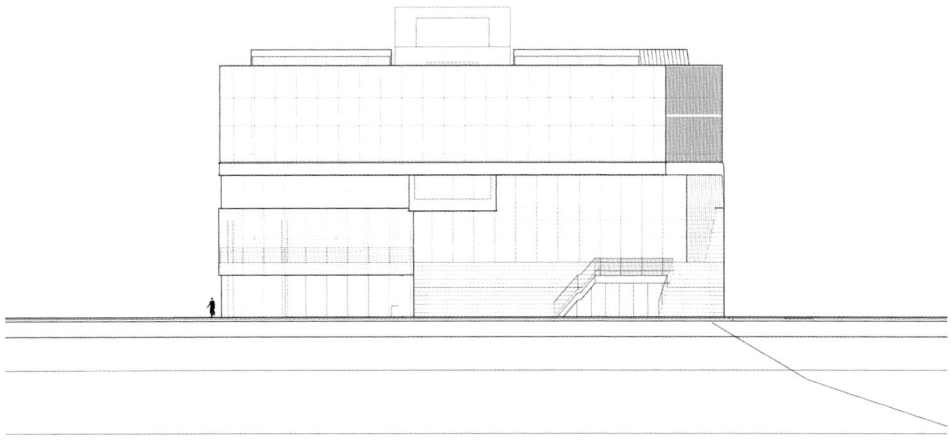

Figure 11.10 Elevation 2

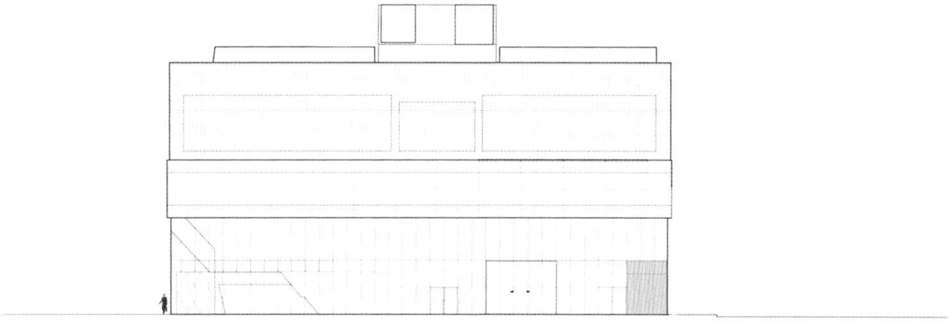

Figure 11.11 Elevation 3

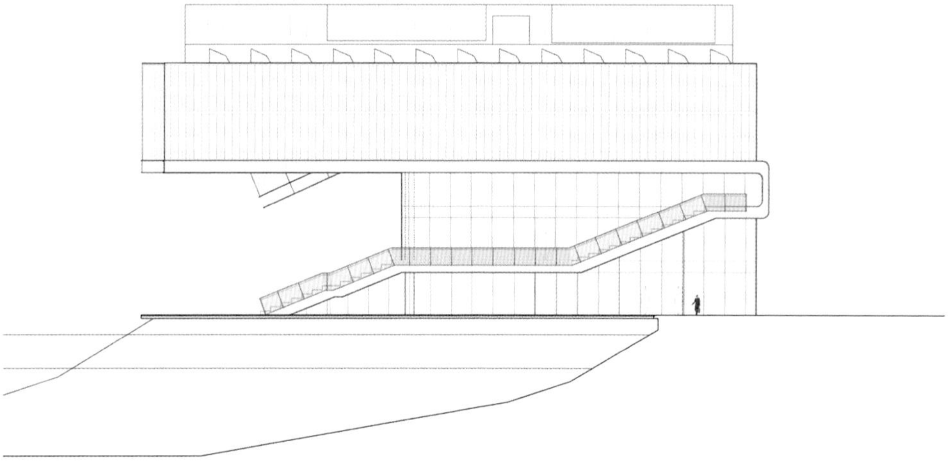

Figure 11.12 Elevation 4

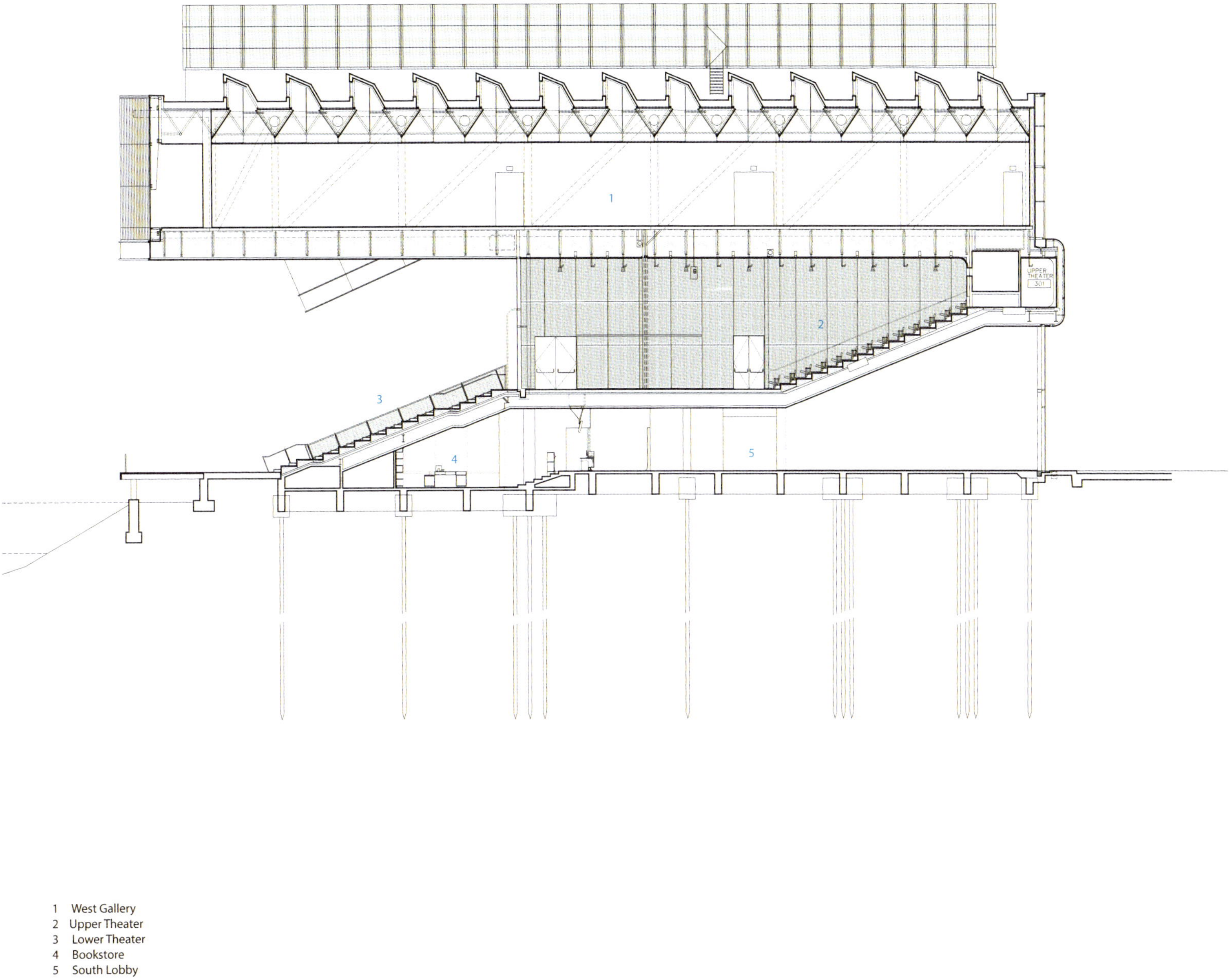

1 West Gallery
2 Upper Theater
3 Lower Theater
4 Bookstore
5 South Lobby

Figure 11.13 Section A

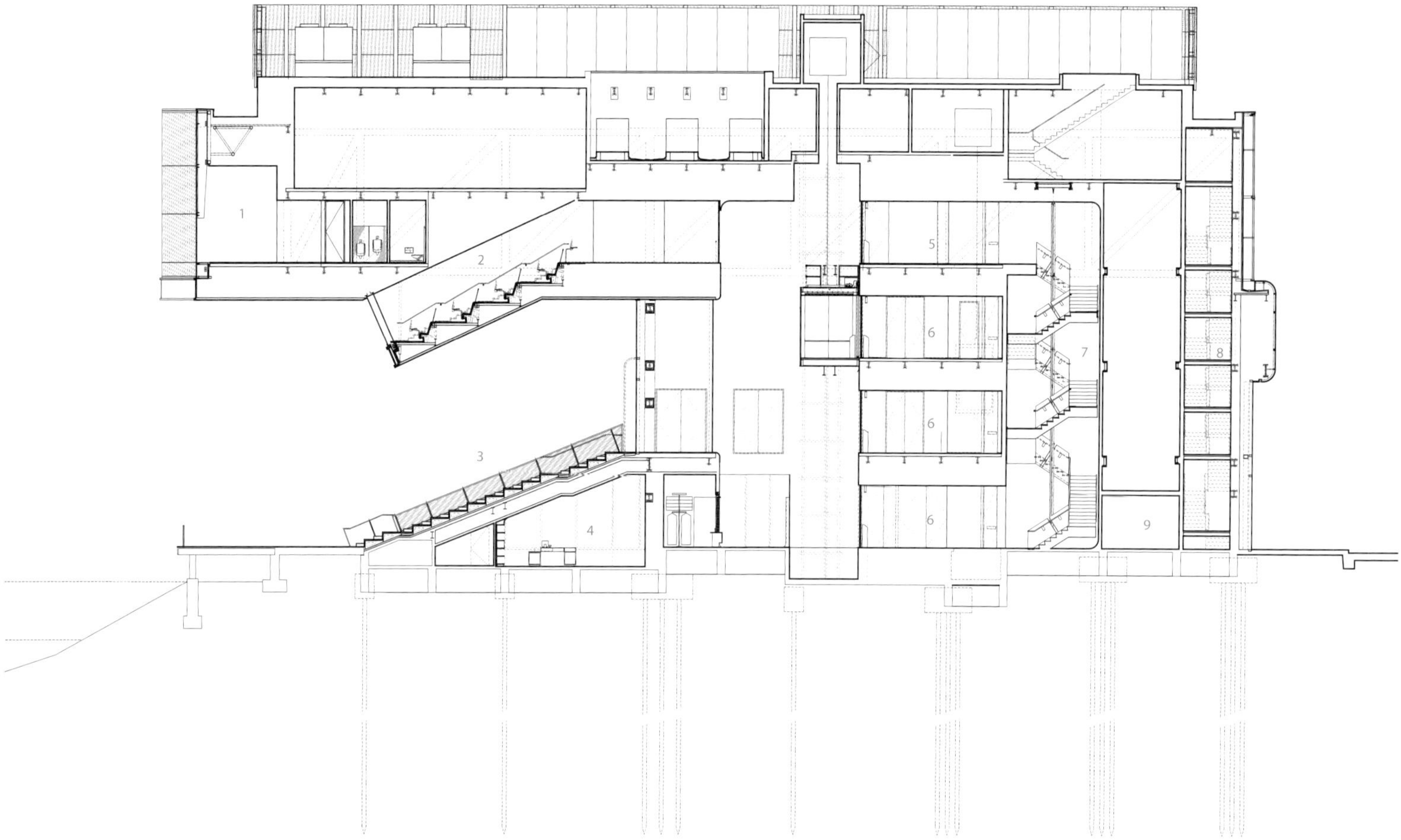

1 North Gallery
2 Bridge
3 Lower Theater
4 Bookstore
5 Gallery Lobby
6 Elevator Lobby
7 Stairs 1
8 Stairs 2
9 Security Control Room

Figure 11.14 Section B

decorative effects in their Brasserie restaurant project at the base of the Seagram Building in New York City. In Boston the film was to create a blurred effect, unveiling the view little by little. The film was opposed by the mayor and was not installed.

High perched spaces for views have become common in many museums from the de Young in San Francisco to the Kunsthaus Graz, the Reina Sofía in Madrid, the New Museum in New York, the Acropolis Museum in Athens, or the MAXXI in Rome. Sometimes they are virtually autonomous from the museum such as at the de Young. Sometimes they are linked to a special events space or a cafe such as at the Reina Sofía or the New Museum. Other times the view is from a major gallery space such as at the Acropolis Museum or the MAXXI. At the ICA the North Gallery is for the most part inevitable within the museum itinerary. It is less an exhibition space than an exhilarating pause between the two major galleries that in itself can "delight and disturb the senses" as the architects seek to do.

At lower levels, the double-height volume of the second and third floors (Fig 11.4 and Fig 11.5) of the west bay (just under the temporary exhibition galleries) is occupied by a 483 m^2 (5,200 ft^2), 325 seat theater that was included in the program to better include and promote the performing and media arts (Fig 11.17). The space is column free and suspended from the trusses above. It can be accessed from both the second and third floors. Within the space, circulation is along the side walls and a control and projection booth is located at the top. The theater has an informal and experimental quality, and more surprisingly, it is totally glazed on two sides: to the north, behind the 15 m (50 ft) wide stage space, the view to the harbor is capped by the cantilevered volume of the gallery box that floats above, and to the west the view is to the skyline of downtown Boston. All of the windows are equipped with two blinds: one for shading and the other for blackout. From the exterior, the activities inside can easily be seen, especially at night.

The corresponding bays on the east side of the building are private spaces. On the second floor, at the theater stage level, there are dressing rooms and other support spaces for the theater as well as offices, meeting rooms, a workshop, mechanical, storage, etc. There is no significant space for on-site art storage. The third floor is devoted to administrative offices and meeting rooms. The second and third floors of the east bay do not contain functions that require large, open spaces, and the structure here is more conventional with intermediate columns that reduce spans.

At ground level (Fig 11.3) the entry space is located in the west bay of the building under the slope of the theater (Fig 11.15). The space lacks generosity and gives the unfortunate impression of arriving by the back side. The glazing of the south wall has a frit pattern on the glass that gives a blurred effect when looking out, and the tall, triangular, east wall is reserved for specifically commissioned art works. A counter for ticket sales and coat check is directly in front of the entrance with the museum store just behind and a few steps down.

A link through the middle bay leads to the cafe on the east side with a glass facade that can slide open to a large wood terrace that borders the water and is sheltered by the gallery box above. The cafe and terrace are lively spaces and surely an asset to the harbor walk. The rest of the ground floor east bay is occupied by food preparation, restrooms, service spaces, and the loading dock. In general, the layout of the building is compact at all floor levels without superfluous or oversized spaces.

As mentioned above, the middle bay is primarily devoted to vertical circulation, and the most spectacular, albeit slow, means of moving to the upper floors is the large, all glass freight elevator (Fig 11.16). The 13 m^2 (140 ft^2) moving room is used for the transportation of works of art and other large objects as well as by the public. It has a playful quality, like a carnival ride, allowing glimpses and changing views to the outside and within the building for visitors going up and down.

Figure 11.15 Interior lobby

Figure 11.16 Interior freight elevator

Figure 11.17 Interior theater

Figure 11.18 Interior gallery

Figure 11.19 Interior Mediatheque

Figure 11.20 Interior gallery

Figure 11.21 Interior north gallery

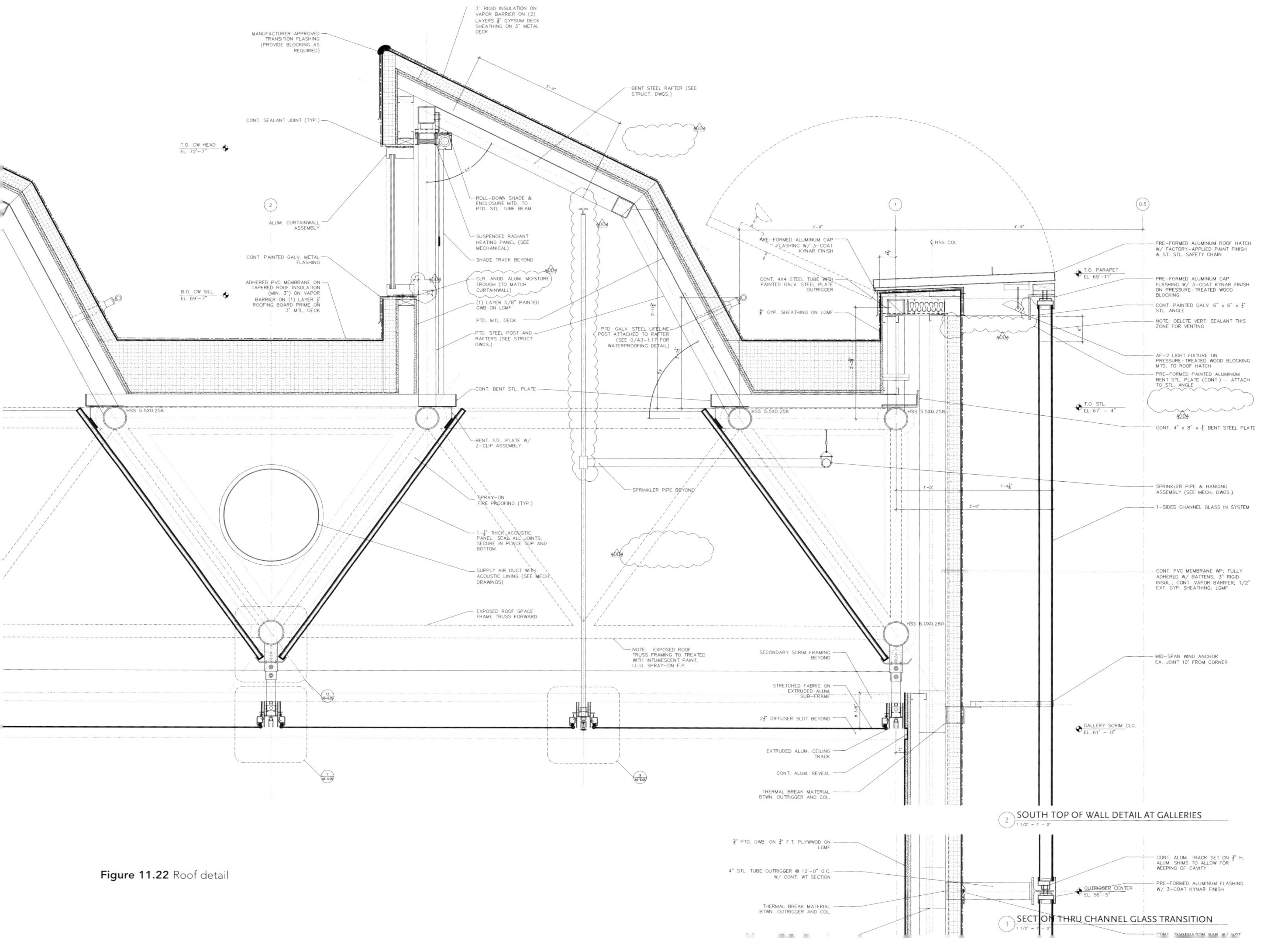

Figure 11.22 Roof detail

Diller Scofidio + Renfro's project is based on vision as the master sense. Circulation is choreographed. Space is scripted. Context is framed. The site is revealed in controlled doses with views turned on or off – opened or denied. Architecture and art should not compete, and museum visitors are assumed to be in a state of increased awareness that the building might help to promote and in turn might magnify the experience of the architecture itself.

The ICA's relation to the water and views is frank. The building clearly fronts the harbor and we imagine an ideal arrival from the waterside, much like an arrival at San Giorgio Maggiore in Venice where visitors may move from a boat, up the stair, and into the building, all in a continuous procession (Fig 11.10). In Boston, access from the waterside appears possible but is in fact blocked. We are inclined to climb the grand stair (the grandstand), but the glass facade at the top has no doors. We are left peering into the theater but unable to enter. Though there is a strong frontal relationship with the water to the north, the actual entry is on the other side of the building. From a practical point of view, limiting the points of entry into the museum is understandable; nonetheless, the result is frustrating and counters expectations and is primarily the consequence of the formal gesture of the "ribbon." Visually, the ribbon is most complete on the west facade where it comes to the ground. For pragmatic reasons, however, it cannot offer physical access directly into the theater. Conceptually, the ribbon should provide spatial continuity. In reality, it disallows it. The entry space, for example, cannot benefit from the harbor view nor have a direct connection with the main urban space along the harbor walk since it is squeezed *under* the ribbon. This makes for a marked distinction between public outdoor space and private indoor space. The form seems to be a vestige of earlier investigations and projects such as Diller Scofidio + Renfro's unrealized Eyebeam Museum of Art and Technology from 2004.

The ribbon form is more evident on the west (theater) side since the infill facade above and below is transparent glass, well recessed behind the plane of the ribbon. On the east side the lower three floors are clad in transparent, translucent, or opaque vertical panels inserted only slightly behind the plane of the ribbon. On the east facade the ribbon appears even more as a graphic treatment. The entry facade to the south (Fig 11.7 and Fig 11.11) seems penalized since it is largely opaque with multiple service doors as well as the loading dock.

Inside the building the ribbon is virtually invisible. In some places it becomes a decorative curve linking floor, wall, and ceiling but disconnected from the exterior form. The continuity of inside and outside space is reinforced, however, by the mahogany wood used for the deck along the harbor walk, the grandstand, the theater floor, and the underside of the gallery box. The wood softens the otherwise metal and glass aspect of the building and is a nod to the wooden architecture of New England.

Sitting atop the central bay of the gallery box is the main mechanical equipment for the entire building. Since there is not a basement, the location, above the servant bay that is sandwiched by two served bays, is perfectly logical when envisioned as part of a mechanical diagram for the project. Its handling makes less visual sense within the overall composition of the building, however. There was little attempt to attenuate the presence of the roof-top equipment or somehow integrate it into the mass of the building. The surrounding dark gray screen transforms it into one large cubic element that vies with the floating glass box below. Its presence and visual impact seem to have been ignored.

For Diller Scofidio + Renfro, projects are derived from site and situation and should be based on concepts rather than formal tendencies. Perhaps the ungainly, top-heavy nature of the ICA illustrates their desire to defy an image of stability and permanence in architecture just as the oversized lantern quality of the building lit at night would affirm an interest in the ephemeral (Fig 11.8). Day or night, inside or outside, the Institute of Contemporary Art/Boston is an exercise in Diller Scofidio + Renfro's notion of architecture as a special effects machine.

CHAPTER 12

The Nelson-Atkins Museum of Art Bloch Building

Kansas City, Missouri

Steven Holl Architects

2007

Figure 12.1 View from north – Lens 2–5

Figure 12.2 Gallery watercolor by Steven Holl

The relatively recent and previously unknown phenomenon of large amounts of light in a city at night is important for Steven Holl because it modifies the perception of individual buildings as well as the larger urban space. A structure or space that is gray by day can glow or radiate in the dark. Night light combined with rain or fog or mist, for example, can produce mysterious effects never experienced before the twentieth century. To shape light is to give new experience. Such matters of perception and phenomenology are at the center of Holl's architectural preoccupations. His extension to the Nelson-Atkins Museum of Art in Kansas City, the Bloch Building, is an iconic illustration of his approach and interests (Fig 12.1).

The original Nelson-Atkins building is a monumental, neoclassical structure realized in 1933 by the architect Thomas Wight with his brother William. Both trained in the office of McKim, Mead, and White. Their limestone-clad museum is to the south of downtown Kansas City and dominates a 89,000 m^2 (square meter; 22 acre) park. In the late 1980s the outdoor spaces were redesigned by the landscape architect Dan Kiley and Jaquelin Robertson. The garden space to the south of the building is now the Kansas City Sculpture Park, where an ever-expanding collection of modern and contemporary sculptures is displayed on the terraced lawns that form a forecourt for the building.

Inside the Wight building, a central, double-story entry space, Kirkwood Hall, traverses the building and divides it in two. Originally the east side was the Atkins Museum of Fine Arts and the west side was the Nelson Gallery of Art. It was only in 1983 that the institution fused into the Nelson-Atkins Museum of Art. The Rozzelle Court, a double-story space on the west side of the building, houses a restaurant, and a long sculpture gallery on the east side now makes the link with the Bloch Building. The galleries that surround these major spaces are introverted and have few openings to the outside. The Nelson-Atkins collection is encyclopedic with one of the most important collections of Asian art in the United States. Wight's building was also renovated as part of the larger project for the museum that included Holl's extension.

In 1999 the Nelson-Atkins invited six architects Tadao Ando, Gigon/Guyer, Steven Holl, Carlos Jimenez, Machado/Silvetti, and Christian de Portzamparc to compete for the design of a 15,330 m^2 (165,000 ft^2 (square foot)) extension. The competition encouraged the architects to place an addition in an open space in front of the north facade of Wight's building. Because of its orientation, the elevation was generally perceived as somber, and it was also little flattered by the nondescript parking lot that occupied the space it faced. The goal of a new project was to make the entire museum livelier and more welcoming. After two days of site visits and orientation sessions, each architect was asked to produce a 50-page sketchbook describing ideas and intentions for the expansion. Holl was inspired by an inscription on the Wight building that says "The Soul Has More Need for the Ideal than the Real." This encouraged Holl and Chris McVoy, Senior Partner and Partner in Charge of the project, to present a design that they felt better suited – or was more ideal for – the situation. Of the six competitors, Holl and McVoy were the only ones *not* to present a scheme to the north of the Wight building. Instead, their proposal placed an elongated extension perpendicular to the original building and to the east in an area that should have remained untouched (Fig 12.3). They also focused on revitalizing the "competition area" while maintaining the north facade of Wight's building intact and visible. They won the competition.

The site plan developed by Holl is intelligent and elegant. The Wight building maintains its central position with both of its principle facades, south and north, untouched. The grand sculpture park is likewise undisturbed. The north side of the site was reconfigured into a lawn and a granite paved plaza where cars are allowed to enter for drop-off and pick-up. The plaza wraps around a site-specific, 41 by 49 m (134 by 161 ft) reflecting pool/sculpture by the artist Walter De Maria, *One Sun/34 Moons*, that sits atop an underground parking lot. The pool is slightly off axis with the earlier building and is shifted toward the new one. A rectangular sun, flat and golden, appears to hover above the surface of the water. At the bottom of the pool there are 34 skylights or moons sprinkled around the slightly curved, gilt bronze sun. Each 91 cm (36 in.) circular moon is lit with neon from the parking garage below. The simplicity and austerity of the new plaza and De Maria's sculpture harmonize perfectly with both buildings, Wight's and Holl's, and become the functional and compositional link of the ensemble (Fig 12.6).

Holl's Bloch Building appears as five autonomous glass volumes placed in the narrow, sloped space between the Nelson-Atkins Building and Rockhill Road to the east (Fig 12.10). In reality it is one, continuous, 256 m (840 ft) long structure with the lower volumes between the glass volumes covered by planted roofs totaling 3,530 m^2 (38,000 ft^2). The planted roof system provides insulation and thermal mass and assists with storm water management. Early design sketches explored the possibility of water between the glass forms rather than grass. Water would have rendered the often-made comparison to icebergs more literal with the glass structures only the tip of something larger that exists below the surface. Holl named the glass volumes "lenses" since they gather light for gallery spaces below. The first and tallest lens (Lens 1) at the northern extremity is the most orthogonal and the most building-like. It sits on the pavement, responds volumetrically to the original building, closes the court on the east side, and has entry doors. The four other lenses are at the

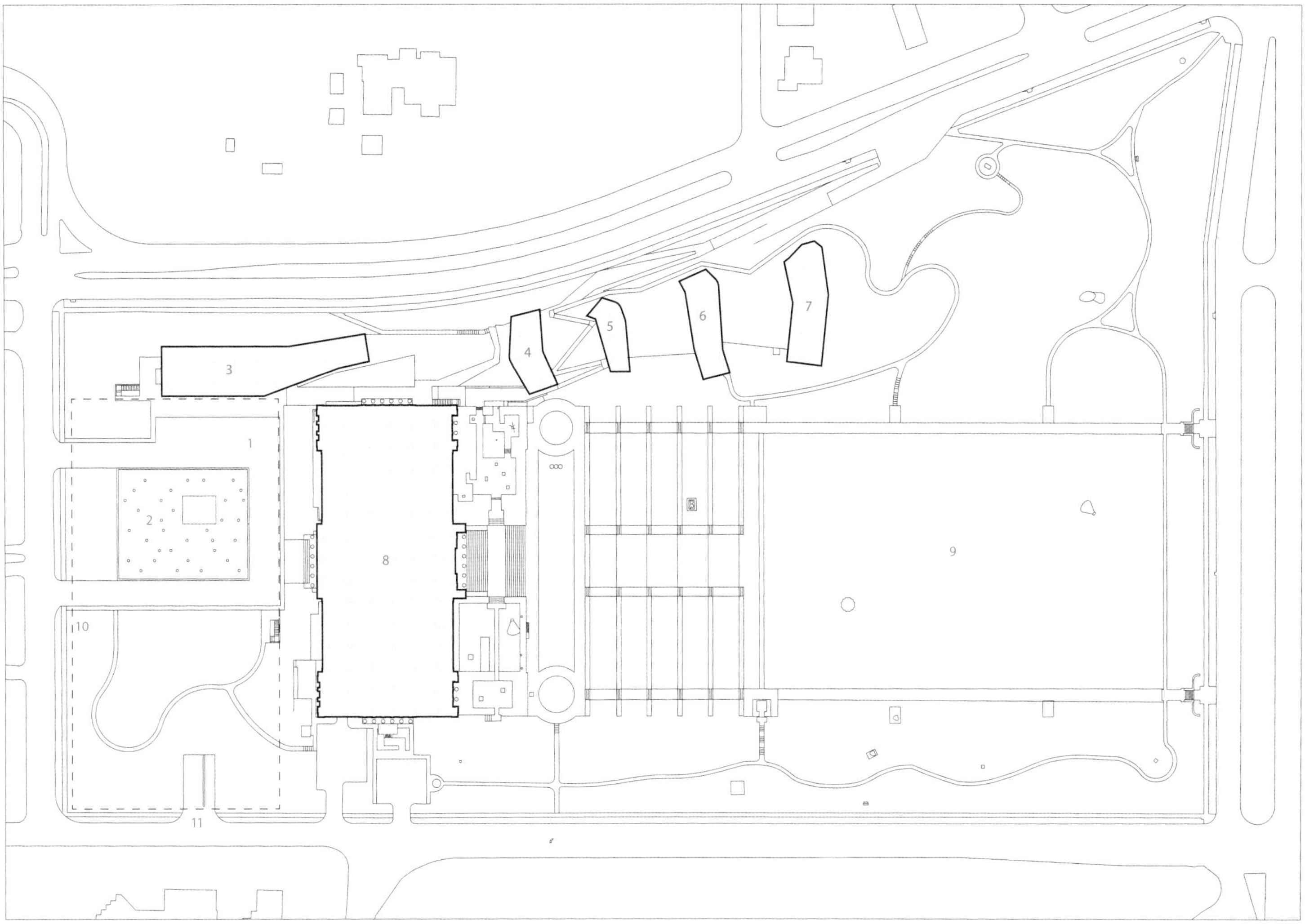

1 Entry Plaza
2 Reflecting Pool
3 Lens 1 Lobby
4 Lens 2
5 Lens 3
6 Lens 4
7 Lens 5
8 Original Museum
9 Sculpture Park Lawn
10 Garage Below
11 Garage Entrance

Figure 12.3 Site plan

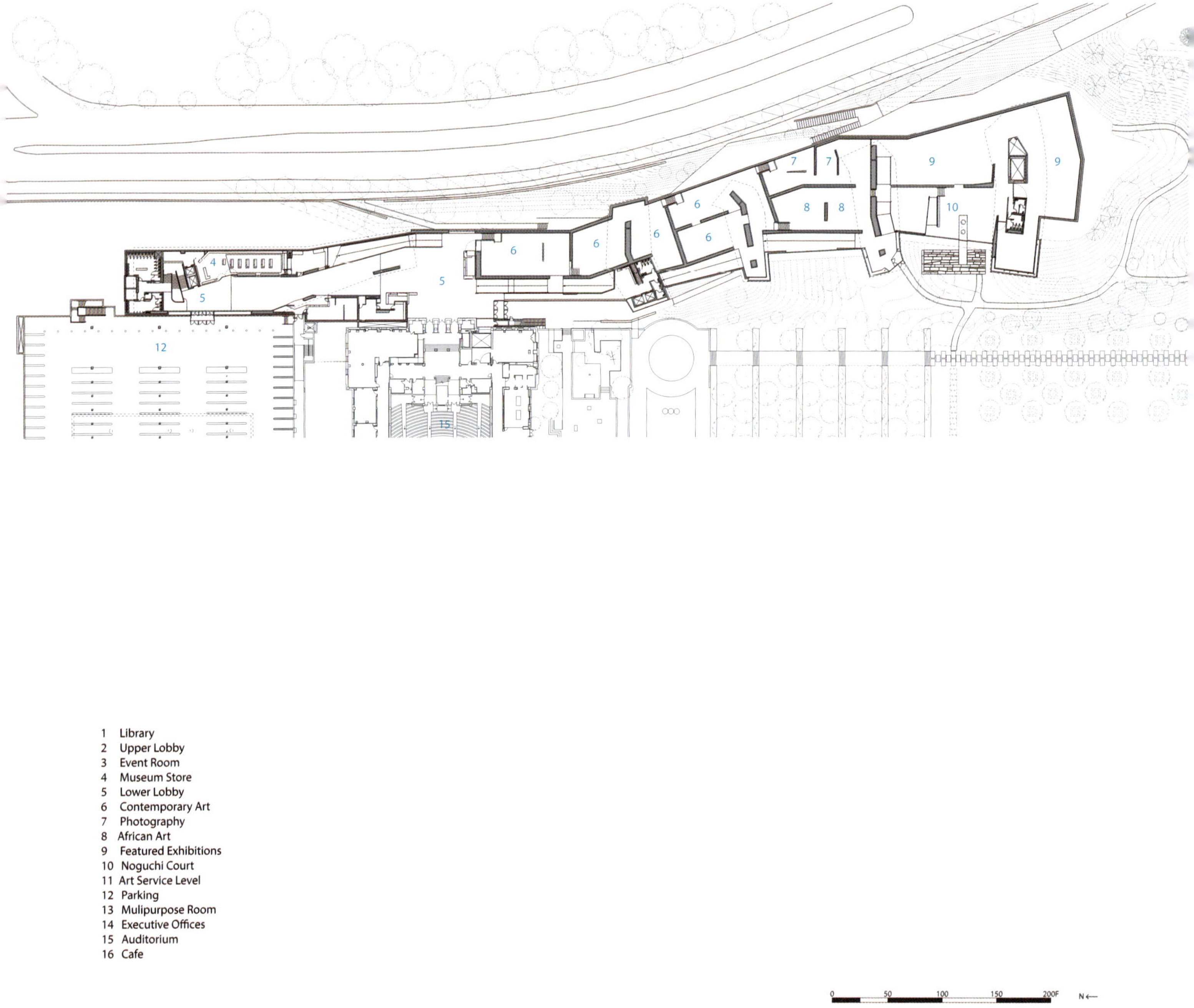

Figure 12.4 First (ground) floor plan

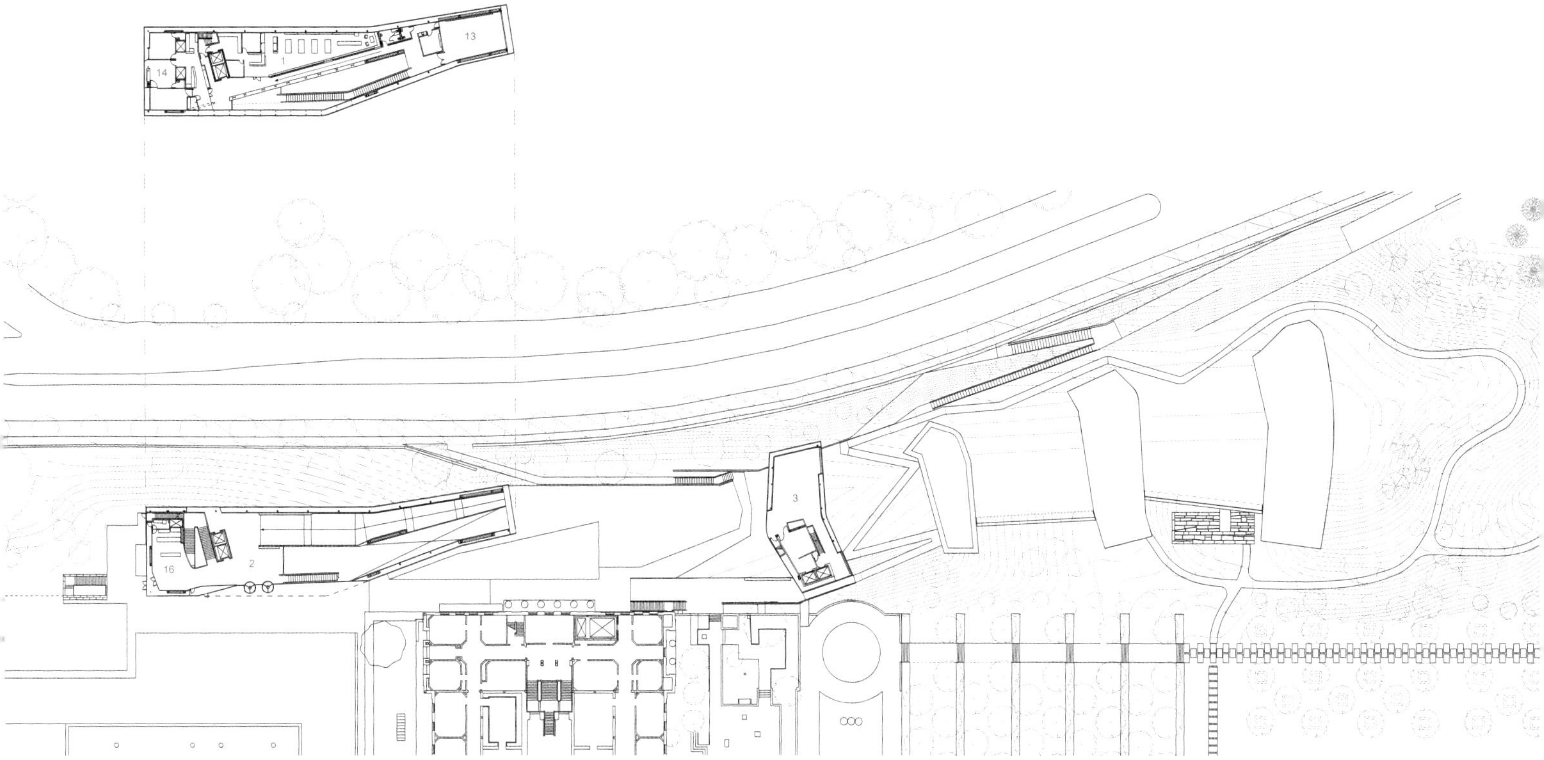

1 Library
2 Upper Lobby
3 Garden Dining Room
4 Museum Store
5 Lower Lobby
6 Contemporary Art
7 Photography
8 African Art
9 Featured Exhibitions
10 Noguchi Court
11 Art Service Level
12 Parking
13 Mulipurpose Room
14 Executive Offices
15 Auditorium
16 Cafe

0 50 100 150 200F N←

Figure 12.5 Second and third floor plans

same time architecture, landscape, and sculpture. Holl and McVoy meant for the project to be a fusion of landscape and architecture. The lenses appear to be set into the ground and become more formally liberated as they progress toward the garden to the south.

To the west of the entry court are the ramp down to the new, two-level parking garage, a delivery area, mechanical equipment masked by vegetation, and a tall ventilation chimney for other mechanical rooms below grade.

From the outside the project is more abstract than sensual. The lawns on the planted roofs between the lenses are impeccable and appear more architectural than natural (Fig 12.7). Only a narrow stainless steel gutter separates the grass from the glass planks of the facades (Fig 12.23). Since the east side merges with the slope (Fig 12.8 and Fig 12.11) while the west side opens to the garden (Fig 12.9 and Fig 12.12), the lower parts of the building are quasi invisible from Rockhill Road. Retaining walls made of concrete and dry stacked stone mix with the plantings to give a more tactile impression. The concrete is horizontally striated and imprinted with wood strip formwork of varying depths giving a strong texture to the wall. Public sidewalks merge with ramped paths that lead up to the outdoor sculpture galleries on the planted roofs.

Holl often uses metaphors or symbolic parallels to describe the concepts for his projects. These have ranged from such cryptic terms as "sliced porosity" to "linked hybrid" to simply "sponge." These expressions should suggest the main theme that will drive a design. In Kansas City, Holl and McVoy arrived at an idea of "complementary contrast" that was expressed through "the stone and the feather." The stone is the original Nelson-Atkins Building; the feather is the new Bloch Building. The contrasts are between heavy and light, opacity and transparency, stable and dynamic,

Figure 12.6 View from north/west – Lens 1

Figure 12.7 View from south/east – Lens 1–4

Figure 12.8 View from east/Rockhill Road – Lens 1

Figure 12.9 View from south/west – Lens 2–5

directed versus open circulation, single mass versus multiple lenses ... The concept of stone and feather guided design choices concerning space, light, form, landscape, materials, etc.

Since the Nelson-Atkins is free of charge, it allowed for multiple entry points and physical links between the galleries and the sculpture garden. Since, however, almost everyone arrives by car, the main entrance is inevitably through the underground parking garage. In car-oriented cities this sometimes means that visitors literally never see the exterior of a museum building. Car access was, nevertheless, well handled. The entry ramp is from Oak Street to the west and is opposite Lens 1 (Fig 12.14). The lens is visible across *One Sun/34 Moons* from a car at the top of the ramp, and its lower level quickly becomes visible again upon descending to the first parking level. This significantly helps orientation. The parking garage of 500 places is well done and an impressive space in itself with a structure of precast undulating concrete "Wave T's" that measure 18 by 3.65 m (60 by 12 ft) and sit on concrete columns and the concrete perimeter walls. The weight of the panels was reduced by casting the concrete around a 61 cm (24 in.), circular Styrofoam core. The first underground level is lit by the 34 moons of De Maria's sculpture. The beams of light passing through the water and skylights give a pleasant and surprising ripple effect within the space.

Unlike his earlier projects for the Kiasma Museum of Contemporary Art in Helsinki or the Bellevue Arts Museum in Washington State, Holl avoided the formula of a central atrium for the Bloch Building mainly due to its elongated plan. Entry into the original Nelson-Atkins Kirkwood Hall from the plaza is still possible. Entry into the Bloch Building from the plaza is through revolving doors into the upper lobby of Lens 1 where there is a cafe to the left and to the right a long stair along the facade that leads up to a library, offices, and a multipurpose room on the second floor (Fig 12.5). Entry into the Bloch Building from the underground parking is through the lower lobby of Lens 1 where a shop and cloakroom are located. Ramps from both Lens 1 entry levels meet at an intermediate lobby level to the south where the main reception area and ticket sales for temporary exhibition are located (Fig 12.16). This space is on the long axis of the original building, and a very logical and comfortable link was made between the old and the new. (Fig 12.15). The limestone wall and what were the side entrance doors of the Nelson-Atkins become part of the new lobby space.

Lens 1 is white and luminous. Inside the lobby we are surrounded by the same translucent glass we saw outside, and exterior form and interior space correspond. Though no works of art were displayed in the space for many years, some sculptures are now exhibited.

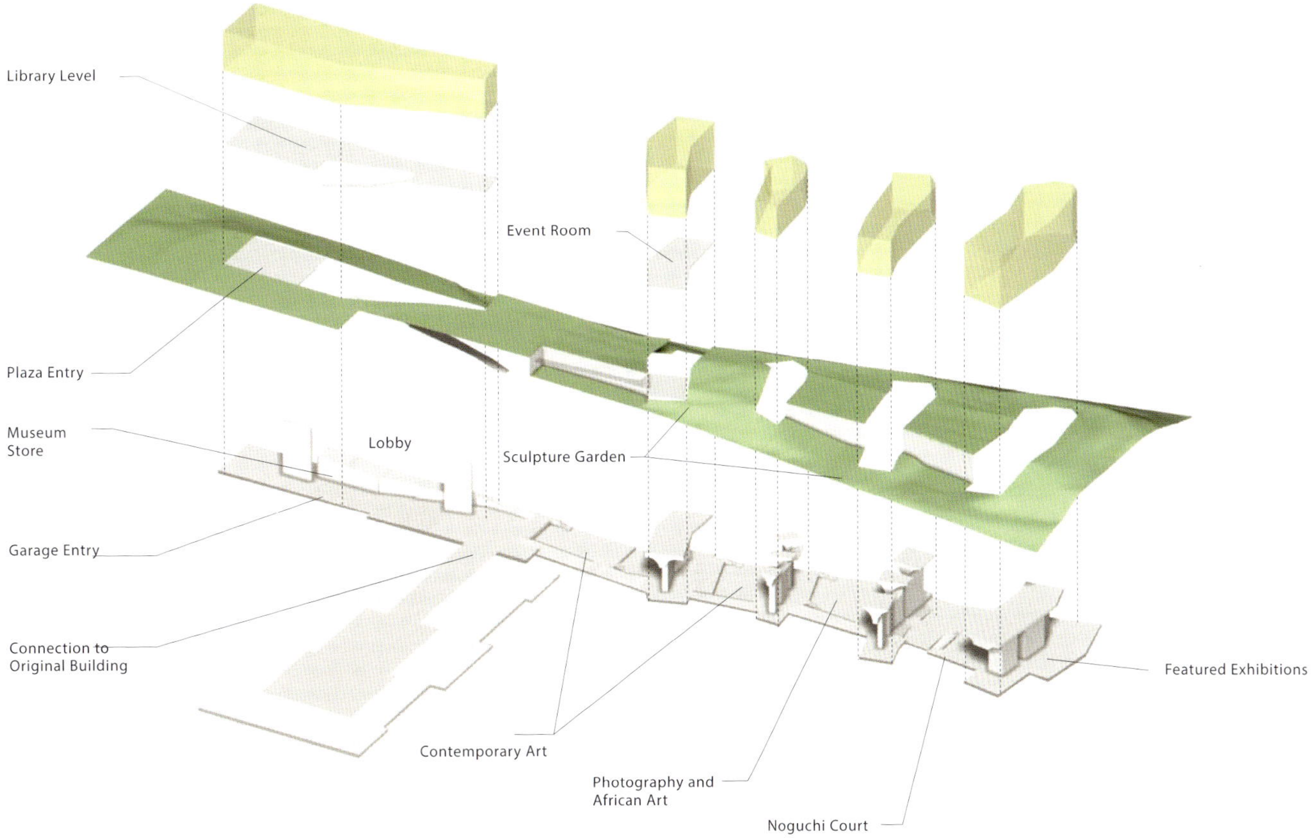

Figure 12.10 Axonometric diagram

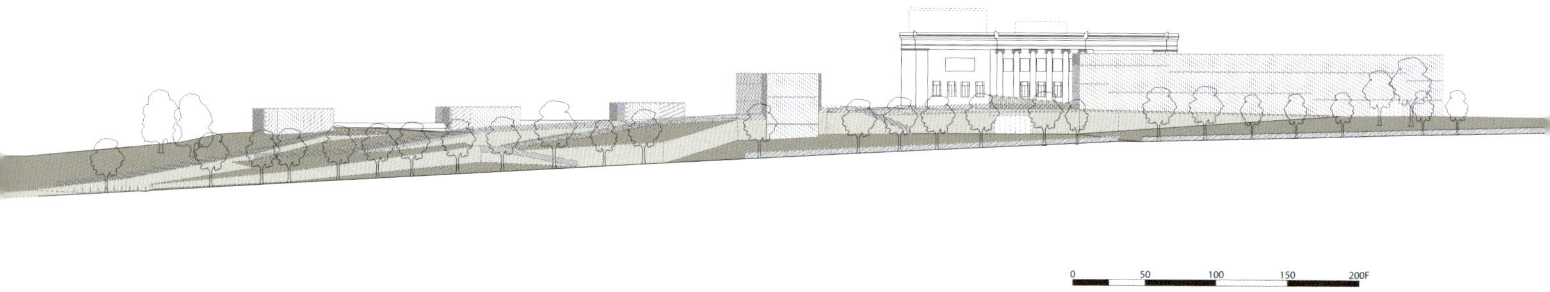

Figure 12.11 East elevation

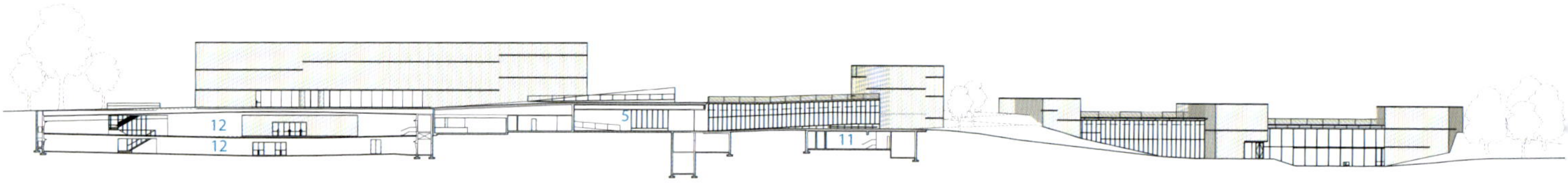

1 Library
2 Upper Lobby
3 Event Room
4 Museum Store
5 Lower Lobby
6 Contemporary Art
7 Photography
8 African Art
9 Featured Exhibitions
10 Noguchi Court
11 Art Service Level
12 Parking
13 Mulipurpose Room
14 Executive Offices
15 Auditorium
16 Cafe

0 50 100 150 200F

Figure 12.12 West elevation

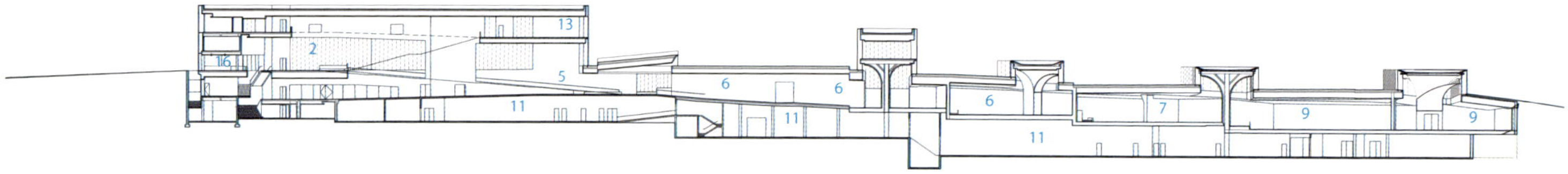

1 Library
2 Upper Lobby
3 Event Room
4 Museum Store
5 Lower Lobby
6 Contemporary Art
7 Photography
8 African Art
9 Featured Exhibitions
10 Noguchi Court
11 Art Service Level
12 Parking
13 Mulipurpose Room
14 Executive Offices
15 Auditorium
16 Cafe

0 50 100 150 200F

Figure 12.13 Longitudinal section

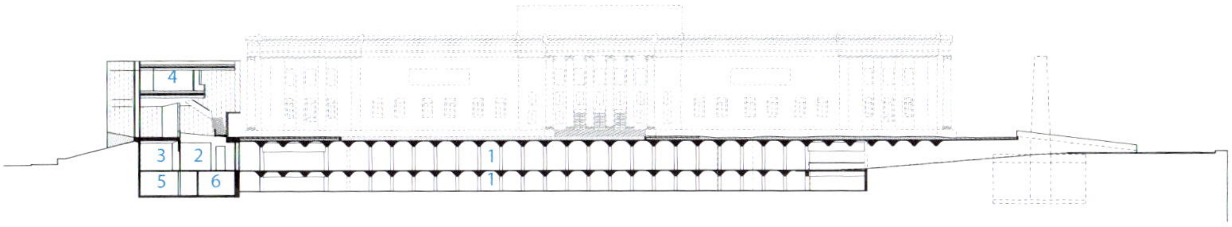

1 Parking Garage
2 Lobby
3 Museum Store
4 Library
5 Stacks
6 Mechanical
7 Contemporary Art
8 Collection Storage
9 Noguchi Court
10 Special Exhibitions
11 Art Receiving
12 Original Building
13 New Opening & Stair
14 European Art
15 Asian Art
16 American Art
17 Auditorium
18 African Art
19 Photography

Figure 12.14 Cross Section – lobby and garage

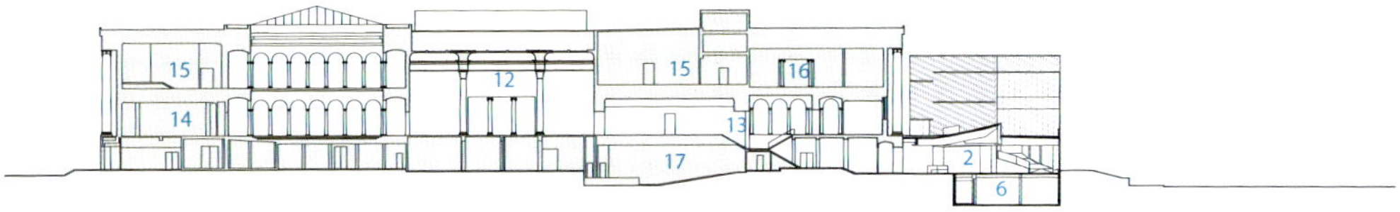

1 Parking Garage
2 Lobby
3 Museum Store
4 Library
5 Stacks
6 Mechanical
7 Contemporary Art
8 Collection Storage
9 Noguchi Court
10 Special Exhibitions
11 Art Receiving
12 Original Building
13 New Opening & Stair
14 European Art
15 Asian Art
16 American Art
17 Auditorium
18 African Art
19 Photography

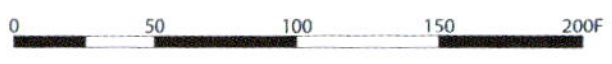

Figure 12.15 Cross Section – lower lobby and original building through cross axis

Though definitely striking, the exterior of the Bloch Building is not flamboyant, and the building rejects another trend in many museums where extravagant exteriors hide more conventional gallery spaces. This is likely because the interior experience of a building, for Holl, should be more important that the exterior. The outside/inside relationship remains complex and somewhat contradictory at the Bloch Building, however. After seeing the five glass volumes from the outside and after passing through the grand space of the lobby lens, we expect to discover little by little during the visit the other glass enclosed spaces. First-time visitors can be overheard saying exactly that. This is not the case, however, since an opaque, structural element called the "T-Wall" that houses ducts, rainwater pipes, and sometimes restrooms was placed at the center of the gallery lenses to reflect light into the spaces below (Fig 12.2 and Fig 12.22). Thus, the lenses are never seen in their entirety. The choice is not by chance since Holl is not necessarily interested in an immediate clarity or readability of his architecture. Ambiguity is a characteristic of our time and there are poetic possibilities in uncertainty. For Holl there is an exterior world and an interior world and one shouldn't necessarily reveal the other. This can make for some disorientation for visitors, however.

From the lobby, galleries cascade down the slope leading from contemporary art (Fig 12.17 and Fig 12.18) to African art (Figure 12.19) and photography, to the Noguchi Court (Fig 12.20), and finally to temporary exhibition spaces at the southern end of the building. Five changes in level are small enough – approximately 91 cm (3 ft) – so that spatial continuity is maintained. The galleries seem to flow with the slope while the perpendicular T-Walls function like dams to slow movement (Fig 12.4 and Fig 12.13). There is a ramped "Gallery Walk" outside of the exhibition spaces along the east facade that is a sort of fast lane down. It is largely a parallel experience to the gallery circulation, and moving back and forth from the galleries to the Gallery Walk can confuse the visit. If the elongated building plan is just right in relation to site planning, it is somewhat problematic for interior circulation. The temporary exhibitions spaces are both a pole of attraction and a dead end. The linear plan obliges visitors to backtrack and retrace their path to return to the lobby.

The galleries are generally rectangular and simple in plan even if there are a few angles and splays. It is only above a height of approximately 3.65 m (12 ft) that the spaces become more complex. Though the walls and ceilings are white-painted gypsum board, they were not conceived as all-purpose flexible spaces. Floors are stained wood or terrazzo and are generally dark. Air conditioning grills are located in a slot near the ceiling and the return is normally at a higher level in the T-Walls. Since the ceilings are often curved or faceted, light tracks are installed as small segments or stich tracks that create a distinct pattern in the surface. Ceiling coves using fluorescent fixtures are located near walls for additional indirect lighting.

The structure of the building is generally steel though the perimeter walls are in concrete. In certain areas double-poured concrete walls provide a cavity for insulation where necessary. The steel columns are commonly spaced from 9 to 18 m (30 to 60 ft) and are located within interior walls. Roof framing is also in steel with concrete on metal decking.

The translucent lenses coupled with the T-Walls are the most notable aspect of the Bloch Building. Though Holl has used translucent facades and channel glass in previous projects such as the Kiasma in Helsinki or the College of Architecture building at the University of Minnesota, there is particular kinship between the Bloch and the ephemeral ice block construction, *Oblong*

Figure 12.16 Interior – foyer Lens 1

Figure 12.17 Interior – Contemporary Art gallery

Figure 12.18 Interior – Contemporary Art gallery

Figure 12.19 Interior – African Art gallery

Figure 12.20 Interior – Noguchi Court

Figure 12.21 View of double of wall cavity

Voidspace, that he realized with the sculptor Jene Highstein as part of the "Snow Show" in Rovaniemi, Finland in 2003. *Oblong Voidspace* sat as an object in the landscape. It had no true function and was created for effect – an experiment in light and space. The ice blocks of the open, 10 by 7.9 by 8.8 m (33 by 26 by 29 ft), cubic structure used fresh water to obtain a crisp blue light through the frozen walls rather than seawater that would have given a greenish tint. Material choice, the subsequent light color, and the overall effect were also critical for the lenses in Kansas City.

"Lenses," in some form, are not uncommon in museum design, and in fact, the original Nelson-Atkins exhibition spaces uses a system of "lay lighting" where a flat, translucent glass ceiling is lit uniquely by incandescent fixtures placed in an accessible cavity above. Actual skylights in Wight's building exist only in non-exhibition spaces such as Kirkwood Hall and Rozzelle Court. Wight's design for the galleries employed polished reflectors and incandescent lights in a double ceiling space that also includes a rolling trolley on tracks used for changing light bulbs and other maintenance. Apparently the Nelson-Atkins ceiling cavity and a double wall system that provides rear access to vitrines made Holl's proposal for double skin lenses in a new building seem like-minded and complementary.

Whereas many museums admit only north light for its evenness and color, the Bloch Building's lenses receive light from all sides. With the lighting consultant Richard Renfro, Holl and McVoy explored ways for mixing and harmonizing the light coming from different directions. Buildings such as José Luis Sert's Maeght Foundation in France were examined, and the marked difference of light color and intensity resulting from clerestories facing in opposite directions was noted. A more homogenous light was sought for the Bloch Building especially at the level of the art. More noticeable differences were embraced at higher levels within the lenses. In order to mix light, the tops of the lens T-Walls were sculpted and sliced into forms dubbed "Fluttering Ts." These elements are meant to direct, deflect, and blend the natural light and allow cool northern light and warm southern light to cross from one side of the lens to the other. Most all of the gallery spaces receive some natural light from the lenses, and care was given to harmonize the fluorescent cove lighting, the halogen spotlights on the stitch tracks, and the natural light entering through the lenses. The exhibition walls are well lit though the centers of the spaces generally appear darker than the perimeter.

The abundance of light coming through the lenses also had to be managed. Models, mock-ups, and computer simulations were made to determine how much light was on each face of each lens throughout the year. Though it was found that the critical condition was the equinox when the lenses received the most light, to design for this case would make for dreary lighting conditions at other times of year. The lenses are composed of a double facade approximately 91 cm (3 ft) thick (Fig 12.21 and Fig 12.23). To the outside there are interlocking, Okalux glass planks with an integrated capillary insulation. They are 40 cm (16 in.) wide, up to 5.5 m (18 ft) high and held at the top and bottom. Intermediate horizontal supports of channels exceeding 5.5 m are connected to catwalks that are suspended within the cavity. To the inside of the glazing complex there is a laminated etched glass panel that also controls ultraviolet light. All of the glass is extra white and the light transmission for the complex is approximately 18 percent.

A system of computer-controlled shades was also integrated within the cavity. In general there is one shade on the north side, two shades of different light transmission on the other sides, and three layers of shades in the temporary exhibition spaces that allow for near blackout. The different shade options are used according to the time of year and the works of art exhibited. The shades are located next to the inside glass panel so that the effect of the fluorescent lights also located within the cavity will always remain the same at night. Though these fluorescent lights cannot be dimmed, there are two rows of lamps that are switched separately in order to vary the lens brightness at night. The lens lighting currently comes on at dusk and shuts off at 10:00pm during the week and midnight on Friday and Saturday. Outside, the color rendering of the fluorescent light is much better than more typical high-pressure sodium street lighting and as a bonus the green of the plants can be seen at night. The cavity of the double-glazing also functions as a thermal buffer.

The Bloch's site placement and concept of merging architecture and landscape were strategies to make a new building defer to the earlier Nelson-Atkins building. As Holl has noted, however, works of architecture may have an entirely different presence by day and by night. After dark, Holl's building has greater presence and the glowing lenses are less deferential and more clearly rival the 1930s architecture.

The structure of the T-Walls at the center of the gallery lenses is composed of steel "T-Frames" at approximately 4.6 m (15 ft) on center that are stabilized by rods located within the double facade cavity and connected to the framing at the level of the green roofs below. The Lobby Lens is somewhat different from the others. Its inner glass layer is sandblasted channel glass rather than the acid-etched glass found elsewhere. Its structure is also different. On the east side, columns are located within the cavity to support the second floor and the roof, while on the west side, the channel glass above the clear glass entry facade is suspended from the roof structure which itself is cantilevered from a large central, north/south truss that runs alongside the second floor walkway.

A basement level exists under the entire Bloch Building and a long technical gallery links the new to the preexisting main mechanical spaces at the north/west corner of the Nelson-Atkins building. The basement houses storage, mechanical rooms, conservation, receiving areas and workshops. Semi-trucks are able to enter into the loading dock at the southern extremity of the building. All of the spaces are generous and well equipped.

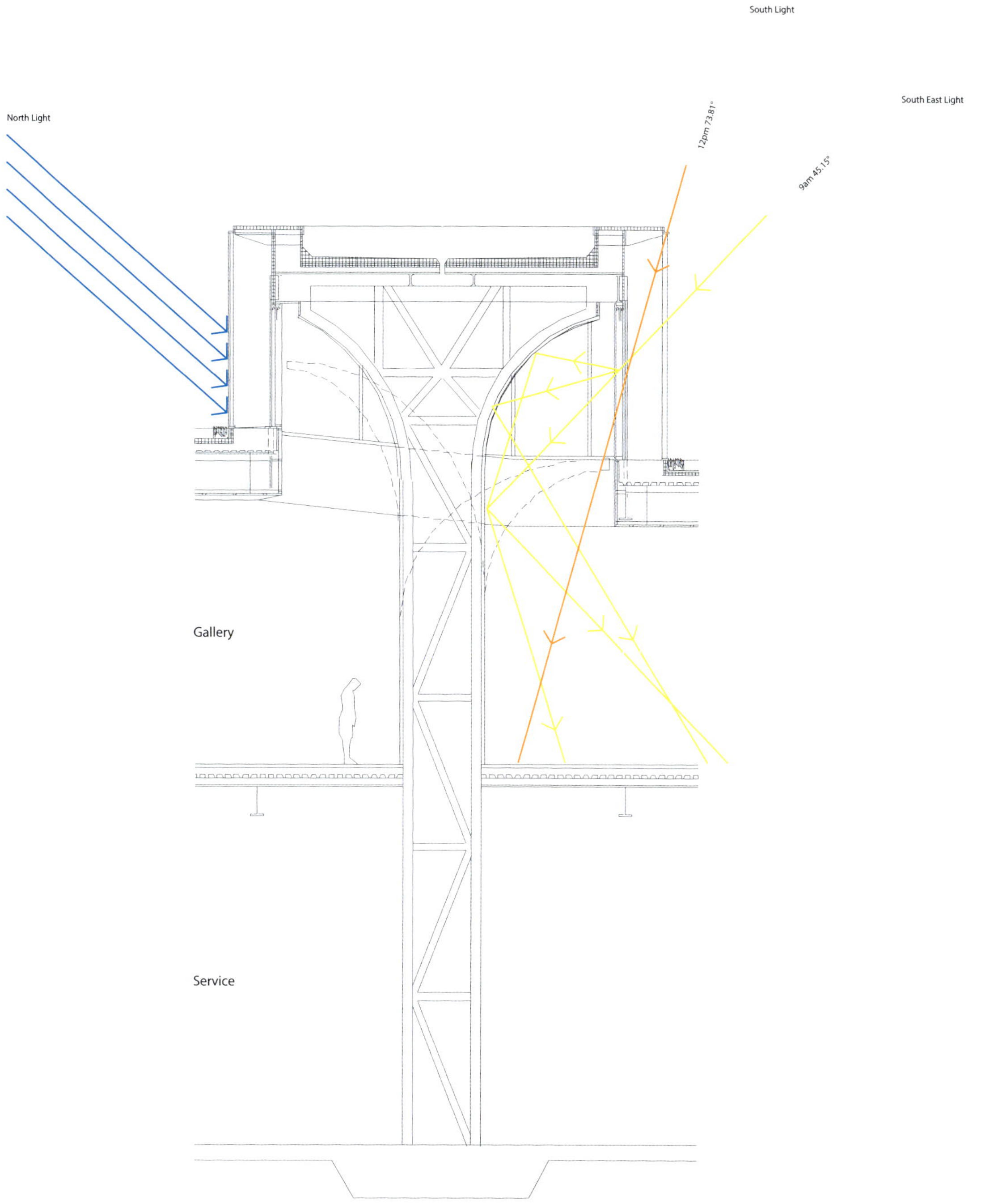

Figure 12.22 "T" section diagram Lens 3

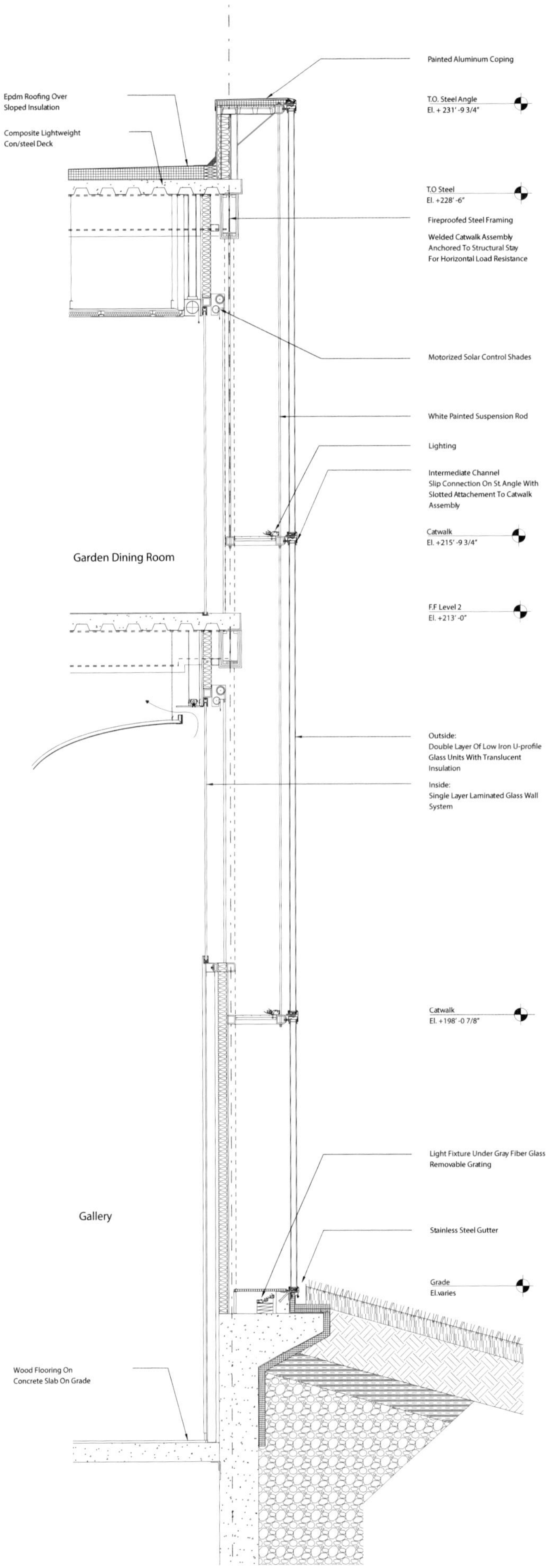

Figure 12.23 Wall section Lens 2

Holl is a follower of the French philosopher Maurice Merleau-Ponty and his theory of phenomenology. He is interested in *Questions of Perception* in architecture and seeks to touch and awaken the senses. Holl succeeded in his design goals in his exceptional Chapel of Saint Ignatius in Seattle, Washington, for example, where in a religious context we more readily accept an architecture that imposes itself emotionally and better appreciate the architect's interests for the dramatic play of light, the symbolic, the pre-logical, and "that inner life which reveals the luminous intensity of the world." An exhibition space is different. Art works have their own presence. In a museum the works of art and the architectural space should ideally coalesce to move and rouse. Holl's narrative architecture does not compete with the art but it sometimes seems detached or indifferent. Inside the Bloch building, the experience of architecture and the experience of art run parallel. The lenses and Fluttering-Ts, for example, are not fundamentally at the service of the display of art. Rather, they are elements to experience virtually independently from the works that are often simply but predominately lit artificially. It is a matter of interpretation if something profound has been created with natural light that stimulates inner and outer perception or if light has been simply aestheticized. The Bloch Building is masterful in numerous ways, yet as a museum, architecture and art mingle but do not coalesce.

CHAPTER 13

Akron Art Museum

Akron, Ohio

Coop Himmelb(l)au

2007

Figure 13.1 Aerial view from south/west

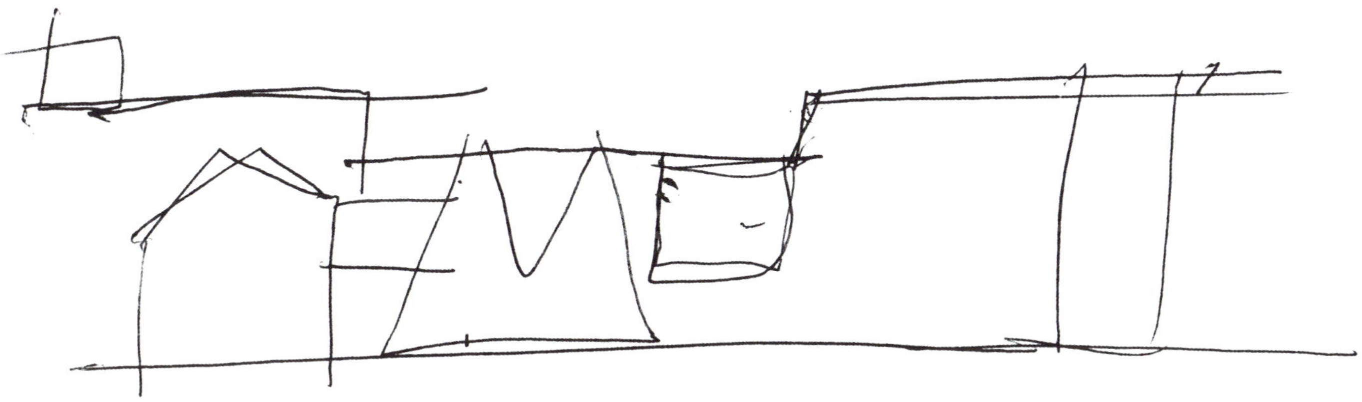

Figure 13.2 Sketch by Wolf Prix

More so than many institutions, the Akron Art Museum clearly expressed its aspirations to create a major symbol for the new century when it embarked on a building project in the year 2000. With a first list of candidates numbering more than 130 strong, a wide net was cast to find an architect sharing like ideas and capable of making an architectural statement for the museum. The selection was reduced to 30 and then narrowed to three: Coop Himmelb(l)au, Snoheta, and UN Studio. In September 2001 the competition winning architect was announced and Coop Himmelb(l)au, led by Wolf Prix, opened their first building in the United States in July 2007 (Fig 13.1). The Austrian architects saw the Akron project as the museum of the future. It should be a three-dimensional sign in the city – a messenger – that signals a major public space. For Coop Himmelb(l)au individual building projects must compensate for the decline of true public space. The museum (or any building for that matter) must make a contribution to the city. It should provide more than simply a place to look at art; it should function as a meeting place, a destination, a place for everyday life. It should also be a place for entertainment. The museum and its architecture should be visible and distinct and should project an energetic, dynamic image.

Akron is a city of 200,000, and like much of Ohio its economy is based on industry and agriculture. Rubber was important to its growth, and The Goodyear Tire & Rubber Company still has its headquarters there. Ohio's important early twentieth-century industrial era resulted in several grand, neoclassic art museums of international renown throughout the state such as those in Cleveland and Toledo. These buildings are often situated in parks outside of downtown and house encyclopedic collections. The Cleveland Museum of Art has expanded its original 1916 building several times over the years, notably with an addition by Marcel Breuer in the 1970s and, more recently, renovations, modifications, and additions by Rafael Viñoly which were completed in two phases in 2009 and 2012. In the 1980s, the Toledo Art Museum hired Frank Gehry to design their Center for the Visual Arts just to the south/east of the neoclassic, 1912 building, and SANAA opened their Glass Pavilion across the street from the original building in 2006. Other significant museum projects in Ohio include Peter Eisenman's Wexner Art Center in Columbus built in 1982, and the Contemporary Art Center in Cincinnati by Zaha Hadid opened in 2003.

The Akron Art Museum began in 1922 as the Art Institute. In 1981, after decades of moves, transformations, and a name change it settled into a red brick and limestone structure that was built as the main post office in 1899. When the museum began to consider a new building, it preferred to remain in its centrally located neighborhood on the north side of downtown since renewal was already well underway in the area. Eventually, a large portion of the same block where the museum occupied only the north/west corner was acquired. This allowed the post office building to be maintained and integrated into a new project in order to reduce costs and assure that the historical building would be preserved. The situation also provided the potential for a striking architectural contrast between the old building and a new, larger addition. Coop Himmelb(l)au's provocative, 1988 rooftop remodeling atop a traditional building in the Falkestrasse in Vienna tipped the scales in their favor.

The squarish site is only one block east of Main Street (Fig 13.3). Following the competition brief, the main entry would be located to the west on High Street. The loading dock and services are located to the east on Broadway Street and a bus drop-off for groups to the north on Market Street. The buildings in the area are generally in brick and only a few stories high. A three-story parking garage sits directly across the street to the west and serves the neighborhood as well as the museum. The immediate surroundings lack density, however, and surface parking lots occupy the area immediately to the south of the museum and another surface parking lot occupies much of the next block to the east which could eventually be used for future museum expansion.

The new 5,880 m^2 (square meter; 63,300 ft^2 (square foot)) building has a clear and logical – virtually self-evident – organization. In plan (Fig 13.4 and Fig 13.5) it is composed of four parts: the original, 1,950 m^2 (21,000 ft^2) post office building that now houses administrative offices and the library; the Gallery Box, an opaque volume devoted to the display of the permanent collection and temporary exhibitions; the grand entry hall named the Crystal that links the post office building and the Gallery Box; and finally an inaccessible, triangular volume to the north/east of the site that houses mechanical equipment but is very important to the overall composition. Since this volume is held back from the street corner it provides for a better view of the preexisting post office building which allows it to remain somewhat autonomous visually in relation to the very prominent addition (Fig 13.6).

In section, the difference in level between the east and west sides of the sloping site is approximately the height of one story (Fig 13.11). The Gallery Box is placed on the ground to the east but advances as a cantilevered volume toward High Street to the west (Fig 13.7). Tucked under it at the lower, entry level are a 160 seat auditorium, a boutique, and a cafe. The Crystal links all the public spaces and various levels (Fig 13.8 and Fig 13.10). Mechanical rooms, art storage, general storage, workshops, preparation areas, etc. are located in generous spaces at basement level. A large freight elevator near the loading dock at the south/east corner of the building services all levels. Unlike many recent museums, a delivery truck cannot enter into

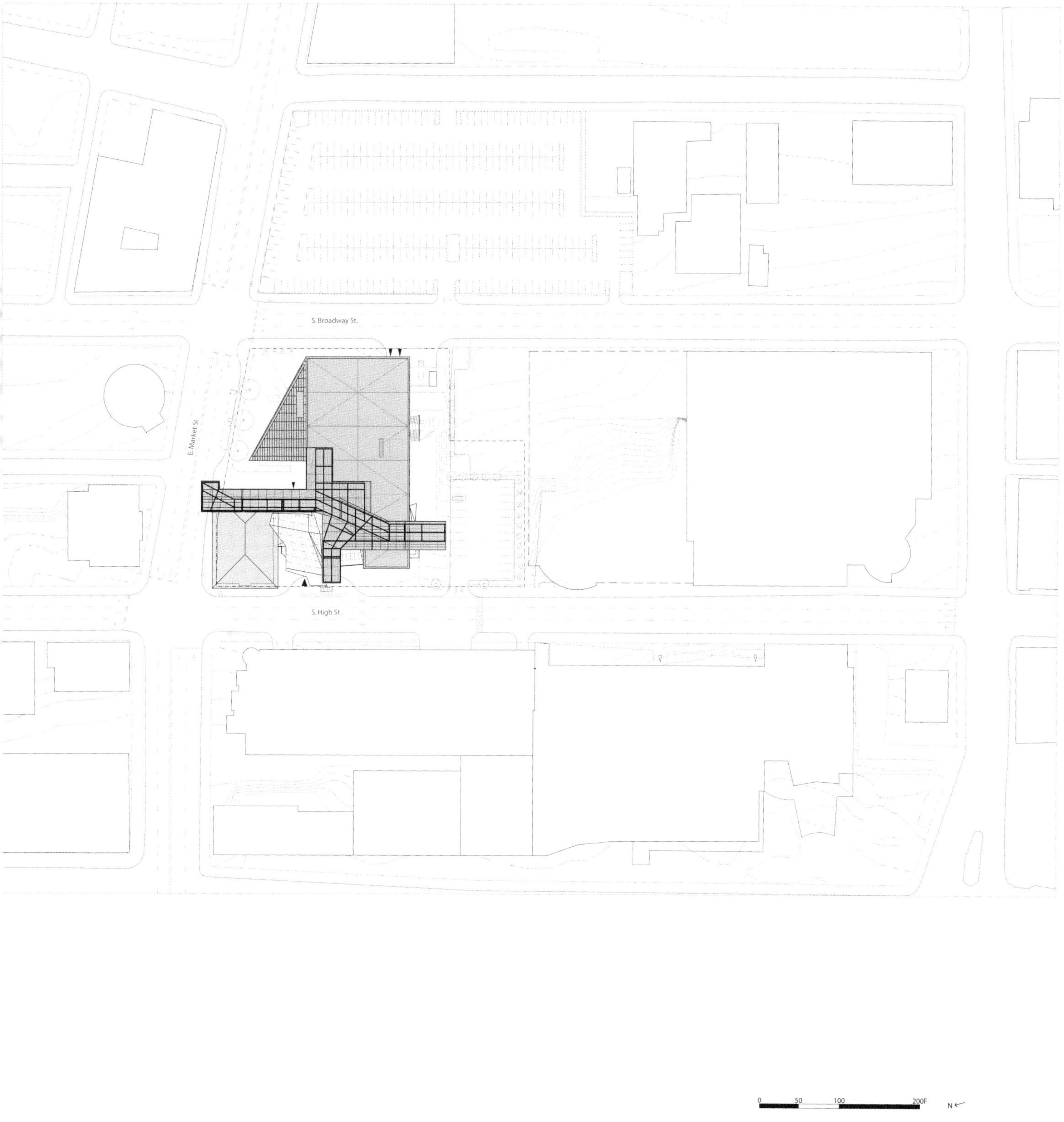

Figure 13.3 Site plan

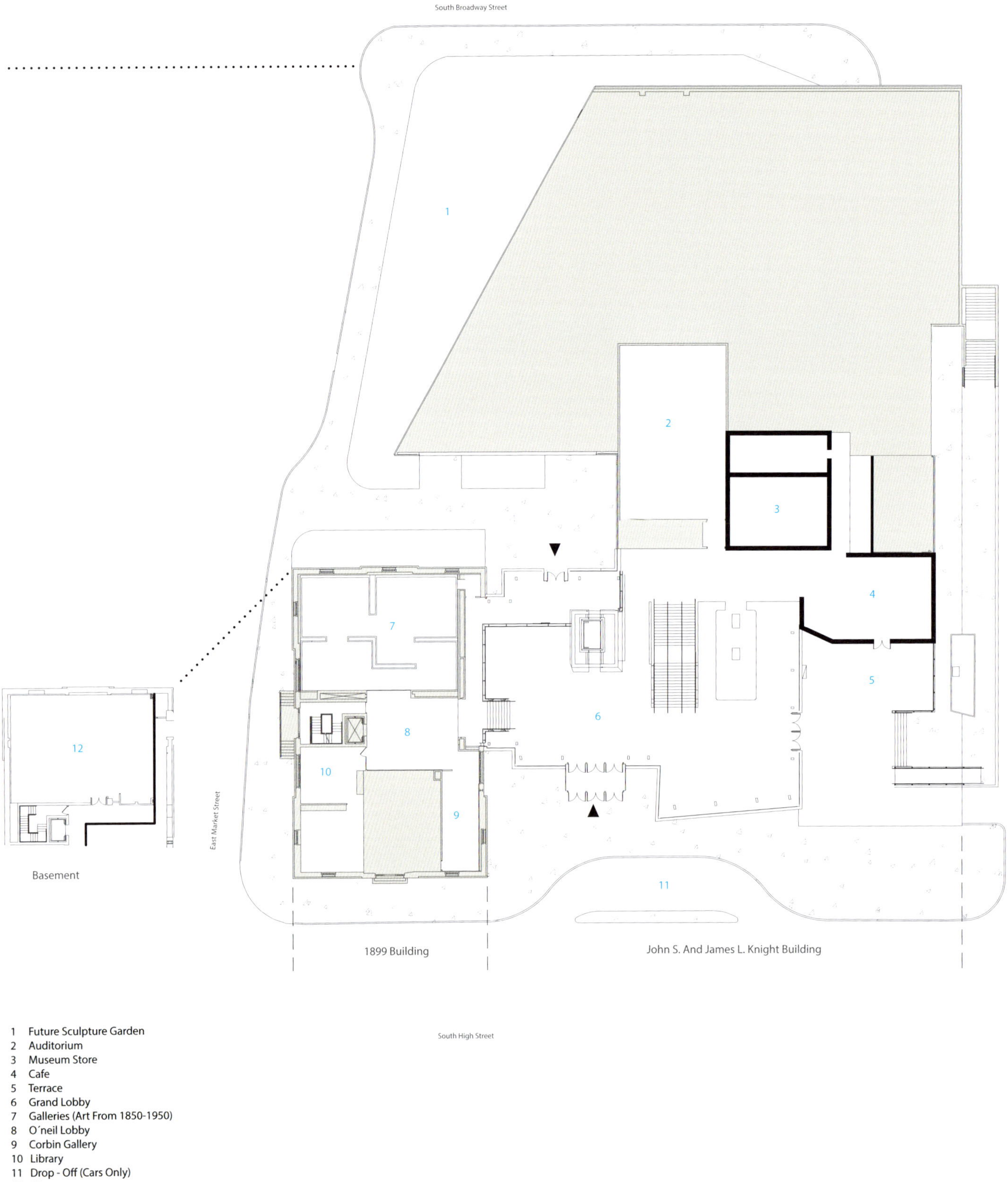

1 Future Sculpture Garden
2 Auditorium
3 Museum Store
4 Cafe
5 Terrace
6 Grand Lobby
7 Galleries (Art From 1850-1950)
8 O'neil Lobby
9 Corbin Gallery
10 Library
11 Drop - Off (Cars Only)
12 Classroom

Figure 13.4 First (ground) floor plan

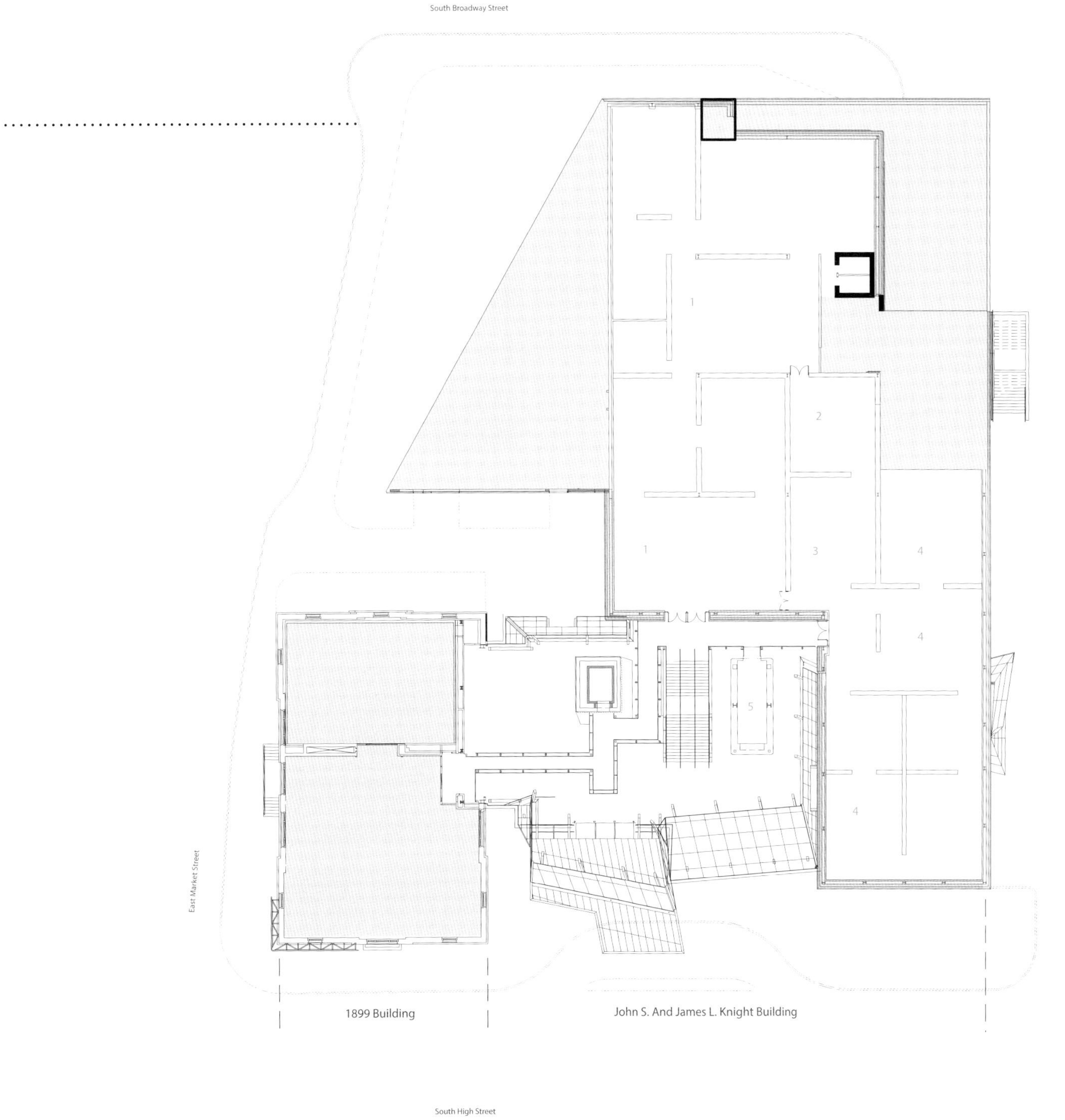

1 Haslinger Galleries (Art Since 1950)
2 Bidwell Gallery
3 Isroff Gallery
4 Arnstein Galleries
5 Video Boot

Figure 13.5 Second floor plan

the building but is simply covered by a canopy for loading and unloading. The building users say that the functional organization of the building is a success.

Function and striking aesthetics were both underscored in the competition brief. In Akron they seem to have been addressed quasi independently. The straightforwardly organized project is counterbalanced and crowned (literally) by a single extravagant gesture: the imposing, cantilevered, 100 m (327 ft) long steel structure that hovers over the post office building and the volumes of Coop Himmelb(l)au's addition (Fig 13.19). The architects named the structure the "Roof Cloud," but it has also been called the "Wing" or the "High Roof." As is often the case for Coop Himmelb(l)au, the project is conceived as distinct, evocatively named elements. Akron is composed of a Crystal, a Gallery Box, and a Roof Cloud with the latter being the most unexpected element of the exterior. For Coop Himmelb(l)au, architecture wants to change society, and unexpected shapes and forms further that aspiration.

Figure 13.6 View from north/east

Figure 13.7 View from south/west

Figure 13.8 West facade

Figure 13.9 East entrance

The Roof Cloud is made of a primary and secondary steel structure skinned with two types of cladding panels that are clipped onto both the top and bottom surfaces. Opaque composite panels are generally located in the middle of the Cloud while metal grating is placed toward the edges and extremities accentuating an appearance of lightness. (The placement of the grating also decreases snow buildup at the cantilevered extremities.) For Coop Himmelb(l)au such elements, even if stationary, defy gravity and make a building dynamic. The entire Roof Cloud sits on four supports: to the south, a steel column sits atop the Gallery Box; a second poured in place concrete "A" Column supports a steel cage that in turn connects to the primary structure of the Roof Cloud above; a third support sits atop the concrete elevator tower located within the Crystal; and a fourth steel column passes through the roof of the post office building to the north. If the attachments related to the new building disappear within the general mass of the project, the support through the roof of the existing building is very visible and compromises the effect of a freely floating cloud liberated from the force of gravity. Conceptually, the large cross that soars above the museum links the new to the old, visually reinforces the internal organization of the building underneath, and projects the museum out toward the city.

As a building element, the roof has been important for Coop Himmelb(l)au at least since such projects/installations as their "House with a Flying Roof" realized in London in 1973 that combined inflatable architecture and floating roofs, and right through more recent projects such as the BMW Welt in Munich completed in 2007 with its dominant, 14,865 m^2 (160,000 ft^2) roof structure that is supported by only 11 columns along with the elevator cores. In Akron the Roof Cloud should function as a horizontal landmark. It gives visibility and an assertive monumentality to the project. If by day the structure appears heavy and we are more impressed by the large cantilevers than by any real lightness or finesse, by night the blue lit structure is liberated of its materiality and becomes an ethereal cloud again.

Though it does somewhat shade the glass lobby below, the cloud is an added, detached element without a precise use or function. (An additional, exterior brise-soleil was considered and studied especially for the west-facing glass but was abandoned for cost reasons.) For the architects its justification is perhaps more metaphysical, and from the competition forward it remained essential for the image of the project. Construction methods were examined and discussed but its existence was never put into question. We imagine that the structure might offer some sort of a spatial or experiential relationship with the city – a panoramic view, perhaps, such as that provided by the project for the Falkestrasse. Unfortunately, it is not possible to enter into the cloud. The structure can only be viewed from below, and it remains primarily a sculptural element.

The entry, or the Crystal, is the center and heart of the project (Fig 13.12 and Fig 13.14). The competition brief requested a large lobby space that could also contain sculptures, and Coop Himmelb(l)au's very high, three-story glazed space that opens onto the city and blurs the boundary between interior and exterior, private and public, seduced the museum. The Crystal is conceived as a flexible space that can also be used for banquets, other museum functions, and private parties.

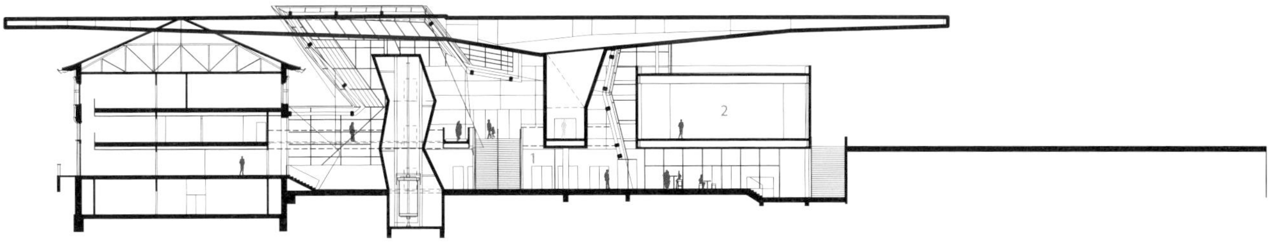

1 Grand Lobby
2 Arnstein Galleries

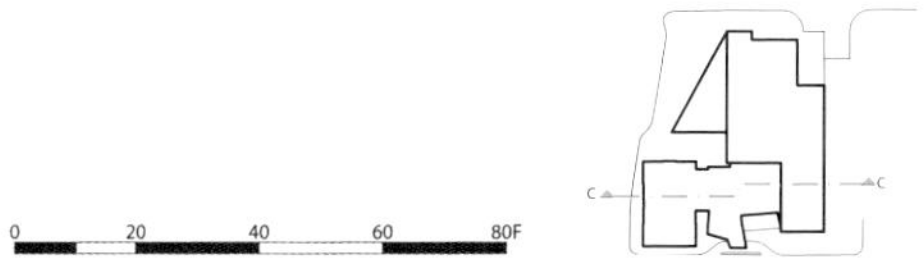

Figure 13.10 Section CC

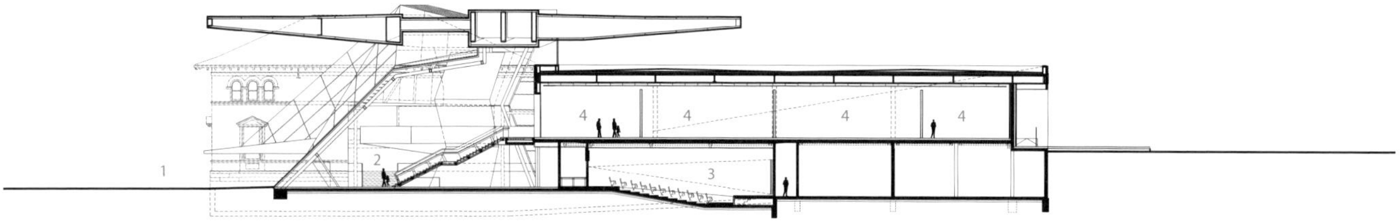

1 Drop-off (Cars Only)
2 Grand Lobby
3 Auditorium
4 Haslinger Galleries (Art Since 1950)

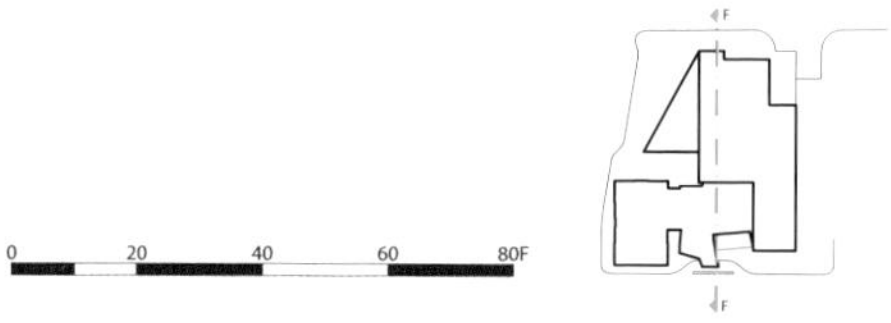

Figure 13.11 Section FF

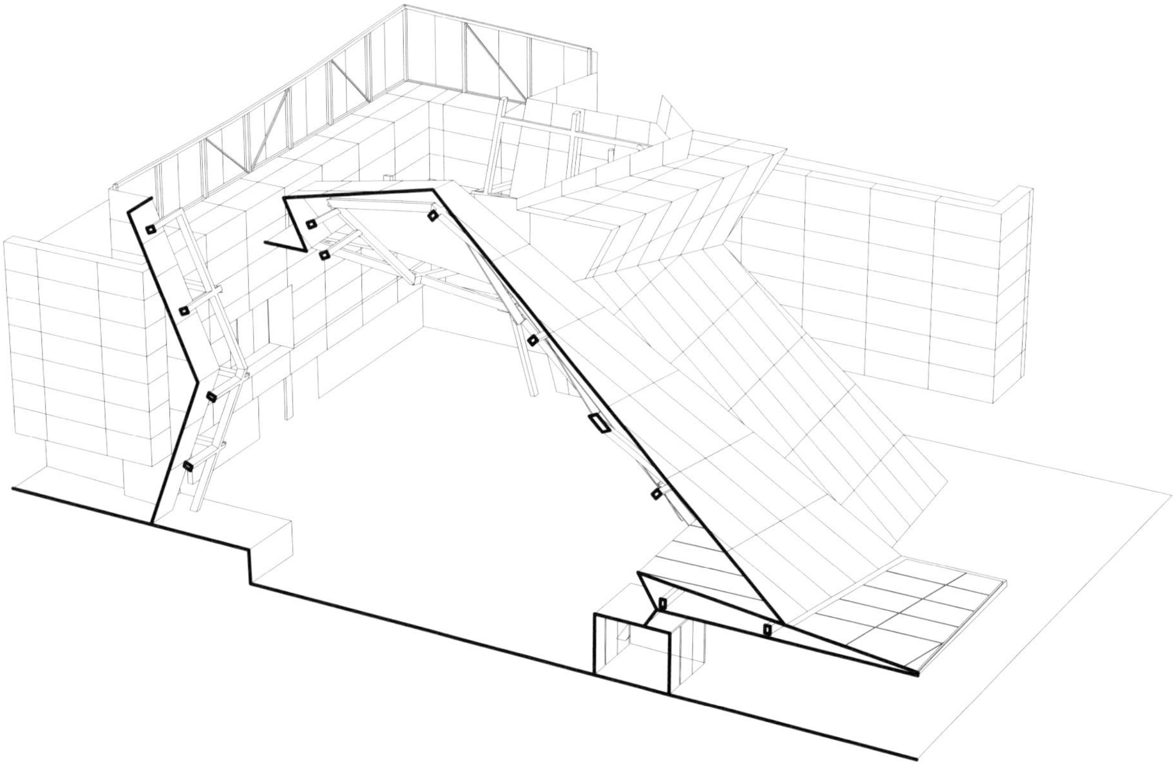

Figure 13.12 Section crystal

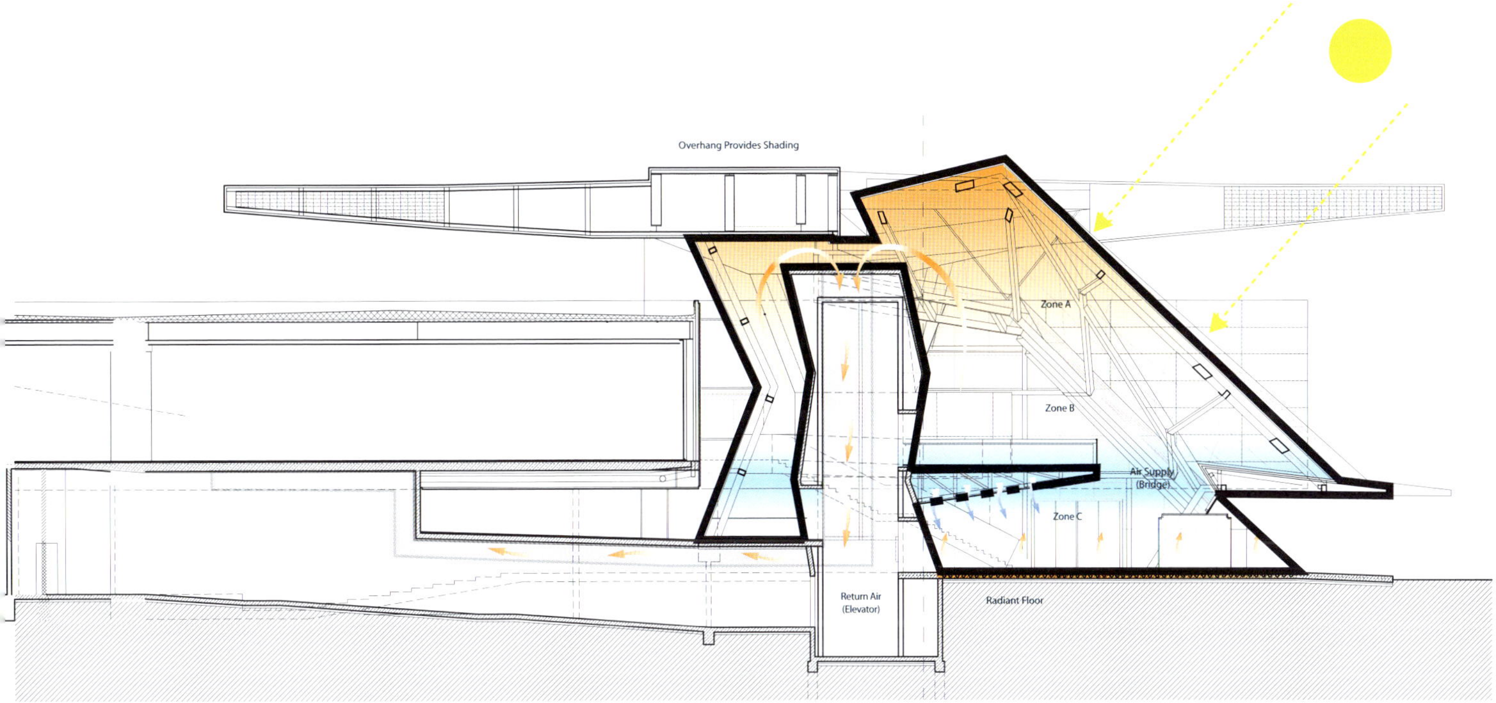

Microclimate Zones:

To optimize running costs the lobby is dived into three stratified layers of climate.

Microclimate Zone A	Space inaccessible to people.
Microclimate Zone B	Optimal climate for circulation and shorter term occupation.
Microclimate Zone C	Optimal climate for activies with long term seating, ie. banquets.

Figure 13.13 Lobby energy concept

The geometry of the multifaceted Crystal is complex but the facade system itself is more standard. The space is spectacular, however, and bathed in light. Finishes are purposely simple and frugal in order to establish continuity with the sidewalk and street outside and make the entry a more urban, transition space. Upon entering, the Crystal provides access to the post office building to the left (the existing building's brick south facade was modified to create larger openings to the entry), the auditorium and museum store ahead, and the indoor cafe and outdoor terrace located under the cantilevered portion of the Gallery Box to the right. A group entrance related to the drop-off area on Market Street is located opposite the main entrance (Fig 13.9). The lobby space can be freely traversed, but there is not enough pedestrian circulation in the area to activate it as a public passageway like we imagine Coop Himmelb(l)au would hope. Two sculptural forms were placed within the glass volume. One is a shifting, tilted concrete tower that houses the elevator and also serves as a plenum for return air (Fig 13.15), and the other is a more cubic form that sits on the concrete "A" Column mentioned above and contains the "video boot," a video gallery that is accessed from the second floor. The monumental stair and the bridges at the upper level also animate the volume (Fig 13.16).

The "crystal" metaphor has been used by Coop Himmelb(l)au for major spaces for projects from Dresden, Germany (the UFA Cinema Center) to Lyon, France (the Musée des Confluences). Akron's Crystal strongly resembles the project for the UFA Cinema completed in 1998 where a similar elevator shaft akin to an oversized *Endless Column* sculpture by Constantin Brancusi was used in an all glass entry space. At a more conceptual level, all such private architectural space in Coop Himmelb(l)au's projects should also be a surrogate urban space – a sort of urban arcade.

The Akron Crystal generally uses a displacement system for heating and cooling so that areas occupied by the public are more precisely controlled climatically, spaces with few people are controlled less, and inaccessible spaces at the top are controlled even less (Fig 13.13). Air is supplied via the second floor bridges, and there is also a radiant system in the floor slabs using water-filled pipes for both heating and cooling that is essential to the system.

In contrast to the exuberant Roof Cloud and Crystal, both the outside and the inside of the Gallery Box are sober – no natural light, no views in or out, no angled or inclined walls. The spaces in Akron are simple and orthogonal, introverted with no link to the outside, and artificially lit with light tracks and incandescent lights (Fig 13.17 and Fig 13.18). Natural light was not considered because of the possible harm to works of art though this problem, of course, has been resolved in other museums. One of Coop Himmelb(l)au's more interesting uses of natural light is in their more recent Martin Luther Church in Hainburg Austria (completed in 2011). There, three spiraling forms in the curved, steel-plate roof direct light inside and at the same time provide views out. The Akron competition asked that the architect respect the preeminent role of the art in the galleries. Coop Himmelb(l)au translated this into spaces where the architecture recedes. The exhibition spaces are a suite of uniform rectangular spaces, well proportioned and serene. There are few columns that could compromise the flexibility of the space that includes 678 m^2 (7,300 ft^2) for temporary exhibitions and 1,208 m^2 (13,000 ft^2) for the permanent collection which is organized in two parts: 1850 to 1950, and 1950 to the present.

The spaces are a constant height of 4.88 m (16 ft); the floors are wood, and the walls are gypsum board painted different colors from one room to another. The technical equipment, such as exit panels, sprinklers, light tracks, etc., is discreet and well integrated, and the air conditioning system that combines ducts in the walls and ceiling with a radiant system in the concrete slab was studied to be particularly quiet. We can imagine that these galleries can be easily adapted to all sorts of exhibitions. It is surprising, however, just how subdued and "white cube" the spaces are. Coop Himmelb(l)au's solution for the exhibition space is extreme in its simplicity, but not radical. The Gallery Box bears a strong resemblance to the "Cinema Block" of the UFA Center. By their very nature, cinemas are logically dark and windowless. Gallery spaces might allow for more of the spatial experimentation that interests the architects that also might somehow enhance their idea of "Seeing by Walking" attributed to Aristotle and others where the mind would be stimulated and perception increased by the body's movement through spaces differentiated by materials, light, etc. There is little invention in the way the public meets art. Coop Himmelb(l)au long rejected modernism's functionalistic box, and as late as 2001 the revealing title given to a published conversation with Wolf Prix, in itself, summarized his thoughts: "The Box as a Burial Site for Art: We Think That's Boring." Still, the Gallery Box tends more toward that functional box than an architecture that changes like clouds.

Over the years and in different contexts, Prix has given his opinion on the museum as an institution and building type like few other architects have. A short text from 1990 entitled "A Museum Is Art" would seemingly place Architecture squarely as the *mother art*.

> I would like to mention three working theories that should prove that a good, timely museum makes art in its conventional form obsolete and that the money for the art collection should instead go to the building costs and the architect's fee. An emotional stock taking could run as follows: we, that is Coop Himmelb(l)au, never liked museums. We used to prefer going to rock concerts, but ever since rock concerts started getting louder and louder (or our hearing worse and worse), we now occasionally escape to a silent, quiet, obliging museum because it is simply more comfortable. Thus, I have arrived at the assumption that museums are something for more mature people. I think our

Figure 13.14 Grand lobby

Figure 13.15 Grand lobby – elevator tower

Figure 13.16 Grand lobby – stair and video boot

Figure 13.17 Interior – gallery

Figure 13.18 Interior – gallery

eyesight is worse than it was before, too; therefore, it is particularly necessary to deal with the lighting in museums. We go to a museum because of its content and architecture. To be honest, we go to a museum more for the architecture and as far as that goes, we prefer, let me put it this way, disobedient museums or disobedient architecture, as opposed to the anticipatory obedience that is frequently found in architecture. Artists love obedient museums and hate disobedient ones. Why? We believe architecture is and ought to be the visual expression of this existing social world and is perhaps and must be an expression of future worlds, too. For this reason, architecture in the future will have to deal intensively with complexity. This is not possible by means of nineteenth-century additive systems of thought. We have to get rid of these systems and find complex design methods in order to create complex architecture. Complexity can be found more readily in art, in the processes of development and emergence of art. Therefore, complex architecture becomes art. And if architecture, namely, the building, is art, then it is a museum in and of itself and for this reason doesn't need any art.

The attitudes expressed here may be more in tune with Coop Himmelb(l)au's earlier Groninger Museum project in Groningen, Netherlands. The pavilion for the museum, completed in 1994, was described as "liquid architecture" by the architects and has much more eccentric gallery spaces than those in Akron.

In general the structure of Coop Himmelb(l)au's new building for the Akron Art Museum is steel. The cantilever of the Gallery Box is formed by two large trusses integrated into the longitudinal walls. The execution of the concrete in the entry space and elsewhere is rough and not particularly well finished. It was specified as such and is not bothersome in the overall context. The exterior and interior cladding panels are in resin covered by a thin veneer of powder-coated aluminum. The panels are used as a rainscreen system and are impeccable. A playful sculptural form within the panels on the south facade was added to face the space reserved for a sculpture garden. In general the structure, materials, and finishes are simple. All of the choices voluntarily stayed within a norm that local contractors were able to realize relatively easily in order to reduce costs and allow for the budgetary extravagance that is the Roof Cloud.

The architecture of Coop Himmelb(l)au often depends on binary opposites: opaque and transparent, heavy and light, useful and useless. This is also the case in Akron. For an architecture that presents itself as a model for the future, however, it is the Roof Cloud, the grand gesture of the project, that presents a problem. It is difficult to see it other than an indulgence, an enormous ornament placed on the building without real concern for integration. Coop Himmelb(l)au has been described as a product of their formative time (the 1960s) and place (Vienna). There is a marked difference with the ideas of another Viennese architect of another time who wrote his most famous essay one hundred years before the Akron Art Museum opened. In the first decade of the twentieth century, Adolf Loos imagined an architecture of the future without ornament. For him, ornament is crime and necessarily too costly. At the time he saw the United States as a model for the architecture of his convictions. Loos' ideas have aged as have their merits and flaws. In today's world we might ask ourselves, however, if provocations that passed as experimental, radical, rebellious, and uncompromising in the last third of the twentieth century are still current and pertinent. It is certainly not the first time or the last we will ask ourselves what constitutes a museum and architecture for the future.

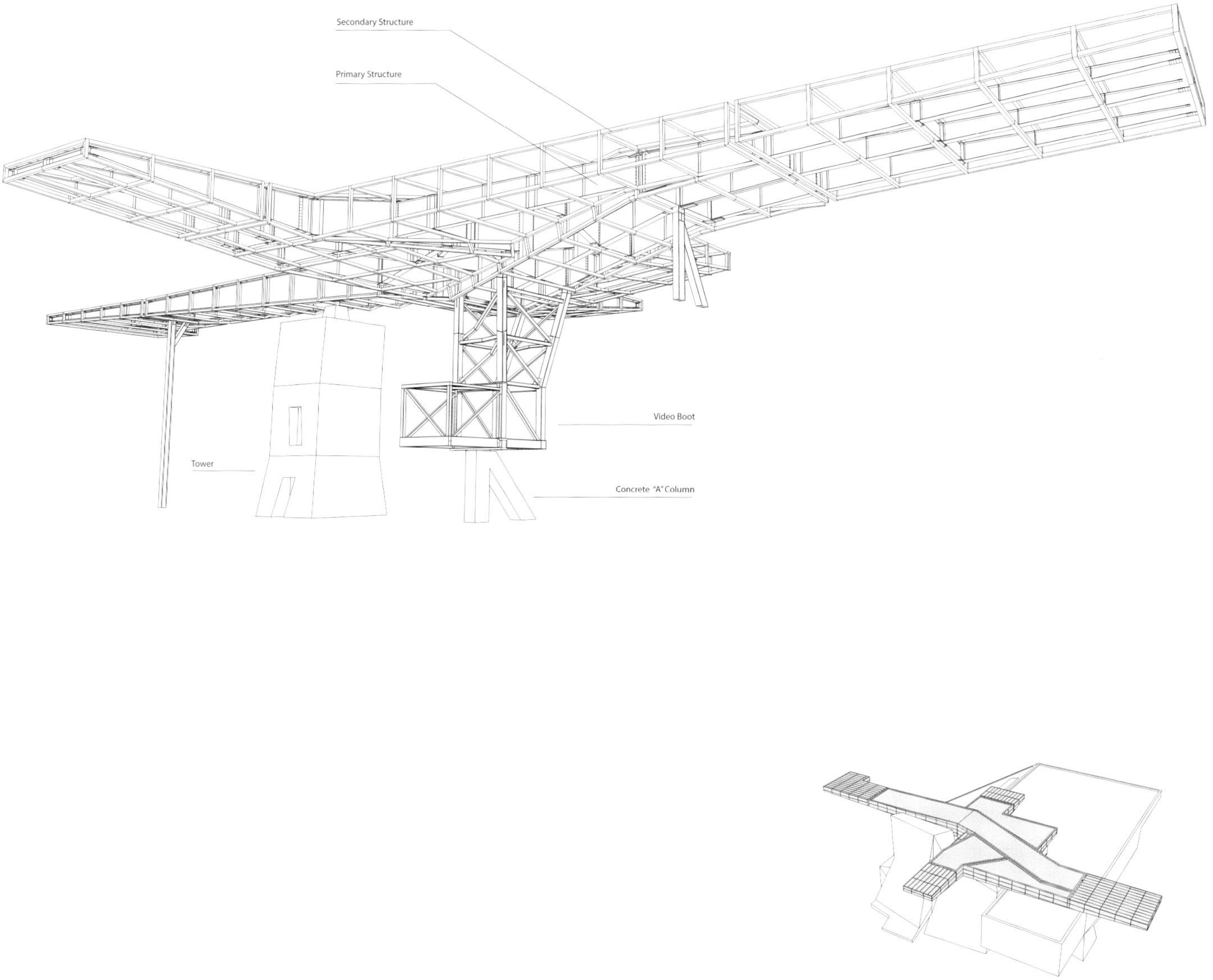

Figure 13.19 Roof cloud structural elements

CHAPTER 14

New Museum

New York

Kazuyo Sejima + Ryue Nishizawa / SANAA

2007

igure 14.1 View from north

At first glance the six stacked boxes of the New Museum of Contemporary Art in Manhattan seem willful and almost naïf (Fig 14.1). As is often the case with Kazuyo Sejima and Ryue Nishizawa (SANAA), however, the design is a reasoned response to the realities of place, site, and program. According to the architects, the cubic forms of the 53 m (174 ft) tall structure were inspired by Manhattan's strict street grid, and the building's shifting silhouette is a pragmatic response to New York's zoning rules and setback requirements. The project was SANAA's first opportunity to build in a dense urban situation. The program of the New Museum made the building inevitably bigger than its neighbors, and the shifts were meant to diminish the bulk of the project.

The New Museum is located in the southern portion of Manhattan at 235 Bowery on a site that was previously a parking lot (Fig 14.2). Since the middle of the nineteenth century the Bowery has had a less than respectable reputation and was known for its flophouses. Artists have had a foothold in the area for decades however. Mark Rothko had a studio there in the 1950s as did Cy Twombly in the 1960s. From the early 1970s up until 2006 the mythical music club CBGB was located only a short distance to the north at 315. The area is clearly in transition and gentrification is now well underway. Already in 1992 the Guggenheim Museum Soho moved into a space on Broadway designed by the architect Arata Isozaki. The Guggenheim was later reduced in size and Rem Koolhaas redesigned a part of the same brick building for a Prada store that opened in 2001. Since then several luxury apartment buildings by architects such as Jean Nouvel, Herzog & de Meuron, and others have been built in the neighborhood. The Sperone Westwater Gallery at 257 Bowery, a remarkable, thin, eight-story "tower" by Norman Foster, opened in 2010. Realizing that transformations in the vicinity were inevitable, SANAA decided that the architecture of the New Museum should present a strong image that could hold its own in the future. To that end the architects investigated possible building envelopes allowed by setback requirements on surrounding sites and the consequences they would have on their own design. SANAA produced an edifice that surprises without becoming overly extravagant formally. The New Museum has often been compared to Marcel Breuer's 1966 Whitney Museum of American Art in Midtown Manhattan that, with its cantilevered, box-like forms, likewise appears daring and surprising in its context.

SANAA won the project by competition. The other architects invited to compete were Abalos & Herreros (Spain), Adjaye Associates (Great Britain), Gigon/Guyer (Switzerland), and Reiser + Umemoto (United States). Of the five competition proposals, SANAA's was the only one that made a strong formal gesture. The others were primarily conceived as infill projects that focused on the treatment of the facade. SANAA's solution takes advantage of its site on axis with Prince Street that allows the project to be seen not only as part of a street facade but also as a freestanding object (Fig 14.4). The ledge created above the first box was conceived to host rotating sculpture installations (Fig 14.5). These facade pieces, visible from Prince Street, mark the entrance and also become a sort of signage for the museum. Ugo Rondinone's *Hell, Yes!* was installed for the opening and replaced in 2011 by Isa Genzken's *Rose II*. The goal of the institution and the architects was to create visibility and recognition. The preservation of the iconic architectural image should be better assured since the New Museum bought the six-story building immediately to its south on the Bowery in 2008.

While the sliding and shifting boxes provide formal variety, the project's rain skin cladding establishes homogeneity for the ensemble. The New Museum was the tallest building SANAA had designed at the time, and the layered skin was meant to give more depth to a building that inevitably would have few windows. All exterior surfaces are clad in anodized aluminum, expanded mesh panels of approximately 1.22 by 2.44 m (4 by 8 ft) (Fig 14.6 and Fig 14.19). If from a distance the building resembles a series of imposing sculptural blocks, from up close the texture of the panels transforms it into a vibrant work of optical art that catches and reflects the changing light. The building's superstructure is steel and concrete. The exterior mesh is clipped to extruded aluminum panels (30 cm or 12 in. wide and 3 mm or 1/8 in. thick) over structural stud walls that form the actual exterior envelope. Even though a certain "roughness" was acceptable considering the building's context on the Bowery, the facade could have been more refined. Because the perforations are large, the stainless steel anchors that attach the mesh panels remain very visible. Though well done, the solution lacks real finesse, and from close up the skin reads more like an object than a surface. Compared to other similar facades in the United States such as Herzog & de Meuron's Walker Art Center, the pattern and execution of SANAA's facade appears less fussy. Yet, even if the simplicity of the New Museum solution is refreshing, a finer texture would have likely assured a similar illusion of mirage, from far or near, like that Herzog & de Meuron achieved in Minneapolis. That said, the complexity, as well as the rigor and successes of the facade, should not be minimized. The grid of the mesh fits the building precisely. One custom-made panel type was studied to adapt to the various facade conditions – the different floor heights, the different box sizes in elevation, the placement of windows behind the mesh, and the fact that the east and west walls are not parallel – so that the perforations fall neatly at each condition. Dimensions of the building itself had to be reconsidered and adjusted in relation to the exterior panel dimensions, grids, and perforations. Likewise, the emergency stairs presented a similar problem inside. Within the given space

Figure 14.2 Site plan

Figure 14.3 Floor plans

of the core they had to adapt in order to fall correctly with the varying floor to floor heights. The exterior facade is power washed yearly to maintain the overall appearance of whiteness.

The New Museum was created in 1977 by Marcia Tucker who, just prior, was a curator at the Whitney Museum of American Art in New York. Today the New Museum is one of the most important institutions of contemporary art in the United States. Before SANAA completed the new 5,574 m^2 (square meter; 60,000 ft^2 (square foot)) building on the Bowery, the museum was located on Broadway not far from its present site.

The six stacked boxes apparent from the exterior correspond more or less to the various interior spaces (Fig 14.8 and Fig 14.9). Even though the striking form might appear to be above all a simple architectural gesture, the architects affirm that the project was conceived from the inside out and was a response to the program requirements. The interior spaces are indeed well organized, optimized, and functional.

The New Museum site is 22 m (71 ft) wide and 34 m (112 ft) deep. The building has seven occupied levels above grade and one below (Fig 14.3). At ground level, information and ticket sales, the museum store, and a cafe are located in a 465 m^2 (1,525 ft^2) lobby behind a full height, 4.6 m (15 ft), glazed facade

Figure 14.4 View from west/Prince Street

Figure 14.5 View of entry

Figure 14.6 View of facade panels

Figure 14.7 View of roof

facing the Bowery (Fig 14.12). The museum store is a curved, freestanding object made of screens also of metal mesh. A narrow, 102 m^2 (1,100 ft^2) gallery with natural top lighting occupies the back of the ground level. A full height glass wall separates this space from the rest of the lobby and allows visitors a first glimpse of works of art immediately upon entering the building. A stair with a glass railing runs parallel to the street and is situated between the boutique and the cafe. It descends to a very simple and pragmatic 180 seat auditorium with white walls and a wood floor that is used for events and lectures as well as for the projection of art videos as part of exhibitions. A small installation space, public restrooms, mechanical rooms, and storage spaces are also located in the basement.

The museum has street access to the Bowery only. Passersby can also glimpse the behind the scenes workings of the museum – delivery, uncrating, storage, etc. – through the two large glazed delivery doors. The ground floor is predominately white. The floors are polished gray concrete. A metal mesh ceiling masks the structure and fluorescent lights above.

The vertical core is pushed to the north side of the building and defines two unequal bays on all levels. It contains a double-sided freight elevator, a passenger elevator, two emergency stairs, and mechanical and service areas. Floors two, three, and four are dedicated to galleries. An education center, classrooms, meeting room, and the Museum as Hub are on the fifth floor. The Museum as Hub is an education and exhibition space meant to create dialogue among museums around the world. Administrative offices occupy the sixth floor. Office spaces are tight but strip windows on the east and south sides provide views and light. The seventh floor, the last level accessible to the public, is a multi-use reception room called the Skyroom (Fig 14.16). This 186 m^2 (2,000 ft^2) space is a destination in itself since the glazed walls and narrow terraces to the east and south offer spectacular views of the downtown Manhattan skyline. The Skyroom has 3.4 m (11 ft) ceilings, gypsum board walls, and a poured epoxy floor.

Mechanical rooms occupy the eighth level. Mechanical equipment is also located on the roof level which is contained within the uppermost box (Fig 14.7). The ubiquitous New York wooden water tanks are also on the New Museum's roof and are unexpected in the context. Air handlers for floors 5, 6, and 7 are located on the roof. Those for the galleries on floors 2, 3, and 4 are located in the eighth floor mechanical room while the air handlers for the ground floor and lower level are located in the basement. The gallery space on the ground floor is conditioned like the lobby space rather than like the other galleries that have strict climate control. This has an influence on the type of artwork that can be exhibited within.

At the New Museum, architectural neutrality was felt to be the best solution for the exhibition of contemporary art, and the three gallery levels are simple and flexible. Without hesitation or unnecessary complication SANAA decided to simply create "white cube" gallery spaces that are generally well proportioned, have no intermediate columns, and are well suited for the exhibition of various types of art. The spaces are somewhat rough and the atmosphere approaches that of an idealized artist's studio. Walls are gypsum board and the floors are concrete. A reveal in the concrete makes the transition between floor and wall. This gap was also conceived as a space to run electrical cables. There is no dropped ceiling and ducts, sprinklers, and beams fireproofed with intumescent paint are left visible. All the interior spaces are white with the exception of the inside of the elevator and freight elevator that are bright apple green. The restrooms in the basement are also an exception and are enlivened by brightly colored mosaic tiles. Even if the vast majority of American museums at the beginning of the new century still use incandescent lighting in exhibition spaces, the New Museum opted for fluorescent tube lighting on light tracks. The galleries often appear over lit, however, which makes the spaces seem severe and un-sensual.

In ascending, gallery spaces become smaller but higher: the second floor gallery (Fig 14.13) is 465 m^2 (5,000 ft^2) and 5.5 m (18 ft) high; the third floor gallery (Fig 14.14) is 372 m^2 (4,000 ft^2) and 5.8 m (19 ft) high; and the fourth floor is 279 m^2 (3,000 ft^2) and 7.3 m (24 ft) high. Since they are separated on different floors, the continuity of materials, details, and color outweighs what remains a subtle change in room proportions, and the exhibition spaces on the three levels resemble each other more than not. It is a veritable challenge to create a coherent whole in a vertical museum, and the stacked galleries can produce disorientation in navigating the building especially when the spatial link is through elevators and enclosed stairs.

The largest gallery on the second floor is autonomous. The core divides it into two areas with the smaller to the north. Those on the third and fourth floors are linked by a surprisingly narrow stair that is squeezed between the core and the north exterior wall (Fig 14.15). At a first landing level a small (1.5 by 2.4 m; 5 by 8 ft) but very high (10.7 m; 35 ft) exhibition niche called The Shaft is on one side, and at a second landing there is a large window oriented toward Midtown. The entire stair space has a playful character. A window at the top of the stair on the fourth floor offers views of the city to the west. Windows are judiciously placed to offer views and a pause in the visit without significantly reducing hanging space.

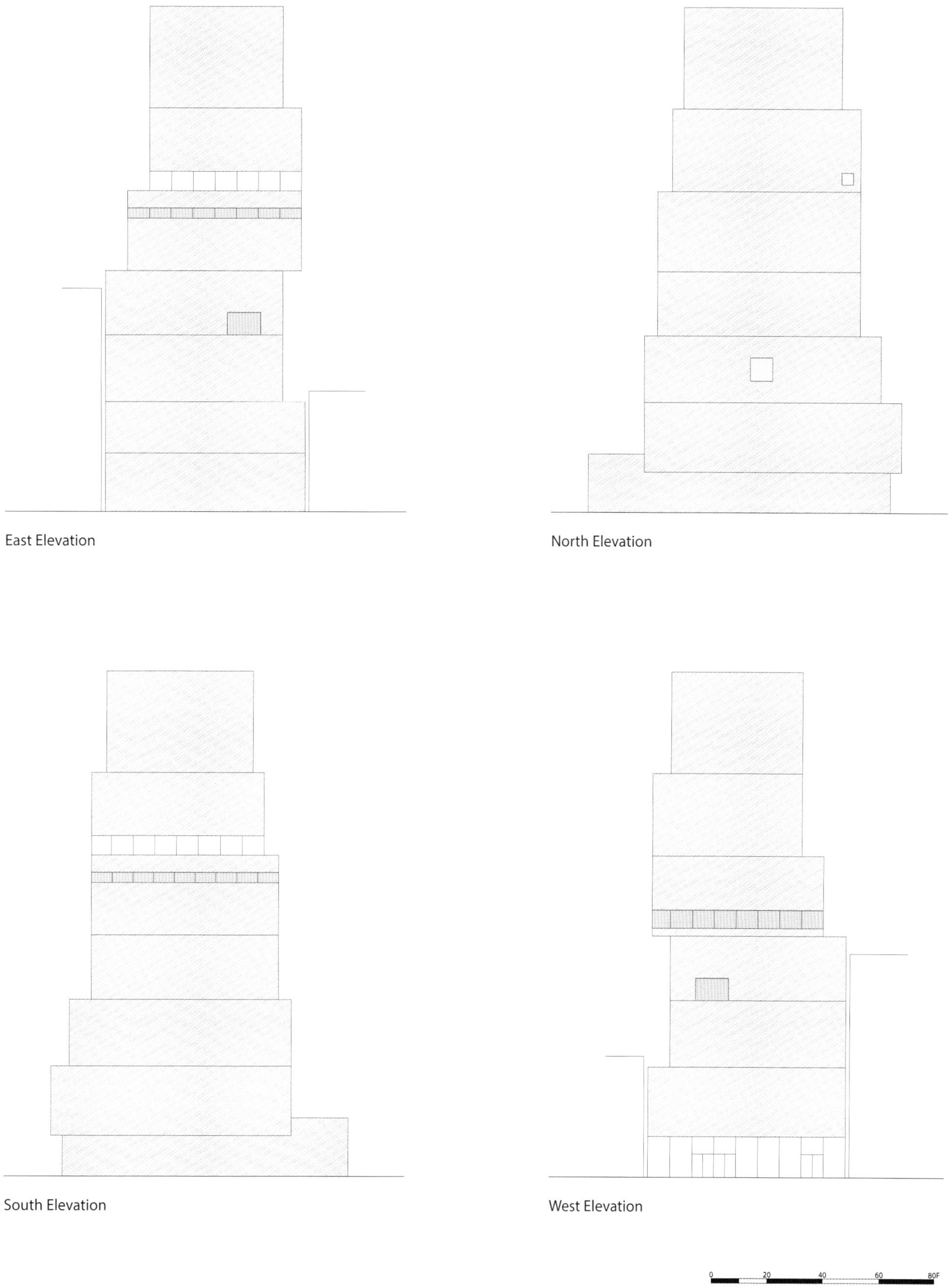

Figure 14.8 Elevations

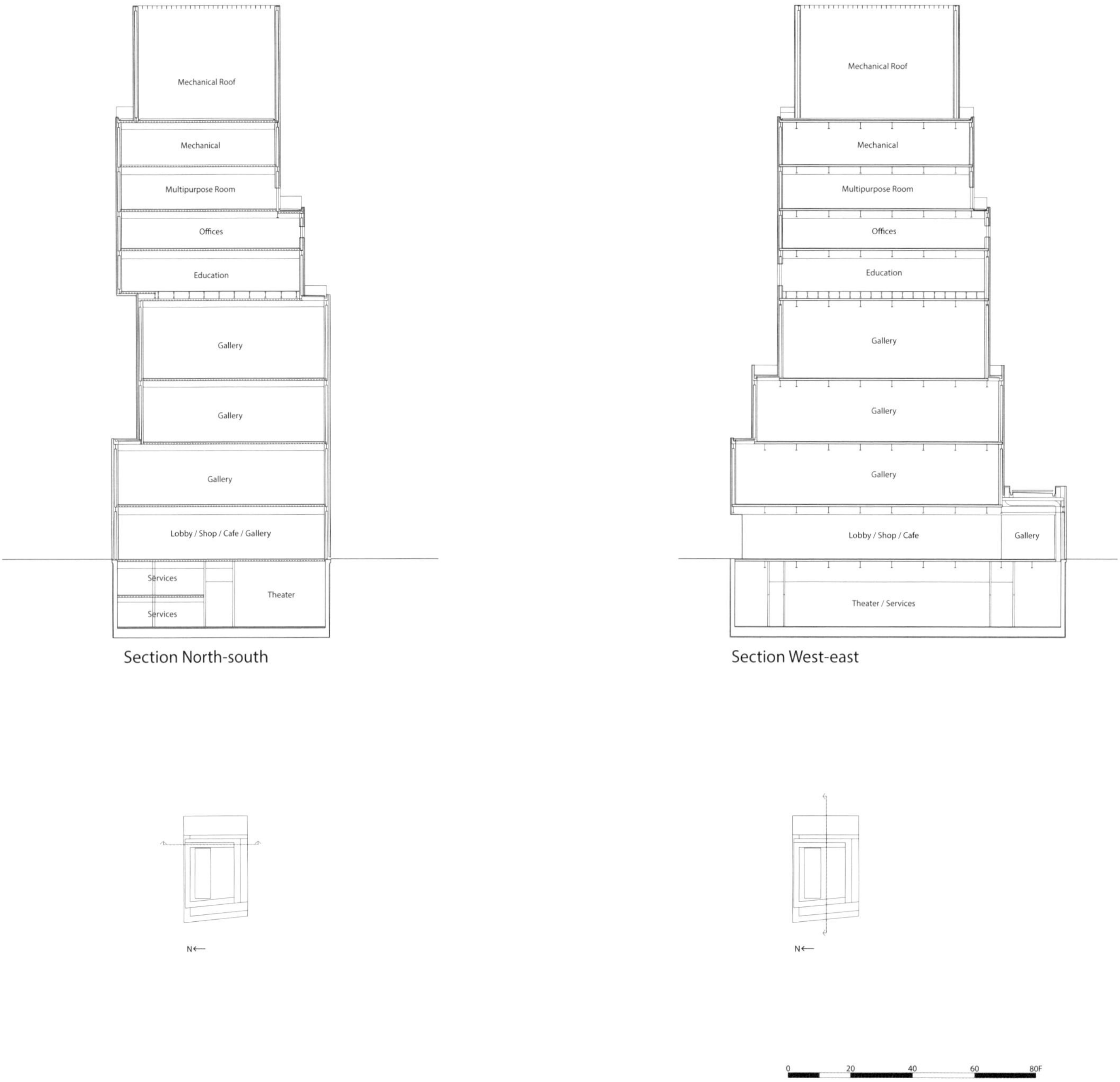

Figure 14.9 Sections

Figure 14.10 Competition model

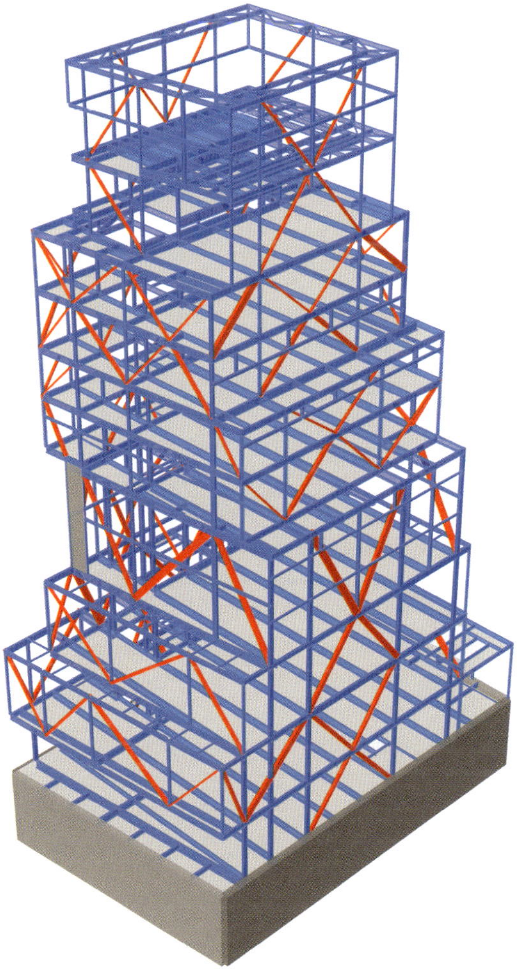

Figure 14.11 Structural diagram

Figure 14.12 Interior – lobby and lobby gallery

Figure 14.13 Interior – second floor gallery

Figure 14.14 Interior – third floor gallery

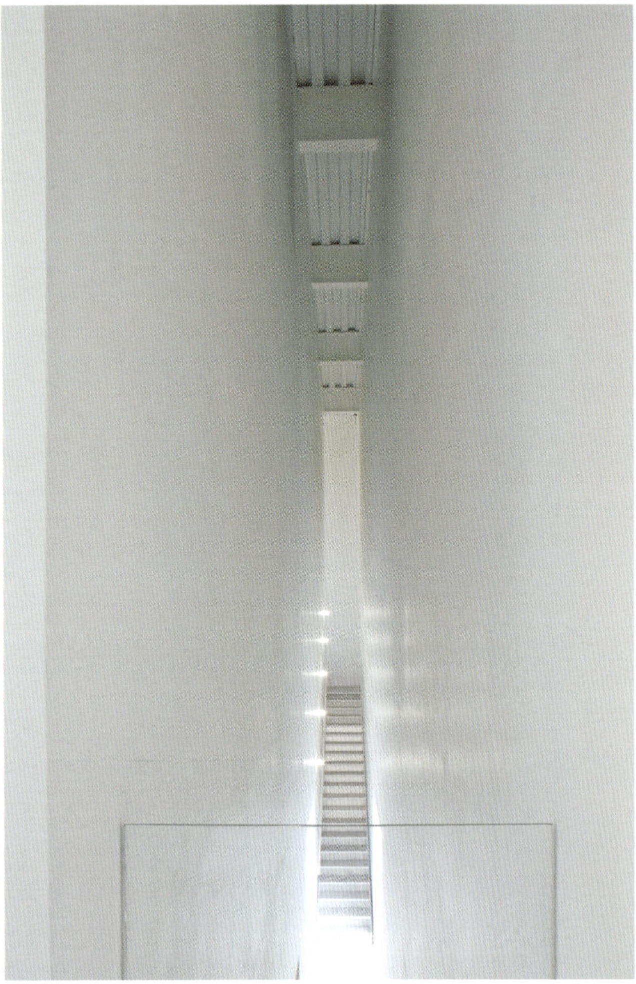

Figure 14.15 Stair between third and fourth floors

Figure 14.16 Skyroom

The vertical circulation by elevators is sometimes slow and the alternative offered by the stairs is functional but not very pleasant. The transition between floors feels abrupt as does the transition between the elevator and the gallery space. When video art is exposed, for example, light from the elevator is a nuisance with every door opening.

SANAA's scheme of shifted boxes also provided an opportunity for integrating natural top lighting into the lower floors of this vertical museum by using the setback spaces for skylights. Yoshio Taniguchi proposed a similar solution for the galleries at the Museum of Modern Art in New York, but it was not retained. At the New Museum, skylights run along the west and north walls on the second floor, the east and west walls on the third floor, and along the south wall on the fourth floor. As ingenious as the solution may be, the natural light washes certain walls but does not provide general, exhibition lighting for the space. All skylights are equipped with horizontal motorized shades that are often closed. The detail of the skylight complex is compact and well conceived (Fig 14.17 and Fig 14.18). Acrylic panels maintain alignments inside while a metal grating outside above the skylights provides shading for the glass and neatly completes the box form.

The offset of the boxes creates a situation where there are no continuous columns other than in the core. The structural complexity is compounded by the skylights that fill the spaces between the boxes. At the ceiling level of the second floor the skylight turns the angle at the north/west corner with six floors hovering above. The competition drawings showed a triangular corner bracket inside under the skylights that transferred the loads from above to the walls below (Fig 14.10). During the elaboration of the project, the engineers, Guy Nordenson and Associates, managed to eliminate the bracket and transfer the loads toward the core without interrupting the horizontal glazing of the roof. All the structure of the building including the core is in steel. Large trusses around the perimeter of the boxes sit on floor beams at mid span (Fig 14.11). At some places the truss diagonals remain visible in front of the windows, but in general the structure is hidden in the walls which were kept as thin as possible so as not to take up valuable floor area. Like at the Toledo Glass Pavilion, the structure of the New Museum is not a regular grid typical of modern architecture. In this case the structure is more scattered throughout the building.

The New Museum was SANAA's second realization in the United States after the Glass Pavilion for the Toledo Museum of Art that opened in 2006. The all glass pavilion appears refined and luxurious. Ironically, its price per square foot represents half that of the more frugal appearing New Museum since, for diverse reasons, the cost of construction in Manhattan is elevated. Nevertheless, the two projects share a method of conception that is often found in SANAA's work. In Toledo, like at the Museum of Contemporary Art in Kanazawa in Japan, the different parts of the program were identified and expressed much like independent buildings placed side by side and then reunited by a glass envelope. In New York the method is similar, but this time done vertically: each program piece is expressed as an independent box and a skin is used to make the ensemble uniform. The color white also unifies the various parts.

Much of the work exhibited at the New Museum shows that the plastic arts occupy a privileged place for exploring and confronting living culture. The museum's architecture, though unusual and surprising, resists overt social comment itself. SANAA's work is more preoccupied with architectural issues such as transparency, lightness, flexibility, simplicity, and program. There is a tranquil nonchalance in the project, and even if SANAA claims logic and pragmatism in their design method, the result is also joyful and full of emotion.

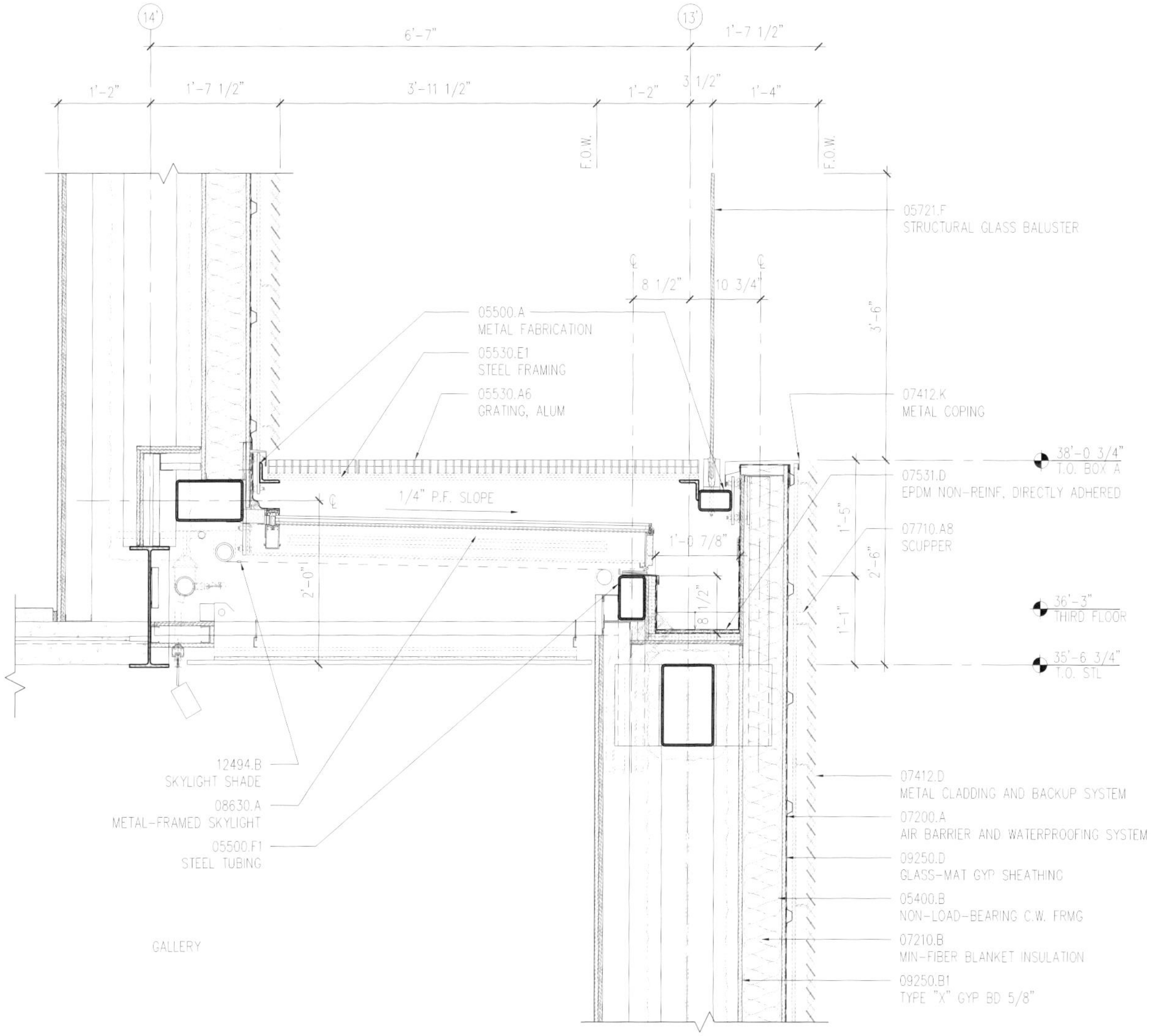

Figure 14.17 Skylight section 1

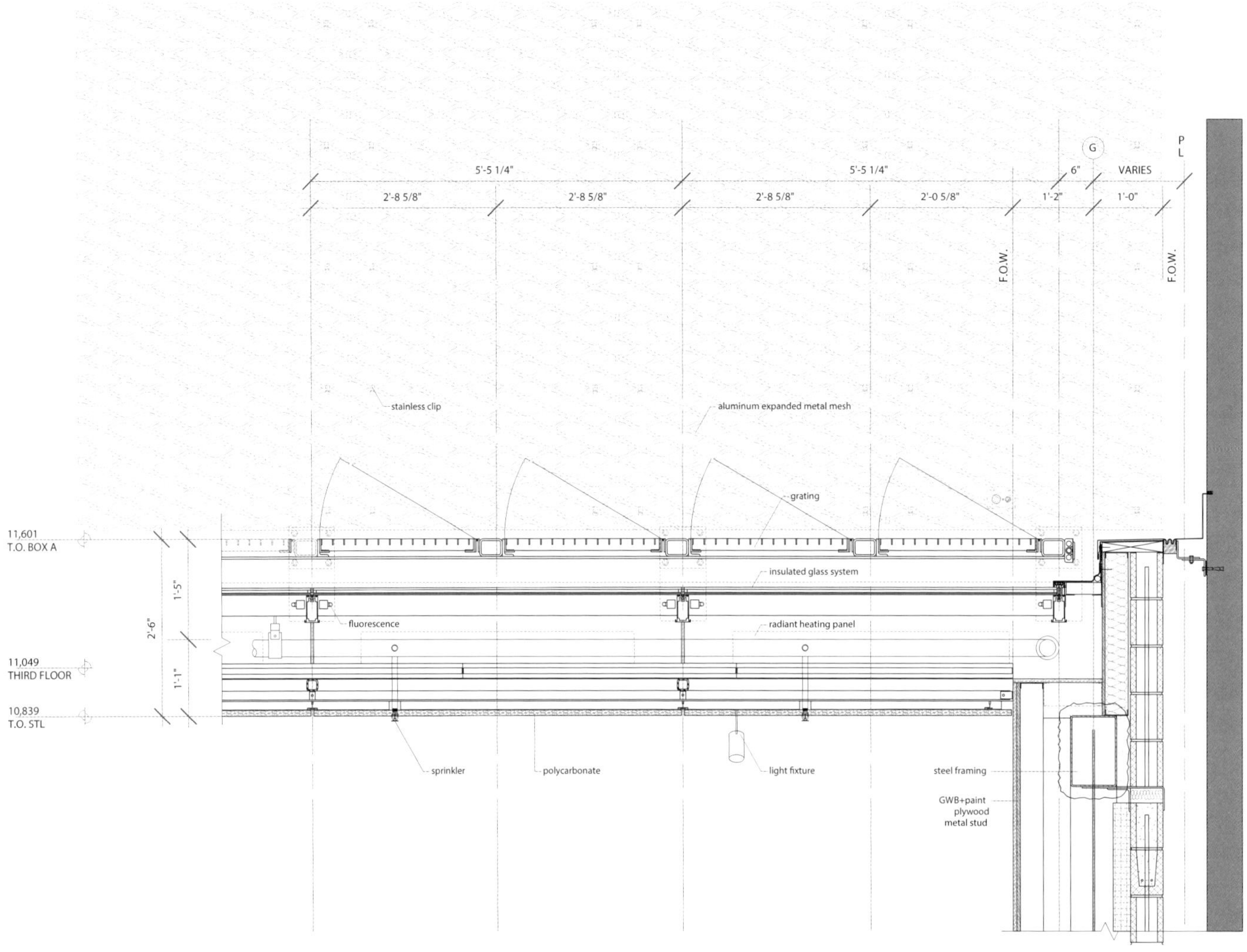

Figure 14.18 Skylight section 2

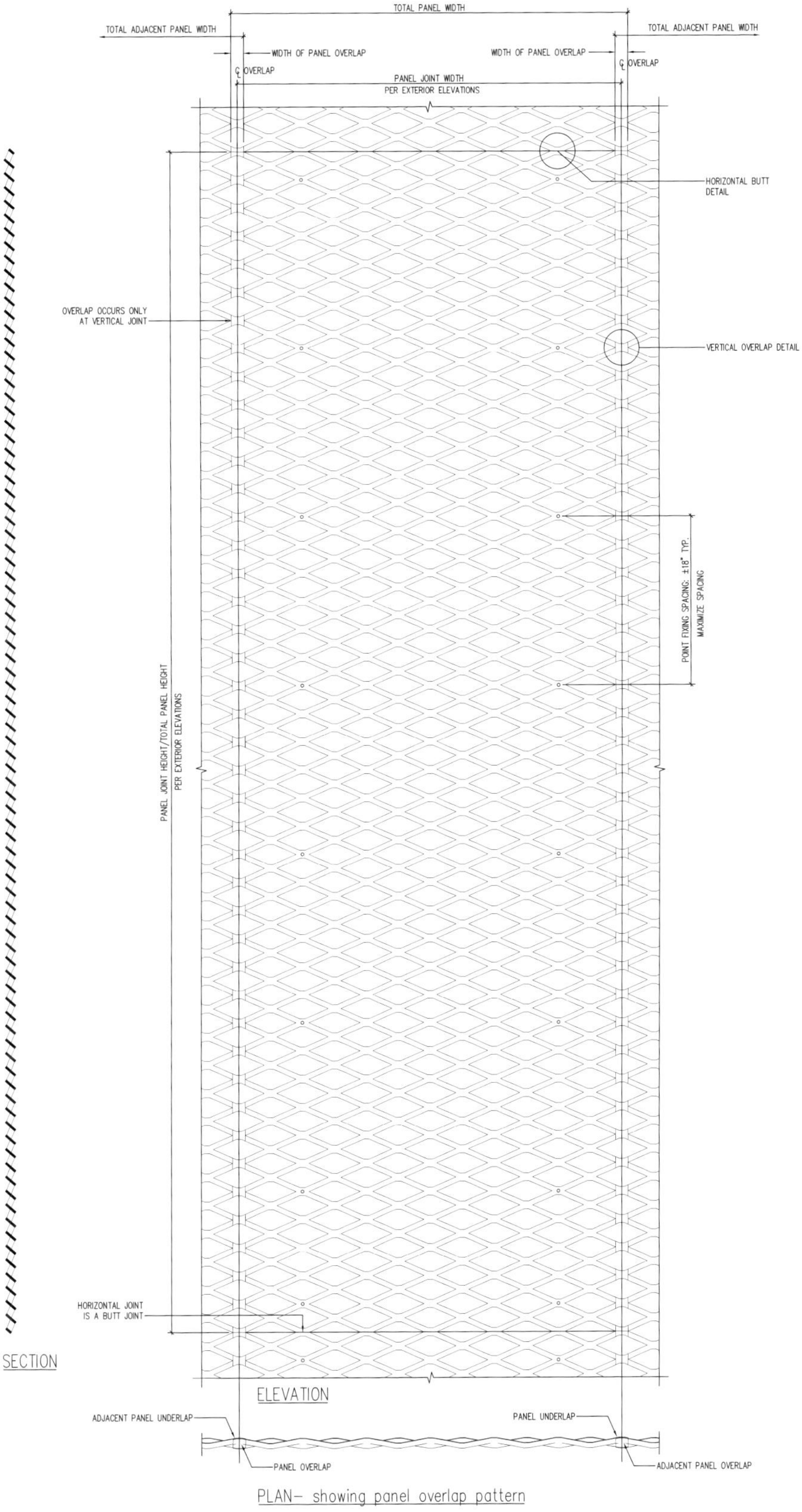

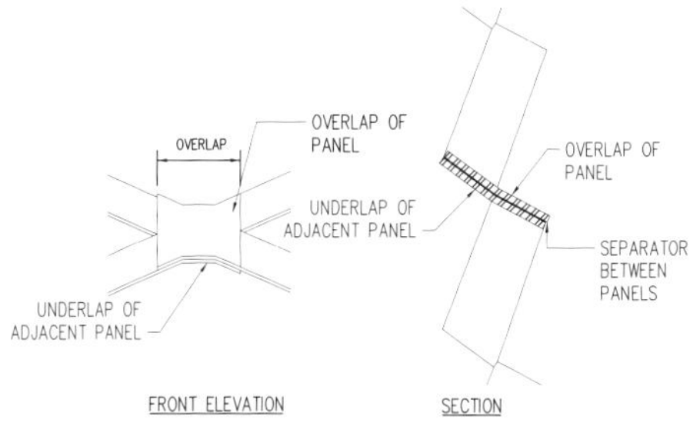

Vertical Overlap Detail

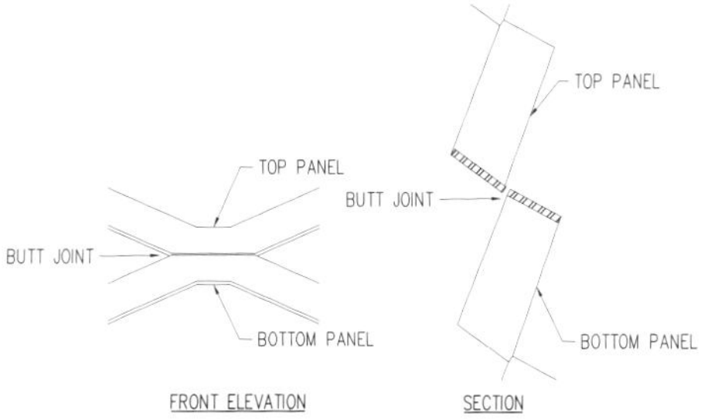

Horizontal Butt Joint

Figure 14.19 Cladding panel details

CHAPTER 15

Acropolis Museum

Athens, Greece

Bernard Tschumi Architects

2009

Figure 15.1 View from north/east

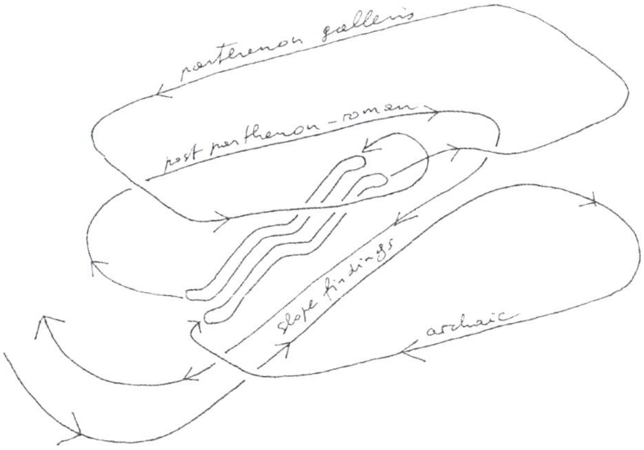

Figure 15.2 Sketch by Bernard Tschumi

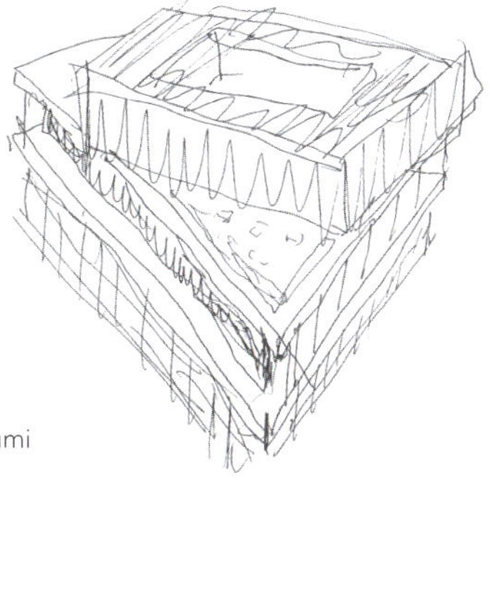

Figure 15.4 Sketch by Bernard Tschumi

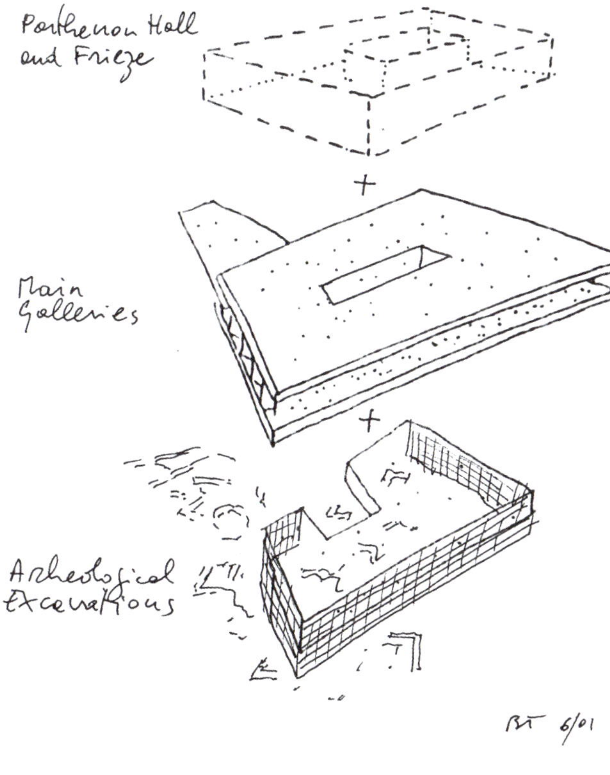

Figure 15.3 Sketch by Bernard Tschumi

> Department stores and museums have one thing in common: the need for seduction through a language of display. Each product exhibited becomes an object of desire, and walking is the preferred means to apprehend such objects of desire. A slow dance begins between two bodies – the dynamic body of the visitor/consumer and the static body of the object of consumption.

Though this statement by Bernard Tschumi in *Event-Cities 2* to describe his concept for a department store in Zurich might trivialize the work of museums and museum professionals, it does somewhat describe the fate of the Elgin Marbles that were such *objects of desire* that Thomas Bruce – Lord Elgin – had them removed from the Acropolis over the period of a decade in the early nineteenth century and shipped to England. Still displayed in the British Museum two centuries later, London desires to keep them, and Athens desires to have them back. The Acropolis Museum (Fig 15.1) provides a more seductive and better controlled environment to exhibit objects that were previously housed in a modest, late nineteenth-century museum located on the Acropolis itself. It also has specifically designed spaces, ready and waiting for the return of the disputed sculptures. The project was meant as a carrot and a stick for the return of the Elgin Marbles as well as sculptures in other museums around the world. It had a clear political goal.

The Acropolis Museum is an archaeological museum. It differs from many art museums in that the curatorial installation is virtually permanent, and the building was designed for specific pieces that are generally arranged chronologically. There is a tight fit between the container and the contained even if many exhibition spaces approach neutrality. Because of this and somewhat because of the architect's own preoccupations, the path, or circulation "loop," through the building is highly prescribed (Fig 15.2). There is not a notion of discovery or alternate path options that some art museums have developed. Though this may also seem contradictory to Tschumi's more general idea that architecture should encourage unpredictability, he had already explored the idea of a circulation loop for a competition entry for the National Maritime Museum in Antwerp in the year 2000. The display of objects in Athens is often analogous in a very direct way to the original location or previous circumstances of the works. Artifacts found on the slopes of the Acropolis, for example, are exhibited on a sloped ramp and the architectural sculptures of the Parthenon are exhibited within an abstracted reinterpretation of the building itself.

A new museum to house the works from the Acropolis had been under consideration since the 1970s. The current site was acquired and three previous architectural competitions were launched over the years. The third competition in the late 1980s was abandoned after important archaeological ruins were found on the site. The fourth and final competition launched in the year 2000 required that the ruins be integrated into the design. Out of 12 competitors, Bernard Tschumi Architects in collaboration with Michael Photiadis of Athens were announced the winners in October 2001. The building was to open for the 2004 Athens Olympic Games; but the project was slowed by opposition from multiple fronts and was completed only in September 2007. The works of art were moved from the old museum on the Acropolis to the new building below by a spectacular relay among three cranes installed on the slopes specifically for the transfer – a true event in the city. The museum opened to the public on June 20, 2009.

The Acropolis Museum is located on a 23,000 m^2 (square meter; 247,500 ft^2 (square foot)) site in the Makriyianni area of Athens that offers an impressive view of the Parthenon to the north-west (Fig 15.5). The primary access is on the north side of the site from the Dionysiou Areopagitou, a pedestrian street that also borders the Acropolis. The building is positioned at the center of the site and several remaining buildings on the block line the surrounding streets. Though Tschumi's project is larger (21,000 m^2 or 226,000 ft^2), taller, and more massive than its neighbors, it is somewhat masked and its impact at street level is diminished by the preexisting buildings. The structure is relatively compact and seems to have found a good equilibrium between its footprint and its height. Gardens and open spaces of approximately 7,000 m^2 (75,500 ft^2) create a buffer between the museum and the surrounding neighborhood, a lively area comprised of apartment buildings, shops, restaurants, etc. The site is gated and does not function as a public park or square. Mechanical equipment is located in an open space along Hatzichristou Street to the south along with several on-grade parking places. Trees have been planted around the building but are still small. There is a second and less used pedestrian site entrance to the west, and service entries are located to the east where a ramp leads down to a loading dock and parking well below the level of the adjacent street. The metro station *Akropoli* is also to the east and within the city block of the museum. Tourists are abundant in the area.

From the street, visitors pass through a planted area between preexisting buildings, descend stairs, and approach the Acropolis Museum via a bridge. A ramp system that appears almost temporary also switches back and forth toward the entry level. Tschumi's north facade is partially hidden by the Weiler Building, a neoclassical structure built in 1836 as a military hospital and used today as offices for the museum. The new structure hovers above the archaeological ruins that date from the fourth to seventh centuries AD in order to disturb them as little as possible; this also entailed discussions and negotiations for the position of each and every structural column. Openings in the

Figure 15.5 Site plan

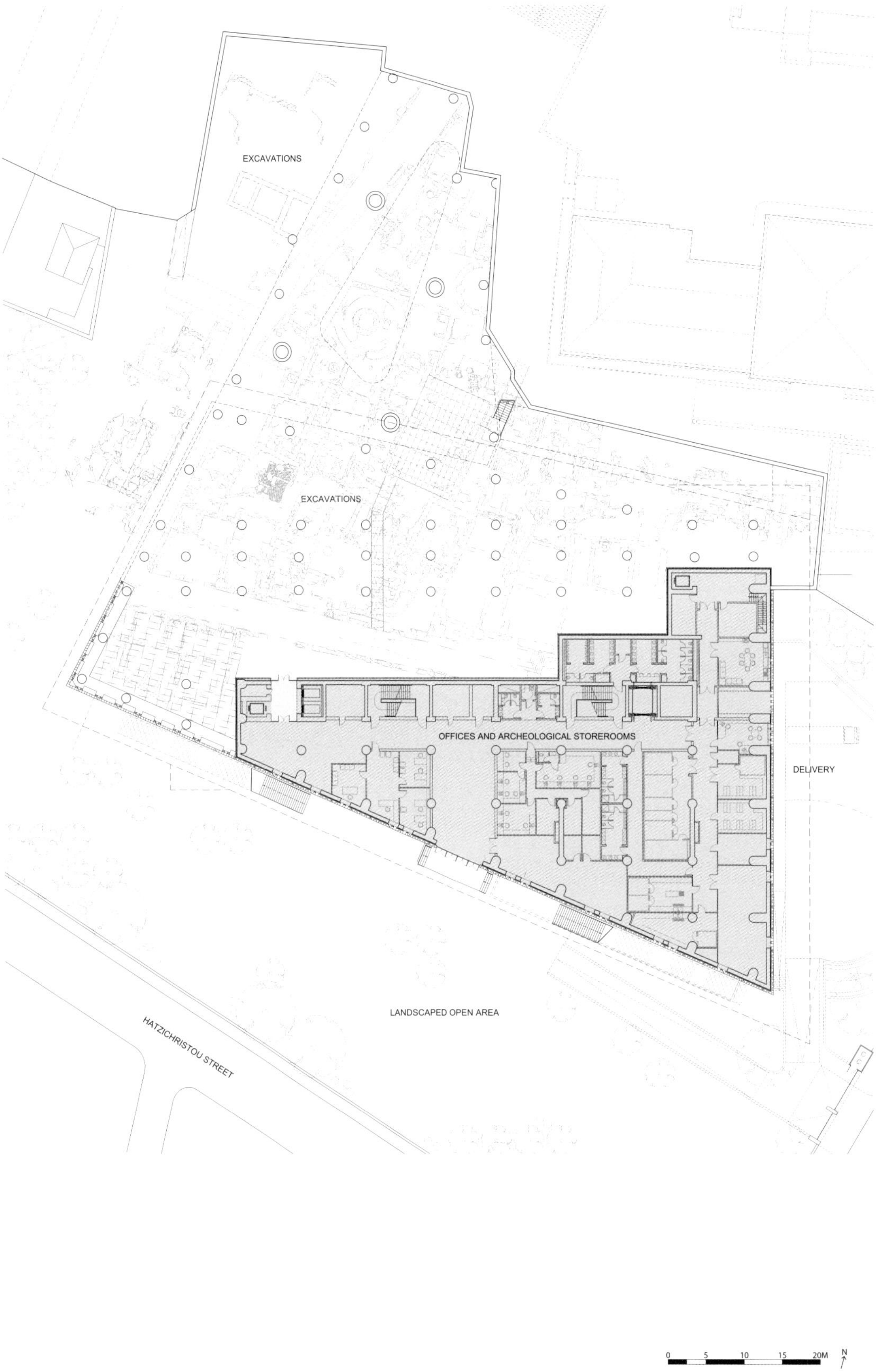

Figure 15.6 Lower level floor plan

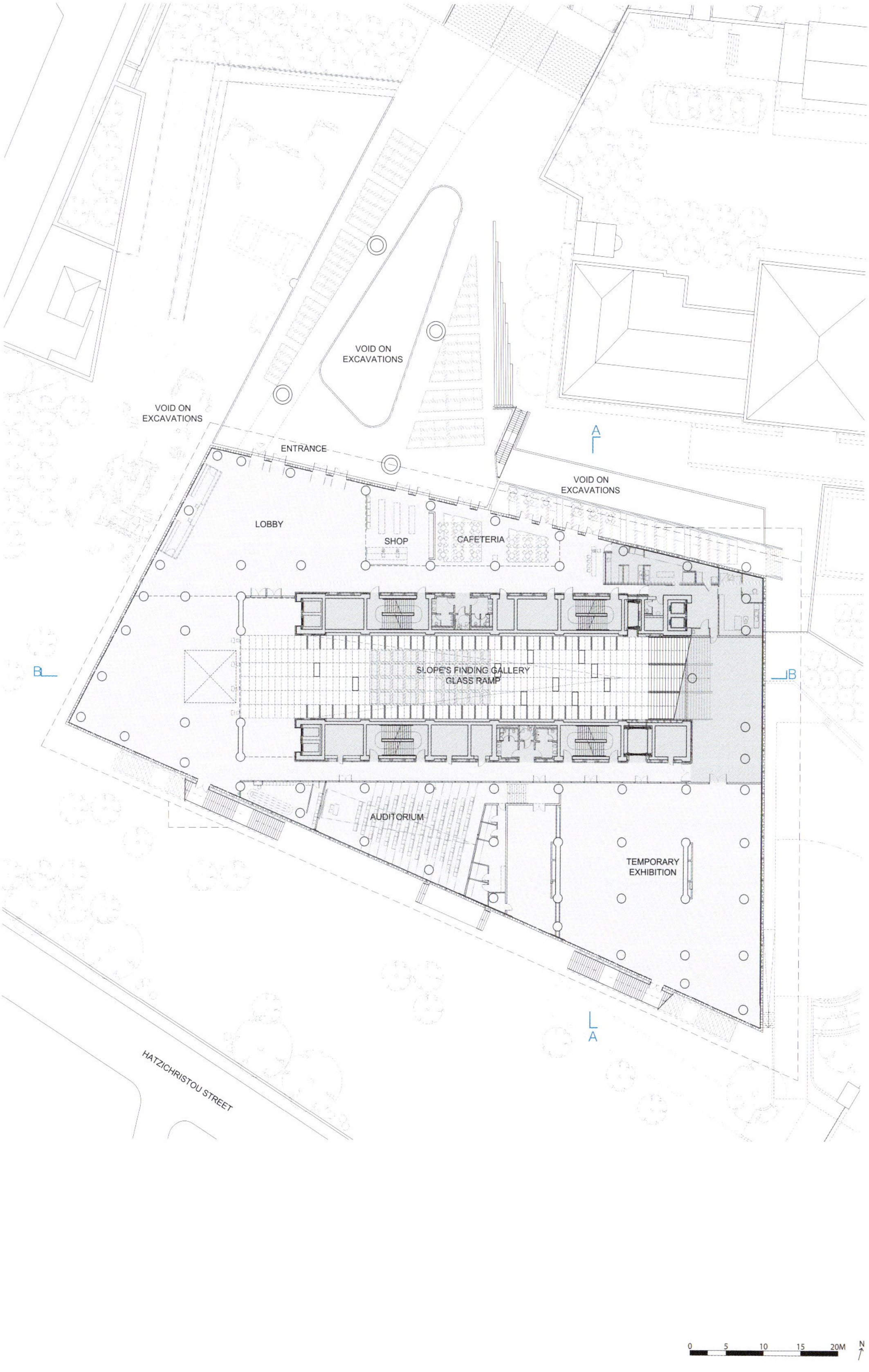

Figure 15.7 First (ground) floor plan

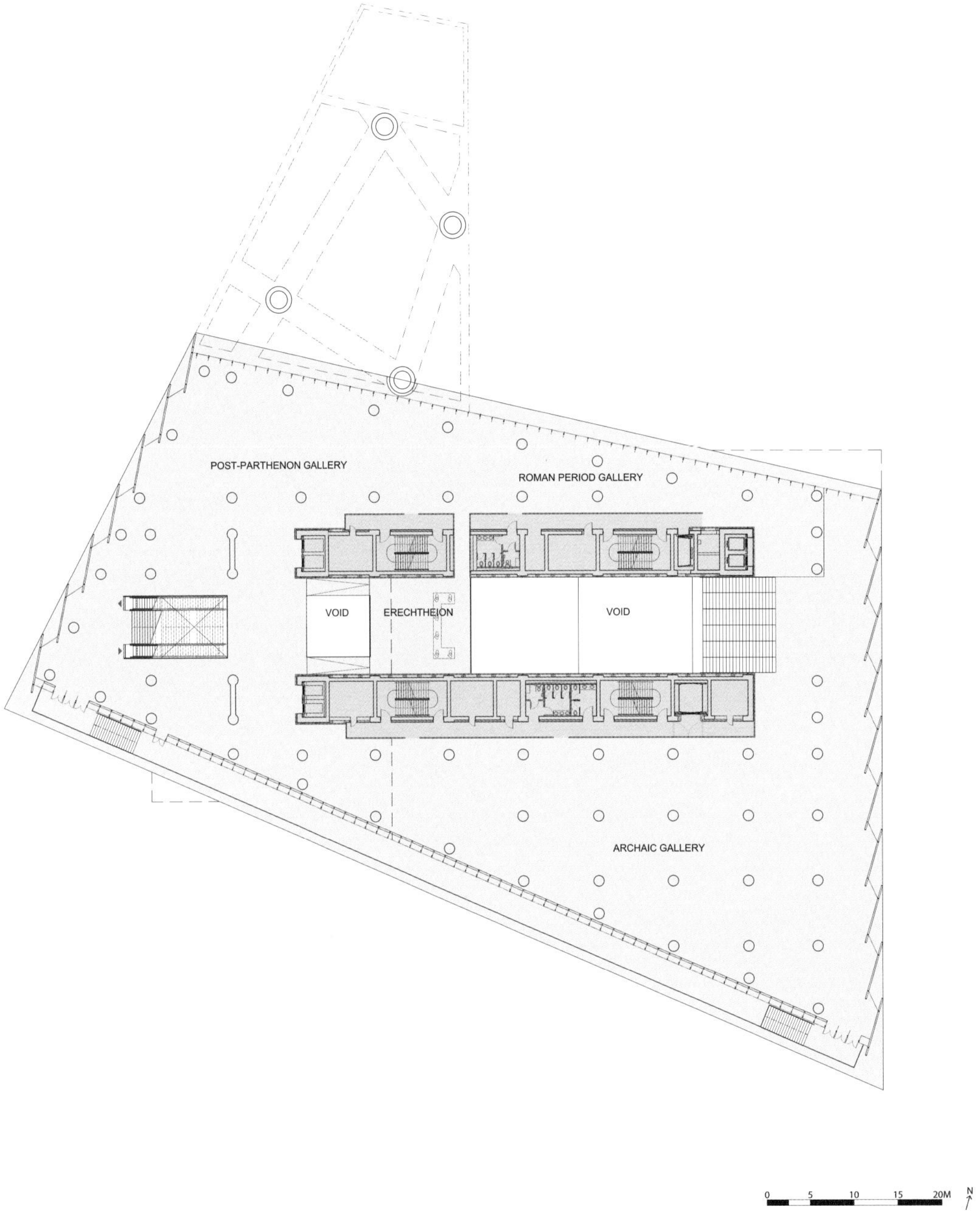

Figure 15.8 Second floor plan

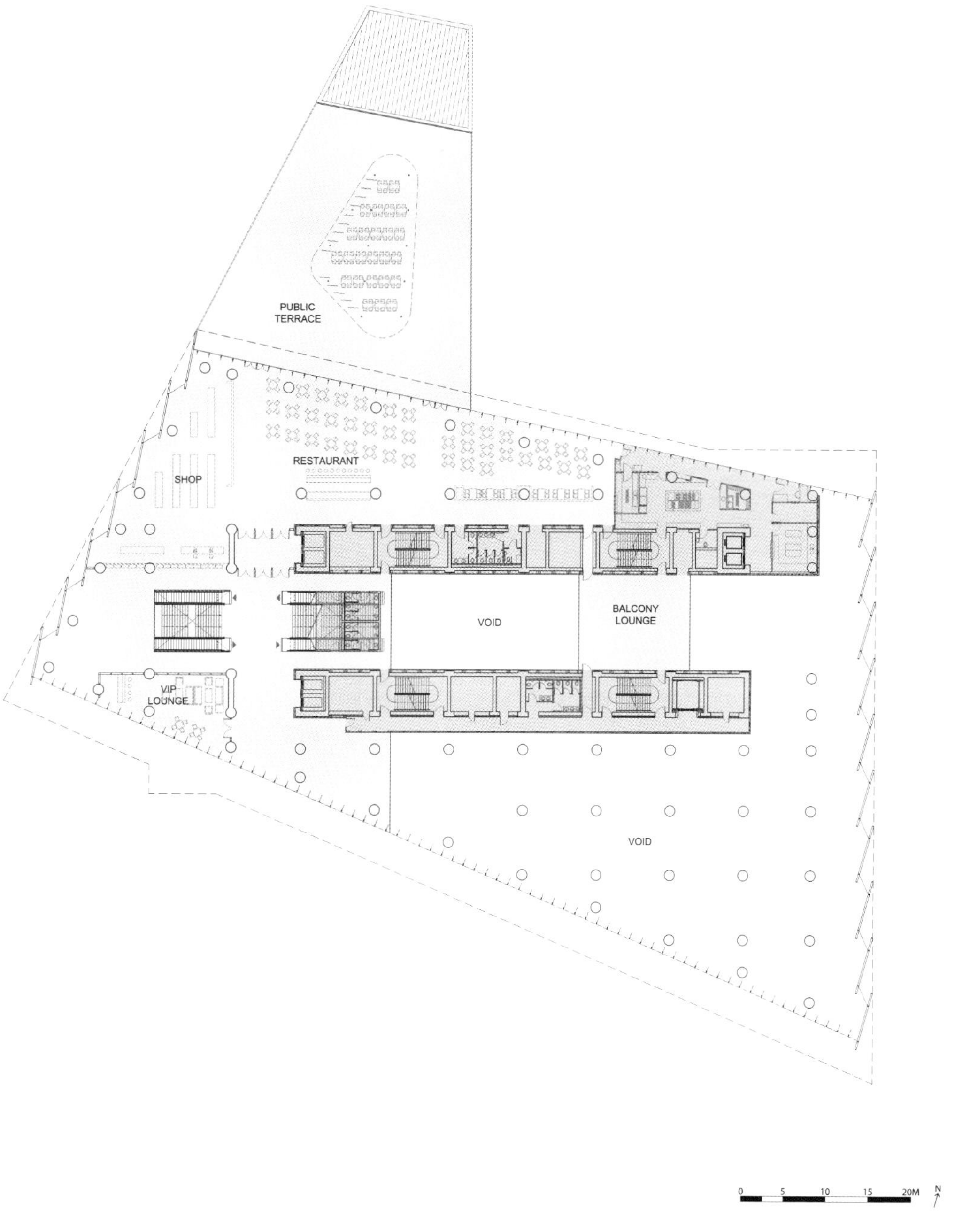

Figure 15.9 Third floor plan

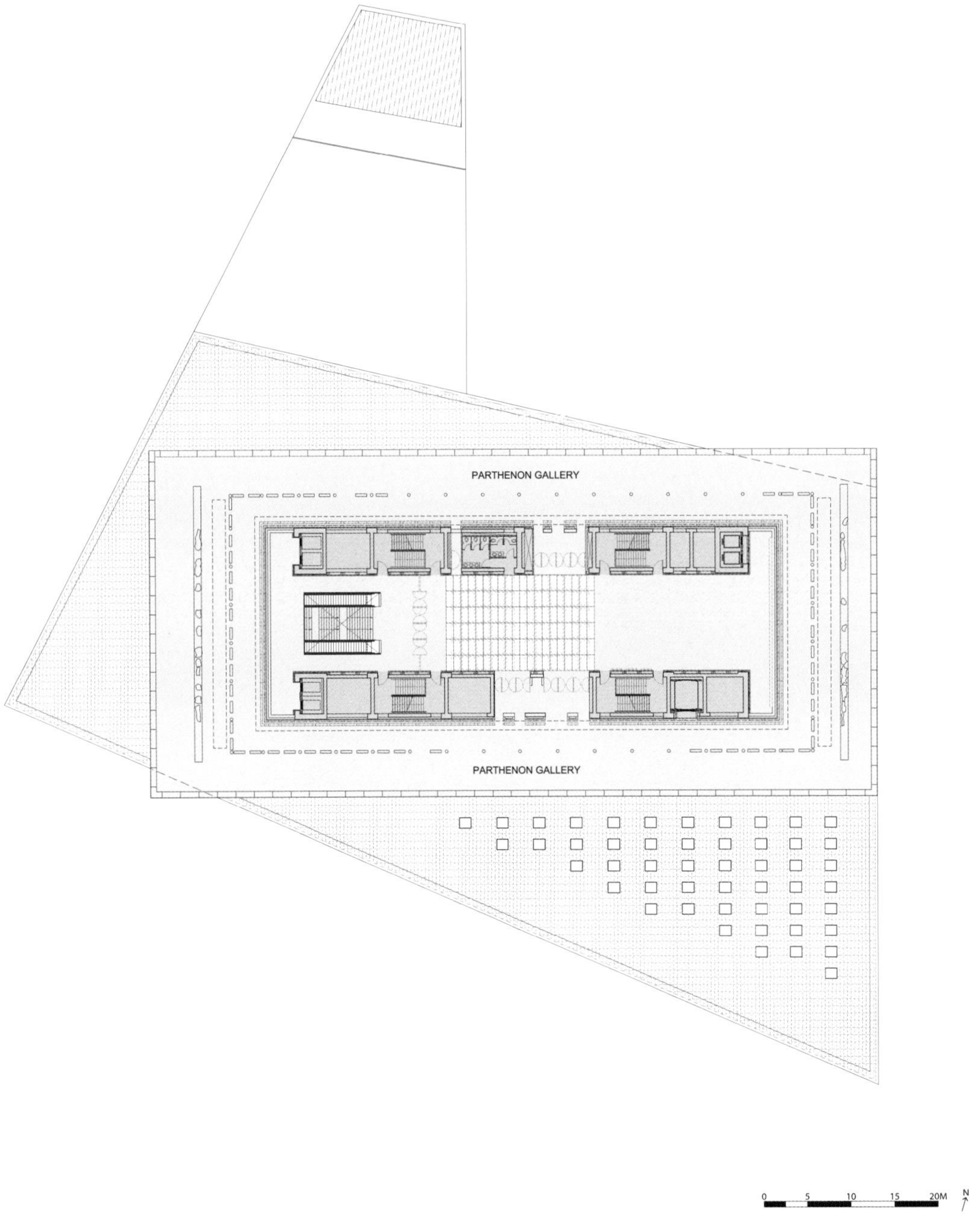

Figure 15.10 Fourth floor plan

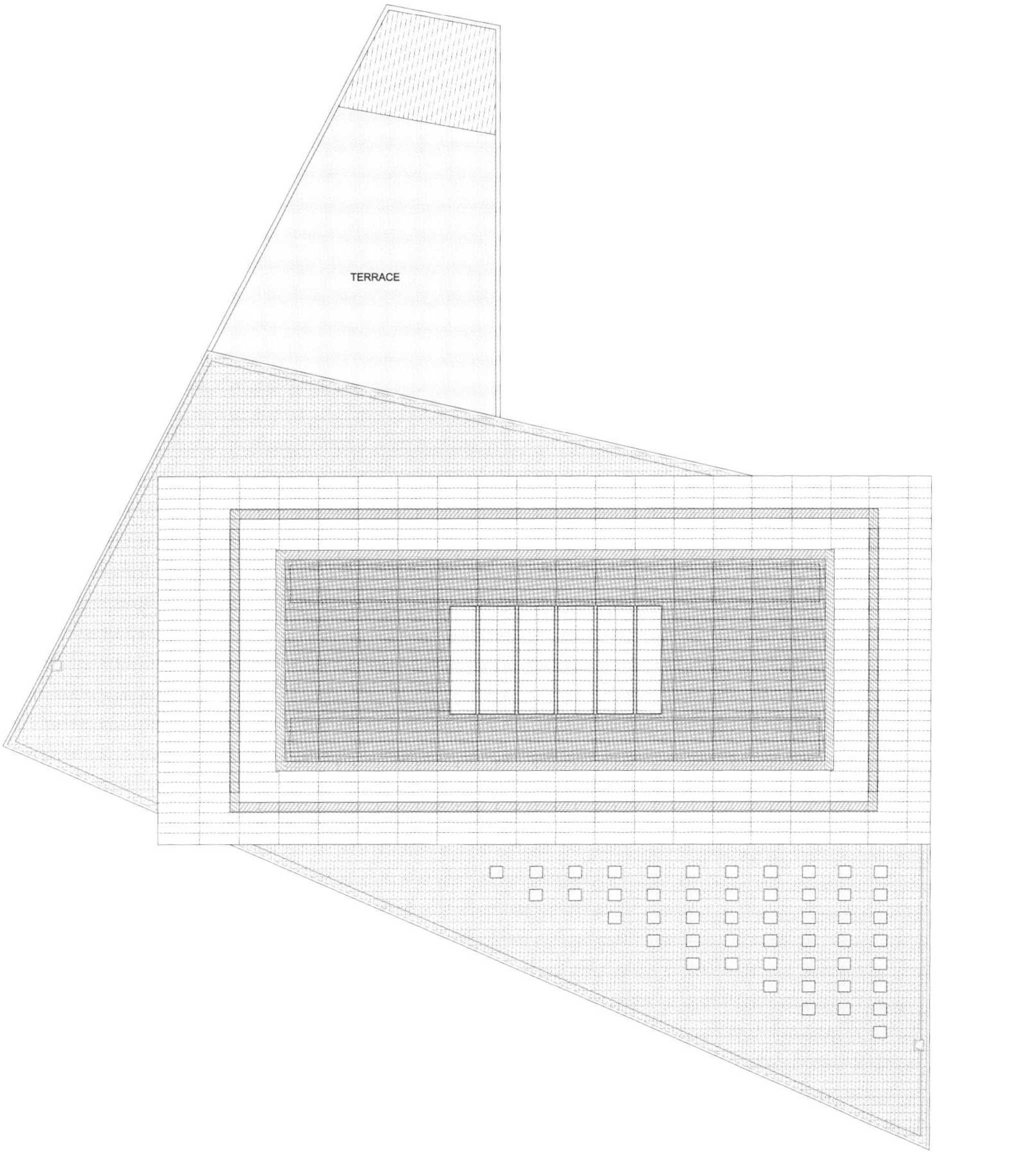

Figure 15.11 Roof plan

ground plane of the bridge and glass floor areas allow views down to the ruins and announce viewing conditions to be found inside the museum. A concrete, trapezoidal canopy supported by four large concrete pillars protects arriving visitors and projects from the main mass of the museum roughly at the same height as the adjacent portion of the Weiler Building (Fig 15.13 and Fig 15.16).

Tschumi's building appears simple, restrained, and solemn. The main material palette of concrete, glass, and stone is already evident as is the composition of the building as three stacked layers (base, middle, top) that also represent three different program areas (Fig 15.3 and Fig 15.4). The expressed floor slabs and the placement of columns behind the glass facade accentuate horizontality. A series of large, double-story, stainless steel-clad fins caps the east and west ends of the building. Two exterior emergency stairs located on the south facade descend from the main gallery level (Fig 15.12). Surrounding buildings are generally light colored, and the museum's dark-colored glass makes it stand out. From the adjacent streets the building sometimes appears only as the uppermost volume of the skewed, elevated black box of the Parthenon Gallery. From other vantage points, the box is completely masked by the lower levels.

Tschumi has elucidated his ideas on architecture in several books and interviews, and the movement of bodies through architectural space (vectors) is likely the most important. Elements such as stairs, ramps, escalators, elevators, bridges, catwalks, etc. are exploited to make buildings dynamic. Movement activates while building envelopes define boundaries. Tschumi strategizes projects in order to avoid "facades," and the necessary envelopes or enclosures should not attempt to impart meaning. Architecture should be less about what it looks like and more about creating events through the conjunction of space and movement. It should be less about form, composition, or the visual and more about concepts. Architecture is seen as the materialization of concepts.

All of these convictions are also evident in the design of the Acropolis Museum. Concerning context, however, Tschumi strayed from his usual principles that architecture should transcend local circumstances and should not necessarily be unique to its context. In the exceptional situation of Athens and the Acropolis, the architect was compelled to develop a project that is inseparable from its context, site, and circumstances.

The way the building is conceived also relies on previously developed and tested strategies or concepts. Just as Tschumi's Parc de la Villette in Paris was based on the superposition of independent systems of lines, points, and surfaces, the Acropolis Museum is also a conceptual layering of autonomous elements. In Athens the strategy translates more directly into recognizable architectural form with a base, a middle, and a top.

Figure 15.12 View from south/west

Figure 15.13 View from north/west

Tschumi's architectural priorities likely explain why the building looks somewhat schematic from the outside. For the architect, the envelope keeps out rain, heat, noise, and burglars. Though the glass facades are refined, their detail does not show up from afar. During the day they appear as homogenous planes. For Tschumi, homogeneity of material should make the concept clearer. There is also an unmediated leap between the robust, horizontal floor slabs and the glass facades. Likewise, the large metal fin elements at the east and west ends of the building appear alien to the ensemble (Fig 15.1). While the rectangular volume at the top makes complete sense conceptually, it seems less resolved architecturally, and the way it pokes over the lower volume is visually awkward. There is little of the articulation, detail, relief, or visual refinement of the building that stands 300 m (980 ft) away that Tschumi acknowledges as one of the most influential buildings of the Western world. The architecture becomes richer at night, however, when the thickness of the curtain walls along with the structure behind becomes visible. Through transparency, flatness is exchanged for depth and the ancient architectural sculptures exhibited behind the envelope enliven the new building and become part of it. The promenade of visitors inside affirms the concept of movement and event. Seeing inside also renders the building more public.

The museum is also highly visible from the Acropolis. The roof surfaces were considered as facades, and there is no mechanical equipment or other noticeable protrusions when viewed from above. The roof of the highest volume of the building, the Parthenon Gallery, is clad in fritted glass on spacers, much like the vertical facades. Areas of stainless steel grating shade skylights below or mask air handling units that are tucked into the central area of the roof (Fig 15.11).

The approach to the building from the north is over the unearthed ruins. Once inside, more utilitarian functions are concentrated on the ground floor with ticketing to the right and a bookstore and cafe to the left (Fig 15.7). The shift in geometry between the envelope that responds to the shape of the site and the core that is determined by the Parthenon Gallery at the top of the museum is felt, but is not pronounced. As an introduction to the museum, there are various models of the Acropolis depicting changes over almost three thousand years. On the south side there is a space for temporary exhibitions and a 200 seat auditorium whose splayed plan is simply (and astutely) the result of the intersection of the two orientations of the building. Lower, non-public levels (Levels -1 and -2) meet the ground and house support spaces such as offices and storage (Fig 15.6). Delivery is located at Level -2. The basement continues to Level -4 which is the primary mechanical level. Level -3 is devoted to parking. The facade of the lower portion of the building (Ground and Levels -1 and -2) is composed of precast concrete panels with a pattern of recessed rectangles. When the rectangles are punched, the facade becomes a screen that allows views out to the surrounding neighborhood. The weight of the facade seems to contradict the floating nature of the building. It is visually strong, and we imagine that it must have some particular symbolic value. Apparently this is not the case since similar solutions were explored for other projects such as the Italian Space Agency in Rome or the museum in Antwerp mentioned above. The facade could be viewed as a gesture to the traditional masonry buildings with punched window openings that surround the museum. Inside, the screen confines the entry space, which contrasts with the very open spaces to be discovered on the upper floors. Insulation is located on the inside of the precast panels and covered by an interior plaster board finish.

The Acropolis Museum has 8,000 m^2 (86,000 ft^2) of gallery space. The visit starts with the large volume of the Gallery of the Slopes that is 10.7 m (35 ft) wide and reaches a maximum height of 14.5 m (48 ft) (Fig 15.17 and Fig 15.18). The space is defined by two long, parallel structural cores (each 53 by 5.6 m or 174 by 18 ft) that contain stairs, elevators, restrooms, and vertical chase spaces for ductwork that originates in Level -4 (Fig 15.14 and Fig 15.15). Artifacts exhibited in the Gallery of the Slopes are in recessed vitrines or hung on the walls. Some are freestanding in the space. All are objects that were found on the slopes of the Acropolis, and many are in clay since most of those of more precious materials were looted over the years. A glass floor over the ruins gives a playful quality to a generally sober space. Visitors appear fascinated. Reflections in the glass floor also provide views up where we see other visitors walking on another glass floor above. Looking up, ahead, and behind to a mezzanine where the caryatids from the Erectheion are located, the extents of the building are understood. The walls of the Gallery of the Slopes are in smooth concrete with a pattern of circular holes in the panels that give texture to the surface. The holes function to reduce noise in a space defined by hard finishes. There is a balance of spectacle and sobriety.

The processional quality of the space suggested by the slope and axis is tempered by the fact that visitors inevitably crisscross the space to look at all of the different objects and that exiting visitors are going in the opposite direction. At the top of the ramp there is a full width, monumental stair, and at the top of the stair there are architectural sculptures from the pediment of the Hecatompedon, the first temple of Athena on the Acropolis.

The works in the Archaic Gallery on the second floor (Fig 15.8, Fig 15.19 and 15.20) are less staged than those in the Gallery of the Slopes. There are no vitrines and visitors have more direct contact with the sculptures. At 8.3 m (27 ft) high, the wedge-shaped space on the south side of the building is wide open and impressive. There is a forest of large, round, concrete columns (1.2 m or 4 ft in diameter) that structure the space. The sculptures are a sort of understory that visitors weave through. They are freestanding and placed on light-colored marble bases like the floor itself. The concrete wall of the core of the building provides a background for the works, but no other exhibition walls were used. Early engineering schemes explored at least one concrete shear wall between columns in the space. Luckily a solution was found using the horizontal mezzanine slabs in the Gallery of the Slopes instead. The works in the Archaic Gallery are presented in a uniform manner even if grouped by theme. The space is flooded with natural light from a grid of square skylights above and an entirely glazed south-facing wall. The view out is veiled by a frit on the glass, but unlike most art museum galleries, there is a strong contact with the outside and distractions are allowed. A link between the works and the city they came from is established. Architectural detail distracts little, however. Exhibition lighting, other technical equipment, and air conditioning grills are located in parallel recessed channels in the ceiling. Likewise, the glass fins for the facade's wind bracing are placed to the outside so that the inside surface is flat. The window frames are black.

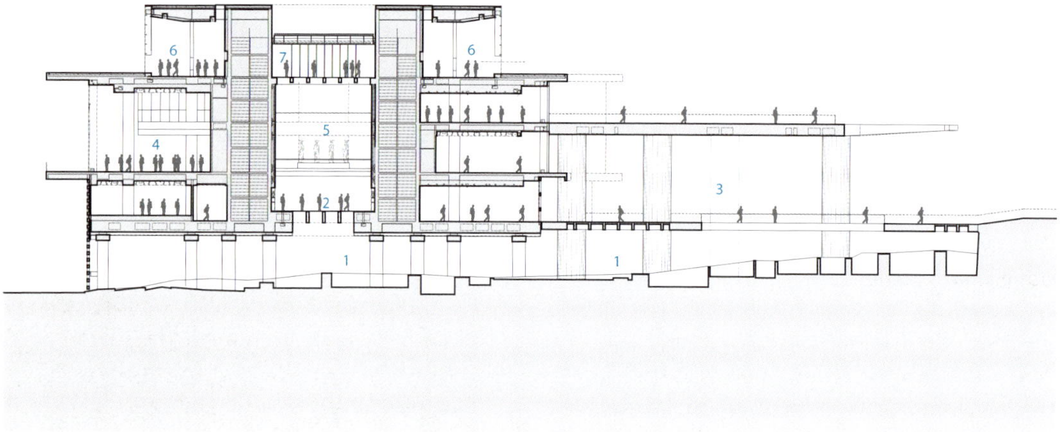

1 Excavation
2 Slopes Finding Gallery (Glass Ramp)
3 Temporary Exhibition
4 Roman Period Gallery
5 Void
6 Parthenon Gallery
7 Balcony Lounge

0 5 10 15 20M

Figure 15.14 Transversal section A

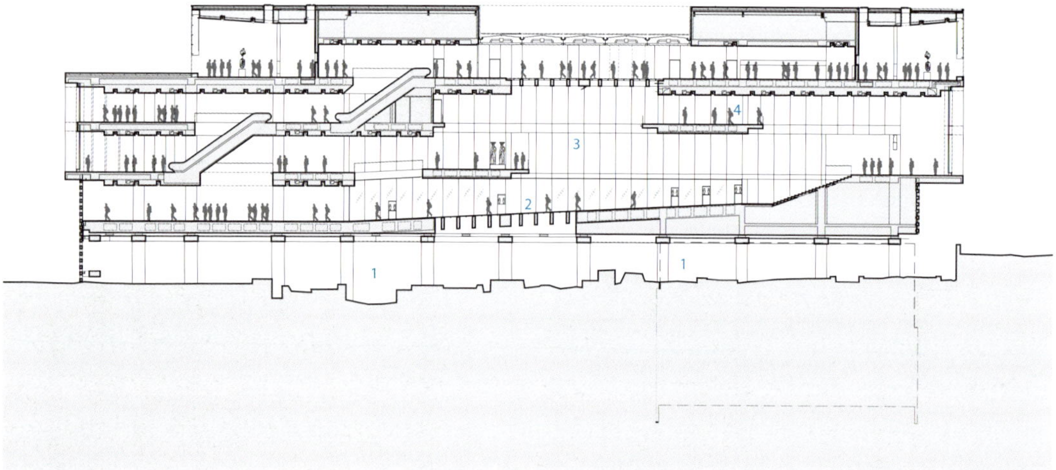

1 Excavation
2 Slopes Finding Gallery (Glass Ramp)
3 Void
4 Balcony Lounge

0 5 10 15 20M

Figure 15.15 Longitudinal section B

The shape of the gallery naturally funnels visitors to the west end of the building where escalators, stairs, or elevators prolong the museum's circulation loop upward. Though they are meant to be visited on the way down along with the galleries on the north side of the core, the caryatids are located on the same level as the Archaic Gallery on a mezzanine within the large volume of the Gallery of the Slopes. The five maidens are crowd pleasers and they hold a privileged position virtually at the center of the museum in both plan and section.

What is a single, high volume on the south side of the core (the second floor Archaic Gallery) is divided into two levels on the north side. Galleries designated as *Propylaia*, *Athena-Nike*, *Erectheion*, and *5th Century BC – 5th Century AD* are located on the second floor. Following the circulation loop, these spaces should be visited after the Parthenon gallery. The third floor (Fig 15.9) is a partial floor and contains lounges, an area that overlooks the Archaic Gallery, a shop, and a restaurant that, along with an outdoor terrace, faces the Acropolis to the north. A simple, kidney-shaped pergola structure on the terrace in painted steel with aluminum, horizontal louvers offers shade for outdoor seating.

The all glass box at the top of the building on the fourth floor (Fig 15.10, Fig 15.21, and Fig 15.22) is devoted to the Parthenon Gallery. It is also a sort of belvedere with panoramic views of the city and especially of the Acropolis. The room measures 84 by 39 m (276 by 128 ft) and is 6.15 m (20 ft) high at the highest point. It is dimensioned to hold a full size, abstracted version of the Parthenon with circulation around it on all sides. The outside dimensions of the double core of the Acropolis Museum are the same as those of the cella of the Parthenon, the inner enclosed chamber of the temple, and the core acts as such for exhibition purposes. The Parthenon Gallery is oriented in precisely the same directions as the Parthenon itself.

Figure 15.16 Lower level

Figure 15.17 Gallery of the Slopes

Figure 15.18 Gallery of the Slopes

Figure 15.19 Archaic gallery

Figure 15.20 Archaic gallery

At the fourth floor level, the escalators of the circulation loop arrive in a space between the two cores of the building, or for exhibition purposes, within the cella of the Parthenon. The ceiling is a skylight and the floor is glass (there are often crews keeping it clean) with views straight down into the Gallery of the Slopes. Ahead there is an area for video projections. The passage from the cella in this case is via side openings that correspond to holes in the original building resulting from an explosion in the late seventeenth century. It was a useful scenario for an exit strategy. The north opening immediately provides a view of the Acropolis. In relation to solar protection, it was fortunate that the primary view is to the north.

Forty-six stainless steel columns approximately 35 cm (14 in.) in diameter surround the core. Their number and spacing are taken from the Parthenon and they form the skeleton of the abstracted exhibition structure. Every other steel column sits directly atop a concrete column below. The others sit on a transfer beam. Thus, the spacing of the Parthenon columns determined the structural grid of the entire museum which is consistently 8.58 m (28 ft) in the east/west direction and generally 7.28 m (24 ft) in the north/south direction.

The Parthenon frieze is displayed on the walls of the core. The steel columns support the metopes. The frieze and metopes are placed so as to allow the original narrative of the suite of sculptures. There are sometimes missing pieces ("cultural holes"), however, and there are copies alongside the originals.

The abstracted structure is less useful for the exhibition of the pediment sculptures which are exhibited on long bases at floor level at the east and west ends of the gallery. The floral akroterion once stood at the highest point at the center of the pediment. A predominately plaster reconstruction was also difficult to integrate into the abstracted structure concept and it also stands on a base at floor level in the south-west corner of the gallery.

The city and the Parthenon are as much the focus of the space as the sculptures, and the views are impressive though not as magical as the panorama from the Acropolis itself. Opinions vary widely whether what is exhibited is sufficient to command the space and audience. The presentation is not kitsch nor does it play on emotions. It is a cogent environment that allows visitors to contemplate the artistic and ancient values of the works. In reference to Bernard Tschumi's quote above, the sculptures are immobile, but not static.

Conceptually, the Parthenon Gallery is an outdoor space. There is abundant natural light, primarily from the all glass facades but also from two narrow skylights that encircle the space – one

Figure 15.21 Parthenon gallery

Figure 15.22 Parthenon gallery

related to the frieze and the other related to the metopes. There is kinship between the square skylights of the Archaic Gallery below that provide an even, non-hierarchical field of light and the entirely glass facades of the Parthenon Gallery that provide non-hierarchical, panoramic views. The skylights in the Parthenon Gallery, however, are directly linked to the works displayed. Their effect tends toward the theatrical rather than the more neutral approach found in the spaces below. The skylight to the south was omitted since there is already abundant light coming through the vertical facade. Inside, the slot in the ceiling was maintained for consistency, and artificial light is located here just as on the other three sides.

The structure of the Parthenon gallery is in steel and the roof cantilevers past the stainless steel columns on all sides in order to avoid columns at the facade. The maximum cantilever is 9.45 m (31 ft). The all glass gallery also proved to be a technical feat in a hot climate. The facade is a ventilated, double skin system hung from the roof structure above by stainless steel suspension rods that also provide wind bracing

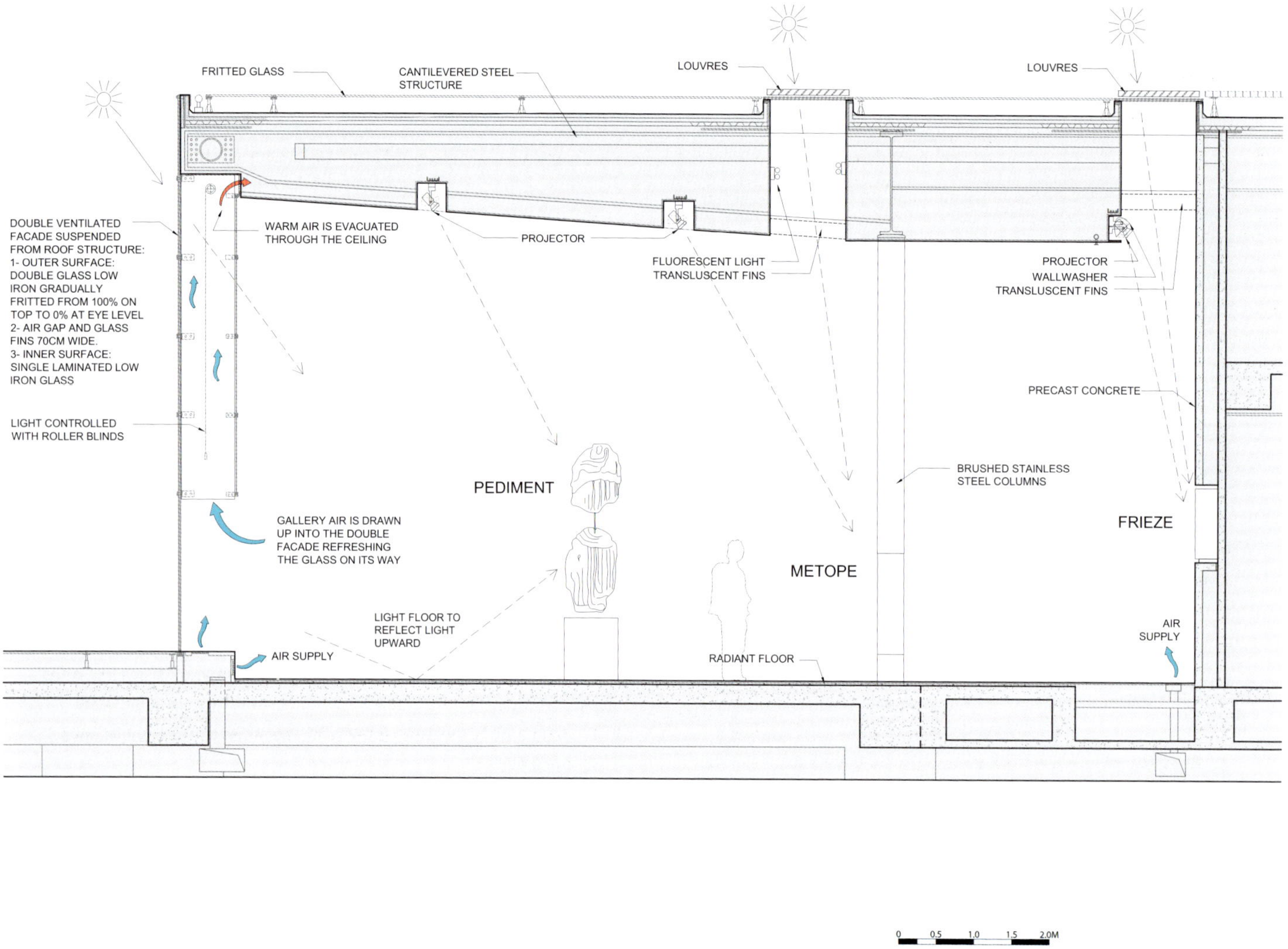

Figure 15.23 Parthenon gallery details

(Fig 15.23). The double glazing of the outer skin and the single-glazed inner skin are connected by perpendicular glass fins and stainless steel pins. The two layers define a 70 cm (28 in.) cavity with integrated operable solar shades. The outside, waterproof layer is low iron, coated glass with a pattern of black, fritted dots to limit heat gain and glare. The inside glass and fins are low iron, laminated glass. All of the glass in the building was manufactured and installed by the Austrian firm Eckelt. The interior skin begins at 2.3 m (7.5 ft) from the floor in order to provide a less obstructed view at eye level. This also allows for conditioned air delivered into the gallery space at floor level to enter the cavity through a displacement ventilation system, rise within the double skin, and then be extracted at the level of the dropped ceiling. Air supply is located near the core and through a continuous ledge at the base of the facade that also doubles as a bench. The ledge is at the same height as the neatly detailed, open-jointed, gray marble paving slabs outside that sit on spacers above the membrane roofing. There is also a radiant floor system of flexible pipes within the concrete slab of the gallery. It was conceived mainly for cooling but is also used for heating.

Because the column spacing for the museum was taken from the Parthenon and generally fixed, the entire building scheme had to be shifted and adjusted during design until an acceptable position was found that would minimize the impact on the ruins on the site. For seismic design, a base isolation system was integrated just below the ground floor slab. Often, systems to protect against earthquakes are placed at ground level. This position, however, reduced ground excavations thereby preserving more archaeological remnants. In the case of an earthquake, the structure below the Ground Level moves with the ground and independently of the structure above that could move up to 15 cm (6 in.) horizontally and 5 cm (2 in.) vertically.

The Acropolis Museum is a more significant and challenging project than many because of its site, because of what it exhibits, and because of its political aspirations. In Athens, Tschumi obviously felt the weight of history, but his project is not self-conscious. It is reasoned yet possesses a certain nonchalance that allows the exhibited works to speak for themselves – as objects of desire or otherwise.

The design was surely difficult to calibrate. There is interdependence between the exhibition strategy, especially for the Parthenon Gallery which is the culminating space and event, and the building's fundamental organization and structure. Having chosen to exhibit the architectural sculptures using an abstraction of the Parthenon wrapped around the core of the building, the technical aspects had to be resolved in a way to give priority to the more symbolic qualities of the project. It is the fusion of concept and technique, and container and contained, that renders the solution self-evident rather than merely facile. Unlike the visual harmony of the Parthenon, there is an unseen harmony in the museum resulting from a meticulous synthesis of concept, display, context, circulation, structure, mechanical, views, conservation of ruins, seismic design, etc. to form a coherent whole.

The architecture of the Acropolis Museum does not overtly strive to impart meaning. It is the relationship between the sculptures and the building, between the building and its context, and the dance between the visitor and the objects that might give significance.

CHAPTER 16

Museum Brandhorst

Munich, Germany

Sauerbruch Hutton

2009

Figure 16.1 Entry facade – view from north

Udo and Anette Brandhorst began collecting art in the 1970s. Their collection is comprised primarily of American and European works from the second half of the twentieth century and is particularly strong in paintings by Cy Twombly and Andy Warhol. In 1999 the Brandhorst collection became part of the Bavarian State Painting Collections through a long-term loan and purchases. Anette Brandhorst died in that same year. Though the couple had lived in Cologne, their collection of over 750 works would be housed in Munich in a purpose-built museum in the city's *Kunstareal* or Museum Quarter.

The *Kunstareal* is located in a dense, lively, affluent quarter of apartments and shops that was developed in the nineteenth century. A site at the intersection of the Theresienstrasse and the Turkenstrasse at the north east corner of the Museum Quarter was chosen for the Brandhorst (Fig 16.1 and Fig 16.2). The *Pinakothek der Moderne* (twentieth-century art) which opened in 2002 is nearby and to the south. The *Alte Pinakothek* (fourteenth- to eighteenth-century art) (Fig 16.4) and *Neue Pinakothek* (eighteenth- and nineteenth-century art) are one block away to the west. There is already talk that a museum devoted to the art of the twenty-first century should eventually replace the university buildings immediately to the west of the Brandhorst along the Theresienstrasse (Fig 16.6).

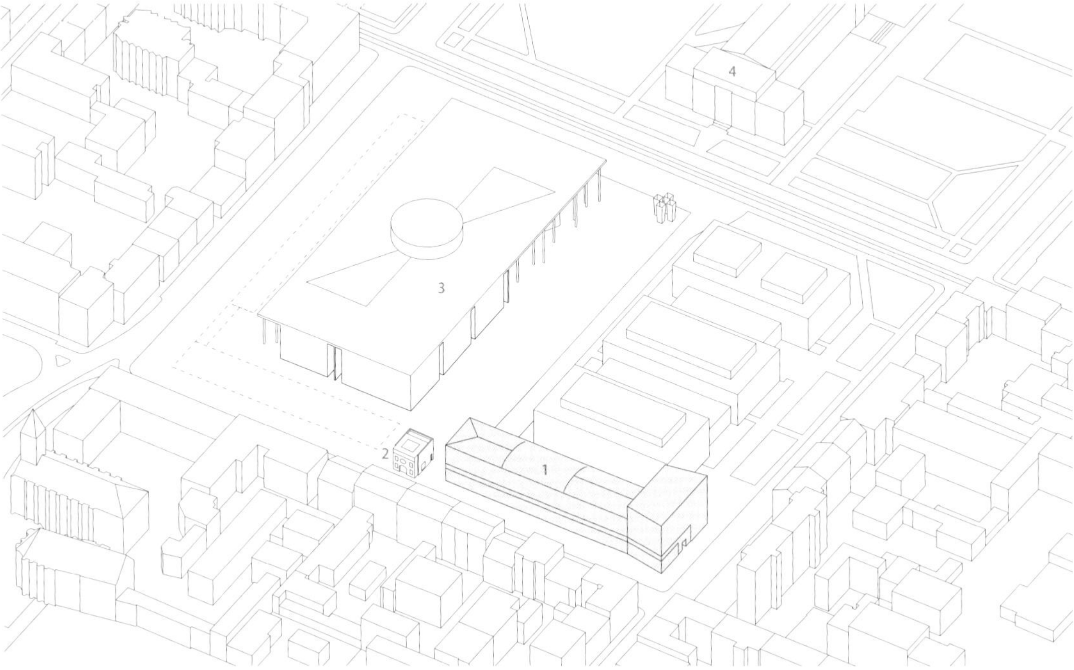

1. Museum Brandhorst
2. Turkentor
3. Pinakothek Der Moderne
4. Alte Pinakothek

Figure 16.2 Isometric site plan

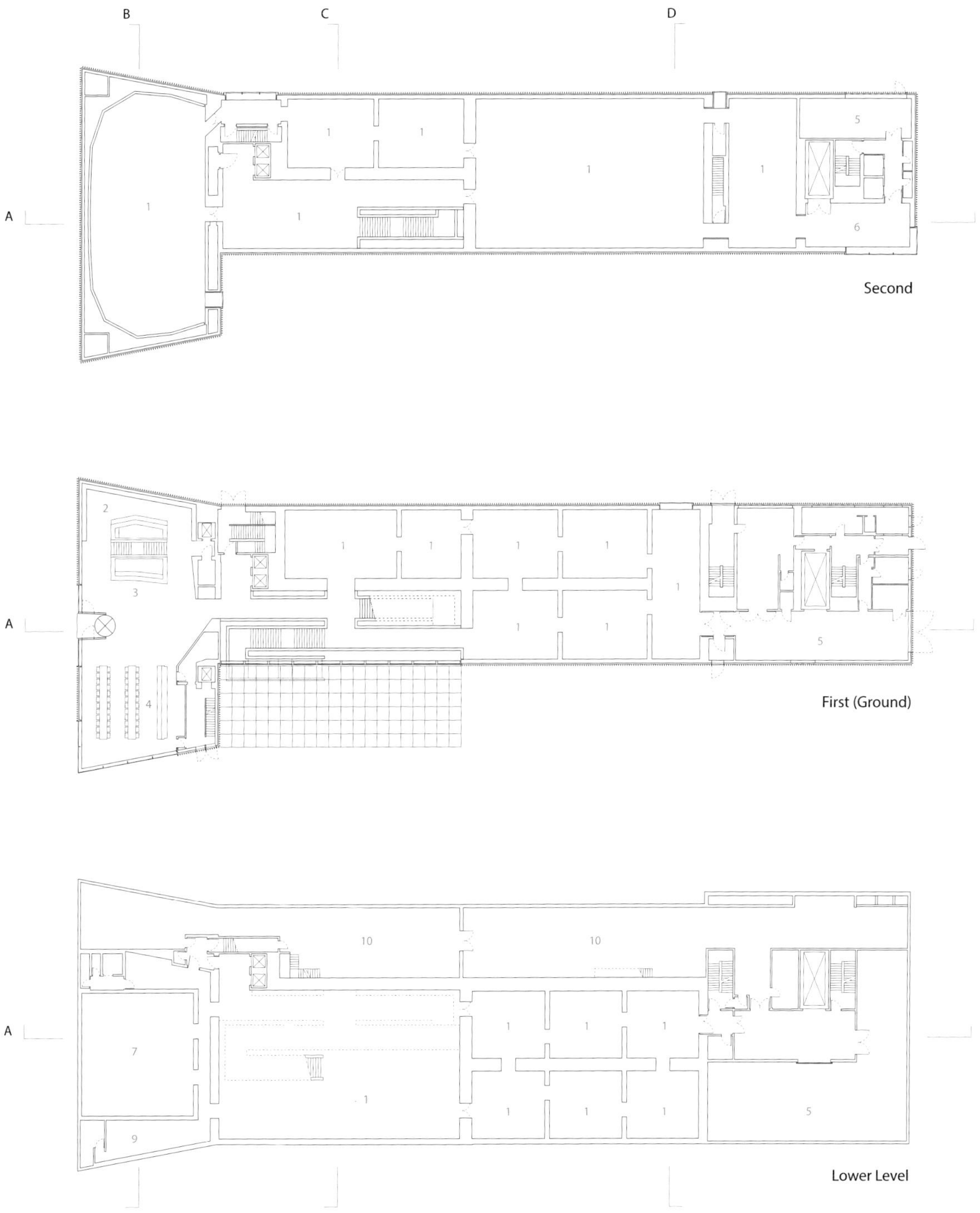

1 Gallery
2 Tickets/information
3 Bookshop
4 Cafe
5 Service/storage
6 Lounge
7 Video Art & New Media
8 Meda Room
9 Video Room
10 Mechanical

Figure 16.3 Floor plans

The entire block along the Turkenstrasse, including the present site of the Brandhorst, was once occupied by the Turkenkaserne, Bavarian army barracks built in the first quarter of the nineteenth century. Like much of the area, the building was heavily damaged during World War II and later demolished. A portion of the central entry tower was preserved and recently restructured and is known as the Turkentor. It is immediately to the south of the Brandhorst and exhibits a single work of art: *Large Red Sphere*, a sculpture by the American artist Walter De Maria that is also part of the Brandhorst collection.

Sauerbruch Hutton was the winner of a three-stage competition for the Brandhorst Museum with the first phase beginning in the spring of 2002 and the final selection announced in December the same year. From 25 initial participants, the number was reduced to four and then to two. The other finalist was Zaha Hadid Architects. Sauerbruch Hutton's project seems refreshingly nuanced and unspectacular for a competition entry. Though the program seems large for the allotted site, the generally rectilinear building mass maintains a low profile and fits comfortably into its context (Fig 16.3 and Fig 16.11). The small site apparently impeded the use of curved forms common in much of Sauerbruch Hutton's work. On the east side, the Brandhorst is set back from the Turkenstrasse by 8 m (26 ft) in order to allow for a row of trees planted in a band of grass and to eventually align with a proposed extension to the *Pinakothek der Moderne*. To the north, at the street intersection, the building mass splays and increases in height, yet remains unimposing. An all white, postwar apartment building by the German architect Sep Ruf occupies the corner just across the Theresienstrasse. Ruf's building is also set back from the prevailing street alignment which provides more space and some greenery in front of the Brandhorst. Sauerbruch Hutton's building responds in plan and in mass to obvious cues from the surrounding context in an unselfconscious manner. The result is an "L" shaped building with a main body along the Turkenstrasse measuring a total of 98 m long, 18 m wide and 17 m high (322 by 59 by 56 ft), and the "head" piece with a street frontage of 34 m (112 ft) along the Theresienstrasse and a height of 23 m (75 ft).

The use of color distinguishes Sauerbruch Hutton's work in general. They honor Gottfried Semper in giving primacy to the building enclosure or skin to dress a structure. Color is more important than form for the architects (Fig 16.5). Vision takes precedent over the other senses, and facades are developed to exploit their two-dimensional qualities. Structure is of lesser importance as a means for architectural expression, and indeed, at the Brandhorst it is not evident how the building is constructed or what it is actually made of.

Sauerbruch Hutton's first proposal for the Brandhorst's dressing was an envelope of colored glass panels similar to other projects they had already realized. Neighbors voiced worries related to noise resulting from such large, hard surfaces at a busy intersection in an urban context. Interestingly, the innovation of this highly "visual" facade stems from acoustical concerns.

The Brandhorst facade is striking. It is a layered rainscreen composed of vertical, glazed ceramic rods held in front of a folded sheet metal plane. The metal (2 mm or 3/32 in. aluminum) makes an accordion form of horizontal bands, and the bands alternate in color (Fig 16.19). The metal also has tiny perforations for added sound absorption. This one facade system is used for all of the opaque walls on all sides of the building. It also masks the large loading dock doors at the south/west corner and other doors for deliveries, emergency exits, the employee entrance at the south/east corner, and some windows. The ceramic rods were fabricated in Germany and are 4 by 4 by 110 cm (1 9/16 by 1 9/16 by 43 3/8 in.). The thickness of the ceramic rod wall is 9 mm (11/32 in.). Within the 110 cm rod height there are four horizontal bands of the sheet metal behind. Each rod is supported at two points by small, threaded steel rods along the lines where the ceramic rods and the accordion sheet metal are closest. There are 36,000 rods in total with 23 different colors. The folded metal is in three pairs of colors. The facade is capped by a simple metal edge covering.

The Brandhorst facade has often been compared to an abstract painting resembling works of artists such as Piet Mondrian or Paul Klee. Works of the Venezuelan Op artists Carlos Cruz-Diez and Jesus-Rafael Soto seem more pertinent, however, since they exploit more than one plane to arrive at optical illusions. The Brandhorst facade is rich in effects. From far away it appears as modulated color only. From near it takes on kinetic qualities and gives a very different impression if viewed straight on or obliquely. The colors of the glazed rods do not appear to repeat in a systematic way giving an organic quality to the ensemble.

Figure 16.4 South-east corner of Brandhorst looking west toward the *Alte Pinakothek*

Figure 16.5 South-east corner of Brandhorst looking north

Figure 16.6 West side of Brandhorst looking north with university buildings to left

Architecturally, the design has taken advantage of a layered rainscreen in an unprecedented way. Most explorations of such systems focus on the outer skin only and relegate any skin behind to the purely technical role of waterproofing. This is true of Herzog & de Meuron's facades for the Walker Art Center and the de Young Museum, for example, as well as for Renzo Piano's many rainscreen facades. Piano's solution for the IRCAM tower in Paris, however, where open-jointed bricks are threaded into stainless steel frames that are hung onto the building, may be a close precedent for the Brandhorst. Piano's reinterpreted brick facade is also meant to respond to the preexisting brick buildings on each side of it. Likewise, the multicolored ceramic rods of the Brandhorst respond to the materials and colors of the surrounding traditional architecture. Sauerbruch Hutton clearly rejected flamboyant forms as a symbol for their museum. The facade is subtle yet powerful and, for the architects, should intimate the purpose of the building. The facade gives a real and illusory depth and its seeming movement fills visitors and passersby with marvel.

The exterior is divided into three tonal areas that correspond to the general building organization (Fig 16.7, Fig 16.8, Fig 16.9, and Fig 16.10). The "head" is a light tone; the ground floor is a dark tone, and the upper floor is a middle tone. A continuous strip window separates the two floors (and the dark and middle tones) of the lower building mass. The window continues into the "head," wraps around the corner of the building, and meets the glazed entrance that opens onto the Theresienstrasse to the north. The entrance is placed away from the other museums of the *Kunstareal* and interacts more directly with the surrounding neighborhood. The written signage for the museum is very discreet.

If Sauerbruch Hutton took a critical position on the form of a contemporary museum, their stance on first encounters with a house for art follows a more conventional and often criticized formula. Upon entering there is little to tell visitors what sort of building they are in. The entry is dominated by the cafe, the bookstore, and a counter for ticket sales (Fig 16.13). The space is handsome with its wood built-in furniture, artificial stone floors, dark maroon wall, and large openings to the outside. No art is visible, however. Though understandable for climate control, the revolving entry door and the relatively small, automatic, glass sliding doors that lead to the galleries lend an institutional character to the space. Beyond ticket control and the sliding doors the space transforms into one for art. Walls and ceilings are white, floors are planks of Danish oak, and the natural light is muted. With a stair on axis leading up and glimpses to the lower level gallery below, the three levels of the building become immediately understandable (Fig 16.14). The oak stair with leather-covered handrails is well executed, and the full height window wall with vertical louvers inside and perforated metal screens outside allows veiled views out.

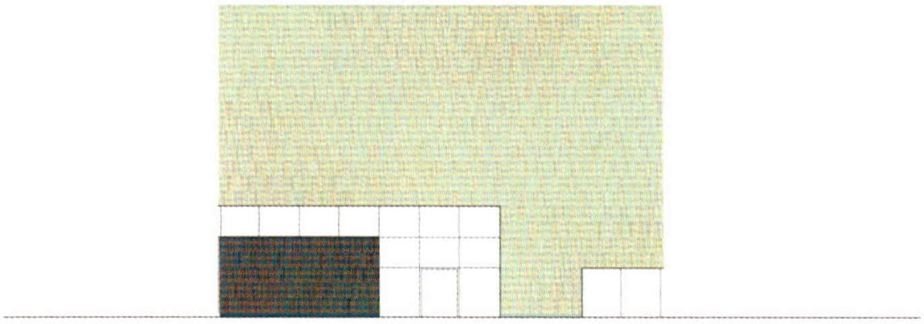

Figure 16.7 North elevation

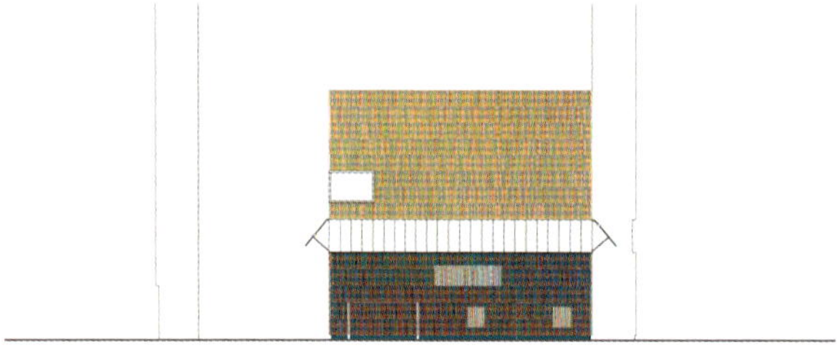

Figure 16.8 South elevation

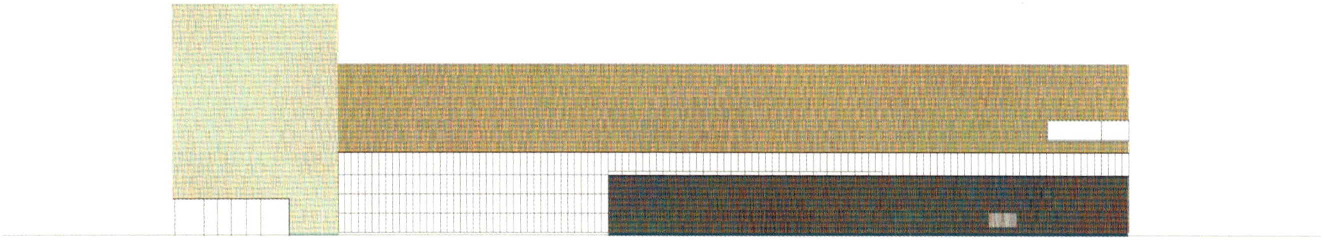

Figure 16.9 West elevation

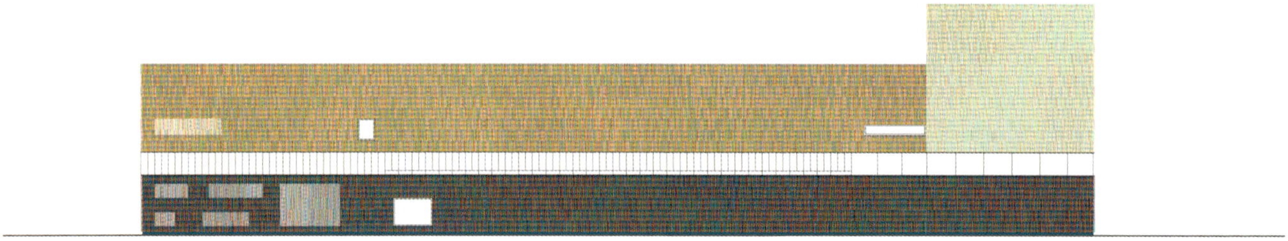

Figure 16.10 East elevation

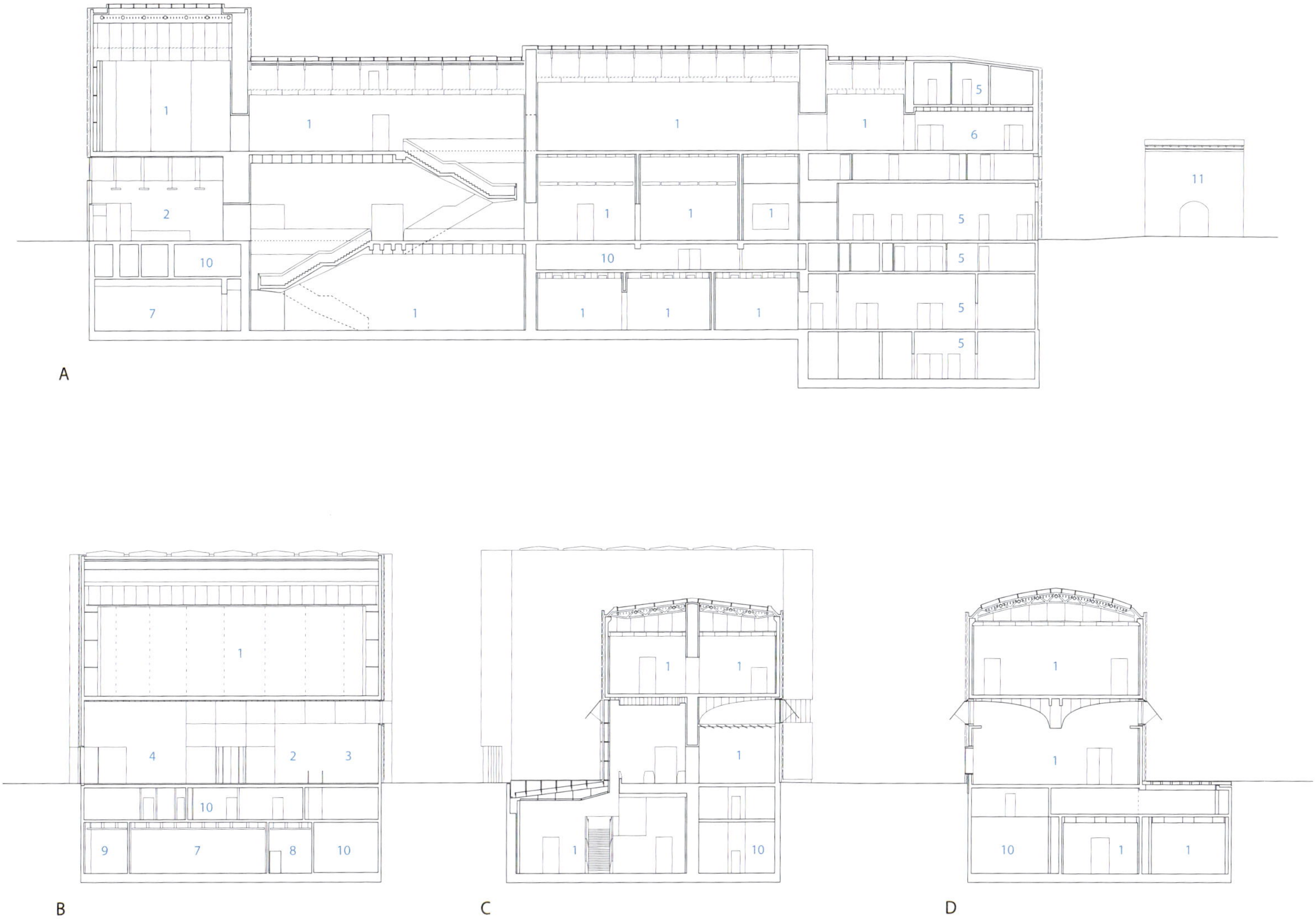

1 Gallery
2 Tickets/information
3 Bookshop
4 Cafe
5 Service/storage
6 Lounge
7 Video Art & New Media
8 Meda Room
9 Video Room
10 Mechanical
11 Turkentor

0 5 10 15 20M

Figure 16.11 Sections

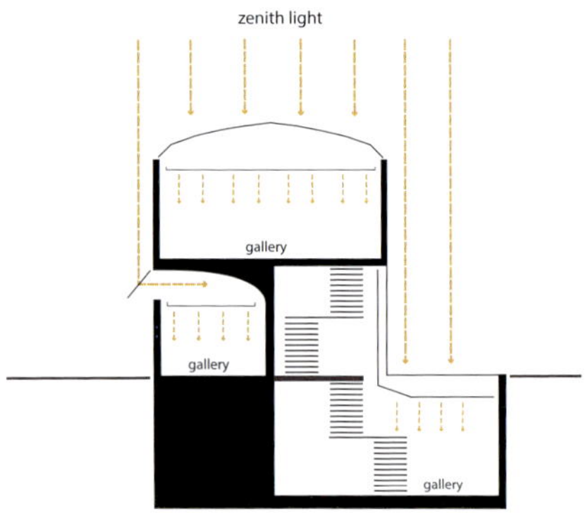

daylight use

HVA	heating, ventilation, air conditioning
CHP	compression heat pump
CCM	compression cooling machine
HE	heat exchanger

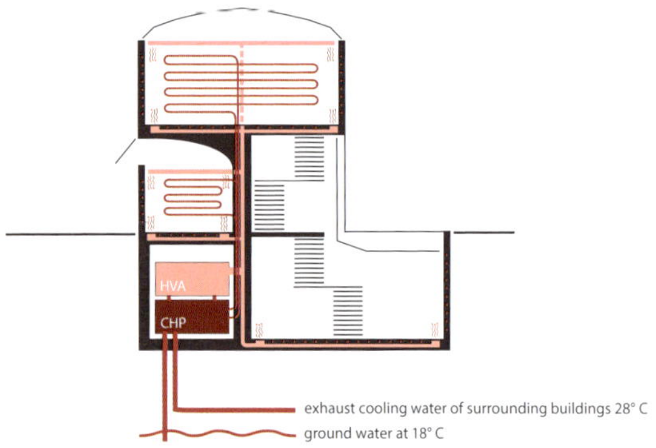

heating
through activated walls and floors

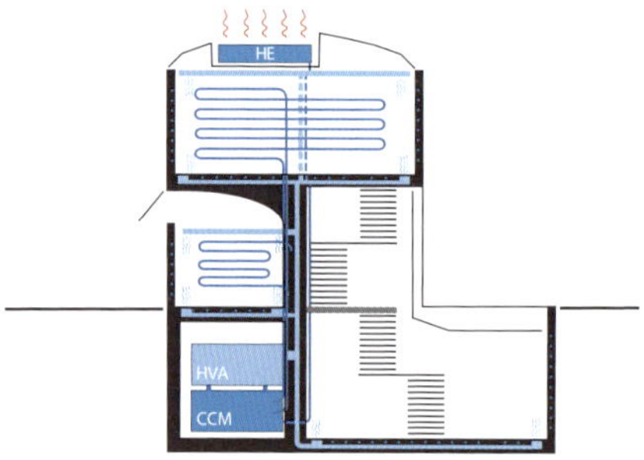

cooling

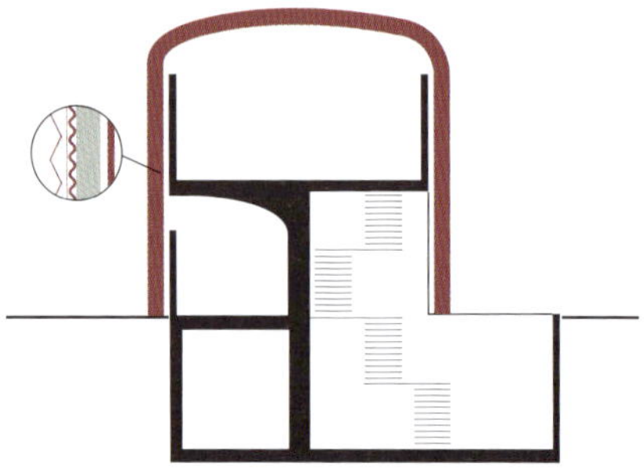

high thermal insulation

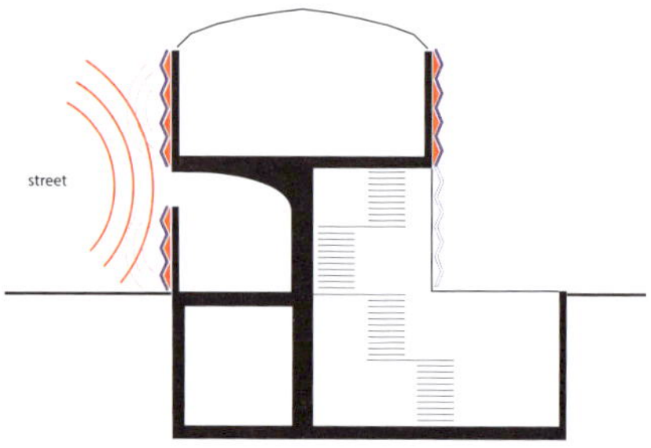

noise absorption

Figure 16.12 Diagrams

The upper floor is the privileged space. Galleries are distinct rooms and are either the half or the full width of the building (Fig 16.15). Linear wooden floor grills are placed slightly in front of the walls and subtly indicate a limit that visitors should not cross. A small reveal joint makes the transition between floor and wall. The thick, 3.5 m (11.5 ft) high passages between rooms are finished in glass for easy cleaning and integrate concealed panels with technical equipment behind. Exit signs are recessed into the walls. The material palette is kept to a minimum and there are few visual distractions.

It is, however, the natural light coming from above that is the strongest quality of the space. The ceiling above the galleries is multilayered. The outer layer is a triple, translucent glass roof. Motorized, aluminum louvers are just below. Bands of fluorescent lights and a steel grating are suspended from the primary steel structure. The grating allows access into the ceiling cavity for maintenance. Ductwork is also in the cavity, and the ceiling depth functions as a climatic buffer for the occupied spaces below. The louvers and fluorescent lights work automatically in tandem to maintain desired light levels. Unfortunately, the movement of the louvers can be heard in the galleries when the system readjusts. During tests for the ceiling complex it was found that the fluorescent tubes should be placed at an angle to the other orthogonal layers in order to avoid a projection of shadows from the metal grating onto the fabric ceiling below. Supports for the synthetic fabric ceiling are suspended in turn from the grating structure and the ceiling itself is composed of two layers of membrane to avoid any accumulation of dust on the layer that is visible from below. From the galleries, the fabric ceiling appears as long, glowing bands with light tracks in the joints between. No spotlights are suspended in the space, however, which results in a perfectly clean ceiling plane. The light quality is pleasant and very even, though with little hint of the sky condition or structure above.

The general atmosphere of the upper floor galleries is one of calm and contemplation. Benches are always provided to encourage pause, and passages are staggered so there is never enfilade. Two of the larger passages have windows that look out to the Turkenstrasse and provide welcome views in this otherwise introverted space. These transition spaces between rooms also give access to emergency stairs thereby keeping the gallery spaces pure. Ceiling heights vary in relation to room size and are 6 to 7 m (19.5 to 23 ft) with the gallery in the "head" reaching 9 m (29.5 ft). At the corner of the building on the upper floor there is a lounge with a corner window facing south and west that looks over a lawn and toward the *Pinakothek der Moderne* and the *Alte Pinakothek*. It is the same dark maroon color as the entry. It is a pleasant place to take a rest and thumb through catalogues that are scattered on the tables.

While the spaces appear to be designed for flexibility, the paintings by Cy Twombly are virtually a permanent installation in the upper floor galleries (Fig 16.16). Twombly's 12-painting Lepanto cycle, created for the 2001 Venice Biennale, is shown in a special, polygonal room in the "head." The architecture allows the works to be seen at their best. Since the galleries are so fine-tuned, every particularity, such as changes in the direction of floor planks or light tracks, takes on importance. The dark, domed surveillance cameras below the fabric ceilings become particularly visible, for example. Sauerbruch Hutton opted for simple forms for the exterior of the museum, and the interior volumes follow suit. The markedly increased height and special shape of the Lepanto gallery is, however, at the verge of calling too much attention to itself.

Figure 16.13 Entry

Figure 16.14 Staircase

Figure 16.15 Second floor gallery

Figure 16.16 Second floor "Head" gallery

Figure 16.17 Ground floor gallery

Figure 16.18 Lower level gallery

The ground floor galleries are similar to those above in concept, design and finish, though smaller (Fig 16.17). Hanging is denser. Some of the passages between galleries have concealed, automatic sliding glass doors that can be used for exceptional climate control for special exhibitions.

The Brandhorst is one of a few museums that attempts to bring natural light into lower floor galleries and distribute it from above. Peter Zumthor's four-story museum in Bregenz, Austria, brings in natural light through translucent facades and channels it into the gallery spaces via cavities above a glass ceiling. This unique solution offers similar top-lighting conditions regardless of floor level. The Brandhorst solution uses the 3 m (9 ft 10 in.) high strip windows of the facade that are 6 m (20 ft) above the floor level to a similar end. An exterior-angled, light-refracting screen made of glass and prismatic acrylic panels is mounted in front of the widow and redirects sunlight onto a curved ceiling inside. Large horizontal louvers further diffuse the light, recreate a ceiling plane, and somewhat mask the curved, perforated ceiling above. The intermediate louver supports integrate light tracks at the bottom and conceal fluorescent tubes at the top that light the curved ceiling above. Light in the ground floor galleries is not exactly even but pleasant. Since the strip windows face east and west, the light quality changes significantly during the day and there are obvious differences from one side of the building to the other. The prismatic panels also project rainbows onto the ceiling and louvers.

A narrow room the full width of the building is reserved for sculptures. There are no horizontal louvers in this space which allows the butterfly section to be fully visible. A large window connects the gallery to the Turkenstrasse and allows the art works to be seen from the street. Large doors in the corner of the gallery lead to the loading area.

The interior vertical metal louvers along the stair descend, turn, and become horizontal louvers for the large glass roof that lights the "patio," the principle gallery of the lower level where many works by Andy Warhol as well as others are exhibited (Fig 16.18). The concrete stair itself is interesting because of its form and long spans. The slot between the stair and the window wall allows a rare view of all three levels.

The lower level pushes beyond the footprint of the building above. It is the largest floor at 98 m (322 ft) long and 27 m (89 ft) wide. Its skylight is at ground level and is covered by steel grating panels that protect the glass and function as a brise-soleil. The blades of the grating are tilted so that direct light will not hit the glass, and some panels are hinged to allow access to the glass roof below. The decision to leave the three layers of the lower level skylight visible – the exterior grate, the transparent glass roof, and the interior louvers – allows visitors to better imagine what might be the roof structure of the upper floor roof that is concealed from view inside and out.

The "patio" gallery is 460 m^2 (square meter; 4,951 ft^2 (square foot)) and 7 m (23 ft) high. It is less formal, less intimate, and seemingly more spacious than the others. It is not as pure since the stair divides the space. To the south of the "patio" there is a series of six galleries of 65 m^2 (700 ft^2) each. Even if artificially lit by rectangular fluorescent fixtures recessed into the ceiling, they are similar in character to the ground floor galleries. To the north and under the "head" of the building there are two black box galleries for media art that total 240 m^2 (2,583 ft^2), along with an education space equipped with computer stations. A large grill under the stair provides additional heating and cooling to control the climate of the large volume that connects all three levels.

Exhibition areas at the Brandhorst total 3,200 m^2 (34,445 ft^2). The building is 12,000 m^2 (129,167 ft^2).

Service is from the south and opposite the public entrance. Delivery trucks arrive in the space between the Brandhorst and the Turkentor, and a delivery bay at the south/west corner allows trucks to enter into the building. A conservation lab is directly adjacent to delivery. It is lit by east-facing windows as well as fluorescent lights. Placing the space to profit from a typical northern orientation was not possible on this tight site.

Of the 750 works in the collection, only about 200 are shown at any one time. Underground levels are occupied by art storage specifically for painting, sculpture, photos, and media with appropriate climate control for each. Above ground there are offices, workshops, security, and various storage rooms.

A freight elevator services the three gallery levels and the six service levels. For very large paintings that do not fit in the freight elevator, there is a 12 m (39 ft) long "basket" that can be suspended from the ceiling of the top floor and maneuvers in the void between the stair and the glazed exterior wall. The system was adapted from window cleaning equipment and can transport narrow objects such as paintings up or down from the ground floor. This system is only assembled when necessary which is normally once or twice a year. In general the building appears functional and well equipped.

Two basement levels of mechanical rooms are located along the east side of the building in a space that is 8 m (26 ft) wide and the entire 98 m (322 ft) length of the project. There are also mechanical rooms sandwiched above the lower level galleries and the ground level.

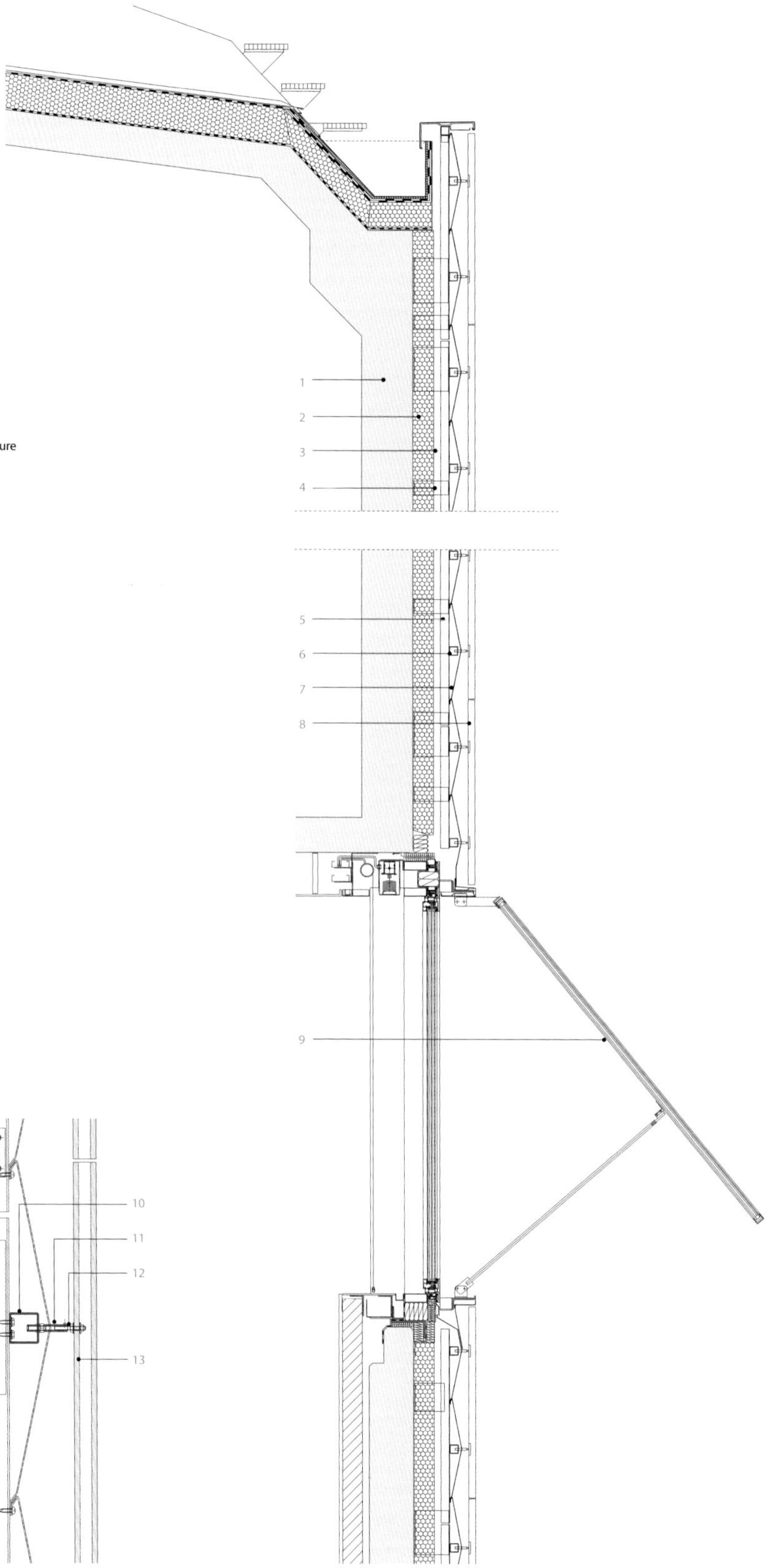

Section Facade

1 reinforced concrete
2 thermal insulation (mineral wool), 120 mm, WLG 040, mounted within the grid of the substructure
3 back ventilation
4 wall bracket, 140 mm
5 wall rail, T 100 x 2 mm
6 square profile, 50 x 3 mm
7 acoustic metal panel with micro perforation, underlayed with acoustic fleece, colour of panel according to colour coding system
8 ceramic rods
9 light reflector (insulating glass)
upper pane: single leaf safety glazing,
lower pane: compound safety glazing,
with inserted acrylic prismatic light reflectors

Fixation Of The Ceramic Rods

10 square hollow aluminium profile, 50 x 3 mm with a riveting nut mounted in a preset grid, M8
11 case mother, M8, over thread staff bolts with riveting mounted nuts
12 inserted threaded rod, M6, bolted over two nuts with polyamide discs to the ceramic rods, tension free, using a transversal headless screw, M4, to secure the position
13 ceramic rod

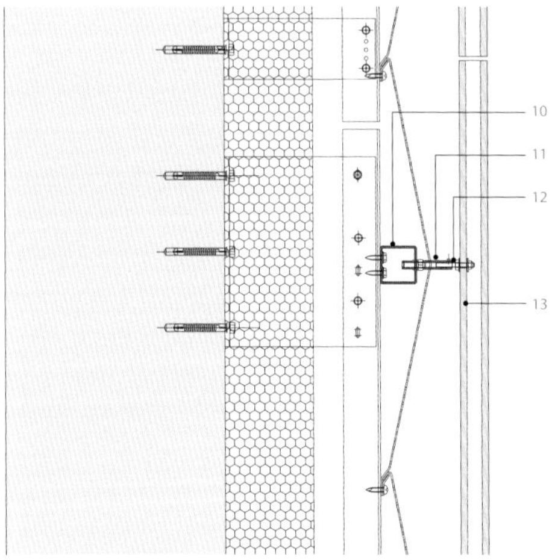

Figure 16.19 Wall section detail

The structure of the Brandhorst is concrete with insulation on the outside. The interior finish is plaster on brick walls. The Brandhorst uses the masonry for thermal inertia with a system of 2 cm (¾ in.) polyethylene (PE-X) pipes spaced at 10 to 15 cm (4 to 6 in.) that circulates warm or cool water in the exterior walls, the interior walls, and the floors (Fig 16.12). In the walls, the pipes are in a grouted cavity and transfer heat or cool into the building itself. The pressure in the pipes is constantly monitored to detect improbable leaks. The system provides superior temperature control thereby minimizing the amount of additional heating or cooling necessary from the forced air system which also controls humidity and filters the air. The ducts are placed in shallow troughs in the concrete slab near the walls.

For heating, an open loop heat pump system uses either water that has already passed through the system of the *Pinakothek der Moderne* and/or water taken directly from the ground. Water coming from the *Moderne* is approximately 35 degrees Celsius (95 degrees Fahrenheit). Ground water is 15 to 18 degrees Celsius (59 to 64 degrees Fahrenheit). Water from the *Moderne*, however, may not always be available or sufficient depending on its own heating or cooling situation. An automatic, intelligent system determines if water from one source, the other, or from both should be used. The warmer the water entering into the Brandhorst heat pump, the better. Water is returned to the ground normally at 12 to 14 degrees Celsius (54 to 57 degrees Fahrenheit). As is often the case in Munich, the *Pinakothek der Moderne* which opened in 2002 uses ground water for cooling as well. Because of its specific location, however, this was not allowed at the Brandhorst. The Brandhorst uses a closed system with a cooling tower on the roof concealed behind a parapet.

The Brandhorst is well conceived, well crafted, and joyful. It is somehow subtle, yet spectacular. Sauerbruch Hutton says that there is a fine line between banality and poetry. The Brandhorst Museum is never banal ...

CHAPTER 17

Centre Pompidou-Metz

Metz, France

Shigeru Ban and Jean de Gastines

2010

Figure 17.1 General view from south

The Pompidou Center – Metz (Fig 17.1) was a first experiment in French cultural decentralization. In the late 1990s, with the prospect of closing Piano and Roger's building in Paris for renovations, the question arose of how to maintain some of the 60,000 works in the collection of the National Museum of Modern Art available for public viewing. A concept of "hors les murs" or "beyond the walls" was developed to exhibit works in other French cities. The temporary closing of the Pompidou Center – Paris spurred reflections on ways to present the national collection to a wider audience in general. Eventually a second Pompidou Center in another French city was imagined. Montpellier, Lille, Caen, and Albi were also interested and hoped to duplicate the effect of the Guggenheim in Bilbao. Metz was appreciated for its proximity to Germany, Belgium, Luxembourg, and Switzerland. With the high-speed train service that began in 2007, Metz and Paris are now only 84 minutes apart, and the site proposed for the new Center is within easy walking distance of the train station. In January 2003 Metz was announced as the chosen city with the ambition of opening the new building for the thirtieth anniversary of the Pompidou Center – Paris in 2007. Metz opened to the public in May 2010, interestingly the same month as the opening of Zaha Hadid's MAXXI in Rome. As a "destination museum" such a project holds great economic and cultural promises for a city and a region. The trend continues, and a Louvre antenna designed by the Japanese architects SANAA opened in 2013 in the northern French city of Lens.

The Pompidou Center – Metz is not an antenna or a satellite of Paris, but a sister institution with its own administration and cultural mission. Nor is it a "museum" since it does not itself possess a collection. It is devoted to the presentation of modern and contemporary art and living performing arts, and all of its exhibitions are temporary. It does have the enormous advantage of having access to the national collection of modern art. Attendance at the Center – Metz has been a success and at times entry projections have been exceeded sixfold. Likewise, the Pompidou Center – Paris has been a huge success since its opening and its sometimes tattered appearance has often been attributed to the sheer numbers of visitors using the building.

Metz has a population of 124,000, and is known for its many parks and open green spaces. One of its selling points was its proposed site very near the city center that became available when a freight train station and related activities were moved. The Pompidou Center – Metz is part of a new 50 hectare (124 acre) redevelopment known as the *Quartier de l'Amphitheatre* named for the 25,000 seat Roman amphitheater that once stood in the vicinity (Fig 17.2). The development is divided into two equal areas on the east and west sides of a remaining freight line. The urban plan developed by the French architect Nicolas Michelin creates a dense, mixed-use district to the west, and a large park, the *Parc de la Seille*, to the east. The 2.8 hectare (7 acre) site reserved for the Pompidou Center is also located in the western half and at the closest point to the city center which is just beyond the train station to the north.

Only a month after Metz was chosen for the new Pompidou Center the architectural competition was launched. Of the 157 responses to the public notice, six teams were chosen to develop projects: Stephane Maupin and Pascal Cribier (Paris); Herzog & de Meuron (Basel); Foreign Office Architect (London); NOX (Rotterdam); Dominique Perrault (Paris), and the winning team of Shigeru Ban (Tokyo), Jean de Gastines (Paris), and Philip Gumuchdjian (London). The 17-member jury was composed of three types of jurors: local elected officials, "qualified personalities" that included specialists related to museums and the arts, and architects. Richard Rogers was one of six architects on the jury.

The brief firmly nudged the competitors toward an iconic project with the hope of attracting visitors. The Metz project should be a building for the twenty-first century and an urban and architectural event comparable to Piano and Roger's building in Paris. The request was for a tall building since the elevated train tracks to the north and east block views to the site which is already in a somewhat low spot. It was felt that the Pompidou Center should be in dialogue with another tall structure of the city, the Cathedral Saint Étienne. The building should not be so tall, however, as to fall into the "high-rise" category of buildings that must meet more stringent public safety requirements. Piano and Roger's building in Paris is such a "high-rise" building.

The program called for a "Forum," the same name as that used for the grand entry space at the Piazza level in Paris. It also required a Grande Nef (Grand Nave), a large, high space on the ground floor. Otherwise the building would contain a variety of exhibition spaces, a multipurpose performance and exhibition space, a conference center with lecture rooms and an auditorium, and other common program elements such as offices, education spaces, a museum store, a cafe and a restaurant, storage, and mechanical spaces. The area of the constructed building is approximately 11,000 m^2 (square meter; 118,000 ft^2 (square foot)) and is roughly one-tenth of the area of its sister institution in Paris. After winning the competition Shigeru Ban and Jean de Gastines set up office in a temporary vaulted building made of cardboard tubes, plywood, and plastic sheeting they designed for an outdoor terrace on the upper floor of the Pompidou Center – Paris. Metz, already short on office space, hopes to acquire the 34.4 by 4.4 by 3.6 m high (113 by 14.5 by 12 ft) structure and place it to the east of their building.

Comparisons between the buildings in Metz and Paris are inevitable. During program development the client identified

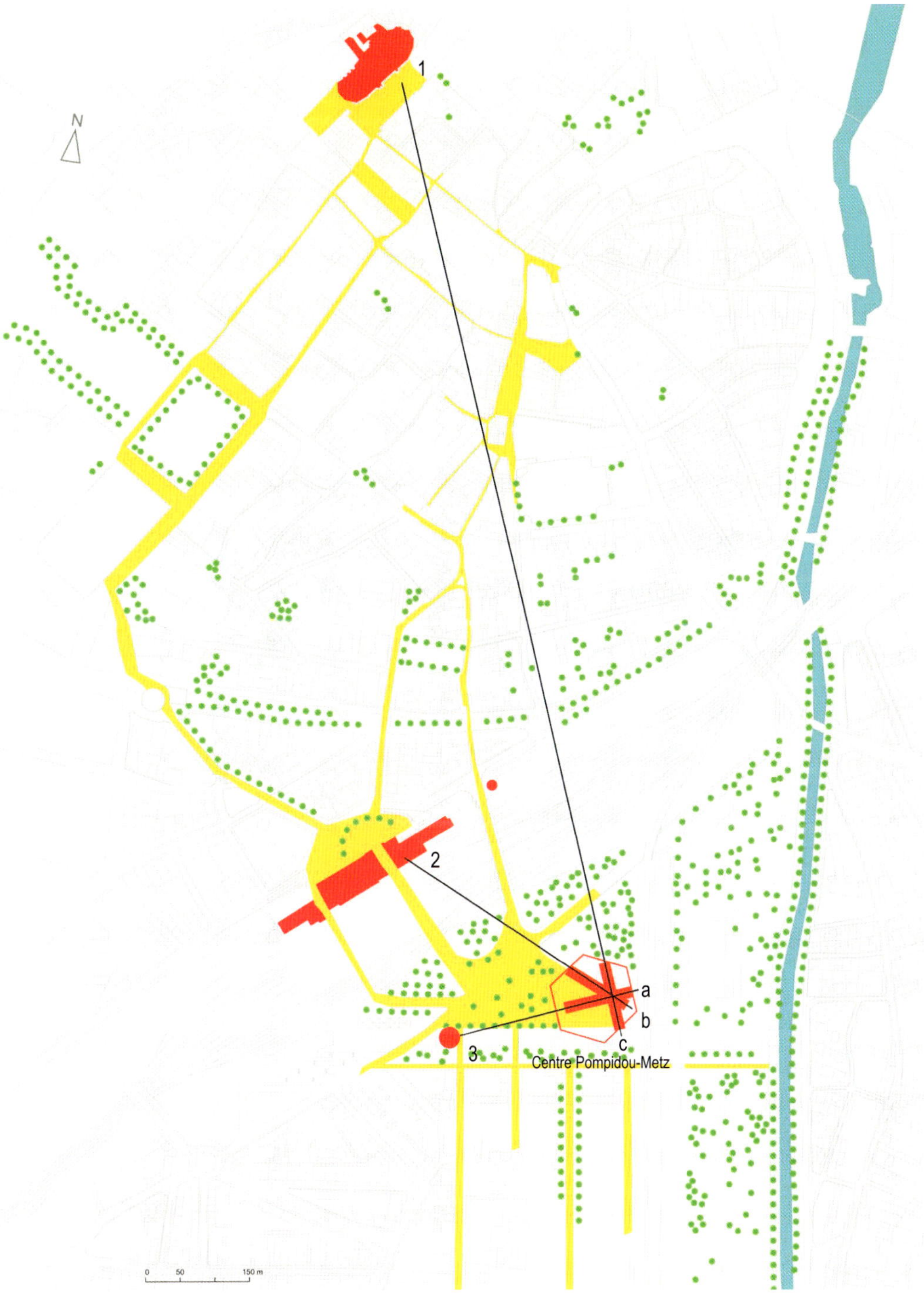

1. Cathedral
2. Metz Rail Station
3. Future Plaza

a. Gallery 1
b. Gallery 2
c. Gallery 3

Figure 17.2 Vicinity plan

Figure 17.3 Site plan

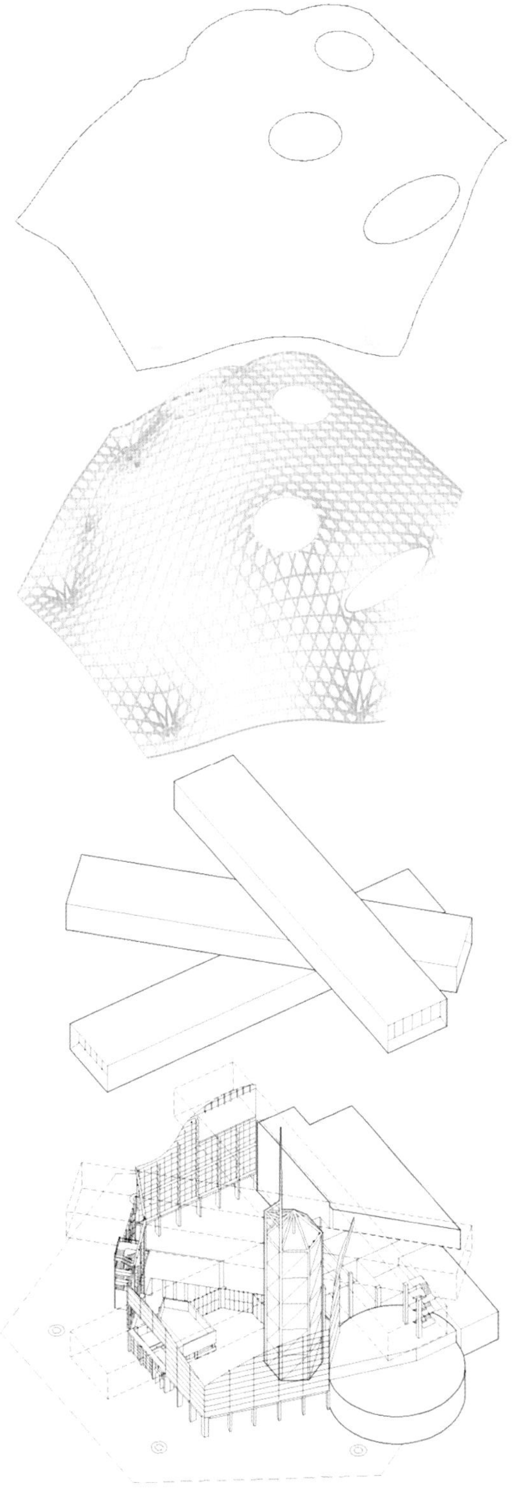

Figure 17.4 Axonometric diagram

1. Exhibition area
2. Hexagonal tower
3. Entry
4. The Forum
5. Administration
6. Creative studio
7. Auditorium
8. Cafe
9. Restaurant
10. Delivery Area
11. Storerooms
12. Exhibition terrace
13. Balcony
14. Void
15. Restaurant terrace

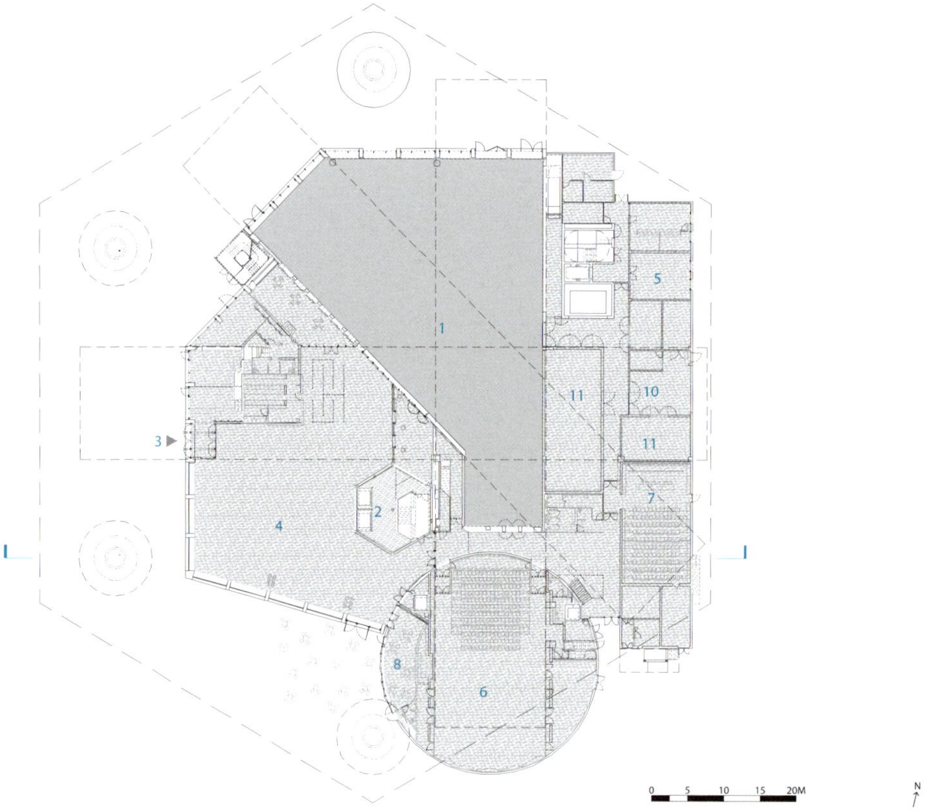

Figure 17.5 First ground floor plan

1. Exhibition area
2. Hexagonal tower
3. Entry
4. The Forum
5. Administration
6. Creative studio
7. Auditorium
8. Cafe
9. Restaurant
10. Delivery Area
11. Storerooms
12. Exhibition terrace
13. Balcony
14. Void
15. Restaurant terrace

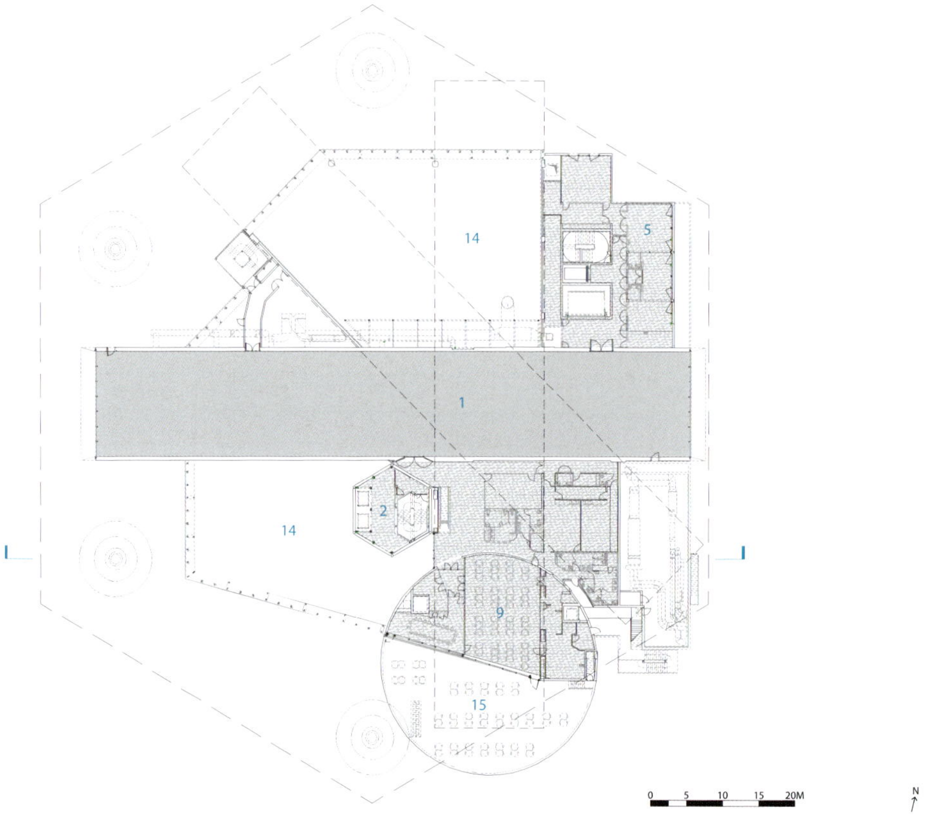

Figure 17.6 Gallery 1 level

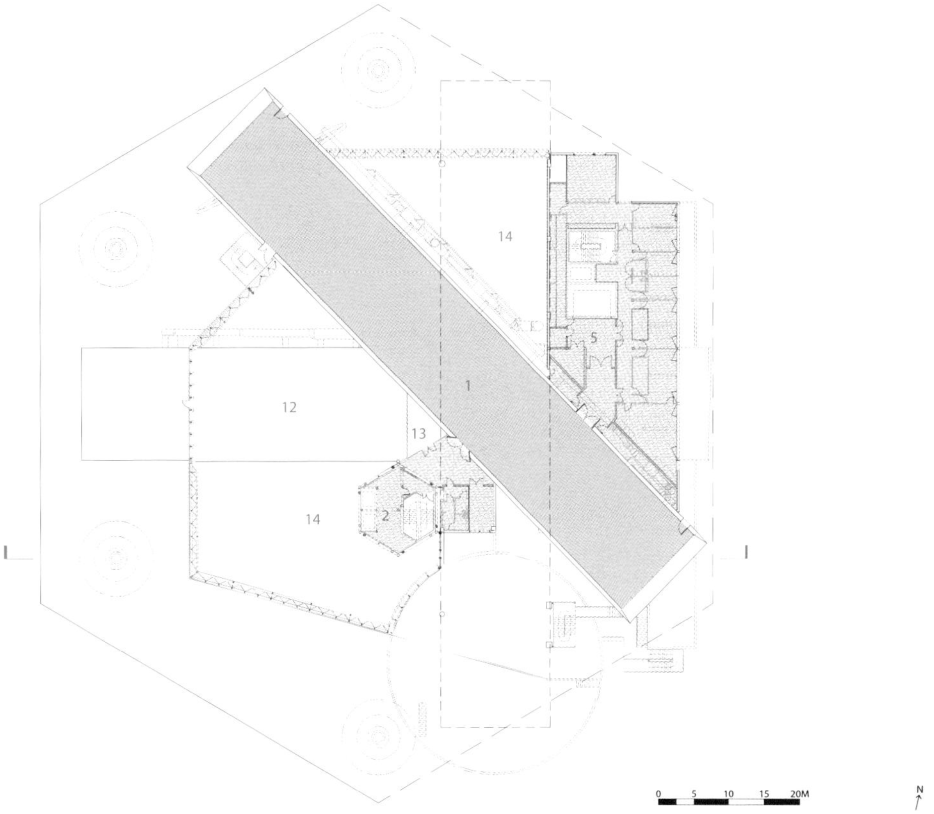

1. Exhibition area
2. Hexagonal tower
3. Entry
4. The Forum
5. Administration
6. Creative studio
7. Auditorium
8. Cafe
9. Restaurant
10. Delivery Area
11. Storerooms
12. Exhibition terrace
13. Balcony
14. Void
15. Restaurant terrace

Figure 17.7 Gallery 2 level

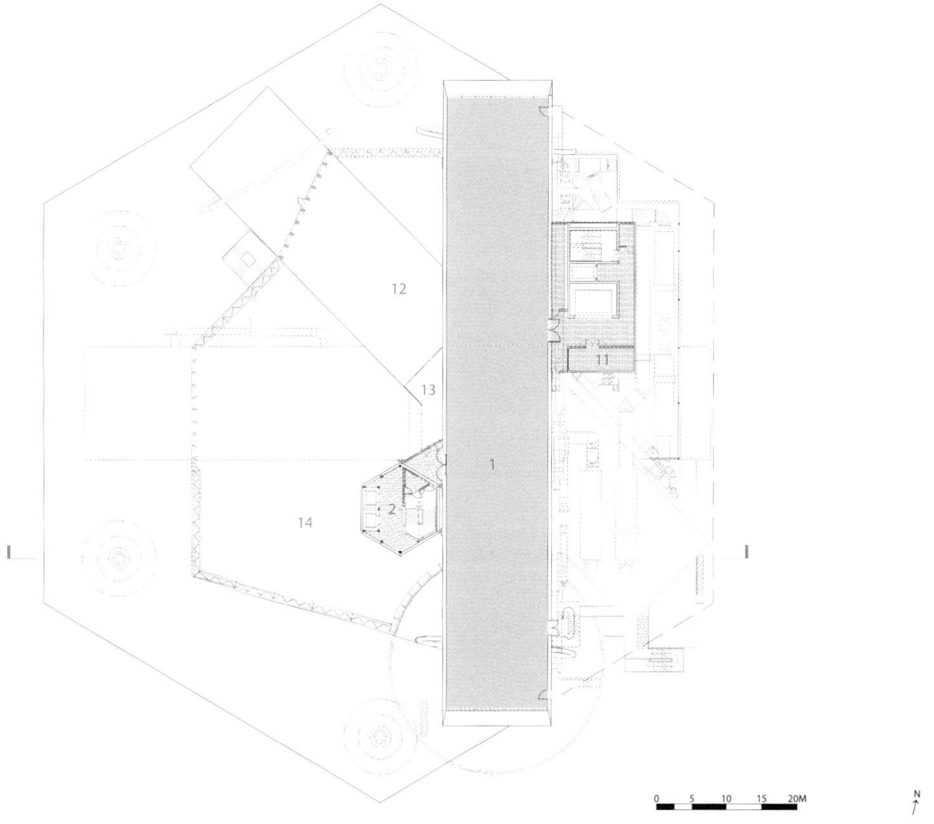

1. Exhibition area
2. Hexagonal tower
3. Entry
4. The Forum
5. Administration
6. Creative studio
7. Auditorium
8. Cafe
9. Restaurant
10. Delivery Area
11. Storerooms
12. Exhibition terrace
13. Balcony
14. Void
15. Restaurant terrace

Figure 17.8 Gallery 3 level

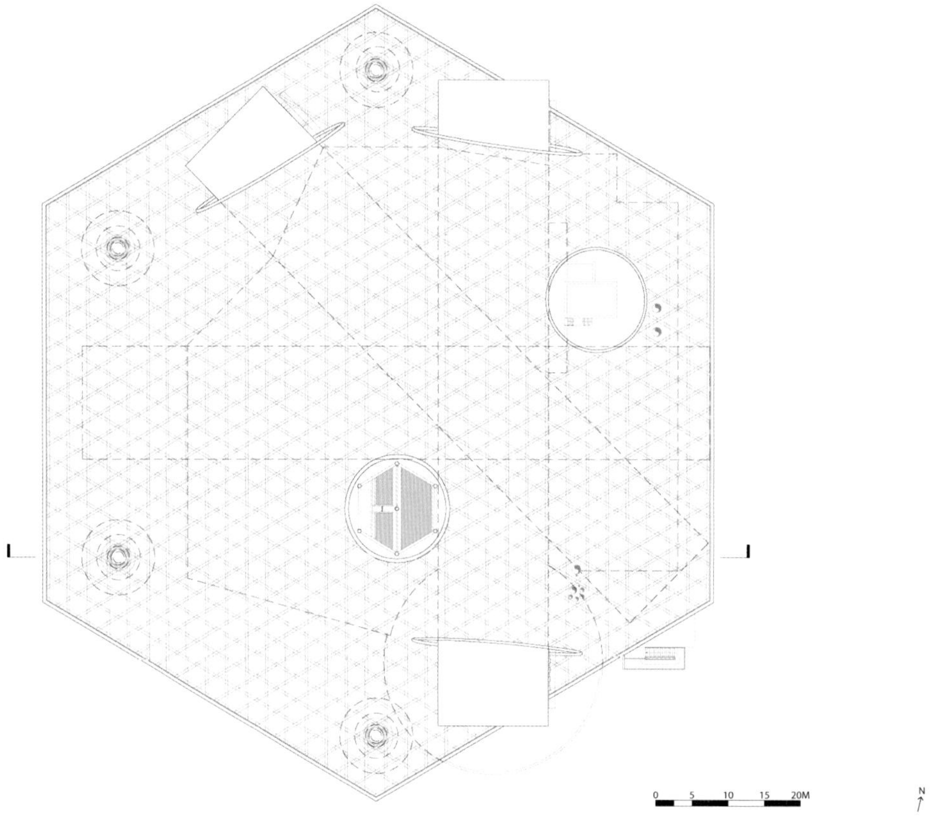

Figure 17.9 Roof plan

qualities of Piano and Roger's building that should be integrated at Metz, and flexibility of the spaces and views out, even from the galleries, were at the top of the list. The large urban space, the Piazza, is also an obvious contribution to the success of the Parisian project. Even if the rotated gallery tubes at Metz mask the likeness, the basic organizational diagram of the two projects is also surprisingly similar. In both designs a large sloped public space, a piazza, with public parking underneath, is located to the west (Fig 17.3). This exterior space flows into an interior Forum that leads to vertical circulation. Vertical circulation is used as a strong architectural gesture and connects identical, stacked, flexible, column-free program spaces. Finally, exterior mechanical spaces with exposed ducts are located along the east facade of both projects (Fig 17.13). Unlike the Pompidou – Paris, Metz has a veritable back side to the east that butts against the train tracks. This side is less tidy than the other sides. Staff parking is also located here as is a fenced technical court that contains delivery and other detached buildings for electrical equipment and trash.

The Metz building negotiates between being tall without becoming a high-rise and being iconic without becoming exactly monumental. The exterior is surprising and spectacular. The rotated, cantilevered gallery tubes seem firmly rooted in contemporary formal investigations and are a strong gesture in themselves (Fig 17.4). Comparisons can be made with SANAA's New Museum in New York or Bernard Tschumi's Acropolis Museum in Athens. The big gesture is obviously the tent roof. An exaggerated roof structure was also the important element for Jean Nouvel at the Museo Reina Sofía in Madrid and for Coop Himmelb(l)au at the Akron Art Museum. At Metz the roof is difficult to classify and seems to march to a different drummer. It also seems somewhat anachronistic – more in tune with the spirit of the 1970s than that of the beginning of the twenty-first century. The lively forms are not of a type that willfully seeks to disturb, yet the resolution of the tubes and the tent does not make immediate visual sense. The project seems to be based on very personal preoccupations. The story is often told of the woven Chinese hat that Ban found in a Paris boutique that became the inspiration for the form and, more importantly, for the structure of the Metz roof. This tale has become a legendary origin for the project and the hat itself is exhibited in the building. Ban and de Gastines' building does not, however, seem to have specific cultural origins. It does not seem "Japanese," a quality often attributed to more serene museum buildings by Yoshio Taniguchi, SANAA, or Tadao Ando, regardless of their location. Like in Piano and Roger's building there is an accumulation of elements and a general exuberance in Metz that distracts attention from any one

Figure 17.10 View from north

Figure 17.11 View from west

Figure 17.12 Exterior Galerie 1

element. Because of this there is a certain unity to the project even though forms, details, and changes of materials may not be meticulously resolved. In certain places it is not easy to discern if particular elements are ducts or columns or rain pipes. The building generally appears somewhat gawky but friendly.

The project builds from a more ordinary base to a more extraordinary roof. The lower part of the building is in concrete. Exterior finishes are primarily stucco and metal cladding. Window frames throughout the building are simple rectangular sections. Corrugated polycarbonate panels enclose the Forum while large garage-like doors allow it to be opened to the outside. All of the surfaces are white which gives unity to the various materials and forms. Exterior escape stairs are in galvanized steel.

A 37 m (121 ft) high hexagonal tower made of tubular steel is located near the center of the building. It contains vertical circulation – two glass elevators and a stair – and provides the top support for the roof structure. It is extended upward by a mast that reaches 77 m (253 ft), an astute way to increase the height and visibility of the structure. The mast is used as a flagpole for the French or European flag, but artists will also have the opportunity to use it for installations related to exhibitions. The height of 77 m is a reference to the year the Pompidou Center in Paris opened: 1977. The hexagonal form found throughout the building is also symbolic. France refers to itself as the "hexagon" because of its general geographic shape. Ban and de Gastines used the hexagon for the shape of the central tower, the module for the wood structure, and even the overall shape of the roof in plan that measures approximately 53 m (174 ft) on each of its six sides (Fig 17.9). The Corian sinks in the restrooms are also hexagonal in shape.

The continuously curved roof required the most study and development to make it feasible both structurally and economically. Shigeru Ban had worked with the German engineer Frei Otto on his paper tube Japanese Pavilion for Expo 2000 in Hanover. Otto is present in the Metz project in spirit. Ban and de Gastines developed the competition project with the engineer Cecil Balmond of Ove Arup, London. After winning the competition, work continued with another team of structural engineers from Ove Arup, but the design of the wood structure was finalized with the Swiss engineer Hermann Blumer.

The roof is made of double, glue-laminated wood beams that are laid horizontally and connected to form a sort of Vierendeel truss (Fig 17.21). These double beams are also double curved and run in three directions forming the hexagonal lattice. In total there are six layers of wood beams woven together, with four layers – two double beams – intersecting at any single connection point. Connections are made with prestressed threaded bars and disk springs.

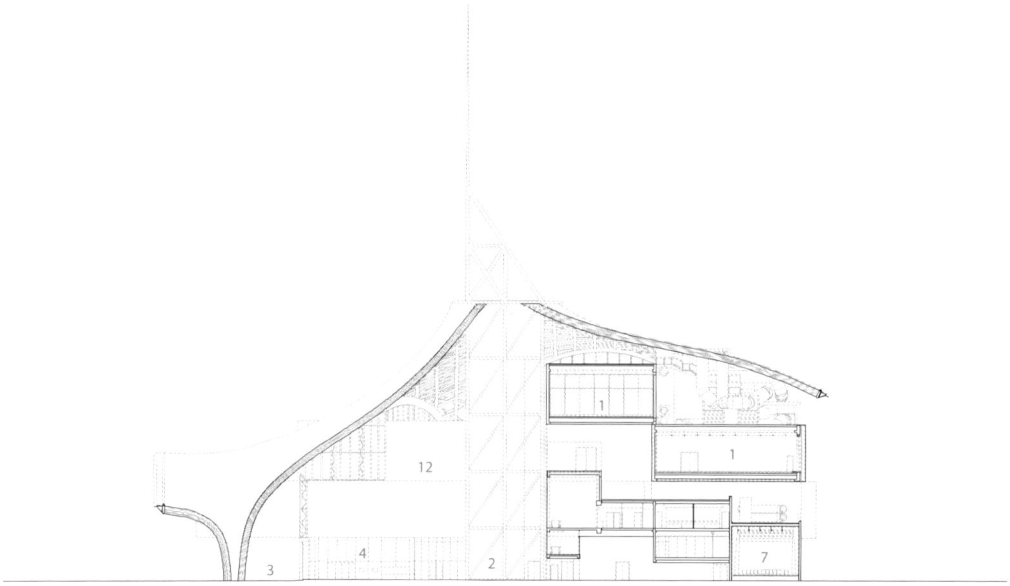

1. Exhibition area
2. Hexagonal tower
3. Entry
4. The Forum
5. Administration
6. Creative studio
7. Auditorium
8. Cafe
9. Restaurant
10. Delivery Area
11. Storerooms
12. Exhibition terrace
13. Balcony
14. Void
15. Restaurant terrace

0 5 10 15 20M

Figure 17.13 Section through the Forum

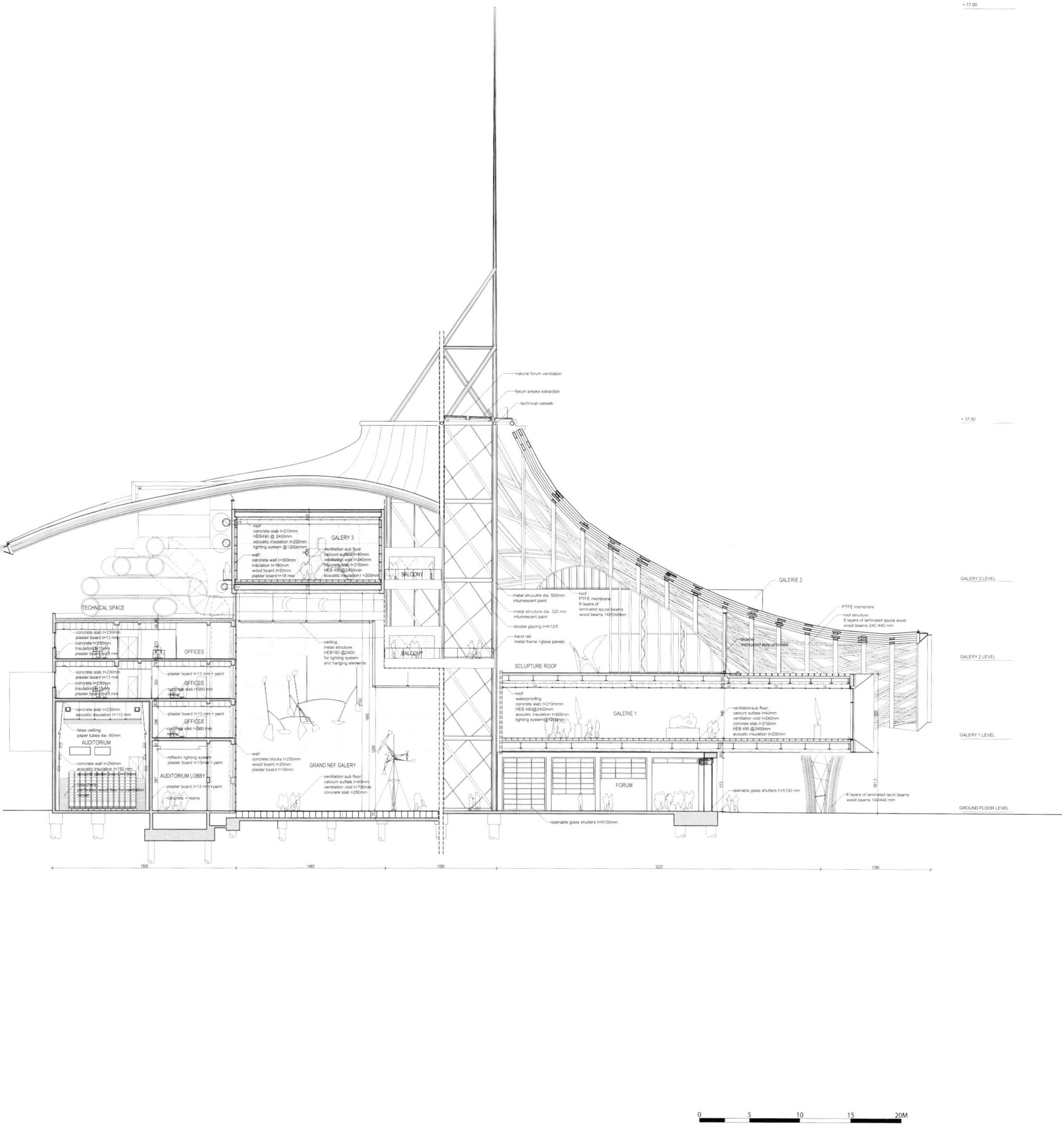

Figure 17.14 Section

The wood structure spans from a steel ring at the top of the hexagonal central tower to woven columns below that have been described as "tulips" or "mushrooms" (Fig 17.12). Maximum spans are approximately 40 m (131 ft). As built, there are four tulip columns. Two columns planned for the east side of the building were eliminated for budget reasons and replaced by a steel beam running the entire length of the east facade that receives the wood structure and transfers the loads into the concrete structure below. The solution is somewhat a *bricolage* but understandable in order to respect a relatively tight budget.

A deeper perimeter wood beam receives all six layers of the lattice. Large steel rings painted white are attached to the concrete gallery tubes. They receive the wood structure and allow the gallery tubes to pass through the roof. Other connecting pieces between wood members are in galvanized steel. Toward the west the roof overhang is generous. In some places on the east side of the building the roof becomes more like a hang nail, barely assuring the continuity of the large hat form.

The wood is predominately spruce and larch from Austria and Switzerland. Wood species were used in relation to their density and the particular loads the beams would be taking in specific structural pieces. The wood frame totals 650 tons. There are 1,600 beams with common lengths of 14 m (46 ft). The shortest beams are approximately 1 m. Common cross section dimensions of the beams are 44 by 14 cm (17 by 5.5 in.), and expansion and contraction of the structure can be up to 30 cm (11.75 in.). Sizes were influenced by the dimensions of milling machines and transportation constraints. The wood structure was manufactured by the German company Holzbau Amann GmbH and required ten months of fabrication and four months of installation. Installation began at the ring at the top of the central mast and worked downward with scaffolding holding the beams in place during construction. The entire realization was highly dependent on computer modeling and CNC fabrication. The membrane was installed just behind the wood structure to limit the time the wood would be exposed to weather. Since the wood is covered, it is expected to maintain its yellowish color rather than turning gray. The structure of the building in its entirety is made more complex because it uses three interrelated systems in concrete, steel, and wood.

The building is covered by 8,000 square meters of PTFE-coated (Poly-Tetra-Fluoro-Ethylene) fiberglass membrane that was manufactured by the Japanese firm Taiyo and installed by their German affiliate in Munich. The membrane panels follow the wood structure below and are connected to the wood by regularly spaced steel supports. The membrane is 0.5 mm thick. Its light transmission is 15 percent and gives a very nice light quality in the spaces below. Rain water is naturally canalized into the "tulip" columns where it is collected by common gray PVC pipes that go to the ground. Likewise, snow accumulates in these low points and a heating element was integrated to melt it and avoid accumulation. The first winter after completion of the building was particularly cold with unusual amounts of snowfall which required a redesign of the heating element.

The result of the roof is striking but does not particularly give the impression of lightness. The space below is vast, but the use of wood humanizes it and avoids monumentality. During the day the membrane appears opaque but changes with the light and time of day. In full sun it is very luminous and can be almost blinding. In other lights it changes to silver-gray or blue and can almost fade into the sky. At night when the roof is lit from below, the membrane becomes translucent and allows the wood structure to become visible (Fig 17.10). The night view better corresponds to the architects' vision of the project.

The "big top" projects up to 20 m (66 ft) beyond the building enclosure. It provides protection for the ticket line and for outdoor cafe seating (Fig 17.11). The roof structure was conceived to create a microclimate for the building, and the 870 m^2 (9,365 ft^2) Forum is an intermediate space that is not insulated, heated, or cooled. Its exterior walls in corrugated polycarbonate stop short of the roof, and the continuous gap between the two was realized by designing the facade as a vertical cantilever with a three-dimensional steel structure sitting atop the concrete wall of the ground level (Fig 17.15). The Forum is used for special events, fundraisers, and exhibition of outdoor artworks. In day-to-day use it is a grand transition space that soars to a height of 37 m (121 ft) at the central tower, only 4 m (13 ft) lower than the interior of the Metz cathedral. At ground level (Fig 17.5), 6 m (20 ft) high, garage-like doors open toward the cafe terrace and the entry plaza and further blur the

Figure 17.15 Interior Forum

Figure 17.16 Forum – elevator tower

Figure 17.17 Ground floor exhibition – Grand Nave

Figure 17.18 Galerie 2

Figure 17.19 Galerie 3

Figure 17.20 Interior Galerie 3 empty

distinction between inside and outside. The Forum provides access to ticket sales, the museum store, an education space, and the cafe at ground level and a restaurant one level above that has its own elevator. A circular shape to the south contains the 370 m^2 (3,983 ft^2) Studio, a multipurpose space with 200 retractable seats that can be used for performances, receptions, exhibitions, or even exhibition preparation. The Studio is also contained within the width of the uppermost, north/south gallery tube that hovers above. Inside, its louvered walls are a frugal system made of medium density fiberboard painted black. The walls provide acoustical control, and ducts are housed in the space behind. An additional 144 seat auditorium is tucked away at the back of the building and is used primarily for cinema and conferences. It is generally gray and black with an undulating paper tube ceiling. Conference rooms and an educational space for children are located on the same level as the restaurant but are accessed by the primary public circulation system of the building.

The 1,200 m^2 (12,917 ft^2) Grande Nef is also located on the ground floor (Fig 17.14 and Fig 17.17). Its triangular shape and varied heights are the result of its position under the splayed gallery tubes above. It is a sort of residual space and its ceiling height goes from 6 to 13 to 21 m (20 to 42.5 to 69 ft). A very tall space was requested in the competition brief. Certain pieces in the collection of the National Museum of Modern Art that are too big to be shown in the Pompidou Center – Paris can be shown in Metz. A large door on the north side allows very large pieces to enter the gallery directly from the outside. Inside, finishes are simple, ducts are exposed, spots are on light tracks, and a steel frame suspended from the ceiling provides support for various exhibition installations.

Vertical circulation is primarily via the two large glass elevators within the central tower that look onto the Forum as they move among the various floors (Fig 17.16). The ride is pleasant and the elevators are only accessible after ticket control. An enclosed stair made of white painted steel and concrete steps is also located within the central tower and serves all levels. A single escalator behind the tower ascends to the Gallery 1 level only. Whereas elevators as the primary circulation in a vertical museum can often create bottlenecks, vertical circulation here seems to function well. Behind the scenes, a 3 by 5 m (10 by 16 ft) freight elevator links all of the levels. It is conveniently placed in relation to the loading dock on the east side of the building. A canopy protects the two loading bays, but unlike many recent museums, trucks do not actually enter into the building at Metz. Since there is no permanent collection there is only limited storage for works of art. A basement was not included in the project so as not to disturb ancient artifacts that might still remain on the site.

The three rectangular gallery tubes (Fig 17.6, Fig 17.7, and Fig 17.8) are rotated by 45 degrees around a point that has no recognizable significance in the building's planning. Gallery 1 is basically oriented east/west, and Gallery 3 is oriented north/south. Orientation is also to capture views of local monuments through the 14 by 5 m (46 by 16 ft) windows at the ends of the tubes. Gallery 3 is privileged and has a surprising view focused on the Gothic cathedral in the city center (Fig 17.20). Visitors are naturally attracted to the light and views making the spaces feel like tunnels to be moved through. Each unobstructed gallery is 1,120 m^2 (12,056 ft^2): 80 by 14 by 5 m high (262 by 46 by 16 ft). If the exterior of the building was meant to be spectacular, the galleries are extremely straightforward spaces that resemble extruded cargo containers (Fig 17.18 and Fig 17.19). They were designed to be flexible and not rival the art, but they rely heavily on temporary exhibition partitions. They are daring in their simplicity, uniformity, and singular approach. Visitors enter on one side near the middle of the tube, and service is from the opposite side. This arrangement is also similar to that of the Pompidou Center in Paris. Small doors near the ends of the tubes open directly to the outside and would provide emergency access for firemen.

Since there is no permanent collection, all of the exhibition spaces are conceived as galleries for temporary presentations of modern and contemporary art – even works that do not yet exist. The spaces appear frugal and somewhat "experimental." Some skylights were shown in competition drawings but the built galleries have a double dropped ceiling and are artificially lit. A metal, 1.2 m (4 ft) grid has light tracks integrated below and fluorescent tubes concealed above for indirect lighting. The grid is suspended below a white acoustical ceiling. Each gallery has 66 lighting zones – 22 zones in the length and 3 in the width – that can be adjusted separately.

The gallery tubes have raised floors with a 25 cm (9.75 in.) plenum below. The plenum in the Grand Nef on the ground floor is 70 cm (27.5 in.) deep. Air conditioning supply is through the plenum and return is through grills in the walls between the two dropped ceilings. Electrical cables also run within the plenum lending more flexibility to the space. The 60 cm (23.5 in.) square floor panels are uniformly perforated with small round holes to allow an even flow of air through the floor. The holes are small enough that they are not perceived within the very large space and no additional pattern has been created by linear or circular grills such as in the Brandhorst Museum or the Kunsthaus Graz respectively. This clever technical solution that allows walls to go anywhere should not be minimized in relation to the success and flexibility of the spaces where exhibition designs have already included diagonal or skewed partitions that sit comfortably on the micro-pattern of the perforated floor. Another result of the solution is that there is no architectural detail required between side walls and the floor. There is no baseboard or reveal joint, and the wall simply continues past the raised floor to the slab below. Visible linear air grills are located in front of the large end windows. They integrate supplemental heat that provides comfort against cold and combats condensation. The combined designated exhibition spaces, the Grande Nef, Galleries 1, 2, and 3, and the Studio, approach 50 percent of the total area of the building. This is high since a more typical ratio is only 25 percent.

The large wood lattice and membrane roof certainly took a bite out of the Metz building budget, and it remains surprising how experientially detached the roof is from the exhibition spaces. Within the galleries, visitors are hardly aware of the roof. Spreading the budget thin, however, has resulted in a building that appears more frugal and casual even if it required very advanced building techniques to realize it. The building is an event in the city – and beyond. It is big, a little rough, a little pudgy, but not ostentatious. Like its sister institution in Paris, it gives the impression that it is accessible to all.

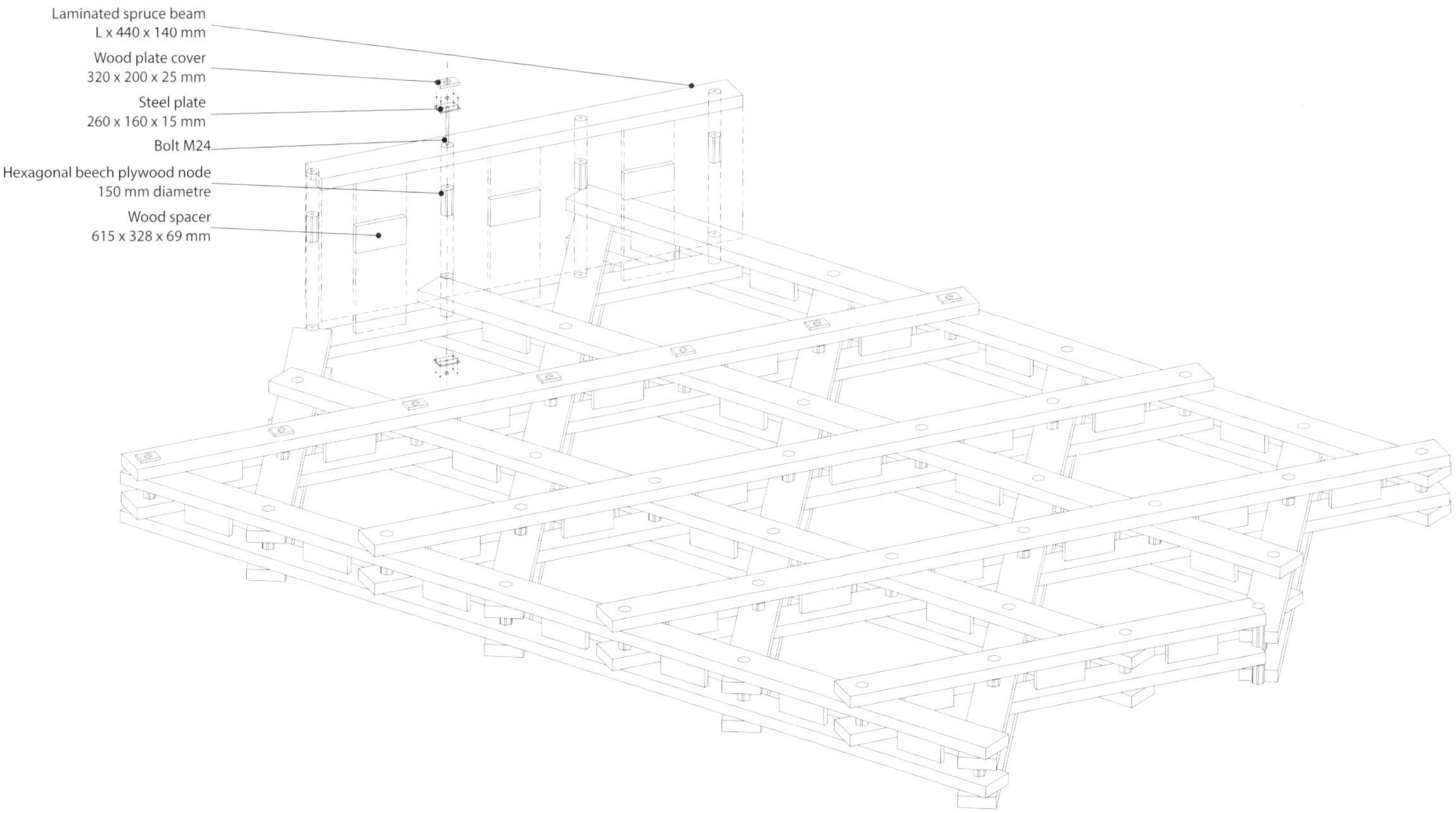

Figure 17.21 Detail – wood roof structure

CHAPTER 18

Museo Nazionale Delle Arti Del XXI Secolo

Rome, Italy

Zaha Hadid Architects

2010

Figure 18.1 Aerial view from north

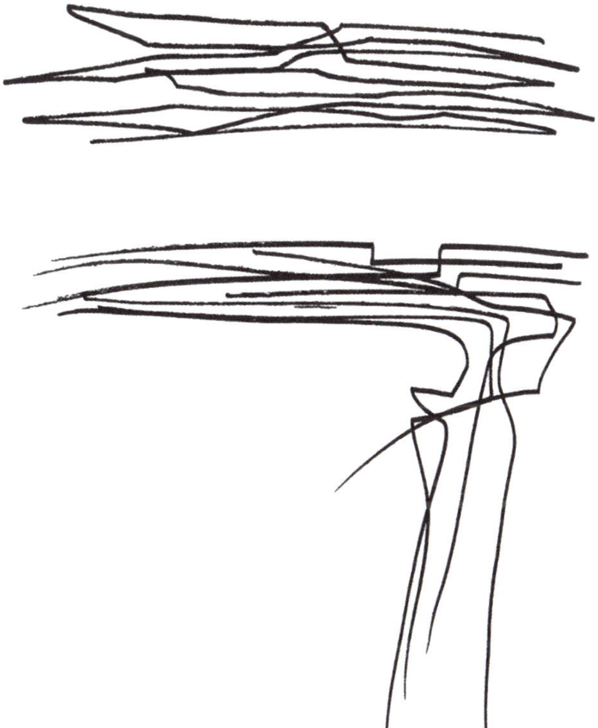

Figure 18.2 Sketch by Zaha Hadid

It might be tempting to look for an evolution in Zaha Hadid's thoughts on museum design between her Contemporary Arts Center (CAC) in Cincinnati and her *Museo Nazionale delle Arti del XXI Secolo* (MAXXI) in Rome. Though the two projects opened approximately seven years apart, they were both conceived at about the same time as competitions. Hadid's office was involved in a flurry of museum competitions at the closing of the twentieth century that also included the extension to the Reina Sofía Museum in Madrid, the Kunsthaus in Graz, and the Brandhorst Museum in Munich. The CAC opened in 2003. Construction began on the MAXXI in the same year. Problems related to budget and financing as well as modifications to norms for seismic design after construction had already begun pushed completion in Rome to 2009. The MAXXI opened to the public in 2010.

The MAXXI is located north of the historic center of Rome in the Flaminio district which is nestled in a bend of the Tiber River (Fig 18.1). The neighborhood around the museum is primarily apartments, shops, and offices. Buildings are mostly from the late nineteenth and early twentieth centuries. The immediate area is defined by three major radial axes that originate at a point near the Tiber and create shifts in the local street grid. The MAXXI's main entrance is located on the central axis, the Via Guido Reni, which is oriented roughly east west (Fig 18.3). As part of the redevelopment of the area a pedestrian bridge, the *Ponte della Musica*, by Buro Happold (2011) now extends the axis of the Via Guido Reni across the Tiber to the west thereby making a more direct link with the *Foro Italico* (previously known as the *Foro Mussolini*), a sports complex built in the 1930s. Indeed, there are numerous sports facilities in the area since several buildings for the Rome 1960 Summer Olympics are also nearby. To the east the Via Guido Reni continues as the Via Pietro de Coubertin, and Pier Luigi Nervi's *Palazzetto dello Sport* and *Stadio Flaminio* are located here. On the same street a little farther east there is another recent cultural institution: the *Auditorium Parco della Musica* designed by Renzo Piano and completed in 2002.

The 3 hectare (7.4 acre), "L" shaped site where the MAXXI now stands was previously a military compound built in the early twentieth century that contained barracks and garage facilities for the repair of military vehicles. In 1997 the defense ministry transferred the site to the cultural ministry for the MAXXI project which was also meant to be an important element in the urban renewal of the district. The site traverses the block from the tree-lined Via Guido Reni to the south toward the Via Masaccio to the north. A tramway runs in the Via Masaccio and a major bus terminus is located within easy walking distance a little farther north. Remaining buildings of the military compound to the west are similar to those demolished to make way for Hadid's building. They have saw-toothed roofs and are industrial in nature. The early twentieth-century Basilica of Santa Croce is just to the east, facing the Via Guido Reni.

Rome was longing for a dose of contemporary art and architecture. The city possessed no major art institution comparable to those in other European capitals such as the Pompidou Center in Paris, the Tate Modern in London, or the Reina Sofía in Madrid. Architecturally, the MAXXI should fulfill a role much like the original, 1930s Goodwin and Stone design for the Museum of Modern Art in New York. It would promote bold architecture in a city lacking significant, contemporary buildings. Recent buildings in Rome such as Richard Meier's Ara Pacis Museum or Piano's Auditorium were viewed as too timid. Meier's ruin-like, stone walls and Piano's "Roman" brick were still too entrenched in the past. The MAXXI should speak more of the future, the twenty-first century, and project a new image of Rome and of Italy.

When the architectural competition was launched the MAXXI possessed no real permanent collection. Today the collection grows, and the building houses two institutions: MAXXI Architecture which is the first national museum of architecture in Italy and MAXXI Art which focuses on contemporary art including performances, film, music, and dance. Competition entrants in a first phase numbered 273. The list of 15 finalists included names such as Vittorio Gregotti, Steven Holl, Toyo Ito, Rem Koolhaas, Jean Nouvel, and SAANA. The Portuguese architect Suoto de Muoro proposed maintaining most all of the existing military buildings and simply renovating them as gallery spaces, and his entry was perhaps the most modest. In contrast, Zaha Hadid's entry was likely the most dynamic (Fig 18.2). The competition brief requested that some of the military buildings be maintained and that a link between the Via Guido Reni and the Via Masaccio be created through the site. Hadid's competition entry integrated both. During the development of the design, the size of the building was decreased which in turn enlarged the unencumbered, public space in front of the museum and makes the link between the two streets even stronger. The scheme makes no allusions to Rome's historical architecture but is sympathetic to its immediate context.

The concept of "movement" and "flow" fundamental to the project and represented by pronounced parallel and concentric lines is most obvious in an aerial view or roof plan of the building where it appears as a distinct object that bends the rules of the preexisting urbanism (Fig 18.7). From the ground level, however, the structure appears as less of a three-dimensional object. In a strict elevation view from the Via Guido Reni it can pass almost unnoticed (Fig 18.11). Likewise, visitors have little reason to go to the west side of the building that is reserved for ramps leading to the basement, fire escapes, and such. From the east and north

Figure 18.3 Site plan

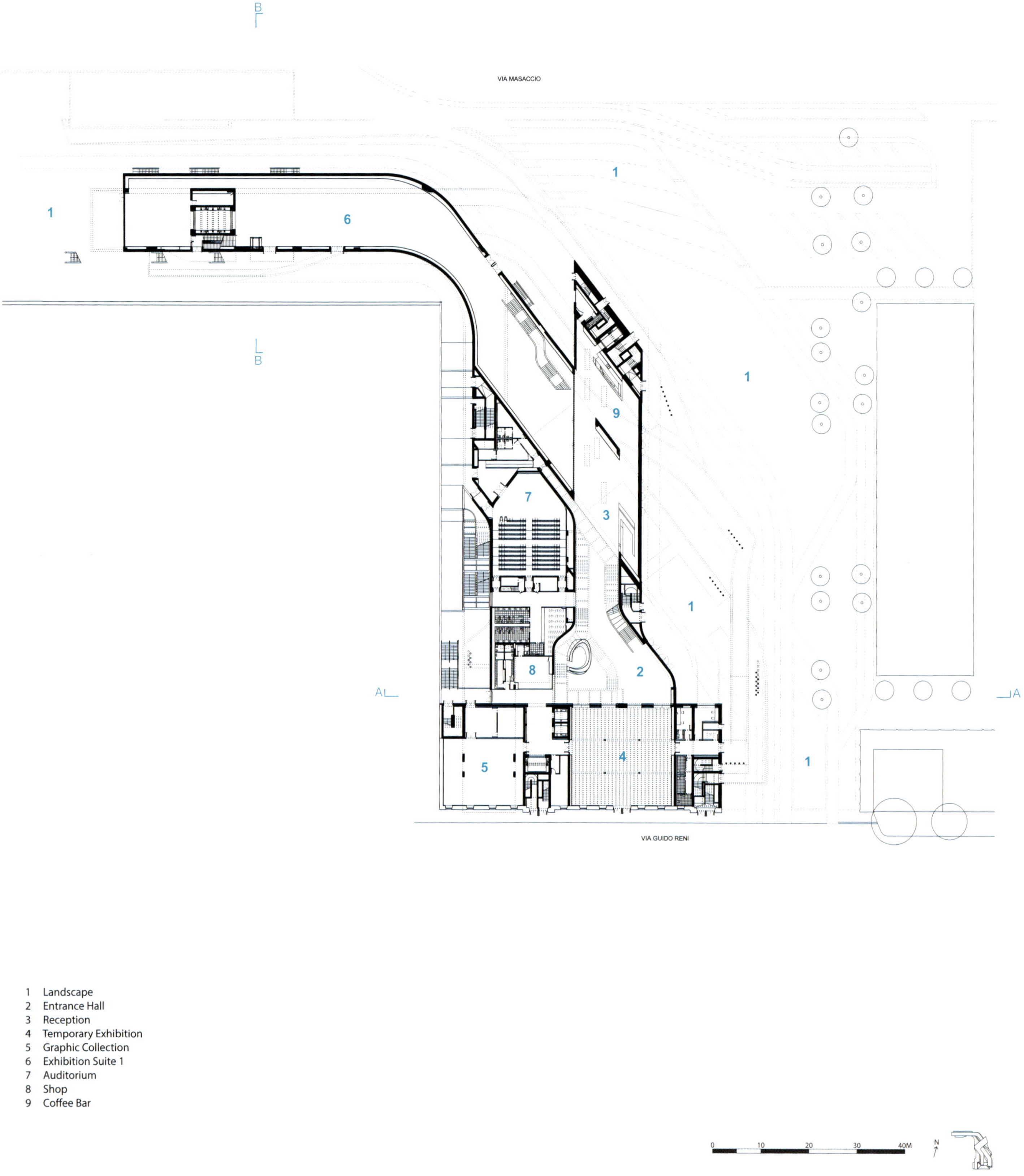

1 Landscape
2 Entrance Hall
3 Reception
4 Temporary Exhibition
5 Graphic Collection
6 Exhibition Suite 1
7 Auditorium
8 Shop
9 Coffee Bar

Figure 18.4 First (ground) floor plan

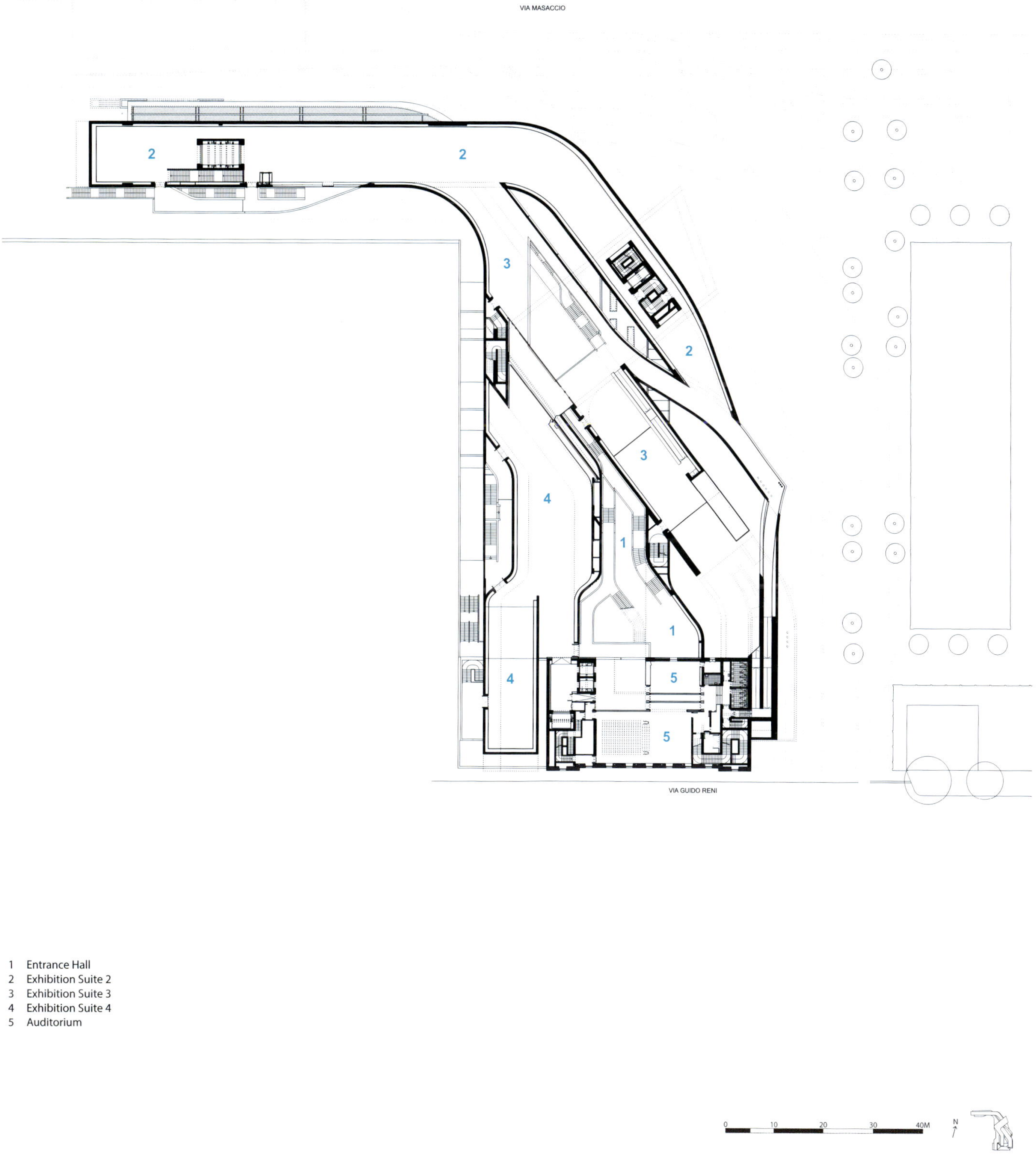

1 Entrance Hall
2 Exhibition Suite 2
3 Exhibition Suite 3
4 Exhibition Suite 4
5 Auditorium

Figure 18.5 Second floor plan

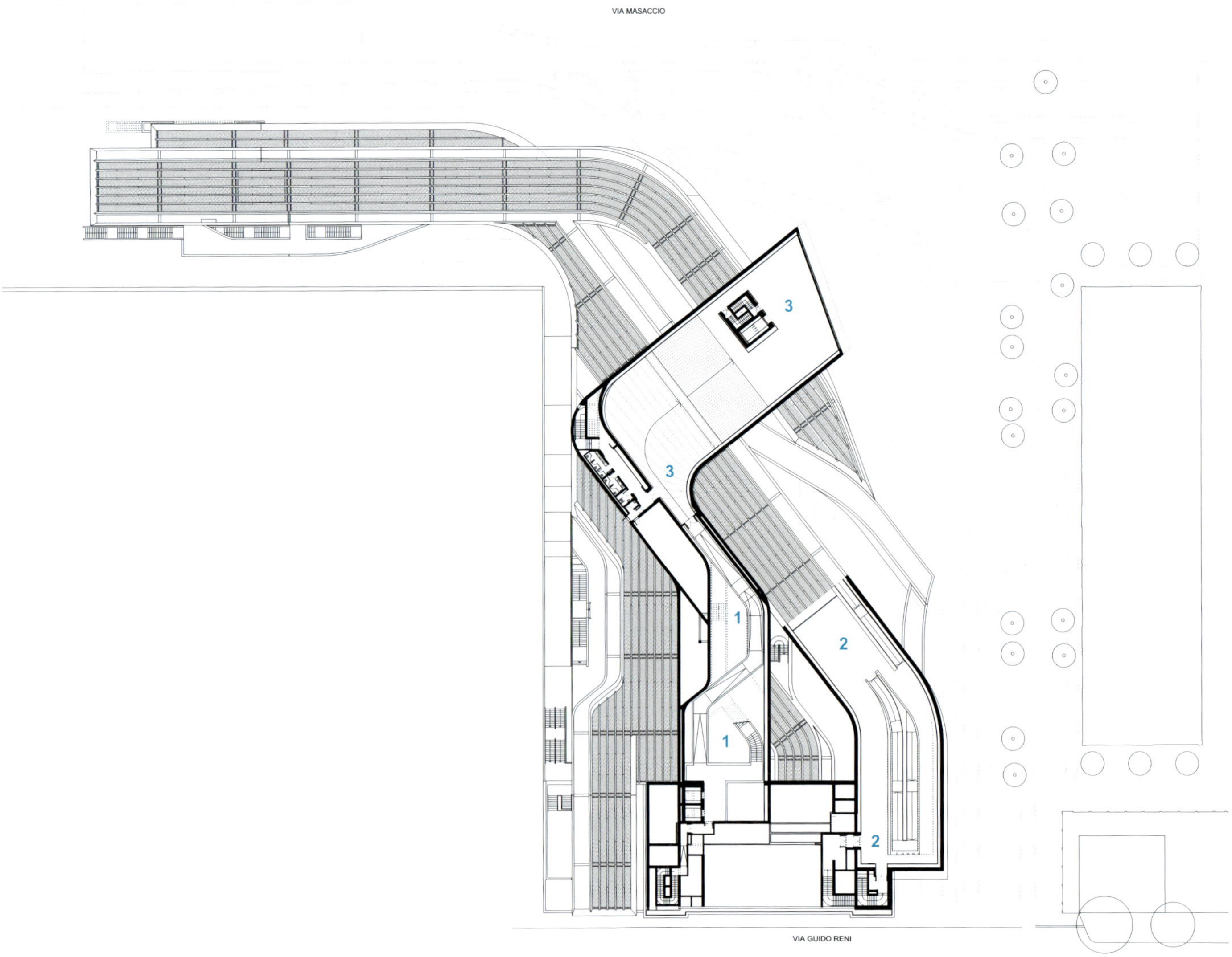

1 Entrance Hall
2 Exhibition Suite 3
3 Exhibition Suite 5

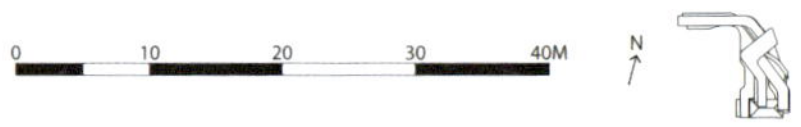

Figure 18.6 Third floor plan

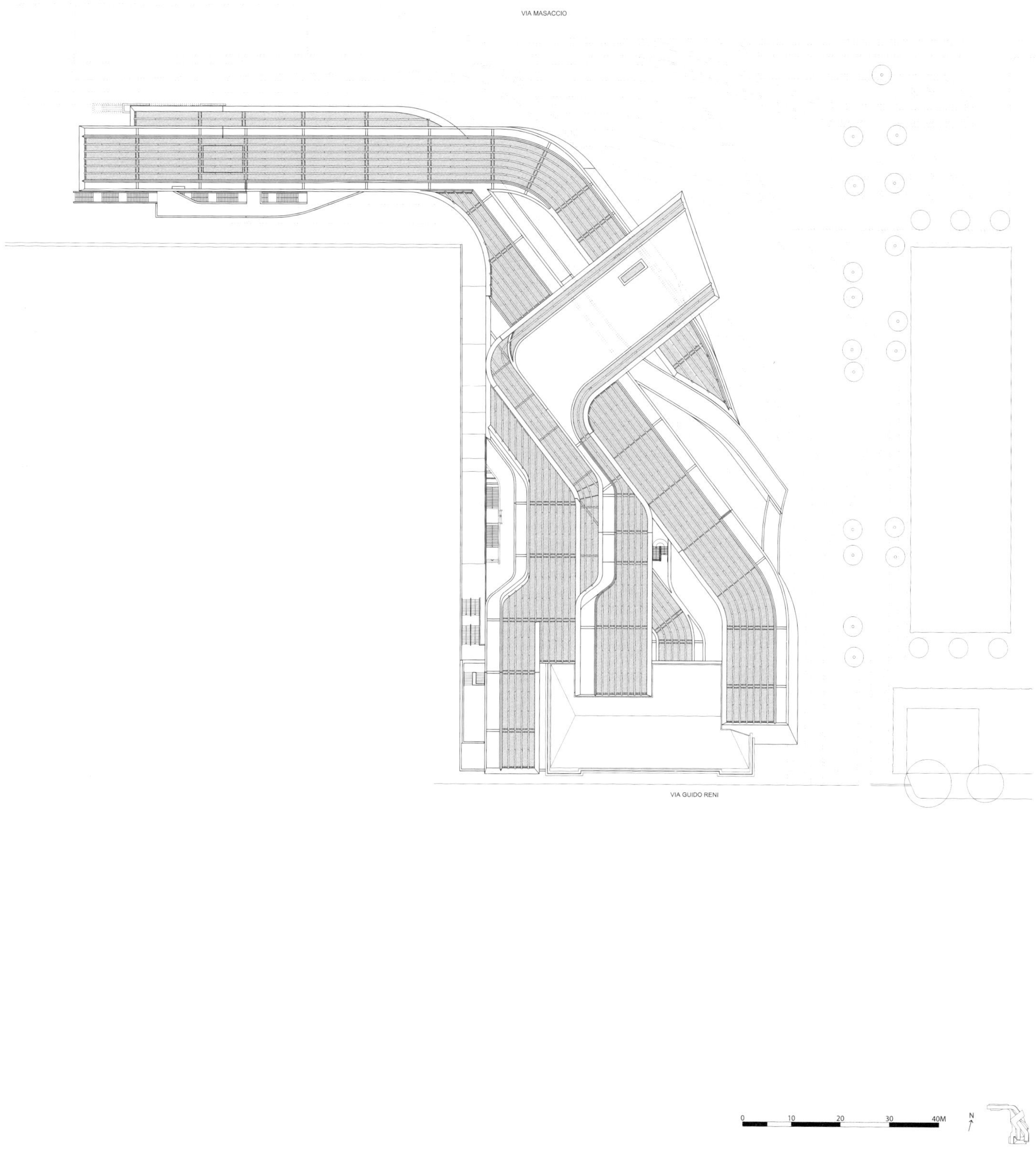

Figure 18.7 Roof plan

sides visitors see an exuberant, waving, deep facade – a sort of bas-relief – rather than a freestanding object (Fig 18.8, Fig 18.12, and Fig 18.13). This is a quality the MAXXI shares with the Contemporary Arts Center in Cincinnati.

Three site strategies made an "alien" object fit surprisingly well into its context. First, two existing buildings were rehabilitated and integrated into the scheme. The new building locks around and into one of them. Second, the new building is sculpted to respond to the shift in the adjacent street grids. Third, the new building generally respects the height of its neighbors. The architectural approach and results are comparable to Cook and Fournier's insertion of their "friendly alien," the Kunsthaus, within the historic center of Graz. The MAXXI combines exuberant, unconventional architecture with more traditional urbanism. The form of the new public piazza is derived from the shift of the street grid and the link through the site, and the space is well rooted, vibrant, and a significant contribution to the success of the project. The renovated stucco building on the east side of the piazza houses a cafe and bookstore on the ground floor and museum offices in the spaces above. This campus character makes for a certain amount of back and forth between the two buildings, and public entrances to all spaces are from the piazza rather than directly from the street. Surface treatments are a graphic pattern of concrete and gravel (uncomfortable to walk on) that corresponds to the flow of the architecture. An alignment of trees softens the generally sober space. It is an everyday space, however, where adults meet and children play. It is also a place for performances, lectures and diverse museum events as well as installations such as the Young Architects Program done in collaboration with the Museum of Modern Art/PS1 in New York.

The building is predominately smooth, abstract concrete, punctuated by five bunched groups of round, concrete-filled steel columns that are one story high (Fig 18.9). Most all of the concrete was cast in place. Formwork was fabricated off-site, however, to assure quality and precision. Exterior walls are generally 40 cm (15.75 in.) thick with 5 cm (2 in.) of thermal insulation on the inside. The overall form cannot be grasped from a single vantage point. There is, however, enough transparency at the ground level to make the structure hospitable, and other glazed areas in the galleries along with the large cantilevered "eye" that culminates at 23 m (75 ft) peak curiosity. The fact that the building is divided into five different sections to allow for movement in the case of an earthquake is little visible, and numerous hydraulic pistons, both vertical and horizontal, that serve as shock transmitters as part of the seismic design are concealed within the structure.

Though much appreciated now, Hadid's project was opposed by neighbors when the design became public. It was nicknamed the "Berlin wall" precisely because of its use of curved concrete. The MAXXI education department was established early on with a role of public relations and advocate for the scheme. The department took up residence on the construction site as a friendly face for the public.

Figure 18.8 View from north/east

Figure 18.9 View from east

Figure 18.10 View from south

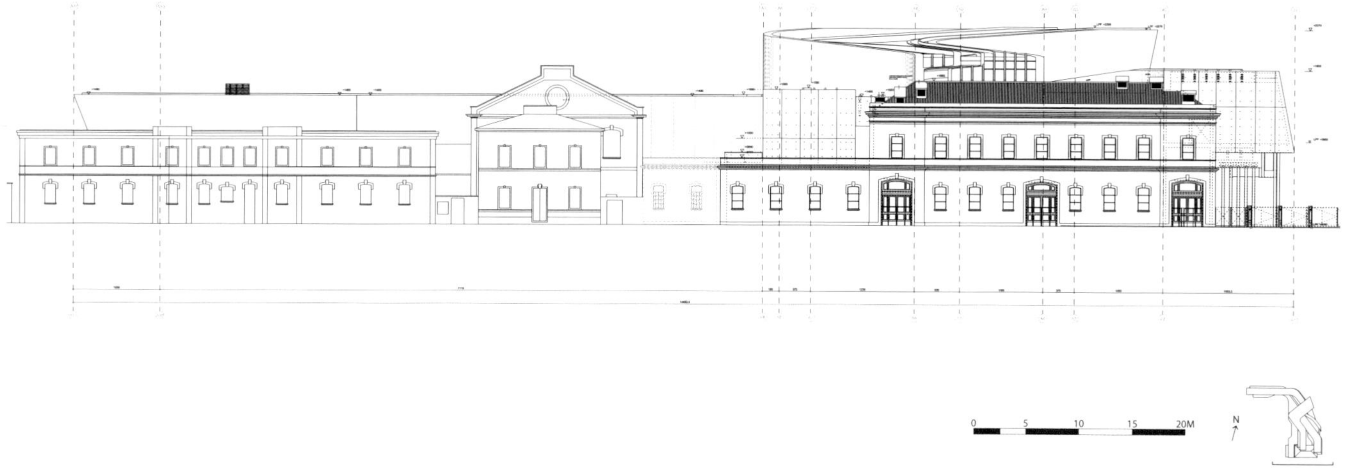

Figure 18.11 South elevation Via Guido Reni

At night the forms of the building are highlighted by lights recessed into the ground (Fig 18.10). The lighting scheme is relatively simple. It does not "perform" like the Kunsthaus in Graz, nor is it integral to the architecture like Steven Holl's glowing glass boxes in Kansas City. Also at night large gates close both ends of the outdoor space when the museum closes. The piazza mediates between the neighborhood and the museum. The gates are a reminder, however, that it is not truly a public space.

The main entry into the 21,200 m^2 (square meter; 228,195 ft^2 (square foot)) building is from the southern end of the piazza just where Hadid's new structure attaches to the preexisting building that faces the Via Guido Reni (Fig 18.4). Upon entering, a white, curved information desk meets the visitor. The eye wanders and follows the curving lines of the crisscrossing stairs upward to the glass roof of a soaring, three-story space (Fig 18.14 and Fig 18.16). The dark, metal-clad stairs and walkways within the entrance hall are impressive by their spatial play and long spans. Backlit translucent panels are integrated into their undersides and provide an abundance, perhaps an overabundance, of light. It is a dynamic, exhilarating space, and visitors appear to be filled with marvel. It can appear somewhat empty, however, because it is so big with so many walkways in need of human animation. Site-specific art works such as Maurizio Mochetti's *Straight Lines of Light in Curvilinear Hyperspace* have been integrated into the volume. Mochetti's piece is composed of suspended red cylinders that project light. It is striking in the otherwise black and white color scheme (Fig 18.17).

The vertical void makes the link between the old building and Hadid's new galleries. The facades of the two story preexisting building were maintained but the interior was demolished and subsequently rebuilt to better function within the overall scheme. This part of the project now contains temporary exhibition spaces on the ground floor and an auditorium above. A small bookstore is located behind the information desk. Galleries can be glimpsed above, but visitors cannot immediately ascend since ticket sales are in a reception area farther to the north with restrooms, lockers, another auditorium, and a seating area with Hadid's *Moon System* sofas found along the way. A small cafe is beyond ticket sales and behind a panel that displays *Wall Drawing #375* by Sol Lewitt. Lewitt's piece is not flattered by its generally somber location at a crossroads of circulation.

With a ticket in hand a visitor has the option of entering the ground floor Exhibition Suite 1 (Fig 18.18) located behind a glass wall directly opposite the ticket counter, or returning to the entrance hall and taking the stair to the upper galleries, or seeking out the elevators that are located beyond the entrance hall in the reconfigured, preexisting building. Visitors should already intuit that there is not one path through the building. The ground floor spaces also present the basic vocabulary of the yet to be discovered galleries: concrete walls and floors and prominent, curving concrete fins suspended below a layered glass roof complex.

No public spaces are located in the full basement of the building that at its deepest descends to 9 m (30 ft) below grade. The basement is devoted to delivery, storage, mechanical rooms, conservation, etc. Boilers are located here as are air handlers, at least one for each of the five exhibition suites. Because of the elongated plan, a total of three freight elevators service different parts of the building above and are linked by corridors at the basement level. Unlike the curved concrete walls in the galleries, the basement structure is generally a grid of concrete columns. A double exterior wall provides a space for emergency stairs to attain the ground level and provides for added control of ground

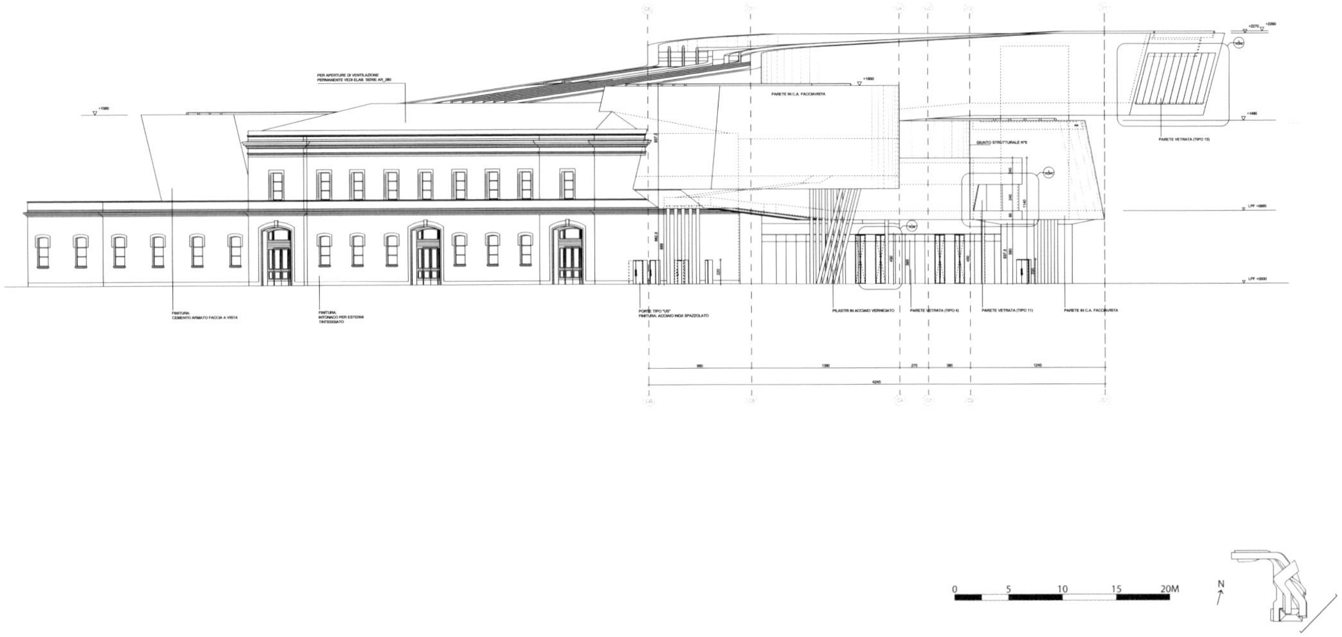

Figure 18.12 East elevation

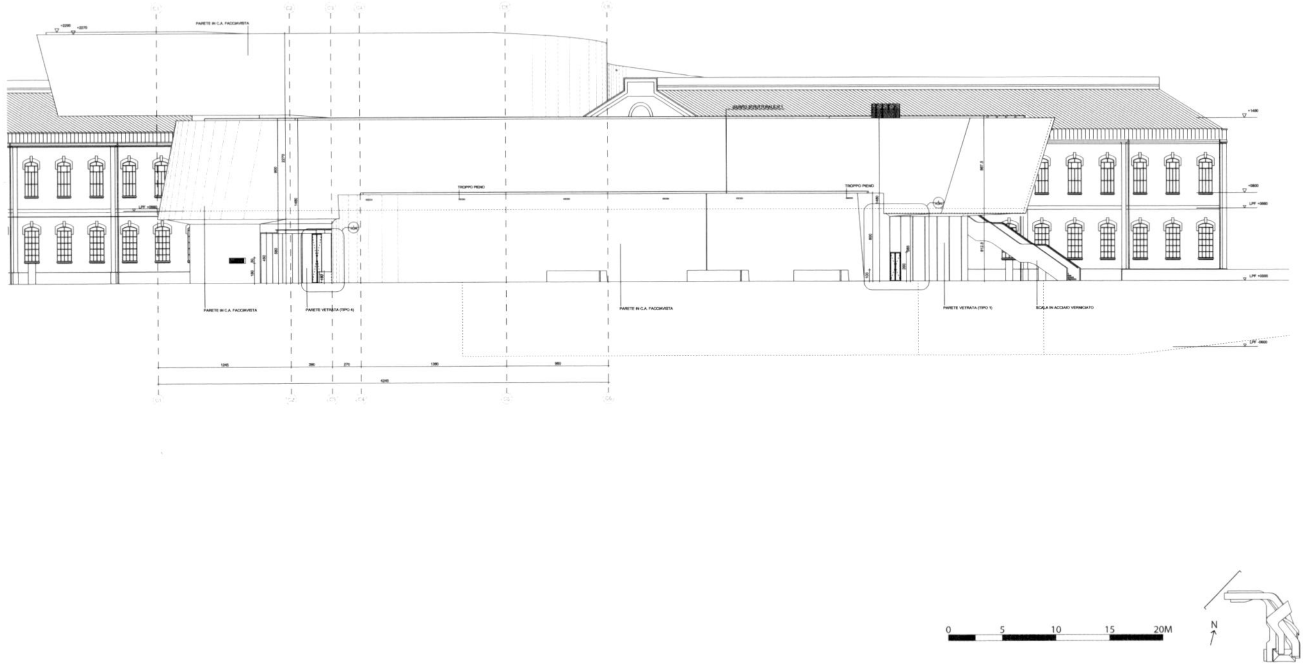

Figure 18.13 North elevation

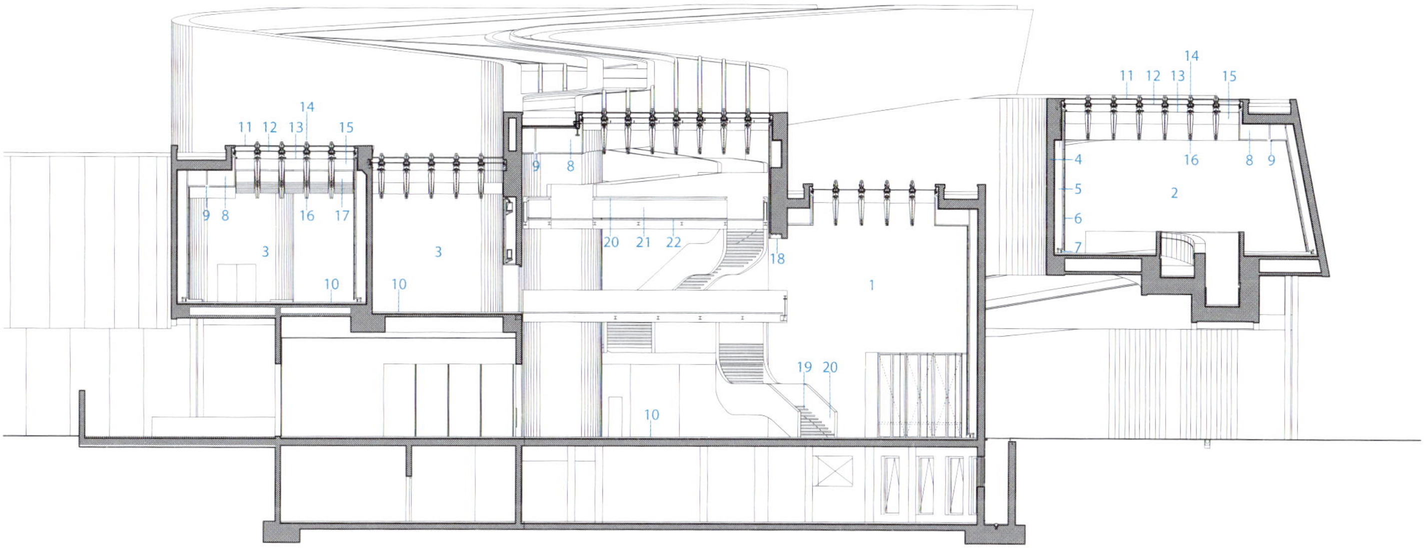

1 Entrance Hall
2 Exhibition Suite 3
3 Exhibition Suite 4
4 Reinforced Concrete + Thermal Insulation Panel
5 500mm Service Cavity
6 Exhibition Wall
7 Electrical System
8 Deep Suspended Ceiling
9 Light Diffusing
10 Resina Continuous Flooring
11 Steel Grating
12 Solar-Protection Glazing
13 High Transparency Toughened Glass
14 Glass-Fibre Reinforced Concrete
15 Steel Truss Supporting Structure
16 Track for Suspensions
17 Aluminium Light-Directing Louvers
18 Steel Plate Anchor
19 Steps and Ramps
20 Parapet and Handrail
21 Supporting Structural Frame
22 Fluorescent Light Ceiling

Figure 18.14 Section main lobby

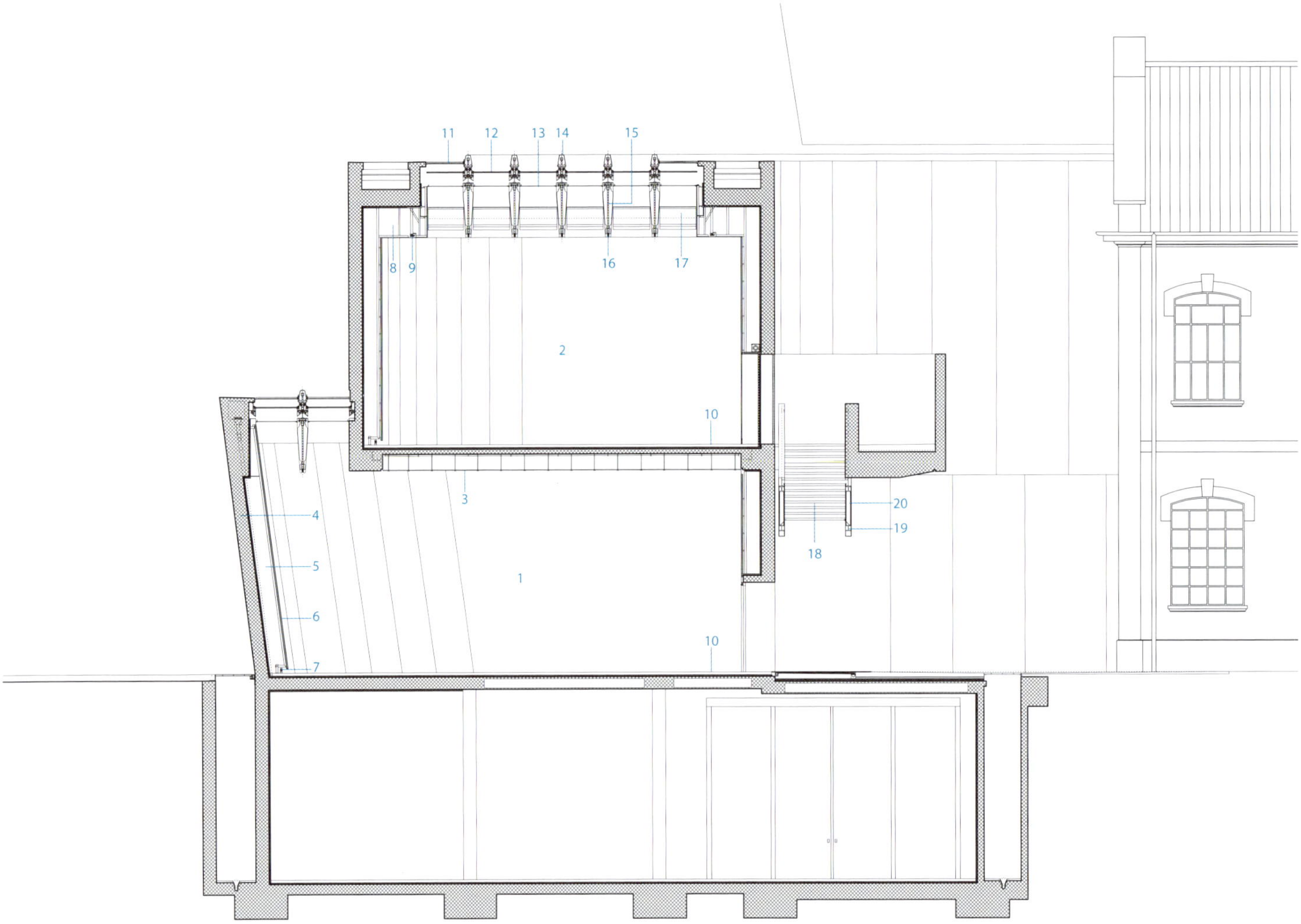

1 Exhibition Suite 1
2 Exhibition Suite 2
3 Sound Absorbtion
4 Reinforced Concrete + Thermal Insulation Panel
5 500mm Service Cavity
6 Exhibition Wall
7 Electrical System
8 Suspended Ceiling
9 Light Diffusing
10 Resina Continuous Flooring
11 Steel Grating
12 Solar-Protection Glazing
13 High Transparency Toughened Glass
14 Glass-Fibre Reinforced Concrete
15 Steel Truss Supporting Structure
16 Track for Suspensions
17 Aluminium Light-Directing Louvers
18 Steps and Ramps
19 Parapet and Handrail
20 Supporting Structural Frame

Figure 18.15 Section galleries

humidity in an area once prone to act as a flood plain for the Tiber River.

Though conceived as a continuous architectural promenade, the exhibition spaces totaling 10,000 m^2 (107,640 ft^2) are divided into five connecting suites on three levels. Architecture is exhibited in Suite 1 on the ground floor. The space appears somewhat as a minor gallery because of its distance from the dramatic entrance hall. Upon entering Suite 1 there is the choice of immediately taking a stair up or carrying on at the same level around a bend to more exhibitions. The space ends with another stair and a glass elevator that ascend to more architecture galleries followed by the art galleries. On the second level (Fig 18.5), galleries weave together, and most all of the Suites 2 (Fig 18.19), 3 (Fig 18.20), and 4 (Fig 18.21) can be visited without necessarily ever coming across the grand volume of the entrance hall. Since the hall is at one end of a linear plan, it does not function as a central focus for the entire building. It is not a point of orientation that is repeatedly encountered like, for example, Yoshio Taniguchi's atrium at the Museum of Modern Art in New York. Hadid's scheme should incite movement and discovery, and there is undeniably a sense of spatial adventure. Though the plan appears relatively simple, there is also a sense of disorientation. Prominently displayed room numbers and diagrammatic models are hung high in the gallery spaces to help visitors orient themselves. Exhibition spaces are surprisingly similar throughout which adds to the confusion, and the building sprawls, partly because of its oddly shaped site. As a critique of the "white box" the MAXXI has reverted back to the very long gallery type (exemplified by the Grande Galerie at the Louvre for example) defined here by continuous parallel or curved walls. The ceiling fins also follow the same geometry. Visitors are pulled through the space and past the works. At the MAXXI the experience should be more akin to navigating the internet or the changing scenes of cinematography. Movement and discovery are, however, at the expense of repose, focus, and meditation.

Figure 18.17 Interior – entrance hall looking north

Figure 18.16 Interior – entrance hall looking east

Figure 18.18 Interior – Exhibition Suite 1

Figure 18.19 Interior – Exhibition Suite 2

Figure 18.20 Interior – Exhibition Suite 3

Figure 18.21 Interior – Exhibition Suite 4

The area where Suites 2 and 3 merge overlooks Suite 1 below and is also visible from Suite 5 above through a glass floor. This space does somewhat provide a point of orientation. Suite 4 is physically separated from the others by a full height glazed wall. At the southern extremity of the suite there is a remarkable permanent installation entitled *Lymph Sculptures* by Giuseppe Penone. It is a rare exhibition space in the museum that is not naturally lit. Indeed, natural top lighting is an important feature of the MAXXI. Even though exhibition spaces are located on three stacked floors, volumes are judiciously offset so that most all spaces have at least a partial glass roof (Fig 18.15).

The 2,600 m^2 (27,986 ft^2) of glass roof is composed of several layers (Fig 18.22). Primary steel beams, 91 cm (3 ft) deep and spaced at approximately 12.5 m (41 ft), span between the parallel concrete structural walls. These beams, encased in folded metal cladding, support 2.2 m (7 ft) deep steel trusses spaced at 1.4 m (4.5 ft). The trusses were originally imagined as concrete beams following the curved and sloped geometry of the roof and in dialogue with the concrete walls. That solution proved too difficult to cast, however. As constructed, the steel trusses are clad with glass reinforced concrete (GRC) panels to maintain continuity of material. The roof fins are a key design element to underscore the ideas of flow and movement. Visually they are very strong. Their design appears to be guided by more conceptual preoccupations rather than their technical role within the layered roof system or their direct influence on the space. Continuous tracks are also integrated at the bottom to hang works of art or to attach temporary walls. (Hadid's use of thin GRC concrete to suggest a heavier cast material is similar in mindset to Tadao Ando's use of GRC panels as a dropped ceiling in the Modern Art Museum of Fort Worth.)

The double-glazed glass roof sits atop the steel trusses and slopes gently to gutters that are integrated within the metal cladding of the primary beams. The glass is treated to filter ultraviolet light that can damage artwork. Outside, above the glass, there is a 5 cm (2 in.) deep steel grating that functions as a brise-soleil and as a surface for maintenance since it can be walked on. The grating is custom-made, and the orientation of the blades assure that direct sun is always blocked while a maximum amount of north light is allowed through for optimal color rendition in the galleries. The grating pattern changes with the curve of the gallery spaces below.

Inside, approximately 40 cm (15.75 in.) below the glass roof, there is another single plane of glass that is open jointed and creates a sort of thermal "loft" buffer space. Return air slots are located here, as are two sets of horizontal roller blinds (one translucent and the other black out), and fluorescent lights, all integrated within the geometry of the tapered GRC cladding. The bottom-most layer of the roof complex is composed of 60 cm (23.5 in.), operable and automated, aluminum louvers that span between the fins. The roof complex provides a well-controlled and very nice light quality. Occasional glimpses of the sky through the various layers also make for a pleasant link to the outside. This is even more important since Hadid wanted the building to be inwardly focused with limited views to the outside. An automated roof washing system was also integrated under the grating. It is linked to a jet washer plant in the basement. As is often the case in museum design, a full-scale mock-up was fabricated by the contractor before construction began. The design proved successful and allowed for a few refinements to be made to certain mechanisms.

Layers of the roof complex are sometimes subtracted or added depending on the location. In Suite 3 the aluminum louvers were omitted since the space was envisioned for sculpture and installations that can receive more light. Suite 3 is the most dynamic space with bridges and ramps and cascading floor plates. Some spaces become awkwardly narrow, however.

The volume of Suite 5 at the very top of the building sits perpendicular to the galleries below, and it is necessarily accessed from the entrance hall (Fig 18.6). A portion of the space has a sloped floor and is used primarily for projections. Here skylights are minimized and form a band along the walls. At the top of the slope, the culminating gallery space is dominated by a full height window wall that reestablishes a connection with the piazza below. The view over the city from this vantage point, however, is less impressive than anticipated. This uppermost volume also contains mechanical spaces for air-cooled chillers that are located on the roof above the gallery. The chillers are concealed below grating in order to maintain the overall roof pattern and profile when seen from above.

In general exhibition spaces feel spacious. Heights and widths vary, with 6 m (20 ft) being an approximate average ceiling height. There is a close relationship between structure (concrete walls) and space. Though the interior gallery walls were originally proposed in concrete, the final design developed with the London-based mechanical engineering firm Max Fordham and Partners has a plasterboard interior finish over a metal frame. Services such as ducts, electrical, and plumbing run in a 50 cm (19.75 in.) plenum space between the concrete and the plasterboard. The plenum often makes a horizontal return at the top of the space to form a partial dropped ceiling also for services. Supply air grills are at the bottom of the wall in a reveal joint that also contains electrical outlets. The galleries use a displacement ventilation system that conditions only the lower portion of the space. Air delivered at floor level slowly moves upward toward return in the loft space of the glass roof complex. Other than the roof there are relatively few windows in the museum and the cast in place concrete makes for an airtight structure.

Vertical circulation is not treated as systematically as the services, and freight elevators and stairs are placed as freestanding blocks within the space in contradiction to the idea of flow. There is no attempt to conceal stainless steel elevator or emergency exit doors within the plasterboard walls, nor elements such as cameras, signage, equipment, etc.

A section of a typical MAXXI gallery has surprising affinities with Renzo Piano's Nasher Sculpture Center. Both buildings have two fundamental components: pronounced, parallel walls that define space, and a glass roof. Likewise, the outer roof layers in Rome and in Dallas are custom-made and oriented toward the more even light of the northern sky.

Zaha Hadid's MAXXI is an urban success. Modern architecture has often been criticized for not fitting in to context. Apparently a lesson has been learned, and Hadid has melded exuberant, abstract, and seemingly foreign forms within a traditional urbanism and has created a functional and vibrant new piazza to boot. The architect's discourse based on energy and flow and layering and pixilation and driftage and geology ... approaches the cryptic. Nevertheless, and perhaps as a result, the building is at ease in its context and actually clarifies the setting in a straightforward manner. The same is not true of the interior, however. The grand entrance hall, for example, is conceptually commonplace in contemporary museums. Such spaces are generally designed for effect. They are not conceived vis-à-vis art works. This is obviously not the case for gallery spaces. Quarrels may rightly be had concerning the advantages and disadvantages of curved and canted walls that appear difficult to hang pictures on as well as sloped floors in exhibition spaces. At the MAXXI what seems more problematic, however, is simply how busy the galleries are visually. This is in large part due to the very present GRC-clad fins throughout the building. Even though the fins do have a functional purpose, it is peculiar that a narrative of flow

Cross Section Of Main Beam

Longitudinal Section Of Fin Trusses

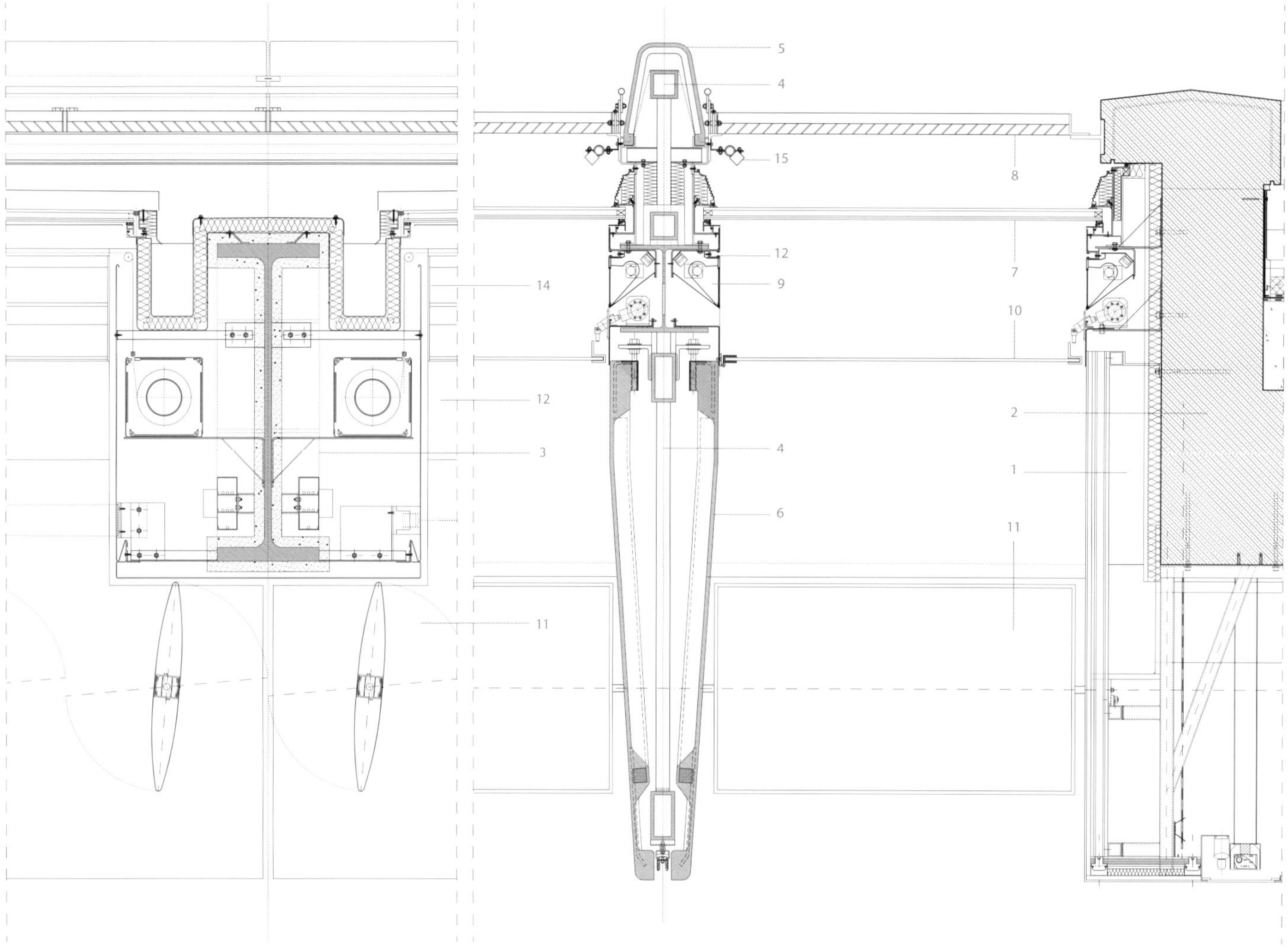

1 Air Extract
2 Parapet
3 Primary Roof Beam
4 Rooflight Fin Trusses
5 Rooflight Fin Capping
6 Rooflight Fin Cladding
7 Glazing
8 Solar Shading
9 Lighting
10 Internal Glazing
11 Adjustable Louvres
12 Blinds
13 Beam Casing
14 Gutter
15 Automated Window Cleaning System
16 Electrical Motor For Adjustable Louvres

Figure 18.22 Roof detail

and movement would be translated so directly into built form without more consideration of the visual impact on the space. Inside there is less reconciliation between the architectural concept and the purpose of the space.

By all reports the 2009 performance by the dance company Sasha Waltz & Guests that took place throughout the MAXXI before art works were installed was spectacular and a huge success. Likewise, artists are apparently inspired by the atypical interior spaces when given the opportunity to create site-specific installations. In these circumstances and for these purposes art and architecture have worked well together. For wall-hung works the advantages of the MAXXI's spaces over other gallery types are less evident. For Hadid, the architecture is meant to challenge curators and visitors. It most likely will do so in both negative and positive ways.

Selected Bibliography

BY CHAPTER

Chapter 1 Modern Art Museum of Fort Worth

Auping, Michael (2002) *Seven Interviews with Tadao Ando*, 1st edn, Fort Worth: Modern Art Museum of Fort Worth.

Jodidio, Philip (2008) *Tadao Ando Modern Art Museum of Fort Worth*, 1st edn, New York: Rizzoli.

Chapter 2 Contemporary Arts Center

El Croquis no. 103 (2001) *Zaha Hadid 1996–2001*, Madrid: El Croquis Editorial.

Dotchantschi, Makus (ed.) (2004) *Zaha Hadid Space for Art*, 1st edn, Zurich: Lars Müller Publishers GmbH.

Chapter 3 Kunsthaus Graz

Bogner, Dieter (ed.) (2004) *A Friendly Alien: Kunsthaus Graz, Peter Cook, Colin Fournier Architects*, 1st edn, Ostfildern, Germany: Hatje Cantz Verlag.

Ilsinger, Renate (ed.) (2003) *Kunsthaus Graz: Documentation of the Competition*, Graz: Haus der Architektur Graz.

Chapter 4 Nasher Sculpture Center

Nash, Steven A. (ed.) (2003) *Nasher Sculpture Center Handbook*, Dallas: Nasher Sculpture Center.

Piano, Renzo (1997) *Logbook*, London: Thames & Hudson.

Chapter 5 The Museum of Modern Art

Elderfield, John (ed.) (1998) *Imagining the Future of The Museum of Modern Art: Studies in Modern Art, 7*, 1st edn, New York: The Museum of Modern Art.

Riley, Terence (2004) *Yoshio Taniguchi: Nine Museums,* New York: The Museum of Modern Art.

Lowry, Glenn D. (2004) *Designing the New Museum of Modern Art*, New York: The Museum of Modern Art.

Chapter 6 Walker Art Center

Blauvelt, Andrew (ed.) (2006) *Expanding the Center: Walker Art Center and Herzog & de Meuron,* Minneapolis: Walker Art Center.

Madison, Cathy (2006) *Art Spaces: Walker Art Center*, London: Scala Publishers.

El Croquis no. 109/110 (2002) *Herzog & de Meuron 1998–2002*, Madrid: El Croquis Editorial.

El Croquis no. 129/130 (2006) *Herzog & de Meuron 2002–2006*, Madrid: El Croquis Editorial.

Chapter 7 Museo Nacional Centro de Arte Reina Sofía

El Croquis no. 112/113 (2002) *Jean Nouvel 1994–2002*, Madrid: El Croquis Editorial.

Baudrillard, Jean, Nouvel, Jean (2000) *Les objets singuliers: Architecture et philosophie*, 1st edn, Paris: Calmann-Lévy.

Holm, Michael Juul (2008) *Jean Nouvel: Louisiana Manifesto*, Humlebæk, Denmark: Louisiana Museum of Modern Art.

Papadakis, Andreas C. (1992) *New Museums (Architectural Design Profile No. 94)*, London: Academy Editions.

Chapter 8 de Young Museum

Ketcham, Diana *et al.* (2005) *The de Young in the 21st Century: A Museum by Herzog & de Meuron*, London: Thames & Hudson.

El Croquis no. 109/110 (2002) *Herzog & de Meuron 1998–2002*, Madrid: El Croquis Editorial.

El Croquis no. 129/130 (2006) *Herzog & de Meuron 2002–2006*, Madrid: El Croquis Editorial.

Chapter 9 Toledo Museum of Art Glass Pavilion

El Croquis no. 121/122 (2005) *SANAA 1998–2006*, Madrid: El Croquis Editorial.

El Croquis no.139 (2008) *SANAA 2004–2008*, Madrid: El Croquis Editorial.

Chapter 10 Denver Art Museum

Libeskind, Daniel, Crichton, Sarah (2004) *Breaking Ground*, New York: Riverhead Books.

Caruso, Laura, Fulton, Andrea Kalivas (2006) *Art Spaces: Denver Art Museum*, London: Scala Publishers.

Chapter 11 The Institute of Contemporary Art/Boston

Incerti, Guido *et al.* (2007) *Diller + Scofidio + (Renfro): The Ciliary Function*, New York: Skira Rizzoli.

Diller Scofidio + Renfro, Medvedow, Jill (2011) *Diller Scofidio + Renfro: Institute of Contemporary Art (ICA) Boston,* Barcelona: Ediciones Poligrafa.

Chapter 12 The Nelson-Atkins Museum of Art Bloch Building

Holl, Steven *et al.* (1994) *Questions of Perception – Phenomenology of Architecture – Architecture and Urbanism Special Issue,* Tokyo: A+U Publishing.

Kipnis, Jeffrey, Wilson, Marc F. (2007) *Stone & Feather: Steven Holl Architects / The Nelson-Atkins Museum Expansion,* Munich: Prestel Verlag.

Holl, Steven, Woods, Lebbeus (2007) *Steven Holl: Architecture Spoken*, New York: Rizzoli.

Chapter 13 Akron Art Museum

Kandeler-Fritsch, Martina (ed.), Kramer, Thomas (ed.) (2006) *Get Off of My Cloud: Wolf D. Prix Coop, Himmelb(l)au Texts 1968–2005,* Ostfildern, Germany: Hatje Cantz Verlag.

Chapter 14 New Museum

El Croquis no. 121/122 (2005) *SANAA 1998–2006*, Madrid: El Croquis Editorial.

El Croquis no.139 (2008) *SANAA 2004–2008*, Madrid: El Croquis Editorial.

Phillips, Lisa *et al.* (2011) *SANAA: Sejima & Nishizawa New Museum New York,* Museum, Barcelona: Ediciones Poligrafa.

Grima, Joseph (ed.), Wong, Karen (ed.) (2008) *Shift: SANAA and the New Museum,* Zurich: Lars Müller Publishers GmbH.

Chapter 15 Acropolis Museum

Tschumi, Bernard (1995) *Event-Cities: Praxis*, Cambridge, Massachusetts: The MIT Press.

Tschumi, Bernard (2001) *Event-Cities 2,* Cambridge, Massachusetts: The MIT Press.

Tschumi, Bernard. (2005) *Event-Cities 3: Concept vs. Context vs. Content,* Cambridge, Massachusetts: The MIT Press.

Bernard Tschumi Architects (ed.) (2009) *The New Acropolis Museum*, New York: Skira-Rizzoli.

Pandermalis, Dimitrios *et al.* (2010) *Bernard Tschumi: New Acropolis Museum Athens*, Barcelona: Poligrafa Ediciones.

Chapter 16 Museum Brandhorst

Detail 04/2010 (2010) *Brandhorst Museum in Munich*, pp.334–340, Munich: Detail.

Hutton, Louisa, Sauerbruch, Matthias (2006) *Sauerbruch Hutton Archive,* Zurich: Lars Müller Publishers GmbH.

2G N.52 (2010) *Sauerbuch Hutton*, Barcelona: Editorial Gustavo Gili.

Schulz-Hoffmann, Carla, Zweite, Armin (2009) *Museum Brandhorst: The Architecture,* Ostfildern, Germany: Hatje Cantz Verlag.

Chapter 17 Centre Pompidou-Metz

Jodidio, Philip (ed.) Le Bon, Laurent (ed.) (2009) *Centre Pompidou-Metz*, Munich: Prestel Verlag.

Chapter 18 Museo Nazionale Delle Arti Del XXI Secolo

Douglas, Charlotte *et al.* (2012) *Zaha Hadid and Suprematism*, Ostfildern, Germany: Hatje Cantz Verlag.

Racana, Gianluca (ed.), Janssens, Manon (ed.) (2010) *MAXXI: Zaha Hadid Architects: Museum of XXI Century Arts,* New York: Skira-Rizzoli.

GENERAL

L'Architecture d'Aujourd'hui No. 6 (1938) *Muséographie*, Boulogne-Sur-Seine, France: L'Architecture d'Aujourd'hui.

Alexander, Edward P. (1979) *Museums in Motion: An Introduction to the History and Functions of Museums*, Nashville: American Association for State and Local History.

Anderson, Gail (ed.) (2004) *Reinventing the Museum: Historical and Contemporary Perspectives on the Paradigm*, Lanham, Maryland: AltaMira Press.

Davis, Douglas (1990) *The Museum Transformed: Design and Culture in the Post-Pompidou Age*, New York: Abbeville Press.

Barreneche, Raul A. (2005) *New Museums*, London: Phaidon Press.

Cerver, Francisco Asensio (1997) *The Architecture of Museums*, New York: Hearst Books International.

Coolidge, John (1989) *Patrons and Architects*, Fort Worth: Amon Carter Museum.

Cuno, James (2011) *Museums Matter: In Praise of the Encyclopedic Museum*, Chicago: The University of Chicago Press.

Englert, Klaus (2010) *New Museums in Spain*, Stuttgart / London: Edition Axel Menges.

Foster, Hal (2011) *The Art – Architecture Complex*, London: Verso.

Hansen, Tone (ed.) (2011) *(Re)Staging the Art Museum*, Berlin: Revolver Press.

Hautecoeur, Louis (1993) *Architecture et aménagement des musées*, Paris: Réunion des Musées Nationaux.

Jodidio, Philip (2010) *Architecture Now! Museums*, Cologne: Taschen.

Jodidio, Philip, Le Bon, Laurent, Lemonier, Aurélien (2010) *Master-Pieces? Museum Architecture: 1937–2014*, France: Centre Pompidou Metz Publications.

Lampugnani, Vittorio Magnago (ed), Sachs, Angeli (ed.) (1999) *Museums for a New Millennium: Concepts, Projects, Buildings*, Munich: Prestel Verlag.

Mack, Gerhard (1999) *Art Museums: Into the 21st Century*, Basel: Birkhauser.

Malraux, André (1965) *Le Musée Imaginaire*, Paris: Gallimard.

Marotta, Antonello (2010) *Contemporary Museums*, Milan: Skira.

Mateo, Josep Lluís (2012) *Expression: Architecture and the Arts: A Pedagogical Interaction*, Zurich: Park Books.

Montaner, Josep Maria (2003) *Museums for the 21st Century*, Barcelona: Gustavo Gili.

Newhouse, Victoria (1998) *Towards a New Museum*, New York: The Monacelli Press.

Newhouse, Victoria (2005) *Art and the Power of Placement*, New York: The Monacelli Press.

O'Doherty, Brian (1986) *Inside the White Cube; The Ideology of the Gallery Space,* Berkeley: University of California Press.

Papadakis, Andreas C. (ed.) (1992) *New Museums (Architectural Design Profile No. 94),* London: Academy Editions.

Stephens, Suzanne (ed.) (1986) *Building the New Museum*, New York: The Architectural League of New York.

Wolf, Eric M. (2010) *American Art Museum Architecture: Documents and Design*, New York: W. W. Norton & Company.

Zeiger, Mimi (2005) *New Museums: Contemporary Museum Architecture around the World*, New York: Universe Publishing.

Credits

DRAWING CREDITS

Fig 1.2–1.5, 1.7, 1.9, 1.10, 1.17: © Tadao Ando Architect & Associates

Fig 2.2–2.12, 2.17–2.21, 2.27: © Zaha Hadid Architects

Fig 3.2–3.9, 3.14, 3.20–3.22: © ARGE Kunsthaus, Spacelab Cook/Fournier GmbH

Fig 4.2–4.5, 4.11–4.13, 4.18: © Renzo Piano Building Workshop

Fig 5.2, 5.3: © Kohn Pedersen Fox Associates: Fig 5.4–5.10, 5.13, 5.14, 5.22: ©Taniguchi and Associates

Fig 6.2–6.6, 6.11, 6.12, 6.18–6.20: © Herzog & de Meuron

Fig 7.2–7.7, 7.12–7.15, 7.22: © Ateliers Jean Nouvel

Fig 8.2–8.7, 8.12–8.16, 8.22–8.24: © Herzog & de Meuron

Fig 9.2, 9.3, 9.6, 9.7, 9.15: © SANAA; Fig 9.16: © Guy Nordenson and Associates

Fig 10.2–10.8, 10.13–10.15, 10.21, 10.22: © Daniel Libeskind

Fig 11.2–11.6, 11.9–11.14, 11.22: © Diller Scofidio + Renfro

Fig 12.2–12.5, 12.10–12.15, 12.22, 12.23: © Steven Holl Architects

Fig 13.2–13.5, 13.10–13.13, 13.19: © Coop Himmelb(l)au

Fig 14.2, 14.3, 14.8–14.10, 14.17–14.19: © SANAA; Fig 14.11: © Guy Nordenson and Associates

Fig 15.2–15.11, 15.14, 15.15, 15.23: © Bernard Tschumi Architects

Fig 16.2, 16.3, 16.7–16.12, 16.19: © Sauerbruch Hutton

Fig 17.2–17.9, 17.13, 7.14, 17.21: © Shigeru Ban and Jean de Gastines

Fig 18.2–18.7, 18.11–18.15, 18.22: © Zaha Hadid Architects

Fig 5.1, 5.11, 5.12, 5.15–5.21: © Timothy Hursley

Fig 6.1, 6.7–6.10, 6.13–6.17: © Roland Halbe

Fig 7.1, 7.9–7.11, 7.16–7.21: © Roland Halbe, Fig 7.8: © Joaquín Cortés/Roman Lores, Courtesy Museo Nacional Centro de Arte Reina Sofía, Madrid

Fig 8.1, 8.8–8.11, 8.17–8.21: © Roland Halbe

Fig 9.1, 9.4, 9.5, 9.8–9.14: © Iwan Baan

Fig 10.1, 10.9–10.12, 10.16–10.20: © Roland Halbe

Fig 11.1, 11.7, 11.8, 11.15–11.21: © Paul Raftery

Fig 12.1, 12. 6–12.9, 12.16–12.21: © Roland Halbe

Fig 13.1, 13.6–13.9, 13.14–13.18: © Roland Halbe

Fig 14.1, 14.4–14.7, 14.12–14.16: © Iwan Baan

Fig 15.1, 15.12, 15.13, 15.16–15.22: © Christian Richters

Fig 16.1, 16.5, 16.13–16.16, 16.18: ©Bayerische Staatsgemaldesammlungen, Museum Brandhorst Munich: Haydar Koyupinar; Fig 16.4: Bayerische Staatsgemaldesammlungen, Museum Brandhorst Munich: Andreas Lechtape; Fig 16.6: © Annette Kisling; Fig 16.17: © Jan Bitter

Fig 17.1, 17.12, 17.15, 17.20: © Roland Halbe; Fig 17. 10, 17.11, 17.16–17.19: © Paul Raftery; Centre Pompidou-Metz © Shigeru Ban Architects Europe and Jean de Gastines Architectes, with Philip Gumuchdjian for the conception of the winning competition project / Metz Métropole / Centre Pompidou-Metz

Fig 18.1, 18.16: © Iwan Baan; Fig 18.8: © Roland Halbe; Fig 18.9, 18.10, 18.17, 18.18, 18.20, 18.21: © Paul Raftery; Fig 18.19: © Francesco Bolis

PHOTO CREDITS

Fig 1.1, 1.6, 1.8, 1.11–1.15: © Mitsuo Matsuoka; Fig 1.16: © Tadao Ando Architect & Associates

Fig 2.1, 2.13–2.16, 2.22–2.26: © Roland Halbe

Fig 3.1, 3.10–3.13, 3.15–3.19: © Paul Raftery

Fig 4.1, 4.9, 4.17: © Timothy Hursley; Fig 4.6–4.8, 4.10, 4.15, 4.16: © Michel Denancé; Fig 4.14: © Shunji Ishida

QUOTE CREDITS

Chapter 1 Page XX: © 2012 Sophie Calle / Artists Rights Society (ARS), New York / ADAGP, Paris

Chapter 13 Page XX: "A Museum is Art", 1990, *Get Off of My Cloud: Wolf D. Prix Coop Himmelb(l)au Texts 1968–2005*

Chapter 15 Page XX: Tschumi, Bernard., *Event-Cities 2*, pp. quote from page 229, for epigraph use., © 2001 Massachusetts Institute of Technology, by permission of The MIT Press

Index

Page numbers in *italic* refer to illustrations.